OAKVILLE GALLERIES
1306 LAKESHORE ROAD EAST
OAKVILLE, ONTARIO L6J 1L6

OCTOBER

OCTOBER
The First Decade, 1976–1986

edited by
Annette Michelson
Rosalind Krauss
Douglas Crimp
Joan Copjec

The MIT Press
Cambridge, Massachusetts
London, England

This book was printed and bound by Halliday
Lithograph in the United States of America.

Library of Congress Cataloging-in-
Publication Data

October: the first decade, 1976–1986.

   1. October (Cambridge, Mass.) 2. Arts,
Modern — 20th century. 3. Art criticism.
I. Michelson, Annette. II. October
(Cambridge, Mass.)
NX456.03 1987   700   87-4200
ISBN 0-262-13222-2

Contents

Acknowledgments   vii

Introduction   ix

The Index

ROSALIND KRAUSS   Notes on the Index: Seventies Art in America   2

NADAR   My Life as a Photographer   16

GEORGES DIDI-HUBERMAN   The Index of the Absent Wound (Monograph on a Stain)   39

ROGER CAILLOIS   Mimicry and Legendary Psychasthenia   58

Historical Materialism

BENJAMIN H. D. BUCHLOH   From Faktura to Factography   76

SERGEI EISENSTEIN   Notes for a Film of *Capital*   114

MARIA-ANTONIETTA MACCIOCCHI   Pasolini: Murder of a Dissident   139

ROSALYN DEUTSCHE
CARA GENDEL RYAN   The Fine Art of Gentrification   151

Critique of Institutions

YVE-ALAIN BOIS
DOUGLAS CRIMP
ROSALIND KRAUSS   A Conversation with Hans Haacke   175

DANIEL BUREN   The Function of the Studio   201

LOUISE LAWLER   Arrangements of Pictures   209

DOUGLAS CRIMP   The Art of Exhibition   223

CHRISTOPHER PHILLIPS   The Judgment Seat of Photography   257

Psychoanalysis

JOAN COPJEC   Flavit et Dissipati Sunt   296

HOMI BHABHA   Of Mimicry and Man: The
                               Ambivalence of Colonial
                               Discourse   317

MARY ANN DOANE   Woman's Stake: Filming the
                               Female Body   326

Rhetoric

YVE-ALAIN BOIS   A Picturesque Stroll around
                               Clara-Clara   342

JOEL FINEMAN   The Structure of Allegorical
                               Desire   373

The Body

BABETTE MANGOLTE   A Portfolio of Photographs of Trisha
                               Brown's Work   394

PETER HANDKE   Blue Poem for B.   407

ANNETTE MICHELSON   On the Eve of the Future: The
                               Reasonable Facsimile and the
                               Philosophical Toy   416

GEORGES BATAILLE   Extinct America   437

HOLLIS FRAMPTON   Erotic Predicaments for Camera   445

ROBERT MORRIS   Fragments from the Rodin
                               Museum   451

Acknowledgments

Throughout the production of this anthology we were constantly aware, as the editors of *October*, of our many debts to those who worked with us on the journal during its first ten years. We therefore wish to thank, collectively, the writers, translators, artists, photographers, editors, proofreaders, designers, and interns who have worked with us at various points along the way. We also want to express our gratitude to those who have provided the financial support for *October*'s editorial production: the Pinewood Foundation, the National Endowment for the Arts, the New York State Council on the Arts, and, for the special issue on Georges Bataille, the J. Paul Getty Trust. The MIT Press Journals Department has provided another constant form of support, and our thanks go to all the members of its staff.

The articles anthologized in this book all appeared originally in *OCTOBER*. They are reprinted with permission.

Notes on the Index: Seventies Art in America © 1977 no. 3, pp. 68–81.
My Life as a Photographer © 1978 no. 5, pp. 6–28.
The Index of the Absent Wound (Monograph on a Stain) © 1984 no. 29, pp. 63–81.
Mimicry and Legendary Psychasthenia © 1984 no. 31, pp. 16–32.
From Faktura to Factography © 1984 no. 30, pp. 82–119.
Notes for a Film of *Capital* © 1976 no. 2, pp. 3–26.
Pasolini: Murder of a Dissident © 1980 no. 13, pp. 11–21.
The Fine Art of Gentrification © 1984 no. 31, pp. 91–111.
A Conversation with Hans Haacke © 1984 no. 30, pp. 23–48.
The Function of the Studio © 1979 no. 10, pp. 51–58.
Arrangements of Pictures © 1983 no. 26, pp. 3–16.
The Art of Exhibition © 1984 no. 30, pp. 49–81.
The Judgment Seat of Photography © 1982 no. 22, pp. 27–63.
Flavit et Dissipati Sunt © 1981 no. 18, pp. 20–40.
Of Mimicry and Man: The Ambivalence of Colonial Discourse © 1984 no. 28, pp. 125–133.
Woman's Stake: Filming the Female Body © 1981 no. 17, pp. 22–36.

A Picturesque Stroll around *Clara-Clara* © 1984 no. 29, pp. 32–62.

The Structure of Allegorical Desire © 1980 no. 12, pp. 46–66.

A Portfolio of Photographs of Trisha Brown's Work © 1979 no. 10, pp. 39–50.

Blue Poem for B. © 1977 no. 3 pp. 26–34.

On the Eve of the Future: The Reasonable Facsimile and the Philosophical Toy © 1984 no. 29, pp. 2–21.

Extinct America © 1986 no. 36, pp. 3–9.

Erotic Predicaments for Camera © 1985 no. 32, pp. 56–61.

Fragments from the Rodin Museum © 1977 no. 3, pp. 3–8.

Introduction

"But why *October*?" our readers still inquire. Briefly *October* is named after Eisenstein's film celebrating the tenth anniversary of the revolution. More fully, *October* is emblematic for us of a specific historical moment in which artistic practice joined with critical theory in the project of social construction. It is this conjunction that we inscribed on our cover: *Art | Theory | Criticism | Politics.* Naming the journal *October* was not, however, a nostalgic gesture. We had no desire to perpetuate the mythology of the revolution. Rather we wished to claim that the unfinished, analytic project of constructivism—aborted by the consolidation of the Stalinist bureaucracy, distorted by the recuperation of the Soviet avant-garde into the mainstream of Western idealist aesthetics—was required for a consideration of the aesthetic practices of our own time.

The 1960s had witnessed, in both Europe and America, extraordinary developments in the visual and temporal arts: in painting, sculpture, dance, performance, and film. This work demanded and sustained the kind of critical theory that had begun to be developed some fifty years earlier. And, as had also occurred in that earlier period, both the new art and its theorization were dismissed with the epithet "formalist." The particular historical moment within which our project took shape was a transitional period in which the modernist canon, the forms and categories that had defined and elucidated it, were everywhere in question. This situation, which we have subsequently come to call postmodernist, required in our estimation an intensive effort of reassessment and analysis. We did not see this juncture as that of the vaunted "death of the avant-garde" and a new "pluralism." We saw it rather as that of late capitalism, a time of continued struggles to radicalize cultural practices, and of the marginalization of those attempts through the revival of traditional artistic and discursive tendencies.

We founded *October* as a forum for the presentation and theoretical elaboration of cultural work that continued the unfinished project of the 1960s. Our task was no more nostalgic with respect to this project than it was in regard to the earlier one. Instead, we considered it the necessary response to what was once again a consolidation of reactionary forces within both the political and cultural spheres. We approached this task on a number of fronts simultaneously, thus establishing the eclectic though hardly "pluralist" character of the journal. We opened our pages to the writings of cultural producers themselves; we published documents from earlier moments in the history of modernism that have a continued relevance for contemporary theory and practice; we commissioned work by critics who shared our interests. In addition, we consistently published texts representing the advanced theoretical efforts made abroad, particularly in France. In this we were not alone; but we made a concerted effort to set a new standard of quality for translation, an effort consistent with our desire to play an active mediating role in that theoretical production, for it seemed to us that the most cogent response to the return to traditional Western values in every sphere of social and cultural life was the critique of the presuppositions of those values made by French theorists, those who had come to be called poststructuralists.

The selection of texts in this anthology, drawn from *October*'s first decade of publication, is structured according to broad and often overlapping areas of theoretical endeavor. Almost from the outset the index, for example, appeared to us as a particularly useful tool. Its implications within the process of marking, its specific axis of relation between sign and referent, made of the index a concept that could work against the grain of familiar unities of thought, critical categories such as medium, historical categories such as style, categories that contemporary practices had rendered suspect, useless, irrelevent. In its status as trace or imprint, the index cut across the rigidly separate artistic disciplines, linking painting with photography, sculpture with performance and cinematography. From the scrutiny of this process in its mute obduracy, its striking independence from categories of form, there seemed to emerge a critical language flexible enough to address the photographic, not photography as a specific medium but a particular mode of signifying that had come to affect all the arts during this historical juncture.

A magazine is a public enterprise, a mode of address, a form of collective speech. The speaker imagines his or her audience. We began by imagining ours as the one for which we had always written. It was an audience specialized in its commitment to the visual arts, one made up of artists, critics, scholars, students. But the audience we imagined as ours was conjured partly out of a milieu whose dissolution was already underway as we prepared our first issues. We had known it in the early seventies, sitting on the floor of the Kitchen, avid for new dance, music, and performance art. We had sensed its presence in the dark of the Anthology Film Archives screening room, watching the cycle of experimental films turn through the twenties and thirties, the forties, fifties, and sixties. We had felt it in the camaraderie experienced in lofts and downtown galleries in the early years of SoHo, and in the enthusiasm of students who saw their subjects being reinvented or constituted afresh.

But that audience was subject to an intensifying process of erosion by the brute logic of the market economy. We in New York saw our community forced out of the SoHo they had helped to create, forced in turn to collaborate in the eviction of even more marginal populations from the Lower East Side, as the creation of a new art district was conscripted as a wedge for real estate development — a condition by no means peculiar to New York. We saw, at the same time, the very artistic experimentation that we had associated with the SoHo community abandoned in favor of the production of luxury objects for consumption and investment, often now by multinational corporations. And at the same time that the interests that art represented were so nakedly displayed, we watched in dismay as art institutions resurrected the claims of disinterestedness. Our attention was therefore redirected toward those institutions — the artist's studio, the gallery and museum, the corporate patron, the discipline of art history.

Our attention also had to be directed toward the operations within these institutions of a system of privilege that rewarded the masculine and ignored the rest, that addressed itself to a male subject that it took as adequate indicator of the universal. A radical ignorance with respect to sexual difference had to be confronted. Women had to be written into historical and contemporary cultural practices as producers and as addressees. This task would entail, however, more than a simple retrieval of women from neglected historical archives or support of contemporary women's work. It would also entail a reconception of the scotoma that kept women from sight not as an impediment to be removed but as a process of vision itself. Feminism would participate in the redefinition of vision as historical and at the same time would help to rethink the very notion of history and our own relation to historical forms.

Historical and political analysis necessitated an engagement with psychoanalysis, as it became increasingly urgent to define the psychical processes, the material, on which social forces work, for social discourses have rhetorical force, which is not simply to say that they affect us as subjects, but more, as psychoanalytic and linguistic theory teaches, that they effect us.

The shift from considerations of affect to those of effect was paralleled by a critique of the notion of the body as pregiven. It was this body and its stages of maturation that had been used as metaphor to support teleological descriptions of artistic practices, scientific invention, history in general. Now we have begun to analyze the body as it is constructed by different discourses — the erotic body, the hysterical body, the sacrificial body, body as screen, as threat: the body as singular no longer. Yet even as we define these constructions of the spoken and speaking body, we encounter, too, heterogeneous configurations of the body as resistant to or as escaping discourse. We have thus allowed the category of the body to mark the point at which theory remains unsatisfied with its own constructions and looks beyond itself. This is the point from which theory must continue, the place where it is most clear that it has not finished speaking.

The end of a decade of publication provides us with the occasion to reflect on our past from a critical vantage not available to us as our positions were being formed. A journal is produced according to the demands of time and in the midst of debates that will intensify, shift, or disappear but whose outcome we cannot, in principle, know. Intellectual work consists, nevertheless, in articulating a position, in defining for oneself a moment, a prospect from which an argument can be made. Every essay assumes some such perspective. At times, though, a single perspective, taken in response to special demands, defines an entire issue of the journal. Thus the new role of photography within the art world became for us a special issue, as did Soviet revolutionary culture, the theoretical film as the "new talkie," and discipleship and psychoanalysis. A *festschrift* honoring the range of Jay Leyda's contributions to scholarship, Leo Steinberg's extended essay on the sexuality of Christ in Renaissance art, Walter Benjamin's diary kept in Moscow in the winter of 1926–27 — these were special issues as well. And the untimely deaths of two independent filmmakers — Rainer Werner Fassbinder and Hollis Frampton — were sad occasions for special issues.

A special issue cannot, of course, be anthologized, although certain essays reprinted here are excerpted from those contexts. We do not, in any case, hope to provide a transcendent view within which our project might be encompassed, but rather another view providing more or less discontinuous perspectives. What is included here, then, is a selection of projects that have functioned over the past ten years to focus our attention — that is, ours and our readers — on cultural production: the index, historical materialism, the critique of institutions, psychoanalysis, rhetoric, and the body.

The Index

ROSALIND KRAUSS

1. Almost everyone is agreed about '70s art. It is diversified, split, factional-ized. Unlike the art of the last several decades, its energy does not seem to flow through a single channel for which a synthetic term, like Abstract-Expressionism, or Minimalism, might be found. In defiance of the notion of collective effort that operates behind the very idea of an artistic 'movement', '70s art is proud of its own dispersal. "Post-Movement Art in America" is the term most recently applied.[1] We are asked to contemplate a great plethora of possibilities in the list that must now be used to draw a line around the art of the present: video; performance; body art; conceptual art; photo-realism in painting and an associated hyper-realism in sculpture; story art; monumental abstract sculpture (earthworks); and abstract painting, characterized, now, not by rigor but by a willful eclecticism. It is as though in that need for a list, or proliferating string of terms, there is prefigured an image of personal freedom, of multiple options now open to individual choice or will, whereas before these things were closed off through a restrictive notion of historical style.

Both the critics and practitioners of recent art have closed ranks around this 'pluralism' of the 1970s. But what, really, are we to think of that notion of multiplicity? It is certainly true that the separate members of the list do not look alike. If they have any unity, it is not along the axis of a traditional notion of 'style'. But is the absence of a collective style the token of a real difference? Or is there not something else for which all these terms are possible manifestations? Are not all these separate 'individuals' in fact moving in lockstep, only to a rather different drummer from the one called style?

2. My list began with video, which I've talked about before, attempting to detail the routines of narcissism which form both its content and its structure.[2] But now I am thinking about *Airtime*, the work that Vito Acconci made in 1973, where for 40 minutes the artist sits and talks to his reflected image. Referring to himself,

1.   This is the title of a book by Alan Sondheim, *Individuals: Post Movement Art in America*, New York, Dutton, 1977.
2.   See my "Video: The Structure of Narcissism," *October*, no. 1 (Spring 1976).

he uses 'I', but not always. Sometimes he addresses his mirrored self as 'you'. 'You' is a pronoun that is also filled, within the space of his recorded monologue, by an absent person, someone he imagines himself to be addressing. But the referent for this 'you' keeps slipping, shifting, returning once again to the 'I' who is himself, reflected in the mirror. Acconci is playing out the drama of the shifter—in its regressive form.

3. The shifter is Jakobson's term for that category of linguistic sign which is "filled with signification" only because it is "empty."[3] The word 'this' is such a sign, waiting each time it is invoked for its referent to be supplied. "This chair," "this table," or "this . . ." and we point to something lying on the desk. "Not that, *this*," we say. The personal pronouns 'I' and 'you' are also shifters. As we speak to one another, both of us using 'I' and 'you', the referents of those words keep changing places across the space of our conversation. I am the referent of 'I' only when I am the one who is speaking. When it is your turn, it belongs to you.

The gymnastics of the "empty" pronominal sign are therefore slightly complicated. And though we might think that very young children learning language would acquire the use of 'I' and 'you' very early on, this is in fact one of the last things to be correctly learned. Jakobson tells us, as well, that the personal pronouns are among the first things to break down in cases of aphasia.

4. *Airtime* establishes, then, the space of a double regression. Or rather, a space in which linguistic confusion operates in concert with the narcissism implicit in the performer's relationship to the mirror. But this conjunction is perfectly logical, particularly if we consider narcissism—a stage in the development of personality suspended between auto-eroticism and object-love—in the terms suggested by Lacan's concept of the "mirror stage." Occurring sometime between the ages of six and 18 months, the mirror stage involves the child's self-identification *through* his double: his reflected image. In moving from a global, undifferentiated sense of himself towards a distinct, integrated notion of selfhood—one that could be symbolized through an individuated use of 'I' and 'you'—the child recognizes himself as a separate object (a psychic *gestalt*) by means of his mirrored image. The self is felt, at this stage, only as an *image* of the self; and insofar as the child initially recognizes himself as an other, there is inscribed in that experience a primary alienation. Identity (self-definition) is primally fused with identification (a felt connection to someone else). It is within that condition of alienation—the attempt to come to closure with a self that is physically distant—that the Imaginary takes root. And in Lacan's terms, the Imaginary is the realm of fantasy, specified as a-temporal, because disengaged from the conditions of history. For the child, a sense of history, both his own and particularly that of others, wholly independent of himself, comes only with the full acquisition of language. For, in joining himself to language, the child enters

3.   See, Roman Jakobson, "Shifters, verbal categories, and the Russian verb," *Russian Language Project*, Harvard University Press, 1957; also, Émile Benveniste, "La nature des pronoms," in *Problèmes de linguistique générale*, Paris, Gallimard, 1966.

a world of conventions which he has had no role in shaping. Language presents him with an historical framework pre-existent to his own being. Following the designation of spoken or written language as constituted of that type of sign called the symbol, Lacan names this stage of development the Symbolic and opposes it to the Imaginary.

5. This opposition between the Symbolic and the Imaginary leads us to a further comment on the shifter. For the shifter is a case of linguistic sign which partakes of the symbol even while it shares the features of something else. The pronouns are part of the symbolic code of language insofar as they are arbitrary: 'I' we say in English, but 'je' in French, 'ego' in Latin, 'ich' in German . . . But insofar as their meaning depends on the existential presence of a given speaker, the pronouns (as is true of the other shifters) announce themselves as belonging to a different type of sign: the kind that is termed the index. As distinct from symbols, indexes establish their meaning along the axis of a physical relationship to their referents. They are the marks or traces of a particular cause, and that cause is the thing to which they refer, the object they signify. Into the category of the index, we would place physical traces (like footprints), medical symptoms, or the actual referents of the shifters. Cast shadows could also serve as the indexical signs of objects. . . .

6. *Tu m'* is a painting Marcel Duchamp made in 1918. It is, one might say, a panorama of the index. Across its ten-foot width parade a series cast shadows, as Duchamp's readymades put in their appearance via the index. The readymades themselves are not depicted. Instead the bicycle wheel, the hatrack, and a corkscrew, are projected onto the surface of the canvas through the fixing of cast shadows, signifying these objects by means of indexical traces. Lest we miss the point, Duchamp places a realistically painted hand at the center of the work, a hand that is pointing, its index finger enacting the process of establishing the

Marcel Duchamp. Tu M'. *1918. Oil and pencil on canvas with bottle brush, three safety pins, and a bolt. 27½ × 122¾ inches. (Yale University Art Gallery, New Haven, Bequest of Katherine S. Dreier, 1952.)*

connection between the linguistic shifter 'this . . .' and its referent. Given the role of the indexical sign within this particular painting, its title should not surprise us. *Tu m'* is simply 'you'/'me'—the two personal pronouns which, in being shifters, are themselves a species of index.

7. In contributing an essay to the catalogue of the recent Duchamp retrospective, Lucy Lippard chose to write a mock short story about a personage she characterized in the title as "ALLREADYMADESOMUCHOFF."[4] Indeed, the seemingly endless stream of essays on Duchamp that have appeared over the last several years certainly does discourage one from wanting to add yet another word to the accumulating mass of literature on the artist. Yet Duchamp's relationship to the issue of the indexical sign, or rather, the way his art serves as a matrix for a related set of ideas which connect to one another through the axis of the index, is too important a precedent (I am not concerned here with the question of 'influence') for '70s art, not to explore it. For as we will see, it is Duchamp who first establishes the connection between the index (as a type of sign) and the photograph.

8. A breakdown in the use of the shifter to locate the self in relation to its world is not confined to the onset of aphasia; it also characterizes the speech of autistic children. Describing the case of Joey, one of the patients in his Chicago clinic, Bruno Bettelheim writes, "He used personal pronouns in reverse, as do most autistic children. He referred to himself as you and to the adult he was speaking to as I. A year later he called this therapist by name, though still not addressing her as 'you', but saying 'Want Miss M. to swing you.'"[5] In an

4. In *Marcel Duchamp*, ed. Anne d'Harnoncourt and Kynaston McShine, New York, The Museum of Modern Art, 1973.
5. Bruno Bettelheim, *The Empty Fortress, Infantile Autism and the Birth of the Self*, New York, 1967, p. 234. My attention to this passage was called by Annette Michelson in the essay cited below.

important essay drawing the parallels between those symptoms that form the psychopathological syndrome of autism and specific aspects of Duchamp's art, Annette Michelson pointed to the autist's characteristic fascination with revolving disks, the fantasy (in some cases) that he is a machine, and the withdrawal from language as a form of communication by means of speaking in private allusions and riddles.[6] All of these features occur, of course, in Duchamp's art with a vengeance. But for the moment I would like to focus on the autist's problem with the shifter—the problem of naming an individuated self—a dramatization of which is also to be found throughout the later work of Duchamp.

Tu m' is one way of signaling this. Another is the division of the self into an 'I' and a 'you' through the adoption of an alter-ego. "Rrose Sélavy and I," Duchamp writes as the beginning of the phrase he inscribes around the revolving disk of the *Machine Optique* (1920). Duchamp's photographic self-portraits in drag, as Rrose Sélavy, announce a self that is split, doubled, along the axis of sexual identity. But the very name he uses for his 'double' projects a strategy for infecting language itself with a confusion in the way that words denote their referents. "Rrose Sélavy" is a homophone suggesting to its auditors two entirely different meanings. The first is a proper name; the second a sentence: the first of the double Rs in Rrose would have to be pronounced (in French) 'er', making Er-rose Sélavy into *Éros, c'est la vie*, a statement inscribing life within a circle of eroticism which Duchamp has elsewhere characterized as "vicious."[7] The rest of the sentence from the *Machine Optique* performs another kind of indignity on the body of language—at least in terms of its capacity for meaning. Overloaded with internal rhyme, the phrase *"estimons les ecchymoses des Esquimaux aux mots exquis"* (we esteem the bruises of the Eskimos with beautiful language) substitutes sheer musicality for the process of signification. The elisions and inversions of the *es*, *ex*, and *mo* sounds upset the balance of meaning through an outrageous formalism. The confusion in the shifter couples then with another kind of breakdown, as form begins to erode the certainty of content.

9. The collapsed shifter announced itself through a specific use of language, and through the doubled self-portrait. But then, up to 1912 Duchamp had been concerned as a painter almost exclusively with autobiography. Between 1903 and 1911 his major subject was that of his family, and life as it was lived within the immediate confines of his home. This series of explicit portraiture—his father, his brothers playing chess, his sisters playing music—climaxes with the artist's own self-portrait as *The Sad Young Man on a Train* (1911).[8] In most of these portraits there is an insistent naturalism, a direct depiction of the persons who formed the

6. Annette Michelson, "'Anemic Cinema' Reflections on an Emblematic Work," *Artforum*, XII (October 1973), 64–69.
7. This is from "the litanies of the Chariot" one of the notes from the *Green Box*. See, *The Bride Stripped Bare by Her Bachelors, Even*. A typographical version by Richard Hamilton of Duchamp's *Green Box*, trans. George Heard Hamilton, London, Lund, Humphries, 1960, n. p.
8. The inscription on the back of this painting reads: *Marcel Duchamp nu (esquisse) Jeune homme triste dans un train/Marcel Duchamp*.

Marcel Duchamp. Machine optique. *1920.*

Duchamp as Rrose Sélavy,
photographed by Man Ray. 1921.

extensions of Duchamp's most intimate world. Only by the end, in *The Sad Young Man . . .* do we find that directness swamped by the adoption of a cubist-informed pictorial language, a language Duchamp was to continue to use for just six more months and then to renounce, with a rather bitter and continuing series of castigations, forever. It was as if cubism forced for Duchamp the issue of whether pictorial language could continue to signify directly, could picture a world with anything like an accessible set of contents. It was not that self-portraiture was displaced within Duchamp's subsequent activity. But only that the project of depicting the self took on those qualities of enigmatic refusal and mask with which we are familiar.

10. The *Large Glass* is of course another self-portrait. In one of the little sketches Duchamp made for it and included in the *Green Box* he labels the upper register "MAR" and the lower half "CEL." And he retains these syllables of his own name in the title of the finished work: *La mariée mise à nu par ses célibataires même*; the MAR of *mariée* linked to the CEL of *célibataires*; the self projected as double. Within this field of the split self-portrait we are made to feel the presence of the index. The "Sieves," for example, are colored by the fixing of dust that had fallen on the prone surface of the glass over a period of months. The accumulation

Elevage de poussière (Dust Breeding). *1920.*
(Photograph by Man Ray.)

of dust is a kind of physical index for the passage of time. *Dust Breeding* (*Elevage de poussière*) Duchamp calls it, in the photograph of the work's surface that Man Ray took and Duchamp included in the notes for the *Large Glass*. The signatures of both men appear along the bottom of the photograph.

Man Ray intersects with Duchamp's career not only in this document for the *Large Glass* but in those other photographic occasions of Duchamp's work: in the production of the film *Anémic Cinèma*; and in the transvestite portraits of Duchamp/Rrose Sélavy. Which is interesting. Because Man Ray is the inventor of the Rayograph—that subspecies of photo which forces the issue of photography's existence as an index. Rayographs (or as they are more generically termed, photograms) are produced by placing objects on top of light-sensitive paper, exposing the ensemble to light, and then developing the result. The image created in this way is of the ghostly traces of departed objects; they look like footprints in sand, or marks that have been left in dust.

But the photogram only forces, or makes explicit, what is the case of *all* photography. Every photograph is the result of a physical imprint transferred by light reflections onto a sensitive surface. The photograph is thus a type of icon, or visual likeness, which bears an indexical relationship to its object. Its separation from true icons is felt through the absolutness of this physical genesis, one that seem to short-circuit or disallow those processes of schematization or symbolic intervention that operate within the graphic representations of most paintings. If the Symbolic finds its way into pictorial art through the human consciousness operating behind the forms of representation, forming a connection between objects and their meaning, this is not the case for photography. Its power is as an index and its meaning resides in those modes of identification which are associated with the Imaginary. In the essay "The Ontology of the Photographic Image," André Bazin describes the indexical condition of the photograph:

> Painting is, after all, an inferior way of making likenesses, an ersatz of the processes of reproduction. Only a photographic lens can give us the kind of image of the object that is capable of satisfying the deep need man has to substitute for it something more than a mere approximation . . . The photographic image is the object itself, the object freed from the conditions of time and space that govern it. No matter how fuzzy, distorted, or discolored, no matter how lacking in documentary value the image may be, it shares, by virtue of the very process of its becoming, the being of the model of which it is the reproduction; it *is* the model.[9]

Whatever else its power, the photograph could be called sub- or pre-symbolic, ceding the language of art back to the imposition of things.

---

9.   In André Bazin, *What Is Cinema?*, trans. Hugh Gray, Berkeley, University of California Press, 1967, p. 14.

Marcel Duchamp. The Bride Stripped Bare by Her Bachelors, Even (The Large Glass). *1915–23. (Philadelphia Museum of Art, Bequest of Katherine S. Dreier, 1953.)*

11. In this connection the preface to the *Large Glass* makes fairly arresting reading. It begins, "Given 1. the waterfall 2. the illuminating gas, we shall determine the conditions for the instantaneous State of Rest . . . of a succession . . . of various facts . . . in order to isolate the sign of the accordance between . . . this State of Rest . . . and . . . a choice of Possibilities . . ." And there follow two other notes: "For the instantaneous state of rest = bring in the term: extra-rapid;" and "We shall determine the conditions of [the] best exposure of the extra-rapid State of Rest [of the extra-rapid exposure . . ." This language of rapid exposures which produce a state of rest, an isolated sign, is of course the language of photography. It describes the isolation of something from within the succession of temporality, a process which is implied by Duchamp's subtitle for *La mariée mise à nu . . .* which is "Delay in Glass."

If Duchamp was indeed thinking of the *Large Glass* as a kind of photograph, its processes become absolutely logical: not only the marking of the surface with instances of the index and the suspension of the images as physical substances within the field of the picture; but also, the opacity of the image in relation to its meaning. The notes for the *Large Glass* form a huge, extended caption, and like the captions under newspaper photographs, which are absolutely necessary for their intelligibility, the very existence of Duchamp's notes—their preservation and publication—bears witness to the altered relationship between sign and meaning within this work. In speaking of the rise of photography in the late 19th century, Walter Benjamin writes, "At the same time picture magazines begin to put up signposts for [the viewer], right ones or wrong ones, no matter. For the first time, captions have become obligatory. And it is clear that they have an altogether different character than the title of a painting. The directives which the captions give to those looking at pictures in illustrated magazines soon become even more explicit and more imperative in the film where the meaning of each single picture appears to be prescribed by the sequence of all preceding ones."[10] The photograph heralds a disruption in the autonomy of the sign. A meaninglessness surrounds it which can only be filled in by the addition of a text.

It is also, then, not surprising that Duchamp should have described the Readymade in just these terms. It was to be a "snapshot" to which there was attached a tremendous arbitrariness with regard to meaning, a breakdown of the relatedness of the linguistic sign:

Specifications for "Readymades."
> by planning for a moment
to come (on such a day, such
a date such a minute), "to inscribe
a readymade."—the readymade
can later
be looked for. (with all kinds of delays)

10. Walter Benjamin, "The Work of Art in the Age of Mechanical Reproduction," in *Illuminations*, New York, Schocken Books, 1969, p. 226.

> The important thing is just
> this matter of timing, this snapshot effect, like
> a speech delivered on no matter
> what occasion but at <u>such and such an hour</u>.[11]

The readymade's parallel with the photograph is established by its process of production. It is about the physical transposition of an object from the continuum of reality into the fixed condition of the art-image by a moment of isolation, or selection. And in this process, it also recalls the function of the shifter. It is a sign which is inherently "empty," its signification a function of only this one instance, guaranteed by the existential presence of just this object. It is the meaningless meaning that is instituted through the terms of the index.

12. There is a late work by Duchamp that seems to comment on this altered relationship between sign and meaning given the imposition, within the work of art, of the index. *With My Tongue in My Cheek* (1959) is yet another self-portrait. This time it is not split along the lines of sexual identity, but rather along the semiotic axis of icon and index. On a sheet of paper Duchamp sketches his profile, depicting himself in the representational terms of the graphic icon. On top of this drawing, coincident with part of its contour, is added the area of chin and cheek, cast from his own face in plaster. Index is juxtaposed to icon and both are then captioned. "With my tongue in my cheek," is obviously a reference to the ironic mode, a verbal doubling to redirect meaning. But it can also be taken literally. To actually place one's tongue in one's cheek is to lose the capacity for speech altogether. And it is this rupture between image and speech, or more specifically, language, that Duchamp's art both contemplates and instances.

As I have been presenting it, Duchamp's work manifests a kind of trauma of signification, delivered to him by two events: the development, by the early teens, of an abstract (or abstracting) pictorial language; and the rise of photography. His art involved a flight from the former and a peculiarilarly telling analysis of the latter.

13. If we are to ask what the art of the '70s has to do with all of this, we could summarize it very briefly by pointing to the pervasiveness of the photograph as a means of representation. It is not only there in the obvious case of photo-realism, but in all those forms which depend on documentation—earthworks, particularly as they have evolved in the last several years, body art, story art—and of course in video. But it is not just the heightened presence of the photograph itself that is significant. Rather it is the photograph combined with the explicit terms of the index. For, everywhere one looks in '80s art, one finds instances of this connection. In the work that Dennis Oppenheim made in 1975 called *Identity Stretch*, the

11.   See *The Bride Stripped Bare by Her Bachelors, Even.* A typographical version by Richard Hamilton, *op. cit.*, n. p.

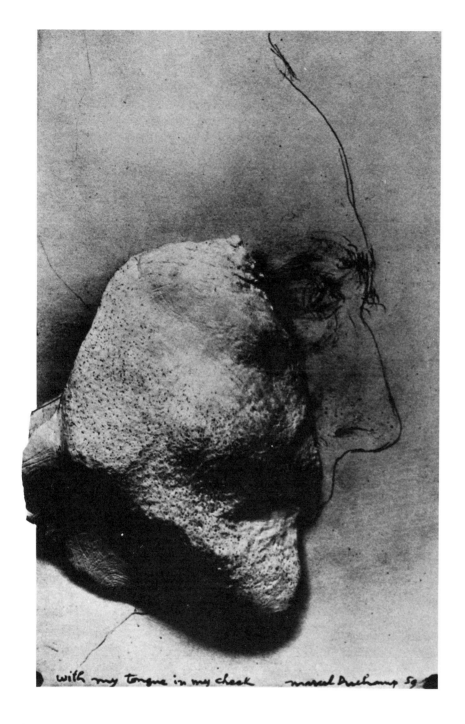

Marcel Duchamp. With My Tongue in My Cheek, *1959. Plaster, pencil and paper, mounted on wood. 9¹³⁄₁₆ × 5⅞ inches. (Coll: Robert Lebel, Paris.)*

Dennis Oppenheim. Identity Stretch. *1975.*
Photographs mounted on board. (Courtesy: The
John Gibson Gallery.)

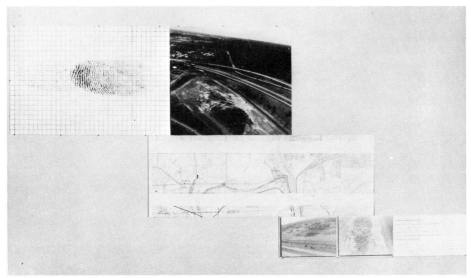

artist transfers the image (index) of his own thumbprint onto a large field outside of Buffalo by magnifying it thousands of times and fixing its traces in the ground in lines of asphalt. The meaning of this work is focused on the pure installation of presence by means of the index. And the work as it is presented in the gallery involves the documentation of this effort through an arrangement of photographs.

Or, the panels that comprise the works of Bill Beckley are also documents of presence, fixed indexically. A recent object combines photographic enlargements of fragments of the artist's body with a panel of text giving us the 'story' of his physical position at a given time and place.

Or, David Askevold's work *The Ambit: Part I* (1975) is likewise made up of photographic panels captioned by text. In his case, like Oppenheim's, we find the index pure and simple: the images are of the cast shadows of an outstretched arm falling onto a luminous plane. The text speaks of an interruption of meaning: ". . . an abstraction within the order of reference which resembles another and also is the identity within this order." The meaning of these three works involves the filling of the "empty" indexical sign with a particular presence. The implication is that there is no convention for meaning independent of or apart from that presence.

This sense of isolation from the workings of a convention which has evolved as a succession of meanings through painting and sculpture in relation to a history of style is characteristic of photo-realism. For there the indexical presence of either the photograph or the body-cast demands that the work be viewed as a deliberate short-circuiting of issues of style. Countermanding the artist's possible formal intervention in creating the work is the overwhelming physical presence of the original object, fixed in this trace of the cast.

14. The functioning of the index in the art of the present, the way that it operates to substitute the registration of sheer physical presence for the more highly articulated language of aesthetic conventions (and the kind of history which they encode), will be the subject of the second part of these notes. The instances involve a much wider field than the types of objects I have just named. They include a shifting conception of abstract art as well, one collective example of which was mounted last spring in the opening exhibition of P.S. 1.

An enormous, derelict building in Long Island City, P.S. 1 was taken over by the Institute for Art and Urban Resources and, renamed Project Studios One, became the site for showing the work of 75 artists, most of whom did "installation pieces." There was tremendous variation in the quality of these works, but almost none in their subject. Again and again this group of artists, working independently, chose the terminology of the index. Their procedures were to exacerbate an aspect of the building's physical presence, and thereby to embed within it a perishable trace of their own.

N.Y., 1976

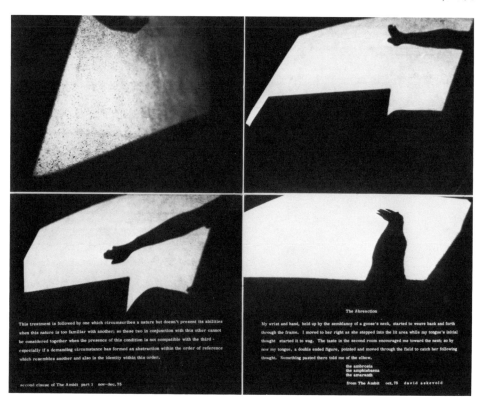

David Askevold. The Ambit. Part I. 1975. Photographs mounted on board. (Courtesy: The John Gibson Gallery.)

Adrien Tournachon. Nadar. c. 1854.
(All Nadar and Tournachon photographs courtesy Alfred A. Knopf, New York.)

My Life as a Photographer

NADAR

TRANSLATED BY THOMAS REPENSEK

I.   *Balzac and the Daguerreotype*

People were stunned when they heard that two inventors had perfected a process that could capture an image on a silver plate. It is impossible for us to imagine today the universal confusion that greeted this invention, so accustomed have we become to the fact of photography and so inured are we by now to its vulgarization.

But not so then. There were some who, like stubborn cattle, refused to even believe that it was possible. What an obstinate race of ill-tempered beings we are: resistant by nature to anything that ruffles our ideas or interferes with our habits; naturally suspicious of everything new, we manufacture menace upon menace until, alas, that tragic irony, "the eagerness to kill," rears its awful head. Why, it seems like only yesterday that one of the learned members of the Institute stood raging in frenzied protest at the first public demonstration of the phonograph. How self-righteously the distinguished professor refused to further dignify with his presence that "ventriloquist hoax," and what a commotion he made stalking out, swearing that the unprincipled charlatan responsible for such a fraud would have to answer to him . . .

Gustave Doré—now there was an incisive, brilliant mind—once said to me, toward the end of his life, his health and spirit broken by disappointment, "What! You mean to say you don't know how much people enjoy finding the one tiny flaw in an otherwise splendid masterpiece?"

As the "Sublime fills us with rioting confusion," so the unknown sends us spinning, shocking us like a slap in the face.

The appearance of the Daguerreotype—which more properly should be called the Niepcetype—was an event which, therefore, could not fail to excite considerable emotion. Exploding suddenly into existence, it surpassed all possible expectations, undermining beliefs, sweeping theories away. It appeared as it remains, the most brilliant star in the constellation of inventions that have already made of our still unfinished century a Golden Age of Science—for lack of any other virtues to recommend it.

Photography sprang to life, in fact, with such splendid haste that its rich profusion of blossoms appeared at once, fully formed: the idea rose complete from the human brain, the first induction becoming immediately the finished work.

Scarcely had the steam engine decreased distance, than electricity abolished it altogether. Bourseul, a lowly employee of the French postal system, glimpsed on the horizon the first sign of the telephone and the poet Charles Cros dreamed the sound of the phonograph. Lissajoux's waves let us actually see the sound that Ader transmitted over long distances and that Edison recorded for us for all time. Pasteur, simply by examining a little more closely the parasitic worms discovered by Raspail, laid down a new order that made all the venerable old books useless. When Charcot opened the mysterious door to the psychic world, a domain whose existence had already been suspected by Mesmer, our time-honored criminal code fell to dust. Marey stole from birds the secret of flight for bodies heavier than air and revealed to man the new realm that would soon be his in the vastness of the universe. Anesthesia placed the divine power of mercy into human hands, staying physical suffering. It is all this, indeed, that Brunetière chose to call "the failure of Science."

Here we find ourselves well beyond the remarkable accomplishments of Fourcroy—at that supreme hour when the embattled Nation *commanded* that discoveries be made; beyond even the achievements of visionaries like Laplace, Montgolfier, Lavoisier, Chappe, Conte, and all the others. So profoundly has Science been transformed in our nineteenth century by these almost simultaneous outbursts of creativity that it is only fitting its symbol be transformed as well: The Hercules of antiquity was a man whose strength was his large, powerful muscles; the modern Hercules is a child reclining on a lever.

But do not all these miracles pale when compared to the most astonishing and disturbing one of all, that one which seems to finally endow man himself with the divine power of creation: the power to give physical form to the insubstantial image that vanishes as soon as it is perceived, leaving no shadow in the mirror, no ripple on the surface of the water? Is it not possible then for man, who today can seize the fleeting flash of vision and cut it into the hardest of metals, to believe that he actually is involved in the process of creation?

To return to the point, Niepce and his shrewd colleague were wise to have waited to be born. The Church has always been cool to innovators, if not too warm, and the discovery of 1839 was suspect from the beginning: this mystery smelled strongly of witchcraft and was tainted with heresy—the heavenly roasting pot had been dragged onto the fire for much less.

Nothing was lacking for a good witch hunt: sympathetic magic, the conjuring up of spirits, ghosts. Awesome Night—dear to all sorcerers and wizards—reigned supreme in the dark recesses of the camera, a made-to-order temple for the Prince of Darkness. It only required the slightest effort of the imagination to transform our filters into philters.

That public admiration was uncertain at first was to be expected; people were bewildered and frightened. The Human Animal needed time to make up its mind and confront the strange beast.

The uneducated and the ignorant were not the only ones to hesitate before this peril. "The lowliest to the most high," so the common saying goes, trembled before the Daguerreotype. More than a few of our most brilliant intellects shrank back as if from a disease. To choose only from among the very highest: Balzac was one of those who could not rid himself of a certain uneasiness about the Daguerreotype process.

He finally pieced together his own explanation for it, seeking refuge somewhat in the fantasist ideas of Cardan. I think I remember seeing this theory developed at great length in a little alcove somewhere in the immense edifice of his work, but I do not have the time to look for it now. I do recall very clearly, however, that he used an exceedingly large number of words to explain it to me on several occasions—he seemed to be quite obsessed with the idea, there in his little violet apartment in the rue de Richelieu—the building had been a famous gambling house during the Restoration and at that time it was still called the Hotel Frascati . . .

According to Balzac's theory, all physical bodies are made up entirely of layers of ghostlike images, an infinite number of leaflike skins laid one on top of the other. Since Balzac believed man was incapable of making something material from an apparition, from something impalpable—that is, creating something from nothing—he concluded that every time someone had his photograph taken, one of the spectral layers was removed from the body and transferred to the photograph. Repeated exposures entailed the unavoidable loss of subsequent ghostly layers, that is, the very essence of life.

Was each precious layer lost forever or was the damage repaired through some more or less instantaneous process of rebirth? I would expect that a man like Balzac, having once set off down such a promising road, was not the sort to go half way, and that he probably arrived at some conclusion on this point, but it was never brought up between us.

As for Balzac's intense fear of the Daguerreotype, was it sincere or affected? I for one believe it was sincere, although Balzac had only to gain from his loss, his ample proportions allowing him to squander his layers without a thought. In any case, it did not prevent him from posing at least for that one Daguerreotype of him that belonged to Gavarni and Silvy before I bought it and that is now in the possession of M. Spoelberg de Lovenjoul.

To suggest that Balzac's fear was something less than real would be to choose one's words very carefully. But, lest we forget, an irrepressible desire to shock has always been the fashionable vice of our brightest minds. These originals, who are still indeed among us today, take such frank delight in making themselves paradoxically ridiculous before our eyes that it would seem to be a mental illness for which we should find a name: *pretentia*. The Romantics coughed languidly at us through their ashen cheeks; the Realists were struck with sudden artless fits of

Nadar. Léon Gozlan. *c. 1855.*

candor; and the Naturalists glared wretchedly with that sordid cast in their eye. Today's generation of decadents and egotists—more tedious by themselves than all the others combined—are afflicted with a shrill screech, the refinement of which only serves to remind us that public madness is not a thing of the past.

Be that as it may, Balzac did not have to look far to find disciples for his new creed. Of his closest friends, Gozlan prudently took cover at once; but good old Gautier and Gérard de Nerval stepped into line immediately. "Faultless" as he was known to be, Gautier never was one to pass up a dubious proposition. Did that writer of elegant and polished verse, floating in an opiate world of Oriental fantasies, forget that the very image of man is forbidden in the lands of the rising sun? As for gentle Gérard, shy and sweet-tempered, always galloping off across some fantastic landscape, he was spoken for well in advance. To an initiate of Isis, an intimate friend of the Queen of Sheba, and a confidant of the Duchesse de Longueville, no dream could be too extravagant. Both of them, however, without any qualms, were among the first to sit—quite successfully I might add—before our camera.

I could not say for how long this trio of mystics resisted the purely scientific explanation of the Daguerreotype, which was accepted very quickly by the public. As was to be expected, our Pantheon of the day protested vigorously at first, but then quickly accepted the inevitable and spoke of it no more.

As the spectral layers appeared, so they disappeared. Neither Gautier nor de Nerval ever brought up the subject again.

Dear Sir,

M. Mauclerc, an actor in transit in our city, has in his possession a daguerreotiped (sic) portrait of himself, which he has shown to me and the patrons of my establishment—the Café du Grand-Théâtre—a portrait he tells us was taken by you in Paris while he was at Eaux-Bonnes by means of the electric process.

Some people who know little of the advances made in the Science of Electricity in recent years have refused to lend credence to the claims of this ill-used young man. My faith in him has never faltered, having dabbled in the process myself for a time.

I beg of you, sir, to kindly make my portrait using the same process, and to send it to me as quickly as possible.

My café is frequented by the best Society, including a large number of English gentlemen and their ladies, especially in the wintertime. I strongly urge you, therefore, to take the greatest possible care with this commission, since it can only be considered favorable to your prospects: numerous persons here have already announced their intention to engage your services.

I would like the portrait in color, if that is possible, taken while I am seated at a table in my salle de billards (sic)—one of the most elegant public rooms in this city.

I am, Sir,

Your obedient servant,

Gazebon,

Proprietor of the Café du Grand-Théâtre, Grande-Place.

Pau, 27 August 1856.

On the back of the folded letter, the practice in those days before the envelope came into general use, with the canceled Imperial seal and stamps of Paris and Pau were the words:

Monsieur Nadar,
Daguerreotype artist,
Rue Saint-Lazare, 113
Paris.

I read and reread this curious letter, which I reproduce here in the original, unable to decide whether I was more amazed at the gullibility of Gazebon or the knavery of Mauclerc.

"Having dabbled in the process myself for a time" set me to thinking, and searching my memory I found there the names of the naïve café proprietor from Pau and the clever itinerant actor.

Some two years before I had received from the same Gazebon—at the instigation of the very same Mauclerc, already then "in transit in our city"—the first of these sensational-sounding epistles. It concerned a gilded copper engraving, a perfect example of Restoration bad taste, entitled *Malek Adel on His Charger*. Poor Malek Adel, it seems, had been passed around from one secondhand dealer to another before being given shelter by Gazebon.

The eternally "in transit" Mauclerc had probably been nosing about one afternoon at the café, and coming across this memorial to the literary taste of the late Mme Cottin, he shrewdly gasped in disbelief, inquiring of the innocent Gazebon whether he was aware that he possessed a treasure of such unquestioned distinction that all the collectors were after it, and that the only other one of its kind belonged to a M. Nadar, Daguerreotype artist, in Paris.

In some such way, I have no doubt, Mauclerc easily coaxed his favorite victim to write to me at once ostensibly about maintaining the market value of our precious masterpieces.

I never answered the letter and the matter was forgotten. It was after this first unsuccessful assault, at least as far as I was concerned, that Mauclerc charged the second time, pushing his trusty Gazebon before him.

So much for Gazebon, whose establishment is "frequented by the best Society, including a large number of English gentlemen and their ladies."—But why *me*? Why this relentless pursuit of me as their chosen vessel? Why contaminate me with complicity in such a foul business? Mauclerc, *"an actor in transit in our city,"* what do you want from me?

Not allowing myself to be swayed by what seemed a marked preference for me—an inclination which I nevertheless choose to consider flattering on the part of M. Mauclerc—I left this second letter unanswered, as I had the first.

And so did I bid them adieu, Mauclerc with his eternal schemes, and heroic Gazebon waiting for his "portrait in color, if that is possible, taken while I am seated at a table in my *salle de billard*(s!)—one of the most elegant public rooms in this city."

But this letter begged to be kept as a rare specimen, and I set it apart Rereading letters like this one at the end of a long and satisfying career is one ol those sweet pleasures which needs no justification.

Yet who would have thought that some twenty years later, old Gazebon would be avenged at last and that . . . but let's not get ahead of ourselves.

Can you imagine anything more satisfying than that hour before the evening meal, after a long day's work? Driven from bed before dawn, you haven't stopped running, your mind has been racing, you've given everything you can, struggling against oppressive fatigue as the day goes on:

I will fall tonight like a slaughtered ox,

and it is only at sundown, when the bell rings, and everyone puts down their work, as the front door turns on its hinges, that a merciful truce is called until tomorrow. It is this cherished hour, satisfied with your day's work—the great human service accomplished—when, restored to yourself at last, you stretch out comfortably in your favorite chair, to harvest the fruit of the day's labor.

But the back door is still open, and if your luck is to be perfect that day, that one with whom you can speak most intimately, who is never far from your thoughts and who thinks always of you, a kindred spirit who has passed through time with you, is suddenly announced into the room. So it was my good fortune one evening to greet the purest soul, the brightest mind, the most quoted person in all of Paris, my dear friend Hérald de Pages; and how nicely our little tête-à-tête was shaping up, leaving fatigue and all the other problems far behind, when, unexpectedly, there came a knock at the door.

"I don't want to see anyone! Will they ever leave me in peace?"

"He has already called three times today, sir, while you were out. He says if you cannot see him now, he will come back later; he says he absolutely must see you."

"Who is he?"

"I don't know; a young man, a workman I'd say, judging from his appearance."

"Send him up," Hérald breaks in—I can tell he has already sensed something interesting.

"All right, let him come up."

*

The young man was shown in, wearing a loosely fitted white shirt tied at the waist, and bare headed. He began by excusing his appearance; he had been working all day and had not had time to go home to change, for he lived with his mother some distance away on the heights of Clignancourt.

He was about twenty years old, at most, a direct, clear look in his eye, reserved, unassuming yet self-assured. He spoke remarkably well, and had none of the drawn-out accent characteristic of the Parisian working class. A fine looking young man, a model French worker: intelligent, responsive, resourceful.

He explained that even though he absolutely had to see me, he would not have persisted if it had not been for the connection that already existed between us: his mother, whose Christian name he mentioned several times, had been in my mother's service in Lyon some years back; in addition, he himself had worked for almost two years for Léopold Léclanché, the son of an old friend of mine.

Nadar. Thérèse Tournachon
(the photographer's mother). c. 1855.

"You nicknamed him *Farouchot*," he laughed so good naturedly, "and a very great loss it was for us all, for me, for everyone, to lose him as we did, for M. Léopold still had great discoveries in front of him, perhaps even more valuable than his electric battery. He was very kind to take me under his wing. I feel a great loss now that he's gone."

"You are an electrician then?"

"Yes, sir. I've always liked my trade, and anything related to it—physics, chemistry, mathematics. I attend courses every evening at the town hall and I read a lot; it's the one thing I really enjoy. I know very little, but I try to keep up with what others are doing. I go to the shops where I can learn something; that's why I left Breguet after a year and a half; it's only a factory; what I am really interested in is the laboratory. I was an apprentice at M. Trouvé's in the rue de Valois while he was working on his duel-motored electric velocipede. I worked with M. Froment on his electric chronometers, and with M. Marcel Deprez, whose generator, I truly believe, sir, is something remarkable that we have not heard the last of. Then there was M. Ader and his telephone . . ."

"Ah! You know M. Ader?"

"Oh, yes indeed sir; a very fine gentleman, sir, and very wise; some day he will have great things to tell us. Yet so unpretentious, so humble."

"Indeed."

"You know him too? Then you know that I am not exaggerating. I was even lucky enough to work with M. Caselli on his autographic telegraphy. Now there . . ."

"But just how old are you?"

"You embarrass me sir; I'll soon be twenty."

"You look younger—but let me see now: you are an electrician; you like to read; you are obviously intelligent; you know my friends *Farouchot* and Ader; and you know your way around—all well and good. But you surely haven't come here this evening only to tell me this?"

There followed a short silence. The young man hesitated, a flush of color coming to his face. Finally, after a great effort:

"I dare not say why it is that I have come to see you, why it is to you and you alone that I *must* come, and why I would have continued to come back no matter how long it took . . . There is nothing more contemptible than flattery, and I want to assure you . . ."

At that moment I must have arched my brow, for he continued:

"Above all, sir, I beg you not to take me for a pretentious fool, which I am not; but what I have to reveal to you is so . . . extraordinary, so incredible, even for one of your experience, so far beyond what is thought to be, that I must beg you to suspend judgment until you have heard me out."

"Yes, please do begin."

"I beg you not to think of me as an inventor, gentlemen. I am only a young man who knows very little, and I don't claim to have made a great discovery—it's only something I happened to find purely by chance while working in the laboratory. You may be surprised by how obvious it will seem. I am speaking, of course, from a scientific point of view; I haven't given a thought to its practical application. I was led to it quite naturally by the recently published accounts on photophony. If MM. Graham Bell and Summer Tainter have indeed established that all bodies can reflect sound under the influence of light, then why do we continue to refuse this gift that light itself holds out to us?"

"And?"

There followed another silence; then resolutely, looking me straight in the eye, he began:

"Suppose for a moment, sir, simply for the sake of argument, as impossible as it may sound to you—but you above all don't have to be reminded that, pure mathematics aside, the great Arago refused to accept that anything was impossible—suppose that a person or an object, anything you like, were in this room at this moment, while your camera technician was in his laboratory, on the same floor or any other floor in the building, unable to see what the object was— not needing to see it! Suppose that a photograph could be taken under these conditions, before your very eyes, over this relatively short distance; would you then grant the possibility of doing the same thing over a considerably greater distance?"

De Pages sprang up as if the young electrician had touched him with a live wire.

Appearing to be surprised, I took the opportunity to examine my interlocutor more closely: his clear, guileless eyes remained fixed on mine.

"And so I have come to ask of you, sir, a favor; a favor that will cost you nothing but that means everything to me. I ask only that you allow one of your own technicians to take, under the conditions I have described, wherever you wish and with whatever model you choose, one photograph to prove or disprove the claims I have advanced. I, needless to say, have none of the photographic equipment necessary, but that end of it has never concerned me.

"Now that I have said it, sir, you see that what I ask is very little. As for my end of it, the little Griscom motor I use—the only equipment I will need—is light enough to hold on my knee.

"I would be eternally grateful if you would do me the honor to witness my demonstration. The profits that could result from it I will not even mention. With absolute trust, I now place myself in your reliable hands."

I dared not move a muscle.

De Pages, in a ferment, sought my eye as eagerly as I avoided his. Clearly, he found me lacking in fervor. Unable to restrain himself, he burst out:

"Do you claim to be able to photograph objects that you cannot even see?"

"I do not claim to be able to do so, sir; I have already done it. But I don't know how else to explain it to you . . . anyway, you will see for yourself. I haven't invented anything; I have only found something that was always there. If I did anything, I discarded what was unnecessary. Do you remember, M. Nadar, what you wrote about Stephenson's first cog wheel locomotive: 'The greatest obstacle to human understanding is the tiresome habit we have of proceeding from the general to the particular'?"

"Now he's quoting from the classics," de Pages laughed.

"I simplified it, that's all. Only . . . gentlemen, I have a confession to make. In conscience I must tell you . . ."

"Yes?"

". . . that I have—kind as you've been I regret it all the more—already demonstrated my experiment publicly. I should have the review of it here somewhere."

He put his hand into his breast pocket, then, with a frown, searched all the others.

"Damn! I must have left it in the workshop!"

Then, smiling again:

"No, here it is."

He unfolded and handed to me a page torn from some *Gazette* or suburban *Review*. At the head of the "Notes and Comments" column we read, de Pages staring intently over my shoulder:

> At two o'clock last Sunday afternoon, in the town hall in Montmartre, a curious experiment took place.
>
> A young man, almost a child, M. M . . . , having obtained the necessary authorizations, demonstrated for the first time publicly his method of electrical photography, with which ingenious process he is able to photograph persons or things beyond his field of vision. The inventor asserted that from Montmartre, he could photograph the town of Deuil, near Montmorency.
>
> His Honor the Mayor and several Council members were on hand, as well as two or three residents of Deuil, who had been called upon to indicate the places to be photographed.
>
> Several exposures were made in rapid succession and the finished pictures were produced at once. The sites represented were immediately recognized by the party from Deuil; houses, trees, and people standing out with remarkable clarity.
>
> The modesty with which the young inventor attempted to escape the enthusiasm of the crowd has only served to increase public interest in this truly remarkable discovery, the practical applications of which already appear to be limitless.

Speechless, we read this extraordinary account a second time.

The very day before, as a matter of fact, de Pages and I had visited the Exposition of Electricity. We had been dazzled and blinded by the miracles we had seen there, yet troubled by this mysterious power we have harnessed, which will be ours to use in the future. Rushing to serve us before, indeed without, being summoned, always there, invisible, like some diabolical servant, it silently indulges our fancies.

We had seen it invisibly discharge all duties and perform all functions, realizing all the dreams of the human imagination, Obedient and ready to execute our commands, this all-powerful yet discreet servant is unrivaled in all its forms, and is known by many names: telegraph, polyscope, phonophone, phonograph, phonautograph, telelogue, telephone, topophone, spectrophone, microphone, sphygmograph, pyrophone, etc., etc. It lifts and carries our burdens, propels our ships, and drives our carriages; it transports our voice from place to place without distortion; it writes far beyond the reach of the human hand; it reads our heartbeat and tells us what time it is; it sounds the alarm before we are aware of the fire and warns us of flood waters before they have begun to rise. Our faithful man-at-arms, it diligently stands the night watch in our stead; it regulates the speed of our missiles and routs our most powerful enemies; it reveals the hidden bullet to the surgeon's knife; it stops dead in their tracks locomotives, galloping horses, and highwaymen all; it tills our soil and winnows our wheat, ages our wine, and captures our game; it monitors the cashier at the same time it guards the cashbox; it prevents electoral fraud and may even someday make honest men of our worthy public officials. A first-class worker, a Jack-of-All-Trades—one at a time or all at once as you like: stevedore, postman, driver, engraver, farmer, doctor, artillery-man, bookkeeper, archivist, carpenter, policeman . . . and why not photographer, even long-distance photographer?

Ah! dear Hérald, always wanting to believe, your fine mind delighting in any new idea—just like our friend Latour-Saint-Ybars, now gone before us—your face, illuminated by the infinite prospect that stretched before us, reproached me with my silent obstinacy.

Yes, of course, I gave in. I would have relented long before if . . . if I had not been in the course of our conversation, visited by a strange creature of the imagination.

Suddenly, as often occurs with optical illusions and certain cases of double vision, the noble features of Hérald's face seemed to merge with those of the honest young worker, becoming a kind of diabolical mask which slowly took on the form of a face I had never seen before but that I recognized immediately: Mauclerc, Machiavellian Mauclerc, "in transit in our city"; the electric image mockingly reared its head at me from the far distant past.

And I seemed to become Gazebon, yes, Gazebon the Gullible. I could see myself seated in my Café du Grand-Théâtre in Pau, still waiting for the portrait to be taken by "the electric process" by M. Nadar in Paris; in the meantime, to pass the time, I raised a toast to "the best Society, including English gentlemen and their ladies."

But the young man was still waiting for his answer, not saying a word now, his eyes still fixed on mine; de Pages continued to effervesce:

"Well Nadar, what do you say?"

"What do you want me to say?"

"But what do you have to lose? What does one exposure more or less mean to you? He asks very little in fact."

At this, the young man, with a smile of sad resignation, replied:

"Oh, no, it's not that. I understand very well what is stopping M. Nadar. Yet, if he could see with his own eyes that it is not true . . ."

"Suppose I do agree . . . where would you install your conducting wires?"

"When I tell you, you will be more skeptical than ever. Still, in conscience, I cannot tell you what is not so. The fact is, sir, that I have no need of wires."

"Well! I should have guessed."

"No, sir, I assure you . . . I am not the first: Bourbouze has proven that tellurian currents exist with a galvanometer. Steinheil used the ground as a conductor as early as 1838, I believe. But the way had been paved long before by the Royal Society of London, when Watson, Cavendish, and a third member whose name escapes me—ah, yes, Martin Folkes!—used the Thames itself as a conductor, not along its current, but across it; they even extended it to include the river bank and some adjacent land. But is not air itself recognized as a conductor? Why do we doubt today what has been known for more than a hundred years? Why do we deprive ourselves of our inheritance? And finally, doesn't the photophone, that miraculous image that speaks and moves, function without conducting wires over great distances? The selenium necessary for its operation was discovered in 1817 by Berzelius: Why has it taken us half a century to put it to use? Yet it is always as you have said, 'the human mind proceeds from the general to the particular.' . . . Not needing conducting wires, sir, I simply dispensed with them."

Speechless a moment ago, I now was absolutely stunned.

But the battle had been won, and our young man knew it, for, to mark his victory, he added more familiarly, with a candid smile:

"And now if you will permit me, M. Nadar, I didn't expect to encounter such resistance in a man known for so many daring initiatives; a man who—thirty years before anyone else dreamed of it—predicted the *phonograph*, even conferring on it its name. For it was in 1856, in an article in the *Musée Français-Anglais*, that you . . ."

"All right . . . enough!"

". . . you who took the first underground photographs by artificial light and the first photographs from an aerial balloon; who in 1863 destroyed the myth of the navigability of lighter-than-air craft and singlehandedly advanced the theory—accepted by everyone today—of aerial locomotion by heavier-than-air machines; you who . . ."

"Have mercy!! Come whenever you like."

"Ah! thank you very much, sir."

"When will you return?" de Pages asked, beside himself with excitement.

"I will return on the sixteenth, if that is convenient, at any hour you choose."

Hérald broke in impatiently:

"The sixteenth . . . but today is only the fourth! Why put it off for twelve days? Why not earlier? tomorrow, or today even?"

"I am sorry, sir; I am unable to come before the sixteenth."

"Why?"

But the young man was already moving toward the door, bowing to take his leave. De Pages grabbed him by the sleave:

"But why wait so long?"

"Excuse me, sir, but I am unable to tell you why; it is a personal matter, of no interest whatsoever. I will return the sixteenth."

"But what possible reason could you have to postpone for twelve days a demonstration that obviously means so much to you?"

"I can only repeat, sir; it is a personal matter and there is no need for anyone to intervene."

But de Pages was not one to be put off and he continued to insist with such energy that the young man, besieged as he was, had to give in:

"Come now, in strictest confidence, among friends, what is it?"

"You persist so kindly, sir, that I am unable to resist any further. Since you wish to know, I will tell you. I must wait until the fifteenth . . . to be paid, so that I can buy the supplies needed for the experiment. Last Sunday at Montmartre I used up the last of my materials. It is an insignificant amount, only about forty francs, but I am sure you understand, sir, that I would rather furnish these myself."

Well, he's finally come out with it, I thought.

This time it was I who looked at de Pages. But nothing escapes the vigilant: the young worker swung around toward Hérald, and stifling a tear that remained suspended in the corner of his eye, he said:

"There! You see, sir, I was sure of it. M. Nadar thinks ill of me. Yet he is my witness: I wanted to say nothing of this; I gave in because you insisted and now I am taken for a schemer, a miserable beggar."

It seemed appropriate to calm and reassure him; and I helped Hérald with the task. To bring the story to a close, the young man left with two louis in his pocket—but how we had to beg him!

He will return tomorrow morning at ten o'clock, *without fail.*

There he goes.

*

Since I said nothing, Hérald began:

"Well??"

"So much for your two louis."

"What do you mean? Do you think all that was only a game, that the boy is a liar, that he won't be back?"

"It wasn't very expensive after all. And what a consummate artist: his entrance, modest and reserved, his attire simple and unaffected—all quite correct; preliminary topic: sentimental evocation of the two mothers—a strategy that never fails; the ingratiating exordium, the elaborate oratorical paraphernalia; the endless list of facts and dates—difficult to verify on the spot—which he manipulates like a circus performer; the flattery, a bit obvious, but always appropriate; and to achieve the well-ordered whole, what endurance! what amazing discipline! And from one still so young! Believe me, he has the makings of a future minister whom even our conservative Republic will be able to use in its political horsetradings."

"But the names of friends he mentioned?"

"Information available only too readily to anyone who happens to be standing next to me or a friend of mine for a few minutes."

"And the newspaper article?"

"How is it, Hérald, that you who know the world of publishing so well, the founder of the *Petit Journal*, with its more than four million readers, how can you let yourself be taken in by an item slipped into one of the last issues of some short-lived tabloid—who knows?—perhaps out of kindness or with the cooperation of a compositor friend? How can you believe as you do in the printed word—and you an editor? In spite of your intelligence you do seem to have retained a certain purity of soul! But no, all this means nothing or very little indeed; what is truly admirable is not so much his acquiring all this pseudo-scientific knowledge but his knowing how to use it—how artfully and dexterously he practices his deception! We have witnessed this evening a first-rate performance, and I for one am pleased to have made the acquaintance of this extremely capable young man. He will go far! . . . Yes, I admit, I am hard to please—but it was amusing: as you watched me allow myself to swallow the bait. At last, Gazebon is avenged—on me!—and by me!!"

Are you satisfied, Mauclerc! you and your hideous smile . . .

"But, my friend, how do you account for all this effort resulting in only the miserable pilfering of two wretched louis?"

"I beg your pardon: you are absolutely right. We were worth more than that; he could have gotten five from us at least—proof that even the best horse falters. But do you think that it was for me alone, for this one performance, that he set up this elaborate theatrical intrigue which must have required serious study and repeated rehearsals? No, it would hardly have been worth it. What this spirited boy has served us here tonight he will ladle out to all the photographers of Paris,

France, and the world, seasoning his rhetoric as a cook does his stew, according to individual taste, and there is no one too humble, I'll wager, for whom he will not prepare this highly seasoned concoction. Since none of those whom he favors with his trust and promise of limitless profits will take it into their head to announce to their neighbor that they have been hoodwinked, the game will go on without end. Now that is what someone of a practical bent would call a 'racket.' And at the same time, it's a great philosophical adventure."

After a moment of silence, de Pages concluded:

"Let's think of it no more. But do you still categorically refuse to believe, you who encourage—which I find reprehensible, I must say—our very charming but detestable friend G. . . . to repeat time and again his favorite conceit, 'Everything is possible, even God!'—do you still refuse to admit the possibility of long-distance photography?"

"I think it would be as rash to deny the possibility as to affirm it. I remain, innocent as I am of absolute knowledge, floating somewhere in the middle. Babinet, in reply to Biot's atheist proposition, has said: 'Then you are absolutely certain that God does not exist? Well, my friend, you are *even more superstitious* than you claim me to be. I really know nothing at all about it.' In conclusion, I will only go so far as to say, this time quoting Biot—no truer words were ever spoken: *'There is nothing easier to do than what I did yesterday; and nothing more difficult than what I will do for the first time tomorrow.'*"

*

P.S. When we wrote these words, we scarcely believed that the technical question presented so imaginatively in this chapter would soon be taken up in actual fact by our eminent correspondent and friend Doctor Ed. Liesegang, of Vienna. Regarding this subject, see his very interesting article in the *British Journal of Photography*, in which we may finally see Mauclerc discredited and Gazebon rehabilitated. Three cheers for Gazebon!!!

P.P.S. This morning the first successful wireless telegraph message was transmitted across the English Channel by Marconi. Is there any dream too extravagant? . . .

Marseilles, June 1899.

Atelier Nadar. Marie, Princess of Solms.

III.   *The Blind Princess*

"Has Mme Ratazzi arrived yet?" I asked glancing over the list of appointments for the day.

"No, sir."

". . . *the Princess of Solms?*"

"Yes, but she is not Mme Ratazzi. The Princess of Solms is the sister of the King of Hanover. Her two children—a son and a daughter—came in person to make the appointment for their mother, who is blind. They said that you knew their family, and that they themselves had some years ago been very close to you."

Some years ago, indeed . . .

In a memoir of this sort it would be impossible to avoid entirely that detestable first person pronoun—it would even be awkward to do so. All the same, I beg the Reader's indulgence while I take a moment to recall an episode that occurred in 1863, which, in spite of the great commotion it raised at the time, has now been completely forgotten.

*

It was during my first attempts to take photographs from a balloon—still very difficult in those days before the trail was cut through, child's play today—that I was struck with the eternal human dream of aerial navigation.

Several abrupt descents, during which the wickerwork basket of my balloon, buffeted by light winds and swinging helplessly, crashed into trees and sideswiped a few buildings, gave me something to think about: "If I can't control my balloon in this light breeze, which tangles my mooring anchors, snaps my cables, and drags me all over creation, how can I ever hope to navigate it?"

This fact and the propositions that logically followed from it, led me to conclude that the aerostat—its very name defined its destiny—could never be an airship. Born a floating bubble, so it would die. Those who claimed it was something more had only taken us up a nettlesome, tortuous path that led nowhere.

Still, I used to think that it was man's birthright, since other animals fly, to range far and wide in the heavens.

It seemed to me that birds and flying insects move through the air precisely because they are unlike balloons. They do not rise in the air because of a difference in specific gravity; they exert pressure on the air itself, and it is this that enables them to fly.

Those learned professors, when I bothered to consult them, quickly taught me that flight, in its strictest sense, that is, aerial self-propulsion, is a harmony of dynamic and static forces.

The invention of the Montgolfier brothers was a lofty yet misleading discovery. It sent man along a road beset with pathetic disappointments and ridiculous failures, a route he nevertheless returned to time and again.* It was necessary, finally—as the homeopaths had turned around allopathic theory—to reverse the proposition in order to extract the essential problem:

To be denser—heavier than air—to command the air—in this as in all other things:—*To be the strongest in order not to be beaten.*

---

* I must ask a question here: How long has it been since that balloon went up one morning in Meudon, without warning, floated over to Chaville, I believe, and returned as quickly as it went, taking advantage of a few precious moments of blissful calm—to gain victory over an *absent* enemy?

There was a minister of public education or rather public ignorance at the time, who had the nerve to utter in peroration to the assembled members of the Institute—to the embarrassment and confusion of all Frenchmen—these disgraceful words: "*Glory to the French Army, which has found the road of the aerial balloon that now stretches out before us.*"

Undoubtedly! Who would not have agreed that this discovery was one of the most precious of human finds? For the fated and commendable inventor never tired of affirming the magnificence of his achievement, attempting to overcome all skepticism with the inauguration of regularly scheduled, daily balloon flights.

Now then, how many times *since* the solemn declaration of that peerless minister has the inventor repeated even once his little jump from Meudon to Chaville and back?

And how much over all these years has it cost us; how much does it continue to add to an already enormous national budget, the abortive ascents of these "floating fish," which do not fly and can never hope to?

It was something and nothing at the same time: only a mathematical formula. Who would breathe life into it? Certainly not me, for I have none of the mathematical fineness, none of the theoretical grace of an engineer; never having been able to tackle logarithms, by nature resistant to symbolic expressions of the sort A + B, reproached from childhood on for knowing how to count, but no more.

Who then will reveal this great unknown to us; which one of us will set in motion this colossal revolution that will overturn the world of today—think about that for a moment—before which all the pride of human knowledge will be swept away?

But can such a superhuman, empyrean task be accomplished by one human being alone?

Faced with this knotty problem, in which the whole range of human knowledge is brought into play, it seemed necessary to appeal to all inquiring minds, in short, to all who believed as I did.

With a dear friend, whom I have since lost, that splendid La Landelle, and Ponton d'Amécourt, struck alas partially mad—*sapientem stultitiam*—I founded the "Society for the Encouragement of Aerial Locomotion by Heavier-than-Air Machines," and with the same stroke, in a reverie of enthusiasm, created our own journal *L'Aéronaute*.

They came from all over, inventors, technicians, mathematicians, physicists, chemists, and more—the Corps of Engineers, the Department of the Navy, professors and students from colleges and universities. At first count, six hundred had responded to the call. Every Friday evening these faithful souls assembled to discuss ideas and present plans of action.

But still it was not enough: experimentation, experimentation without end was necessary to create from Nothing this Vast Synthesis.

Money was needed, a lot of money . . .

But where to find it? . . .

The only fortune I ever had was my work, and I would not have accepted even one penny from the government of that day—although they bore me good will, a remarkably insistent good will that I recall, which I must in conscience give them credit for today.

I was the only one to encourage my Society for Encouragement, and I was not sufficient to the task.

The idea came to me then that the treasure I was seeking was to be found precisely in what I was trying to get rid of. I therefore had built at great expense to myself an aerostat of previously unheard of dimensions, the balloon of which, containing 6,000 cubic meters of gas, was able to lift forty-five artillery soldiers— which it actually did—standing in the two-story wicker basket. And I called this monster the *Géant*.

I had hoped the ascents of this colossal balloon in every capital and great city of the entire universe would fill the coffers of our Society, allowing, at the same time, for everyone to pay a part of the ransom of future aerial navigation.

In fact, Paris twice, then all of Brussels, Lyon, and Amsterdam, tried to elbow their way into this oddity. I had been right after all, except on one essential point; forgetting to be a wise virgin, my lamp untrimmed, hundreds of thousands of francs poured in only to disappear immediately into thin air . . .

All my great plans came to nothing, except a grim struggle to pay everyone that went on for ten years.

But this concerns only me.

Dear Reader, you must wonder what all this has to do with the Princess of Solms—well, in fact, I am rushing toward her under full sail.

But how can I resist such memories, especially when I find myself standing again before the GREAT CAUSE, there where I will walk no more . . .

The second time we went up in the *Géant*, we left the Champ de Mars at seven o'clock one evening, and at eight o'clock the next morning, through an error in judgment on the part of one of the crew members, we were dropped out of the sky near Hanover, Germany, some 650 kilometers away. For 28 kilometers in the space of 30 minutes—the normal speed of the average express train—we were dragged bouncing across the German countryside. Try to imagine covering the same 28 kilometers in a half hour, sitting in a basket in tow behind a speeding train, and you can see what a lively little dance it was.

There were, surprisingly, no casualties. One person suffered a broken arm; I fractured a leg and had a few sprains; but my dearest wife who had gallantly chosen—in the words of the canon—"to follow her husband wherever he went," was cruelly bruised. The other passengers got off with minor injuries.

We were taken in rather great pain to the city of Hanover which was nearby, where we were installed in too princely a manner on the *premier étage* of the Grand-Hôtel, reserved for our little group—by the order of the King.*

I am unable to describe the concern and kindness that flowed both from the Palace and the French embassy. Baskets of fruit and bouquets of flowers were dispatched by the Queen to my poor wife morning and night—that same queen I was to encounter in Paris several years later, in exile, half mad with grief, keeping vigil over her dying husband in a rented house the two of them had taken in the rue de Presbourg.

Twice a day, without fail, an aide-de-camp of the King came to inquire after

---

*   These expenses, like all the others, including the specially heated train that we had not requested, were all paid back—every last *silbergroschen*—which the King most *certainly* was unaware of. We also paid for all the medical attention we received, except that administered by Doctor Muller—an excellent fellow—who declined all payment for his services, and to whom our government presented several days after the incident the *ruban rouge* of the Legion of Honor.

I kept all the receipts, amounting to some 6000 francs—six thousand francs!—the cost of one week's stay, including transportation, compensation for damages, and incidentals.

All this by way of reply to the Prussian newspapers: It was because they resented the success of my aerial postal service during the siege of Paris and were trying to get even with me for an article I wrote in which I expressed no great love for Germany, that they all rushed to accuse me then of ingratitude—that most detestable of human perversions.

us. He was a giant, whose large frame appeared even more menacing under his white uniform. I was perfectly free, as he sat at my bedside, to observe that this great body of war concealed a remarkably fine intelligence molded by an excellent scientific education. Needless to add, my presence there in a hospital bed served quickly to enlist him as another adept in our Society.

I had not seen this officer since the adventure in Hanover, when looking through the newspapers one day, I came across his name. I read with regret that Count Wedel, for so he was called, had suddenly left the personal service of the King, and Hanover itself, following an unfortunate duel in which he had shot a duke to death—whose name I have lost somewhere in the *burg, stein,* or *berg* endings, the ones that evoke the names of old German families.

*

At last, after being so long in the past, we have finally arrived back in the present: The Princess of Solms is announced. The son and the daughter enter leading and sustaining their mother; eyes closed and smiling in the way of the blind, the Princess slides her feet carefully across the floor.

I had seen the same absent expression on the face of her brother, the King, who was also blind—although I never did find out if their affliction was hereditary. But the King refused to accept his condition; and everyone remembers the innocent deception he frequently practiced with his glasses at the Opéra. He was his sister's twin in another way; he also had a guardian angel, his daughter the Princess Frederika, who never left his side while he lived. Like twin Antigones, both daughters had forever renounced marriage out of the jealous self-devotion of filial duty.

When the Princess had been seated, the laboratory procedures got under way. Between poses I sat with the children, whose friendliness and warmth I was attracted to immediately, both of them being more pleasant than I had been led to believe. They never took their eyes off their dear *maman,* whom they hovered over attentively.

They spent the time retelling the details they remembered of our stay in Hanover: their many visits to see the shattered basket, and the shredded material that was all that remained of the balloon; the questions they asked about the terrible catastrophe; the games they played good-naturedly with my son, who was much younger than they were at the time—he had been brought from Paris as soon as the accident had happened; the Queen sent for him every morning, and off to the Palace he would go. The two of them did not stop asking me questions, inquiring about what I had been up to since then, and what my plans were for the future.

While answering their questions as best I could, dashing back and forth to complete my work, I inquired about a few things that had continued to intrigue me from the time of my convalescence.

And from the rear of the studio, separated from us by a great distance, the Princess sometimes joined in our conversation.

One last time I returned to sit with them, just as they were about to leave. "Oh, by the way, can you tell me anything about a charming gentleman whom I had the pleasure to meet during my stay; he seems to have disappeared since his tragic duel: Count Wedel? . . ."

A thunderbolt striking us on the spot could not have created such chaos.

The two children sprang up, as if charged by an electric current, stretching every muscle in their body toward one point: *maman*. Deathly pale, holding her breath, the daughter pleaded with her hand for silence, and the young man quickly screamed in a whisper, *"No!!!"*

Not understanding, I said nothing.

But already they had turned back toward one another—what thoughts they saw in each other's glance!—and trembling, they breathed a sigh of relief.

Their mother, still smiling, had heard nothing.

Then the young man whispered into my ear, so quietly that I had to strain to hear: "The man killed by Count Wedel two years ago was our older brother . . . We are able to hide this terrible thing from our mother because of her blindness. But we have always feared—we always will fear—that with the Count gone, she may someday suspect . . . Our mother thinks that our brother has been traveling around the world for the last two years. Every two weeks we read her *his* letters—every word of which she knows by heart—letters written by my sister and me . . . She is counting the days until he returns . . . another word could have taken her from us forever . . ."

Tragic frailty of human existence! All these stories lovingly created, carefully intertwined, and dutifully carried on; the patient lies, the breathless intensity—all could have been suddenly undone, cruelly annihilated in a moment: the tender hope of a mother, the heroic consolation of her children, fallen in ruins to be swallowed up in darkest despair, beyond the power of the human word . . . all because of a chance encounter, a word casually spoken on a visit to a photographer's studio, in a strange city . . .

The memory of it still makes my blood run cold.

The Index of the Absent Wound
(Monograph on a Stain)*

GEORGES DIDI-HUBERMAN

translated by THOMAS REPENSEK

Almost Nothing to See

It is a large piece of linen serge, covered with stains. Lined with red silk (one side is therefore covered over), it has been carefully rolled up and placed in a silver reliquary. The reliquary itself is locked behind a metal grating within a monumental altar that stands beneath Guarini's soaring black marble dome in Turin. None of the sheet (*lenzuolo*) itself, therefore, is visible. One kneels before a photographic negative, as it were, enshrined in the altar and illuminated from within.

Sometimes — though very rarely — it is carried in a procession, an ostentation of the object, in person, if we can call it that. But even then nothing can be seen. All the faithful express the same dissatisfaction: ". . . I was disappointed: *non si vede niente* (you can't see anything) everyone was saying. We tried. . . ."[1] But the dissatisfaction and the attempt to see constitute *something*. In fact, *almost* nothing was visible. "We tried to see something else," the spectator goes on to say, "and little by little we could see."[2] Almost nothing was visible, that is to say: already something other than *nothing* was visible in that *almost*. One actually saw, then, something else, simply in the looking forward to it or the desiring of it.

But the modalities of the desire to see are extremely refined. The little-by-little of this "discovery" itself takes on the form of a dizzying spiral that is both precise, as dialectic, and overwhelming, as unending baptism of sight. Following it to its source raises the very question of the advent of the visible. And that involves an entire constellation of ideas, conventions, and phantasms, which I will deal with here only partially, from the point of view of a single stain.

---

* This text is a summary of a paper presented at Urbino in July 1983 at the colloquium "Rhetoric of the Body," in response to the well-developed arguments of Louis Marin on Nicole and the Veronica question.
1. Pierre Vignon, reply to M. Donnadieu, in *L'Université catholique*, XL, no. 7 (1902), p. 368.
2. *Ibid.*

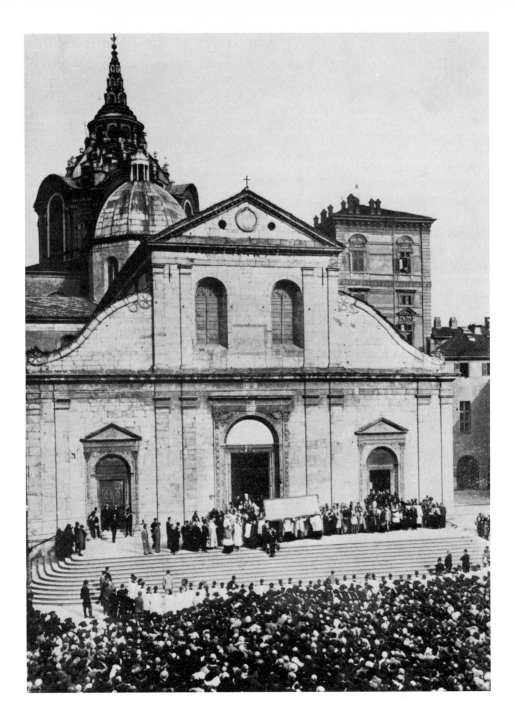

Ostentation (Enrie, 1931).

Let us recall that the historic impetus that rendered the shroud of Turin visible — or more precisely, figurative — is found in the history of photography.[3] When Secondo Pia immersed in the chemical bath his last attempt to produce a clear photograph of the holy shroud — his earlier attempts had all been underexposed — this is what happened: there in the dark room, the moment the negative image took form (the inaugural glimpse), a face looked out at Pia from the bottom of the tray. A face he had never before seen on the shroud. A face that was, he said, *unexpected*. And seeing it he almost fainted. The event took place during the night of the 28th to the 29th of May, 1894.[4]

It was after this "amazing" occurrence (just as the negative coalesced) that the pattern of stains on the shroud of Turin took on a recognizable form. The photographic negative revealed what one had never hoped to see on the shroud itself. As the photographic "evidence" objectified an aspect of the shroud, it became proof of a miracle. Not only did it sanction an unprecedented sort of expository value for this relic heretofore hidden from view, it reestablished the *aura* of the shroud, investing the object itself with a counterpart to its semiotic status. The holy shroud became the *negative imprint* of the body of Christ, its *luminous* index miraculously produced and miraculously inverted in the very act of resurrection, henceforth to be conceived of in photographic terms.[5]

The stain we are concerned with here remains, with others, outside the confines of this splendid hermeneutical elaboration, since it cannot be explained by the theory of a negative flash of light, *achiropoïete*, that would reconstitute the actual appearance of the Christly body. It doesn't seem to lend itself to being raised up (in the sense of the dialectical *Aufhebung*) into something figurative; it seems to defy comprehension as a recognizable image. It says nothing about the economy of its support (which would at least establish the hypothesis of a luminous-negative index). It seems to exist only in terms of its tonal variations, only as an effect of its support. Yet the tonal variations of the fabric have no precise limits, sequence, or articulation. It seems to exist, therefore, only as the uncertain effect of something as undifferentiated background. Between the *spatium* (the background in question) and the pure surface, this stain reveals itself only in the precarious opening of the becoming visible; it is deployed only as a closing of signification, a closing to signification. It says nothing. It doesn't seem made to be understood (whereas a figure, a recognized image, a facial ap-

---

3.   I use the term *impetus* rather than *origin* because it concerns the universalizing moment of this *making visible*. Before the camera was passionately focused on the shroud of Turin and the train of its hermeneutic or polemical effects (the thousands of articles written on the topic since 1898), few authors devoted themselves to the study of a relic that had been exceedingly discreet and stingy in its allocation of miracles. They include: Pingone (1581), Paleotto (1598), Chifflet (1624), Capré (1662).

4.   Cf. especially A. Loth, *Le portrait de N.S. Jésus-Christ d'après le Saint Suaire de Turin*, Oudin, Paris, n.d. [1900], pp. 25–27.

5.   The reader is referred to my study, "Le négatif et al relève de figurabilité — Note sur un drap photographié," forthcoming.

pearance always point to or at least carry the promise of meaning). It seems to arise from pure contingency. It tells nothing in itself about its origin. Would segmenting or scanning it give it meaning? Yet it appears to be outside the bounds of scansion or any sort of narrativity. It is only a chain of nonmimetic, chance occurrences, neither imperceptible nor yet perceptible as figures.

The stain (Vignon, 1938).

The Indexical Presupposition, Retracement

What we need is a concept of figurative *Aufhebung*. We would have to consider the dichotomy of its field and its means, and how they deploy a dialectical mimesis as initiation of absolute knowledge; how it attempts to transform sensible space[6] and to begin a movement (Hegel would have said automovement) in the direction of certitude, figural certitude. An absolute seeing that would transcend the scansion of seeing and of knowing; an absolutely reflexive representation. Confronted with its formless stains, interpreters of the shroud imagined such a *transformation*, which photography would actually accomplish. A phantasm associating Christ's passion with the medium of photography would *hallucinate* such a transformation (with all the beauty, rigor, and insane precision the term implies).

We have to look at this stain again, but this time with the "foresight" of such figural certainty in mind, or its "phantasm," its *phantasia* in the Hegelian sense; for Hegel considered *Phantasie* an *Aufhebung*, and spoke of the movement of truth as a delirium of absolute translucidity.[7]

But first it must be stated that in that very place where figuration abolishes itself—as in this stain—it also generates itself. This, in a way, amounts to setting forth a transcendental phenomenology of the visible, which would describe with regard to this stain, appearance (*phaïnesthai*, which, however, has the same root as *phantasia* in the element signifying light) as the very process of *dis*figuration; it would describe how this stain came *not* to possess a figurative aspect. That requires in any case inventing a structure of substitutions, returns, and representations: a structure of *retracement*. Retrace, in other words, tell, *retell* a story, but also trace *a line* over it, a line that, let's say, will make the original trace "represent a subject for other traces," those traditional narratives known as the gospels.

The prodigality (sophism) of hermeneutics consists therefore in laying this trace over a story which it does not in any way represent. If this constitutes an aporia, then it must be noted that a hermeneutic enterprise is able to override any semiotic aporia that threatens to impede the automovement of its figural certainty. This movement has its premise in the hypothesis declared earlier (it is a ravishing hypothesis in any case), that there, just where figuration effaces itself, it generates itself as well. But the unlooked-for corollary, the supplement, would be the following: the effacement of all figuration in this trace is itself the guarantee of a link, of *authenticity;* if there is no figuration it is because *contact*

6. Hegel considers every signifying process an *Aufhebung* of sense-space intuition. Cf. Jacques Derrida, "The Pit and the Pyramid: Introduction to Hegel's Semiology," in *Margins of Philosophy*, trans. Alan Bass, Chicago, University of Chicago Press, 1982.
7. Cf. Georg Wilhelm Friedrich Hegel, *The Phenomenology of Spirit*, trans. A. V. Miller, London, Oxford University Press, 1977; and J.-L. Nancy, *La remarque speculative*, Paris, Galilée, 1973, pp. 137–140.

has taken place. The noniconic, nonmimetic nature of this stain guarantees its *indexical value*. I might add that the word *authenticity* is common to the vocabulary used by Peirce to describe the index[8] and to the cultural discourse of theologians concerning relics (the stain itself is like a micro-session — and no less important for that — in the great authenticating process focused on the shroud of Turin, a process that never ends).

The absence of figuration therefore serves as proof of existence. Contact having occurred, figuration would appear false. And the signifying opaqueness itself reinforces the *it was* of an object (in the Peircian sense, we know that an index does not cease to be an index when the interpretant fails to account for it, whereas the existence of its referential object — the illness related to a symptom, for example — is semiotically essential[9]). Every figure has its origin where it is effaced, if that place of origin is a place of contact.

But that also means that an *act* is thereby — though no less originarily — set in motion. Peirce defines the symptom as a paradigm of the index, because the symptom locates on a semiotic plane an illness in the process of acting[10] — a *drama*, that is, an action fraught with consequences; in Greek there is a word for murder and a word for ritual. Figuration is effaced just where drama provides its index; this means, in its fullest sense, that the more fully drama is freighted with consequence, the greater, and more beautiful, will be the splotch, the disfiguration, the stain.

For in fact we are dealing here with crime, blood, and ritual. Figural certitude takes the decisive step of *seeing* substance in this brownish stain. Henceforth it will see a bloodstain. Thus is established the existence of a sheet of linen as a shroud.

The third stage of the argument: If all physical contact calls to mind the act that establishes it (in an indexical relationship), every act calls forth as well, and imperatively, the proper name of the *actor*: he who left some of his blood on this linen sheet (Peirce also considers the proper name to be a paradigm of the index, because it is associated with an absolutely specific subject; he says, however, that the proper name is also a "legisign," because it is a sign that legalizes its relationship to the subject; it is there precisely as an imperative; elsewhere Peirce writes that "if an index could be translated into sentence form, that sentence would be in the imperative or exclamatory mood, as in *Look over there!* or *Watch out!*").[11] Now since we are dealing with him in whose Name the shroud is placed in the reliquary altar, and with the drama of his Passion, such as it is found written for all eternity in the books of the gospels, the imperative takes

---

8.   Charles Sanders Peirce, *The Collected Papers,* vols. I–VI, ed. Charles Hartshorne and Paul Weiss; vols. VII–VIII, ed. Arthur Burks, Cambridge, Harvard University Press, 1931–1935; 1958.
9.   *Ibid.,* 2:304.
10.   *Ibid.,* 8:119.
11.   *Ibid.,* 3:361.

on another meaning, that of dogma. As for the index, it acquires an added dimension, as a prescription to a treasure-trove of symbols. If there is any paralogism it is to be found here: the index reduced to the symbolic imperative of a story in which the possibility of a theology of the resurrection of the body must — semiologically speaking — play a part. The disappointing tenor of this line of thought is felt at once, for it consists of "affirming" the indexicality of a visible sign for the sole purpose of making it shine forth as a beacon of symbolic law.

Elaboration of Detail

It is necessary, *in spite of everything*, to subject this contingent stain to law (concatenation), a passage to discreet order — a division. A *discernment*, a word whose root, *cernere*, contains the three signifying vectors "sifting," "seeing," and "deciding," which is exactly what is involved here.

Decidedly, then, let us look at this stain once again; let us draw close to it again, to discern, to define an order of detail and articulation. Yet this stain is, in its physical conditions as in its perceptual effects, inseparable from the texture of its support. Looking closely at a stain on the shroud of Turin results unfortunately in a total loss of perspective. The weave "eats up" all effect of outline, and even tonal distinction. An intimate knowledge of this stained fabric is therefore an obstacle to discernment; because it gives priority to the materiality of the fabric, it compromises the hermeneutical process.

This is undoubtedly, in one sense, an aspect of the epistemic nature of detail. Detail, Bachelard recalled, is anti- and ante-categorical. In order to describe a detail, "you have to judge material disturbances beneath the surface. And then, conclusions fluctuate. The first conclusion [from a distance] was correct; it was qualitative, it developed in the discontinuity of numerous predicates. . . . [Detail] is richness, but also uncertainty. Along with its subtle nuances occur profoundly irrational disturbances. . . . At the level of detail, Thought and Reality appear to be set adrift from one another so that as Reality is distanced from the scale at which our thinking normally takes place, it loses its solidity in a certain way, its constancy, its substance. Finally, Reality and Thought are engulfed in the same nothingness."[12] It should be noted in passing that interpretation (*Deutung*), in the Freudian sense, is established in the contemplation of this very uncertainty of detail (uncertainty thought of henceforth in terms of an attempt at overspecification); this doesn't in the slightest set it in opposition to a hermeneutic enterprise that functions only "en masse."[13]

But this "voracious burst" of detail seen at too close a range has a place in

12.   Gaston Bachelard, *Essai sur la connaissance approchée*, Paris, Vrin, 1927, pp. 253, 257.
13.   Cf. Sigmund Freud, *The Interpretation of Dreams* (1900) in *The Standard Edition of the Complete Psychological Works*, trans. James Strachey, London, Hogarth Press and The Institute of Psycho-Analysis, vols. IV & V; Hubert Damisch, "Le gardien de l'interprétation," in *Tel Quel*, no. 44 (1971), p. 78; Naomi Schor, "Le détail chez Freud," in *Littérature*, no. 37 (1980), pp. 3–14.

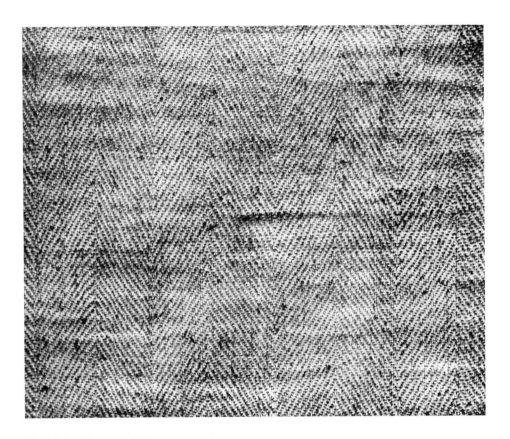

The fabric (Vignon, 1938).

the phenomenology of visible discernment. From among many possible sources, we could cite Ernst Bloch's *Experimentum mundi*, which develops the theme of the closely considered surface as a "contamination" of the space and a blinding hold on the eye. *Proximity* is with all justification thought of as an *obstacle*, an obscurantist view, an alienating immediacy. I would like to call it the effect of *surface* (to distinguish it from *ground*, which can be apprehended in its parts; to suggest also its anguished, even catastrophic, terror-striken nature, as a space become wall, wall become sky, sky become hole, intimate dizziness). Now, since obstacles are there to be surmounted, we ought to sense the inevitable appeal of *Aufhebung*. Bloch calls it mediation, elevation, negation, ostentation, rotation by seeing. And this is how, he says, a figure will "appear" or "reappear." He calls this process finally an *elaboration*.[14] And that alone tells us that the problem

14. I am summarizing the general theme of his argument. Cf. Ernst Bloch, *Experimentum mundi. Frage, Kategorien d. Herausbringens, Praxis*, Suhrkamp, 1975.

of detail does not have its source only in the problematic of pure perception. The problem here is not one of a *Gestalttheorie*, in as much as, according to Merleau-Ponty's critique, *Gestalttheorie* uses a concept of "form" as pure cause or something "real," given.[15] It is a question rather of considering the appearance of figuration or recognizable form as a process of *elaborated distancing*. Distancing creates visibility, in as much as it involves elaboration.

I think it is necessary to understand this word in its Freudian sense as elaboration or working through (*Verarbeitung, Bearbeitung*); an associative process that presupposes its object, rendering it suitable to support a fantasy. Case in point: a fantasy of the Christly body, filigreed in discernment, on the sheet, a (double) "silhouette." We may get some understanding of this presupposition and of this elaborated distancing from Paul Vignon, one of the principal inter-preters of the holy shroud, in a passage where he attests to the appearance of a recognizable image on the stained fabric: "Close up, *in place of the images*, he [he is referring to himself] hardly saw anything except formless spots, similar to mildew or rust stains, which several persons also reported seeing. From a dis-tance however. . . , all these stains blended together and harmoniously arranged themselves so as to constitute the two images *which since then have become well known. . . .*"[16]

Now to return to the close-up view, this time with figural certainty provi-sioned (previsioned) well in advance. Vignon provides this detailed view of the fabric: "One area beneath the left hand . . . at first seemed void of any impres-sion. . . . By looking from rather far away, you could make out shadowy im-pressions caused by the first phalanxes of the index finger and the middle finger of the right hand, which extend on the diagonal from the upper right to the lower left."[17]

The Dramaturgical Deduction: The Wound

"Getting near involves playing at getting farther away. The game of far and near is the game of distance," writes Maurice Blanchot.[18] Elaboration makes the detour possible. The detour involves distancing. It calls forth its own *return*; it invokes the story of something rising up from "the depths of time," something that fills up a period of waiting. Something unique and far away, however near it may be.[19] In this game of near and far, therefore, there is an effect of *aura*, in-

15. Cf. Maurice Merleau-Ponty, *The Structure of Behavior*, trans. Alden L. Fisher, Boston, Beacon Press, 1963, p. 144.
16. Vignon, reply to Donnadieu, p. 370. I have italicized the words that seem to designate the presupposition of knowledge in the illusion of its afterthought.
17. Vignon, *Le Saint Suaire de Turin devant la science, l'archéologie, l'histoire, l'iconographie, la logique*, Paris, Masson, 1938, p. 33.
18. Maurice Blanchot, *Le pas au-delà*, Paris, Gallimard, 1973, p. 99.
19. Cf. Walter Benjamin, "Some motifs in Baudelaire," in *Charles Baudelaire, A Lyric Poet in the Era of High Capitalism*, trans. Harry Zohn, London, New Left Books, pp. 107–154.

volved in the surface of the photograph itself (the shroud of Turin reproduced on film realizes the delicious paradox of glorifying its cultural value). There is finally, in this game of near and far, the ubiquitous presence of the Christly body, which is in the shroud, there without being there, doubly absent, as dead body and body brought back to life, and present in the terrible signs of its Passion. So it is that the power of narrative is grafted eternally to seeing.

This is possible precisely because the elaborated distancing of view locates the shroud on a *screen*. It aims to orthogonalize the indexical vector, to make it projective. If the bloodstain is both the index of a contact and the vector of a projection, then anything is possible.

And the first thing possible for this trace is its tracing, in the sense of *trace drawing*. For it becomes possible actually to draw the unfigurable, to plot it, in as much as it appears to be projectable. By reducing *background* to *surface* we are led to believe that we are actually seeing everything in its smallest detail. The detour of a "transfer drawing" provides the context therefore for some very precise captions: "P: orifice, half filled with flesh from wound made when nail removed. 1: path where blood first flowed from hand and quickly dried. 2: last blood, diluted by serum, along same line. S: serum from wound after blood had dried."[20]

20.   Vignon, *Le Saint Suaire*, p. 3.

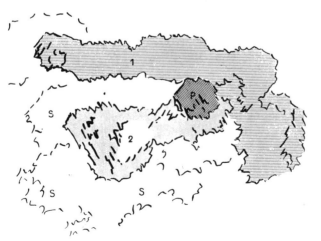

Trace drawing (Vignon, 1938).

From this sort of "photographic" detail, the tracing can easily be seen as a "photograph" of a *scene*. As a dramatic event. The unfigurability of this stain will therefore be the index not only of a contact, not only of a substance (blood), but of a "living" wound which interpreters of the shroud have agreed is that of the left hand of Christ, believed to be placed on the right side, at the level of the groin, at the time of burial.

This absent wound will therefore set the stage, by the simple expedient of the tracing of a stain, for the excruciatingly precise scenario of the insertion and removal of the nail, the opening and partial closing of the flesh. A paradigm perhaps of any originating event. This will unquestionably have benefited from the incalculable power of having preestablished a sense of *figurability*, understood as a *means of staging*—a translation suggested by Lacan for what is generally called the consideration of representability, which Freud refers to as *Rücksicht auf Darstellbarkeit*. This is where the field I referred to as *figurative Aufhebung* has its fantasmatic extension, in thoughts expressed as images or, as Freud says, as pseudothoughts; in substituting for logic pure relationships of formal contiguity; in the play of displacements of plastic intensity, in their ability to focus and fascinate (referred to here as the "center of the hole," marked P—P as in *plaie* [wound], P as in *profondeur* [depth]—on Vignon's diagram; enchanting the view as long as one takes care to imagine *more*, to the bottom of the hole, the very "bottom" of the body of Jesus); finally, in its ability to use "concrete words," according to Freud, as "links" in a chain[21] (the word *serum*, for example, which reengages the visibility of the stain in its entirety).

The appeal to *Rücksicht auf Darstellbarkeit* of course presupposes its extension to *Rücksicht auf Verstandlichkeit*, a "coming to grips with intelligibility" (what is also known as secondary elaboration), which, Freud writes, draws figurability out from a dream, from the side of fantasy, which redisplaces the visual intensities, limits them or uses them—he says—as a means of "rebuilding a façade," of subsuming the intense image, even the scene, into *scenario*.[22] Into coherence, narrative logic.

Our *figurative Aufhebung* functions therefore on the one hand as the "regressive attraction" of a memory (here, a visual phantasm of the Passion as related in the gospels) in the light of its reappearance, its restaging (essentially this is how Freud establishes his definition of coming to grips with figurability[23]); on the other hand, it is an operation dialectalized by the "dramaturgical deduction" of a secondary elaboration. But it is not "secondary" in the sense of appearing after the fact, for this elaboration is inscribed at the very outset of this entire operation.

And this operation is constructed so as never to stop. Because it is *Aufhebung*

---

21. Cf. Freud, "The Means of Representation in Dreams," pp. 310–338.
22. *Ibid.*, "Secondary Revision," pp. 488–508.
23. *Ibid.*, "Considerations of Representability," pp. 339–349.

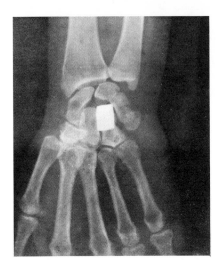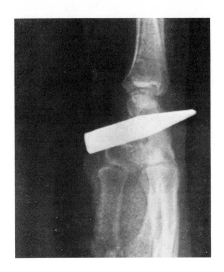

itself. It will henceforth account for all stains and all traces. It will determine a system of traces that will tell the history of the shroud itself, and of its accidents (water stains, for example, or scorch marks from fires that it miraculously escaped); a system of traces of the blood of the Passion, blood that the commentators call "living,"[24] and "dead"—deposited on the shroud during the process of burial; and even a system of traces of the partial obliteration of traces, that is, a system that can account for the "white" areas. Thus Paul Vignon saw, beneath "our" stain, "under the left hand (the one with the wound), an organic liquid that stained the sheet with pale, irregularly shaped, circular marks. This liquid partially redissolved the imprint—as it was being formed—of the fingers of the left hand, washing before it the already brownish-colored substance."[25]

In fact, this operation is made to stop only at the moment of grace when not only status, substance, and act would be characterized from every trace and even every absence of trace, but even the exact reference to every passage in the gospel concerning the way of the cross, the death, and the resurrection of Christ. It is the *entire* Passion which, imagined, must be *called up* (both in the reference point and in the sense of *Aufhebung*) from the holy shroud. "Geometry" and "experimental science" will be the means employed by this will to an absolute vision.

Abject Proof

A fantasy of referentiality sustains this entire will to see. Actually, to re-see. The hermeneutic of the holy shroud lodges its power of verification in the "reality" (in fact, in the photographic visibility of a stained piece of cloth) of the gospel text. This is why it demands an *experimental verification* of its own semiotic hypotheses.

24.   Cf., for example, A. Legrand, *Le Linceul de Turin*, Desclée de Brouwer, Paris, 1980, p. 156.
25.   Vignon, *Le Saint Suaire*, p. 35.

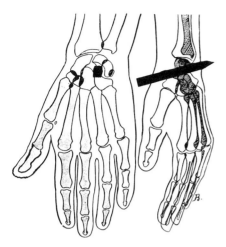

Opposite: X-rays of crucified hands (Barbet, 1935).
Left: Diagram of hand wound (Barbet, 1935).

The problem arises then concerning "our" stain and its *localization*, that is, its exact position on the "body-assumed-visible" beyond the fabric (the body of Christ). This stain, we are told, is the blood of the crucified hands. The problem is to find out where exactly the nails made their entry. Pierre Barbet, a surgeon at the Hôpital Saint Joseph in Paris, wrote a work in 1935 entitled *Les cinq plaies du Christ, étude anatomique et expérimentale*,[26] in which he frankly stated that his purpose was to "find out where the nails had been driven through; what I did was to *reconstruct* the crucifixion and then X-rayed and dissected the parts."[27] Attempting to prove that Jesus had been crucified from the wrists rather than the palms, he experimented nailing the arms of corpses to a cross by the palms; when he pulled on them, the wound always tore open and the limb would fall to the ground. And then: "After amputating an arm I quickly took an 8-millimeter-square nail, like those used for the crucifixion, which I had shortened to a 5-centimeter length for easier X-raying. With the hand lying flat, face up against the plank, I placed the point of the nail in the middle of the wrist joint, and, holding it straight up, hit it with a large hammer, carefully driving it in straight, and then hard like an executioner."[28] Since the result was conclusive—it "held" —Barbet claimed he "held" proof that it was indeed from the wrist (the Destot opening, in fact) that crucifixion took place. He produced X-rays and diagrams in support of this proof.

We have seen how the figurative elaboration of the stain on the shroud of Turin essentially required a denial of the materiality of its support (in that it necessitated its idealization as screen). But here with Barbet's act there is a denial of the very surface, since it attempts to explore the fabric as a thickness ca-

26.   Pierre Barbet, *Les cinq plaies du Christ. Étude anatomique et expérimentale*, Dillen/Tertiaires Carmélites de l'Action des Grâces, Paris, 1935, 45 pp. (reprinted and expanded in 1950: *La Passion de Jésus-Christ selon le chirurgien*, Apostolat des éditions, Paris, 10 ed., 1982, 262 pp.).
27.   *Ibid.*, p. 11. Author's emphasis.
28.   *Ibid.*, p. 15.

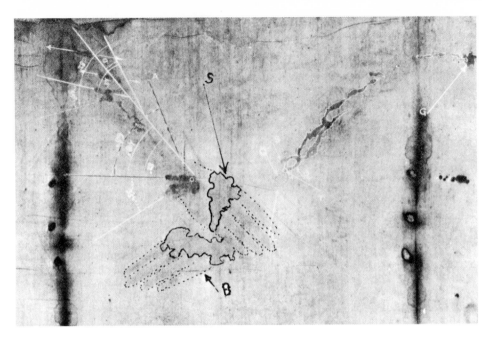

"Geometry" of the stain (Ricci, 1972).

pable of being the object of surgery; it digs into the surface as one would penetrate a body. Photographic elevation of the X-rayed stain of a wound produced
by piercing.

The locale of our stain is now clearly identified, in terms of the sort of
ground that subsumes it: the divine proportions of the Christly body.[29] In addition, the formulation of the ground makes it possible to organize the scattered
stains into a system; to plot a "geometric figure" that will correlate each stain to
each dramatic event of bodily contact, that is, to each "monad" of its suffering
— finally to each *moment* in the Passion of Christ. Elevation of a locus of points
into quasi-medico-legal narrative terms. In this way we can arrive at the total
number of lashes received in the flagellation (although the number varies, depending on the source, from 90 to 121). From this "geometry" we will attempt
to make an inference as to the posture of the brutally beaten body, of the body
crucified, of the body entombed. We will add a supporting cast of characters
having the "right" proportions (deduced from the shroud itself) to *reconstruct*
every ritualized moment of the Passion. And in addition to a ground plan, there
will be a staging. Proof garnered from the scene for experimental verification.
But the staging possesses a logic of its own, and so from a simple stained sheet

29.   That the body of the holy shroud is not only the body of a "real" Christ, but also the ideal
one of religious iconography, is another bridge cast out over the abyss in studies by Vignon, *Le
Saint Suaire*, pp. 115–192; I. Wilson, *Le Suaire de Turin, linceul du Christ?*, trans. Albeck, Albin
Michel, Paris, 1978, pp. 128–165; L. Ferri, *La Sindone vista da uno scultore*, La Parola, Rome,
1978, passim.

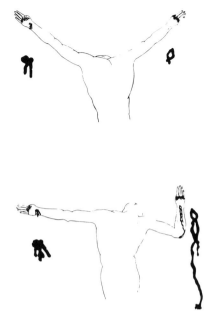

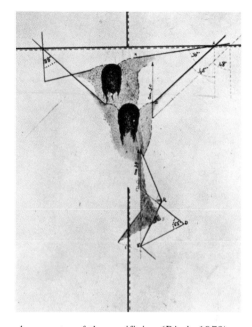

Postural inference (Ricci, 1972).   *Axonometry of the crucifixion (Ricci, 1972).*

the entire story of the gospel will be told, and what the gospels don't tell as well: the saliva of the last utterance, the shackle on the left foot of Christ on the Way of the Cross, its precise appearance, etc.[30] It is not for nothing that the shroud of Turin is dubbed the *fifth gospel.*

Our stain will therefore have proven itself susceptible to "geometrization." And this "geometry" will not only facilitate certain postural inferences (position of the nails in the hand, shape and size of the cross), but perhaps will identify something at the source of this entire agonizing fantasy: the very rhythm of Christ's mortal expiration. Interestingly enough, Monsignor Ricci, one of the principle contemporary "sindonologists," uses the term *axonometry* to describe the reconstitution of the spasm. His analysis also provides the principle of formal emergence of the stain, attempting, as it does, to demonstrate why the stain has the appearance that it does, or rather, how it came to have such an appearance, at a given moment of the Passion.

One might perhaps think we have come full circle here. But no. This is movement made never to stop. Pierre Barbet gives a last and abject proof at the conclusion of his work; "one more for good measure," although you sense that in addition to its retrospective function there is also a foundational function: "I apologize for including these last two photographs, which even I think are hideous and blasphemous. . . . I found some human tatter in the Anatomy cloak-

30.   Cf. G. Ricci, *Via Crucis secondo la Sindone*, Centro Romano di Sindonologia, Rome, 1972 (French trans., 1981), pp. 17–19, 54.

Experimental restaging of a crucifixion (Barbet, 1935).

room, perfectly fresh and supple";[31] and he actually crucified it, according to his theory of crucifixion. The photographic visibility of a pure effect of the weave of the fabric was finally transformed into the pure and abject effect of the "real" thing (a "real" person crucified). This is what I was referring to as a fantasy of referentiality.

This abject part of the proof at least signifies that what is called the dramaturgical "deduction" is not a deduction, and not even an induction (in the Aristotelian sense of inductive syllogism). It is really something more like an *abduction*. This is what Aristotle calls a syllogism whose major premise is evident (it is evident that if there are stains on the shroud of Turin they are the index of something), but whose minor premise is only likely (probable); the probability of the conclusion, therefore, is only as great as that of the minor premise.[32] For Peirce, an abduction is any sort of reasoning whose conclusion is only probable. In the rhetoric of proof generated from the shroud of Turin, the minor premise would consist of the stage of simulation, of the probability of the reconstruction of the drama of the Passion. The probability of the minor premise is that abduction would therefore be pure *scenic verisimilitude*: a pure resemblance. And

31.   Barbet, *Les cinq plaies du Christ*, p. 43.
32.   Aristotle, *The Prior Analytics*, trans. John Warrington, New York, Dutton, 1964, II, 25, pp. 71–73.

we see what an *abject* effect it has, this "too highly detailed"—that is, perverse—restaging of an event.

I will cite one last sindonological avatar, Father Côme, whose thesis is defended in *La Sindone e la Scienza*, a small work published by the author, which was presented at a congress in Turin in October 1978.[33] According to his theory there is on the shroud an *ultimate detail*, which is waiting to be seen, *underneath* the stain we have been dealing with: "In order to fold the hands of the victim over the pubic region, which conceals the sexual organs, it would have been necessary to draw the arms back along the body and bend the elbows in spite of the advanced rigidity of rigor mortis and the effect of tetanus due to crucifixion. The persons who first prepared the body for burial were therefore concerned to conceal something they thought should not be seen."[34] No one had ever seen what it was, because, Côme writes, no one had dared to look that closely. He tells us what it is: "the most atrocious detail of the Passion of Christ." This something is Christ's sperm. This reflex response is documented in medical accounts of crucifixions and hangings: "the ultimate spasm of erection and ejaculation of the crucified," of which there is, he continues, "on the holy shroud, within view, the means of direct verification, *if one only wishes to avail oneself of it. . . .*"[35]

Baptism by Sight

The historic value of this theory is unimportant. It is no less exemplary, however, for all its eccentricity.

On the one hand, it effects a passage to the limit of what I referred to as a fantasy of referentiality, the very one contained in the indexical presupposition relating to the stains on the holy shroud, and "elevated" into what could be called "the game of greatest naturalism." Now there is nothing more "naturalistic" than detail as it functions in fantasy (Freud stresses this in regard to screen memories). It is interesting that all this hermeneutical analysis of stains—non-iconic signifiers, pure effects of support or tonality—tends to define, in fact, a new art of *iconic devotion* (in every sense of the term). Most sindonological studies include illustrations of drawings or models that purport to represent the real Christ crucified (in its iconographic sense).[36] Verisimilitude regarding the Passion—an act of torture—cannot logically operate within an economy of abjection; these new icons are remarkable rather for the baroque obscenity of the wound and, in particular, its secretion.

Yet it is also true that this excessive naturalism (which has its paradoxical

---

33.   R. P. Côme, *La suprême abjection de la Passion du Christ*, F. Tanazacq, 1955, 2nd rev. ed., 1975, 22 pp.; "Le détail le plus atroce de la Passion du Christ," in *La Sindone e la Scienza*, ed. Paoline/Centro Internazionale di Sindonologia, Turin, 1978, pp. 424–427.
34.   Côme, "Le détail le plus atroce," p. 425.
35.   *Ibid.*, p. 424.
36.   Cf. Barbet, Ricci, Ferri.

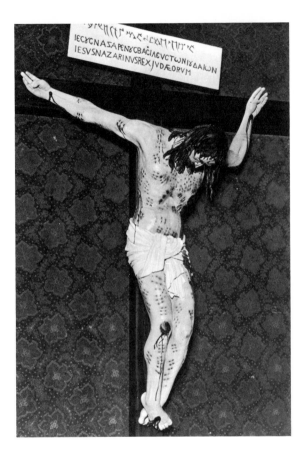

Crucifixion: wood sculpture based on data taken from the holy shroud (Ricci, 1972).

source in the historicist and positivist criticism of religion contemporary with the implementation of photography) is entirely contained within a theological order. Côme offers his hypothesis as a veritable *télos* of faith, because it carries compassion to the level of atrocity, that is, he believes, "to the limit of total truth."[37] *Télos* of the eucharistic communion; the drops of divine sperm being the "innumerable sacred fragments of our communion."[38] *Télos*, finally, of the incarnation; Jesus rendering the forfeiture of his death absolute in extremity. This also has its logical confirmation. The "ultimate detail," writes Côme, "finally allows us to feel we are looking at a complete portrait."[39]

37.   Côme, *La suprême abjection,* p. 6.
38.   *Ibid.*, p. 18.
39.   *Ibid.*, p. 16.

It is in fact the picture that is complete. The indefinite retracing of the index actually permits its own reversal, its iconic and symbolic elevation. It is like a *baptism of sight* that the hermeneutic of the holy shroud demands in the sense that as in baptism, "by receiving the imprint (*to antitupon*: the index) of the Holy Spirit, everything is accomplished in you as image (*eikonikôs*: as icon), because you are the images (*eikones*) of Christ."[40]

In summary then there was a piece of stained linen. A determination was reached as to its nature: it was blood. Through the fact of contact, the act was described and the actor identified. And his death recreated. Bloodstains made it possible to imagine the meaning and the drama of Christ's Passion.

Lest we forget: the blood itself may only be a product of the imagination. To continue the logic of the index, the experimental fantasy and love of verification, we should perhaps wonder whether it really is blood at all. The infallible method of peroxydation (used in legal medicine to test *even invisible* stains or very old stains) reveals nothing, nothing at all.[41] To this day there is no known blood to be found on the holy shroud.

It goes without saying that in this logic of an indexical assertion, whose aim is to be overwhelmed by the iconic and symbolic dimensions, this does not really constitute an objection to "authenticity" (to divinity). For the index of the glorious body is not an index. It is an *achiropoïete* icon; the blood-substance will in all cases be transformed by a *luminous* vector, and in all cases the contact, implied by the trace, will be transformed by a vector of *virgin passage* (crossing a surface without touching it: the birth of Christ, Pentecost, and his resurrection, all from the linen shroud). An argument found in Saint Thomas Aquinas could, I believe, be used to characterize this hermeneutical question (and in a certain way, theologically speaking, it rescues it) regarding the substance of our stain. Is it or is it not the blood of Christ? Thomas would say that the blood of Christ is in its entirety *elsewhere*: although blood is a humor, and therefore susceptible to corruption, the blood of Christ is not tainted by original sin; it is wholly revived and glorified. There is a problem, however: "Certain churches preserve as a relic a small amount of Christ's blood. His body is therefore not revived in the integrity of all its parts." Solution: "As for the blood that certain churches preserve as a relic, it did not flow from the side of Christ, but miraculously, they say, from an image of Christ (*imagine Christi*) that someone had struck."[42] It is therefore *imag(inary) blood*. And no less miraculous for that.

40. Cyril of Jerusalem, *Catéchèses mystagogiques*, ed. Piedagnel, Cerf, Paris, 1966, II, p. 1.
41. Cf. Wilson, *Le Suaire de Turin*, pp. 101–105.
42. Thomas Aquinas, *Summa*, III, Qu. 54. Art. 3.

Mimicry and Legendary Psychasthenia

ROGER CAILLOIS

translated by JOHN SHEPLEY

Prends garde: à jouer au
fantôme, on le devient.

From whatever side one approaches things, the ultimate problem turns out in the final analysis to be that of *distinction*: distinctions between the real and the imaginary, between waking and sleeping, between ignorance and knowledge, etc. — all of them, in short, distinctions in which valid consideration must demonstrate a keen awareness and the demand for resolution. Among distinctions, there is assuredly none more clear-cut than that between the organism and its surroundings; at least there is none in which the tangible experience of separation is more immediate. So it is worthwhile to observe the phenomenon with particular attention and, within the phenomenon, what is even more necessary, given the present state of our knowledge, is to consider its condition as pathology (the word here having only a statistical meaning) — i.e., all the facts that come under the heading of mimicry.

For some time now, for various and often undesirable reasons, these facts have been the object of those biologists with a heavy predilection for ulterior motives: some dream of proving metamorphosis, which, fortunately for that phenomenon, rests on other foundations,[1] others, the clear-sighted providence of the famous God whose bounty extends over the whole of nature.[2]

Under these conditions, a strict method is essential. First of all, it is important to list these phenomena very rigorously, for experience has shown that there are too many bad explanations pushing them toward confusion. It is also not a bad idea to adopt as much as possible a classification that relates to facts and not to their interpretation, since the latter threatens to be misleading, and

1.   Alfred Russell Wallace, *Darwinism*, London, 1889.
2.   L. Murat, *Les merveilles du monde animal*, 1914.

©Editions Gallimard

is moreover controversial in almost every case. Giard's categories[3] will thus be mentioned, but not retained. Neither the first: *offensive mimicry* designed to surprise the prey, *defensive mimicry* designed either to escape the sight of the aggressor (mimicry of dissimulation) or to frighten it away by a deceptive appearance (mimicry of terrification); nor the second: *direct mimicry* when it is in the immediate interests of the imitating animal to take on the disguise, *indirect mimicry* when animals belonging to different species, following a common adaptation, a *convergence*, in some way show "professional resemblances."[4]

. . .†

It has been assumed that, in order to protect itself, an inoffensive animal took on the appearance of a forbidding one: for example, the butterfly *Trochilium* and the wasp *Vespa Crabro*—the same smoky wings, the same brown legs and antennae, the same black and yellow striped abdomen and thorax, the same vigorous and noisy flight in broad daylight. Sometimes the imitative creature goes further, like the caterpillar of *Choerocampa Elpenor*, which on its fourth and fifth segments has two eye-shaped spots outlined in black: when it is alarmed, its front segments retract and the fourth swells considerably, achieving the effect of a snake's head capable of deceiving lizards and small birds, which are frightened by this sudden apparition.[5] According to Weismann,[6] when the *Smerinthus ocellata*, which like all hawk moths conceals its hind wings when at rest, is in danger, it exposes them abruptly with their two large blue "eyes" on a red background, giving the aggressor a sudden fright.[7]

The butterfly, wings spread, thus becomes the head of a huge bird of prey. The clearest example of this kind is surely that of the *Caligo* butterfly in the jungles of Brazil, described by Vignon as follows: "There is a bright spot surrounded by a palpebral circle, then by circular and overlapping rows of small radial feathery strokes of variegated appearance, imitating to perfection

3.   Alfred Giard, "Sur le mimétisme et la ressemblance protectrice," *Arch. de Zool. exp. et gén.*, 1872, and *Bulletin Scientifique de la France et de la Belgique*, vol. XX (1888).
4.   Felix Le Dantec, *Lamarkiens et Darwiniens*, third edition, Paris, 1908, pp. 120ff.
†   For this essay's publication in *Minotaure*, Caillois shortened the text by removing some of the descriptive passages, indicated by ellipsis points. These indications are retained in the version printed here, taken from the original *Minotaure* publication. The longer version of the essay was published in *Le mythe et l'homme*, Paris, Gallimard, 1938.—ed.
5.   Lucien Cuénot, *La genèse des espèces animales*, Paris, 1911, pp. 470–473.
6.   Weismann, *Vorträge über Descendenztheorie*, vol. I, pp. 78–79.
7.   This terrifying transformation is automatic. One might compare it to cutaneous reflexes, which do not always tend to a change of color designed to conceal the animal, but sometimes end by giving it a terrifying appearance. A cat in the presence of a dog bristles its fur so that, because it is frightened, it becomes frightening. Le Dantec, who makes this observation (*Lamarkiens et Darwiniens*, p. 139), thus explains the phenomenon in man known as *gooseflesh*, which occurs especially in cases of great fright. Made inoperative by the atrophy of the pilose system, it has nevertheless survived.

Phyllium bioculatum (polygonal leaf insects disguised by solar green).

the plumage of an owl, while the body of the butterfly corresponds to the beak of the same bird."[8] The resemblance is so striking that the natives of Brazil affix it to the doors of their barns as a replacement for the creature it imitates.

It is only too obvious that in the previous cases anthropomorphism plays a decisive role: the resemblance is all in the eye of the beholder. The objective fact is fascination, as is shown especially by *Smerinthus ocellata*, which does not resemble anything frightening. Only the eye-shaped spots play a role. The behavior of the Brazilian natives only confirms this proposition: the "eyes" of the *Caligo* should probably be compared to the apotropaic *Oculus indiviosus*, the evil eye that can not only harm but protect, if one turns it back against the evil powers to which, as an organ of fascination par excellence, it naturally belongs.[9]

Here the anthropomorphic argument does not apply, since the eye is the vehicle of fascination in the whole animal kingdom. It is, on the other hand,

---

8.   P. Vignon, "Sur le matérialisme scientifique ou mécanisme anti-téléologique," *Revue de Philosophie*, 1904, p. 562. Cf. Alfred Giard, *Traité d'entomologie*, vol. III, p. 201; and A. Janet, *Les papillons*, Paris, 1902, pp. 331–336.
9.   On the evil eye and animals as fascinators, see the famous work by Seligmann, *Der bose Blick und Verwandtes*, Berlin, 1910, especially vol. II, p. 469. On the apotropaic use of the eye, see Paul Perdrizet, *Negotium perambulans in tenebris: études de démonologie gréco-orientale*, Strasbourg, 1922.

decisive for the biased declaration of resemblance: besides, even from the human point of view, none of the resemblances in this group of facts is absolutely conclusive.

. . .

For the adaptation of form to form (*homomorphy*), there is no lack of examples: box crabs resemble rounded pebbles; chlamydes, seeds; moenas, gravel; prawns, fucus; the fish *Phyllopteryx*, from the Sargasso Sea, is simply "torn seaweed in the shape of floating strands,"[10] like the *Antennarius* and the *Pterophrynx*.[11] The octopus retracts its tentacles, curves its back, adapts its color, and thus comes to resemble a stone. The green and white hind wings of the *Aurora Pierid* simulate umbelliferae; the bumps, knots, and streaks of symbiotic lichens make them identical with the bark of the poplars on which they grow.

One cannot distinguish *Lithnius nigrocristinus* of Madagascar and Flatoids from lichens.[12] We know how far the mimicry of mantises can go: their legs simulate petals or are curved into corollas and resemble flowers, imitating by a slight instinctive swaying the action of the wind on these latter.[13] The *Cilix compressa* resembles bird droppings; the *Cerodeylus laceratus* of Borneo with its leafy excrescences, light olive-green in color, a stick covered with moss. Everyone knows the Phyllia, or leaf insects, so similar to leaves, from which it is only a step to the perfect homomorphy represented by certain butterflies: first the *Oxydia*, which places itself at the end of a branch at right angles to its direction, the front wings held in such a position as to present the appearance of a terminal leaf, an appearance accentuated by a thin dark line extending crosswise over the four wings in such a way as to simulate the leaf's principal veins.

Other species are even more improved, their hind wings being furnished with a slender appendage that they use as a petiole, acquiring by this means "a sort of insertion into the plant world."[14] The combination of the two wings on each side represents the lanceolate oval characteristic of the leaf: here, too, a spot, but longitudinal this time, continuing from one wing onto the other, replaces the middle vein; thus "the vital organic force . . . has had to shape and cleverly organize each of the wings since it thereby achieves a fixed form, not in itself, but by its union with the other wing."[15] These are chiefly the *Coenophlebia Archidona* of Central America[16] and the various kinds of Kallima in India and

10.   Murat, pp. 37–38.
11.   Cuénot, p. 453.
12.   left fig. 114.
13.   Cf. references in Roger Caillois, "La Mante Religieuse," *Minotaure*, no. 5 (1934), p. 26.
14.   Vignon, p. 562.
15.   *Ibid.*
16.   Delage and Goldsmith, *Les théories de l'évolution*, Paris, 1909, fig. 1, p. 74.

Coupling of Smerinthus ocellata.

Malaysia, the latter deserving further study. The lower side of their wings reproduces, following the pattern indicated above, the leaf of the *Nephelium Longane* where they prefer to alight. Furthermore, according to a naturalist employed in Java by the London firm of Kirby and Co. for the trade in these butterflies, each of the different varieties of Kallima (*K. Inachis, K. Parallecta,* etc.) frequents a specific kind of bush that it most particularly resembles.[17] Among these butterflies, imitation is pushed to the smallest details: indeed, the wings bear gray-green spots simulating the mold of lichens and glistening surfaces that give them the look of torn and perforated leaves: "including spots of mold of the sphaeriaceous kind that stud the leaves of these plants; everything, including the transparent scars produced by phytophagic insects when, devouring the parenchyma of the leaves in places, they leave only the translucid skin. Imitations are produced by pearly spots that correspond to similar spots on the upper surface of the wings."[18]

*

These extreme examples have given rise to numerous attempts at explanation, none of them truly satisfactory.

Even the mechanism of the phenomenon is unclear. One can certainly observe with E.-L. Bouvier that mimetic species depart from the normal type by the addition of ornaments: "lateral expansions of the body and appendages in Phyllia, modeling of the front wings in Flatoids, development of tuberosities in the larva of many geometer moths, etc. . . ."[19] But this is a singular abuse of the word *ornament*, and above all it is more an observation than an explanation. The notion of *preadaptation* (insects seeking out milieux that match their dominant shade of color or adjusting to the object they most resemble) is insufficient on its side in the face of equally precise phenomena. More insufficient still is the recourse to chance, even in Cuénot's subtle fashion. He attaches himself in the beginning to the case of certain Phyllia of Java and Ceylon (*Ph. siccifolium* and *Ph. pulchrifolium*) that live by preference on the leaves of the guava tree, which they resemble by the subterminal constriction of their abdomens. The guava, however, is not an indigenous plant but has been imported from America.

So if similarity exists in this example, it is fortuitous. Without being disturbed by the exceptional (not to say unique) nature of this fact, Cuénot goes on to say that the similarity of the Kallima butterfly is no less the result of chance, being produced by the simple accumulation of factors (appendage in the shape of a petiole, lanceolate front wings, middle veining, transparent and mirror areas) that are found separately in nonmimetic species and are there

17.   Murat, p. 30.
18.   Rémy Perrier, *Cours de zoologie*, fifth edition, Paris, 1912, quoted in Murat, pp. 27–28.
19.   Eugène Louis Bouvier, *Habitudes et metamorphoses des insectes*, Paris, 1921, p. 146.

unremarkable: "resemblance is therefore obtained by the sum of a certain number of small details, each of which has nothing exceptional about it and can be found isolated in neighboring species, but whose combination produces an extraordinary imitation of a dry leaf, more or less successful depending on individuals, which quite notably differ among themselves. . . . It is *one combination like any other*, astonishing because of its resemblance to an object."[20] Likewise, according to this author, the *Urapteryx samqucaria* caterpillar is *one combination like any other* of a characteristic attitude, a certain skin color, tegumentary rough spots, and the instinct to live on certain plants. But properly speaking, it is hard to believe that we are dealing here with *combinations like any other*, since all these details can be brought together without being joined, without their contributing to some resemblance: it is not the presence of the elements that is perplexing and decisive, it is their *mutual organization*, their *reciprocal topography*.

*

Better to adopt under these conditions a shaky hypothesis that could be drawn from a remark by Le Dantec,[21] according to which there may have been in the ancestors of the Kallima a set of cutaneous organs permitting the simulation of the imperfections of leaves, the imitating mechanism having disappeared once the morphological character was acquired (that is to say, in the present case, once the resemblance was achieved) in accordance with Lamarck's very law. Morphological mimicry could then be, after the fashion of chromatic mimicry, an actual photography, but of the form and the relief, a photography on the level of the object and not on that of the image, a reproduction in three-dimensional space with solids and voids: sculpture-photography or better *teleplasty,* if one strips the word of any metapsychical content.

. . .

There are reasons more immediate, and at the same time less to be suspected of sophistry, that keep mimicry from being taken for a defense reaction. First of all, it would only apply to carnivores that hunt by sight and not by smell as is often the case. Carnivores, moreover, do not generally bother with motionless prey: immobility would thus be a better defense, and indeed insects are exceedingly prone to employ a false corpselike rigidity.[22] There are other

20.   Cuénot, p. 464. In the last edition of his work (1932), Cuénot doubts that this sum of small details could be directed by an "unknown factor," but the recourse to chance continues to seem to him the most likely hypothesis, pp. 522–523.
21.   Le Dantec, p. 143.
22.   Cuénot, p. 461.

Praying mantis devouring the male.

means: a butterfly, in order to make itself invisible, may do nothing more than use the tactics of the *Satyride asiatique*, whose flattened wings in repose appear simply as a line almost without thickness, imperceptible, perpendicular to the flower where it has alighted, and which turns simultaneously with the observer so that it is only this minimum surface that is always seen.[23] The experiments of Judd[24] and Foucher[25] have definitely resolved the question: predators are not at all fooled by homomorphy or homochromy: they eat crickets that mingle with the foliage of oak trees or weevils that resemble small stones, completely invisible to man. The phasma *Carausius Morosus*, which by its form, color, and attitude simulates a plant twig, cannot emerge into the open air without being immediately discovered and dined on by sparrows. Generally speaking, one

23.   Murat, p. 46.
24.   Judd, "The Efficiency of Some Protective Adaptations in Securing Insects from Birds," *American Naturalist*, vol. XXXIII (1899), p. 461.
25.   Foucher, *Bull. Soc. nat. acclim.* left 1916.

finds many remains of mimetic insects in the stomachs of predators. So it should come as no surprise that such insects sometimes have other and more effective ways to protect themselves. Conversely, some species that are inedible, and would thus have nothing to fear, are also mimetic. It therefore seems that one ought to conclude with Cuénot that this is an "epiphenomenon" whose "defensive utility appears to be nul."[26] Delage and Goldsmith had already pointed out in the Kallima an "exaggeration of precautions."[27]

We are thus dealing with a *luxury* and even a dangerous luxury, for there are cases in which mimicry causes the creature to go from bad to worse: geometer-moth caterpillars simulate shoots of shrubbery so well that gardeners cut them with their pruning shears.[28] The case of the Phyllia is even sadder: they browse among themselves, taking each other for real leaves,[29] in such a way that one might accept the idea of a sort of collective masochism leading to mutual homophagy, the simulation of the leaf being a *provocation* to cannibalism in this kind of totem feast.

This interpretation is not so gratuitous as it sounds: indeed, there seem to exist in man psychological potentialities strangely corresponding to these facts. Even putting aside the problem of totemism, which is surely too risky to approach from this point of view, there remains the huge realm of sympathetic magic, according to which like produces like and upon which all incantational practice is more or less based. There is no need to reproduce the facts here: they can be found listed and classified in the classic works of Tylor, Hubert and Mauss, and Frazer. One point, however, needs to be made, the correspondence, fortunately brought to light by these authors, between the principles of magic and those of the association of ideas: to the law of magic — *things that have once been in contact remain united* — corresponds association by contiguity, just as association by resemblance corresponds quite precisely to the *attractio similium* of magic: *like produces like.*[30] Hence the same governing principles: here the subjective association of ideas, there the objective association of facts; here the fortuitous or supposedly fortuitous connections of ideas, there the causal connections of phenomena.[31]

26.   Cuénot, p. 463. On the effectiveness of mimicry, see Davenport, "Elimination of Self-Coloured Birds," *Nature*, vol. LXXVIII (1898), p. 101; and Doflein, "Über Schutzanpassung durch Aehnlichkeit," *Biol. Centr.*, vol. XXVIII (1908), p. 243; and Pritchett, "Some Experiments in Feeding Lizards with Protectively Coloured Insects," *Biol. Bull.*, vol. V (1903), p. 271. See also the bibliography in Cuénot, p. 467.
27.   Delage and Goldsmith, p. 74.
28.   Murat, p. 36.
29.   *Ibid.*, and Bouvier, pp. 142–143.
30.   Of course, the same correspondence exists for association by contrast and the law of magic: *opposites act on opposites.* In either realm, it is easy to reduce this case to that of resemblance.
31.   Cf. Henri Hubert and Marcel Mauss, "Esquisse d'une théorie générale de la Magie," *Année sociologique*, vol. VII (1904), pp. 61–73.

Prestigious magic in the Manta mendica.

The point is that there remains in the "primitive" an overwhelming tendency to imitate, combined with a belief in the efficacy of this imitation, a tendency still quite strong in "civilized" man, since in him it continues to be one of the two conditions for the progress of his untrammeled thought. So as not to complicate the problem unnecessarily, I leave aside the general question of *resemblance*, which is far from being clear and plays a sometimes decisive role in affectivity and, under the name of *correspondence*, in aesthetics.

*

This tendency, whose universality thus becomes difficult to deny, may have been the determining force responsible for the present morphology of mimetic insects, at a time when their organisms were more plastic than they are today, as one must suppose in any case given the fact of transformation. Mimicry would thus be accurately defined as *an incantation fixed at its culminating point* and having caught the sorcerer in his own trap. No one should say it is nonsense to attribute magic to insects: the fresh application of the words ought not to hide the profound simplicity of the thing. What else but *prestigious magic* and *fascination* can the phenomena be called that have been unanimously classified precisely under the name of mimicry (incorrectly as I see it, one will recall, for in my opinion the perceived resemblances are too reducible in this case to anthropomorphism, but there is no doubt that once rid of these questionable additions and reduced to the essential, these facts are similar at least in their origins to those of true mimicry), phenomena some of which I have reported above (the examples of the *Smerinthus ocellata*, the *Caligo*, and the *Choerocampa Elpenor* caterpillar), and of which the sudden exhibition of ocelli by the mantis in a spectral attitude, when it is a matter of paralyzing its prey, is by no means of the least?

Recourse to the magical tendency in the search for the similar can only, however, be an initial approximation, and it is advisable to take account of it in its turn. The search for the similar would seem to be a means, if not an intermediate stage. Indeed, the end would appear to be *assimilation to the surroundings.* Here instinct completes morphology: the *Kallima* places itself symmetrically on a real leaf, the appendage on its hind wings in the place that a real petiole would occupy; the *Oxydia* alights at right angles to the end of a branch because the arrangement of the spot representing the middle veining requires it; the *Clolia*, Brazilian butterflies, position themselves in a row on small stalks in such a way as to represent bell flowers, in the manner of a sprig of lily of the valley, for example.[32]

*

32.   Murat, p. 37.

It is thus a real *temptation by space.*

Other phenomena, moreover, such as so-called "protective coverings," contribute to the same end. The larvae of mayflies fashion a sheath for themselves with twigs and gravel, those of *Chrysomelidae* with their excrements. *Oxyrrhyncha* or spider crabs haphazardly gather and collect on their shells the seaweed and polyps of the milieu in which they live, and "the disguise seems like an act of pure automatism,"[33] since they deck themselves in whatever is offered to them, including some of the most conspicuous elements (experiments by Hermann Fol, 1886). Furthermore, this behavior depends on vision, since it neither takes place at night nor after the removal of the ocular peduncles (experiments by Aurivillius, 1889), which shows once again that what is involved is a disturbance in the perception of space.

In short, from the moment when it can no longer be a process of defense, mimicry can be nothing else but this. Besides, there can be no doubt that the perception of space is a complex phenomenon: space is indissolubly perceived and represented. From this standpoint, it is a double dihedral changing at every moment in size and position:[34] a *dihedral of action* whose horizontal plane is formed by the ground and the vertical plane by the man himself who walks and who, by this fact, carries the dihedral along with him; and a *dihedral of representation* determined by the same horizontal plane as the previous one (but represented and not perceived) intersected vertically at the distance where the object appears. It is with represented space that the drama becomes specific, since the living creature, the organism, is no longer the origin of the coordinates, but one point among others; it is dispossessed of its privilege and literally *no longer knows where to place itself.* One can already recognize the characteristic scientific attitude[35] and, indeed, it is remarkable that represented spaces are just what is multiplied by contemporary science: Finsler's spaces, Fermat's spaces, Riemann-Christoffel's hyper-space, abstract, generalized, open, and closed spaces, spaces dense in themselves, thinned out, and so on. The feeling of personality, considered as the organism's feeling of distinction from its surroundings, of the connection between consciousness and a particular point in space, cannot fail under these conditions to be seriously undermined; one then enters into the psychology of psychasthenia, and more specifically of *legendary psychasthenia,* if we agree to use this name for the disturbance in the above relations between personality and space.

Here it is possible to give only a rough summary of what is involved, and Pierre Janet's theoretical and clinical writings are moreover available to every-

---

33.   Bouvier, pp. 147–151. Likewise the conclusion for insects: "the insect that disguises itself requires the contact of foreign bodies and the nature of the bodies producing the contact is of little importance" (p. 151).
34.   Cf. Louis Lavalle, *La perception visuelle de la profondeur,* Strasbourg, 1921, p. 13.
35.   In the end, for science everything is milieu.

Giant phasma.

one. I will, however, briefly describe some personal experiences, but which are wholly in accord with observations published in the medical literature, for example with the invariable response of schizophrenics to the question: where are you? *I know where I am, but I do not feel as though I'm at the spot where I find myself.*[36] To these dispossessed souls, space seems to be a devouring force. Space pursues them, encircles them, digests them in a gigantic phagocytosis. It ends by replacing them. Then the body separates itself from thought, the individual breaks the boundary of his skin and occupies the other side of his senses. He tries to look at *himself from* any point whatever in space. He feels himself becoming space, *dark space where things cannot be put.* He is similar, not similar to something, but just *similar.* And he invents spaces of which he is "the convulsive possession."

All these expressions[37] shed light on a single process: *depersonalization by assimilation to space,* i.e., what mimicry achieves morphologically in certain animal species. The magical hold (one can truly call it so without doing violence to the language) of night and obscurity, the *fear of the dark,* probably also has its roots in the peril in which it puts the opposition between the organism and the milieu. Minkowski's analyses are invaluable here: darkness is not the mere absence of light; there is something positive about it. While light space is eliminated by the materiality of objects, darkness is "filled," it touches the individual directly, envelops him, penetrates him, and even passes through him: hence "the ego is *permeable* for darkness while it is not so for light"; the feeling of mystery that one experiences at night would not come from anything else. Minkowski likewise comes to speak of *dark space* and almost of a lack of distinction between the milieu and the organism: "Dark space envelops me on all sides and penetrates me much deeper than light space, the distinction between inside and outside and consequently the sense organs as well, insofar as they are designed for external perception, here play only a totally modest role."[38]

This assimilation to space is necessarily accompanied by a decline in the feeling of personality and life. It should be noted in any case that in mimetic species the phenomenon is never carried out except *in a single direction*:[39] the animal mimics the plant, leaf, flower, or thorn, and dissembles or ceases to perform its functions in relation to others. *Life takes a step backwards.* Sometimes

36.   Cf. Eugène Minkowski, "Le problème du temps en psychopathologie," *Recherches philosophiques,* 1932–33, p. 239.
37.   They are drawn from introspective notes taken during an attack of "legendary psychasthenia," deliberately aggravated for purposes of ascesis and interpretation.
38.   Eugène Minkowski, "Le temps vécu," *Etudes phénoménologiques et psychopathologiques,* Paris, 1933, pp. 382–398: the problem of hallucinations and problems of space.
39.   We have seen for what reasons it was advisable to exclude cases in which the animal mimics another animal: resemblances poorly established objectively and phenomena of prestigious fascination rather than mimicry.

assimilation does not stop at the surface: the eggs of phasmas resemble seeds not only by their form and color, but also by their internal biological structure.[40] On the other hand, cataleptic attitudes often aid the insect in its entry into another realm: the immobility of weevils, while bacilliform Phasmida let their long legs hang, and not to mention the rigidity of geometer-moth caterpillars standing bolt upright, which cannot fail to suggest hysterical contraction.[41] On the other hand, is not the automatic swaying of mantises comparable to a tic?

Among others in literature, Gustave Flaubert seems to have understood the meaning of the phenomenon, when he ends *The Temptation of Saint Anthony* with a general spectacle of mimicry to which the hermit succumbs: "plants are now no longer distinguished from animals. . . . Insects identical with rose petals adorn a bush. . . . And then plants are confused with stones. Rocks look like brains, stalactites like breasts, veins of iron like tapestries adorned with figures." In thus seeing the three realms of nature merging into each other, Anthony in his turn suffers the lure of material space: he wants to split himself thoroughly, to be in everything, "to penetrate each atom, to descend to the bottom of matter, to *be* matter." The emphasis is surely placed on the pantheistic and even overwhelming aspect of this *descent into hell*, but this in no way lessens its appearance here as a form of the process of the *generalization of space* at the expense of the individual, unless one were to employ a psychoanalytic vocabulary and speak of reintegration with original insensibility and prenatal unconsciousness: a contradiction in terms.

One does not need to look far to find supporting examples in art: hence the extraordinary motifs of Slovak popular decoration, which are such that one does not know whether it is a question of flowers with wings or of birds with petals; hence the pictures painted by Salvador Dali around 1930, in which, whatever the artist may say,[42] these invisible men, sleeping women, horses, and lions are less the expression of ambiguities or of paranoiac "plurivocities" than of mimetic assimilations of the animate to the inanimate.

Beyond doubt some of the above developments are far from offering any guarantee from the standpoint of certainty. It may even seem questionable to compare such diverse realities as homomorphy and the external morphology of certain insects, sympathetic magic and the concrete behavior of people of a certain type of civilization and perhaps a certain type of thought, and finally psychasthenia and the psychological postulations of people belonging, from these points of view, to opposite types. Such comparisons, however, seem to me not only legitimate (just as it is impossible to condemn comparative biology) but even indispensable as soon as we approach the obscure realm of un-

40. Works by Henneguy (1885), for the Phyllia.
41. Cf. Bouvier, p. 143.
42. Salvador Dali, *La femme visible*, Paris, 1930, p. 15.

conscious determinations. Besides, the solution proposed contains nothing that should give rise to suspicions of dogmatism: it merely suggests that alongside the instinct of self-preservation, which in some way orients the creature toward life, there is generally speaking a sort of *instinct of renunciation* that orients it toward a mode of reduced existence, which in the end would no longer know either consciousness or feeling — the *inertia of the élan vital*, so to speak.

*

It is on this level that it can be gratifying to give a common root to phenomena of mimicry both biological and magical[43] and to psychasthenic experience, since the facts seem so well to impose one on them: this *attraction by space*, as elementary and mechanical as are tropisms, and by the effect of which life seems to lose ground, blurring in its retreat the frontier between the organism and the milieu and *expanding to the same degree the limits within which*, according to Pythagoras, *we are allowed to know, as we should, that nature is everywhere the same.*[44]

43.   This parallel will seem justified if one thinks that biological necessity produces an instinct or in its absence an imagination capable of performing the same role, i.e., of arousing in the individual an equivalent behavior.
44.   In this brief account, I have had to leave aside certain related questions, for example those of obliterating coloration and dazzling coloration (cf. Cuénot, *La genèse des espèces animales*, third ed., 1932), and discussion of a secondary interest as well: the relation between the instinct of renunciation, as I have called it, and the death instinct of the psychoanalysts. Above all, I have been able to give only a limited number of examples. But here I refer the reader to the impressive and exciting pages by P. Vignon, *Introduction à la biologie expérimentale*, Paris, 1930 (*Encycl. Biol.*, vol. VIII), pp. 310–459, as well as the numerous accompanying illustrations. Here one can read with especial interest about the mimicry of caterpillars (pp. 362 ff.), mantises (pp. 374 ff.), and leaf hoppers (*Pterochrozes*) of tropical America (pp. 422–459). The author shows on each occasion that if the mimicry is a process of defense, it goes well beyond its purpose: that it is "hypertelic." It leads therefore to an infra-conscious activity (so far it is possible to agree) working to a purely aesthetic end "for the setting." "This is elegant, this is beautiful" (p. 400). It is hardly necessary to discuss such anthropomorphism. For my part, however, if one wishes to reduce the aesthetic instinct to a tendency of metamorphosis in the object or in space, I have no objection. But is that what Vignon wants?

Historical Materialism

El Lissitzky. Photomontage for catalogue accompanying Soviet Pavilion at Pressa *Exhibition,* Cologne. 1928.

From Faktura to Factography

BENJAMIN H. D. BUCHLOH

As the first director of the Museum of Modern Art, Alfred Barr largely determined the goals and policy of the institution that was to define the framework of production and reception for the American neo-avant-garde. In 1927, just prior to the founding of the museum, Barr traveled to the Soviet Union. This was to have been a survey journey, like the one he had just completed in Weimar Germany, to explore current avant-garde production by artists working in the new revolutionary society. What he found there, however, was a situation of seemingly unmanageable conflict.

On the one hand, he witnessed the extraordinary productivity of the original modernist avant-garde (extraordinary in terms of the number of its participants, both men *and* women, and in terms of the variety of modes of production: ranging from Malevich's late suprematist work through the Laboratory Period of the constructivists, to the Lef Group and the emerging productivist program, as well as agitprop theater and avant-garde films screened for mass audiences). On the other hand, there was the general awareness among artists and cultural theoreticians that they were participating in a final transformation of the modernist vanguard aesthetic, as they irrevocably changed those conditions of art production and reception inherited from bourgeois society and its institutions. Then, too, there was the growing fear that the process of that successful transformation might be aborted by the emergence of totalitarian repression from within the very system that had generated the foundation for a new socialist collective culture. And last of all, there was Barr's own professional disposition to search for the most advanced, modernist avant-garde at precisely the moment when that social group was about to dismantle itself and its specialized activities in order to assume a different role in the newly defined process of the social production of culture.

These conflicting elements are clearly reflected in the diary that Barr kept during his visit to the Soviet Union:

> . . . went to see Rodchenko and his talented wife. . . . Rodchenko showed us an appalling variety of things—suprematist paintings

(preceded by the earliest geometrical things I have seen, 1915, done with compass)—woodcuts, linoleum cuts, posters, book designs, photographs, kino set, etc. etc. He has done no painting since 1922, devoting himself to the photographic arts of which he is a master. . . . We left after 11 p.m.—an excellent evening, but I must find some painters if possible.[1]

But Barr was no more fortunate in his search for painting during his visit with El Lissitzky: "He showed also books and photographs, many of them quite ingenious. . . . I asked whether he painted. He replied that he painted only when he had nothing else to do, and as that was never, never."[2]

And, finally, in his encounter with Sergei Tretyakov, it became clear that there was a historical reason for the frustration of Barr's expectations. For Tretyakov enunciated the position these artists had adopted in the course of transforming their aesthetic thinking in relation to the emerging industrialization of the Soviet Union: the program of productivism and the new method of literary representation/production that accompanied it, *factography*. "Tretyakov," Barr's diary tells us, "seemed to have lost all interest in everything that did not conform to his objective, descriptive, self-styled journalistic ideal of art. He had no interest in painting since it had become abstract. He no longer writes poetry but confines himself to reporting."[3]

This paradigm-change within modernism, which Barr witnessed from the very first hour, did not make a strong enough impression on him to affect his future project. He continued in his plan to lay the foundations of an avant-garde art in the United States according to the model that had been developed in the first two decades of this century in western Europe (primarily in Paris). And it was this perseverance, as much as anything else, that prevented, until the late '60s, the program of productivism and the methods of factographic production from entering the general consciousness of American and European audiences.

In 1936, when Barr's experiences in the Soviet Union were incorporated in the extraordinary exhibition *Cubism and Abstract Art*, his encounter with productivism was all but undocumented. This is particularly astonishing since Barr seems to have undergone a conversion towards the end of his journey, one which is not recorded in his diary, but which he publicly expressed upon his return in "The Lef and Soviet Art," his essay for *Transition* published in the fall of 1928. Surprisingly, we read in this article, illustrated with two photographs of Lissitzky's exhibition design for the 1928 *Pressa* exhibition in Cologne, the following, rather perspicacious appraisal of the ideas and goals of the Lef Group:

1.   Alfred Barr, "Russian Diary 1927–1928," *October*, no. 7 (Winter 1978), p. 21.
2.   *Ibid.*, p. 19.
3.   *Ibid.*, p. 14.

The *Lef* is more than a symptom, more than an expression of a fresh culture or of post-revolutionary man; it is a courageous attempt to give to art an important social function in a world where from one point of view it has been prostituted for five centuries. The *Lef* is formed by men who are idealists of Materialism; who have a certain advantage over the Alexandrian cults of the West—the *surréaliste* wizards, the esoteric word jugglers and those nostalgics who practice necromancy over the bones variously of Montezuma, Louis Philippe or St. Thomas Aquinas. The *Lef* is strong in the illusion that man can live by bread alone.[4]

But western European and American interests in the modernist avant-garde refused to confront the implications seen so clearly by Barr. Instead, what happened at that moment, in the process of reception, was what had been described in 1926 by Boris Arvatov, who along with Alexei Gan, Sergei Tretyakov, and Nikolai Tarabukin made up the group of productivist theoreticians. Arvatov wrote about the painters who refused to join the productivists, "Those on the Right gave up their positions without resistance. . . . Either they stopped painting altogether or they emigrated to the Western countries, in order to astonish Europe with home-made Russian Cézannes or with patriotic-folkloristic paintings of little roosters."[5]

It is against this background that I want to pursue the following questions: Why did the Soviet avant-garde, after having evolved a modernist practice to its most radical stages in the postsynthetic cubist work of the suprematists, constructivists, and Laboratory Period artists, apparently abandon the paradigm of modernism upon which its practice had been based? What paradigmatic changes occurred at that time, and which paradigm formation replaced the previous one?

For the sake of detail and specificity I will limit myself in what follows to a discussion of only some aspects of the respective paradigms that generated the crucial concern for *faktura* in the first period, and that made *factography* the primary method in the second period of Russian avant-garde practice.

Faktura was first defined in the Russian context in David Burliuk's futurist manifesto, "A Slap in the Face of Public Taste," of 1912, and in Mikhail Larionov's "Rayonnist Manifesto" of the same year. In the works of Malevich from 1913–1919 *faktura* was a major pictorial concern, as it was at that time for painters such as Lissitzky, Popova, and Rozanova, who had their origins in synthetic cubism and who had been profoundly influenced by Malevich's suprematism. Further, it remained the central concept in the nonutilitarian ob-

4.   Alfred Barr, "The Lef and Soviet Art," *Transition*, no. 14 (Fall 1928), pp. 267–270.
5.   Boris Arvatov, *Kunst und Produktion*, Munich, Hanser Verlag, 1978, p. 43. All translations from the German, unless otherwise noted, are my own.

jects produced by Rodchenko, Tatlin, and the Stenberg brothers, sometimes referred to as the Laboratory constructivists. During an extremely hectic period of approximately seven years (from 1913–1920) the essential qualities of *faktura* were acquired step by step and developed further by the individual members of that avant-garde.

By 1920 it seemed to them that they had brought to their logical conclusion all the major issues that had been developed during the preceding fifty years of modernist painting. Therefore the central concern for a self-reflexive pictorial and sculptural production was abandoned after 1920 — gradually at first, then abruptly — to be replaced by the new concern for factographic and productivist practices that are indicative of a more profound paradigmatic change.

Faktura

Attempts are being made in the recent literature to construct a genealogy for the Russian vanguard's concern for *faktura*, claiming that it originates in Russian icon painting. Vladimir Markov's 1914 text "Icon Painting" — after Burliuk and Larionov the third to address *faktura* explicitly — had established this specifically Russian source, arguing that "through the resonance of the colors, the sound of the materials, the assemblage of textures (*faktura*) we call the people to beauty, to religion, to God. . . . The real world is introduced into the icon's creation only through the assemblage and incrustation of real tangible objects and this seems to produce a combat between two worlds, the inner and the outer. . . ."[6]

---

6.   Yve-Alain Bois, in his essay "Malévich, le carré, le degré zéro" (*Macula*, no. 1 [1976], pp. 28–49), gives an excellent survey of the original discussion of the question of *faktura* among the various factions of the Russian avant-garde. More recently Margit Rowell has added references such as Markov's text, quoted here, that had not been mentioned by Bois. In any case, as Bois has argued, it is pointless to attempt a chronology since the many references to the phenomenon appear simultaneously and often independently of one another.

As early as 1912 the question of *faktura* is discussed by Mikhail Larionov in his "Rayonnist Manifesto," where he calls it "the essence of painting," arguing that the "combination of colors, their density, their interaction, their depth, and their *faktura* would interest the truly concerned to the highest degree." A year later, in his manifesto "Luchism" he argues that "every painting consists of a colored surface, its *faktura* (that is, the condition of that colored surface, its timbre) and the sensation that you receive from these two aspects." Also in 1912 we find David Burliuk differentiating between "a unified pictorial surface A and a differentiated pictorial surface B. The structure of a pictorial surface can be I. *Granular*, II. *Fibrous*, and III. *Lamellar*. I have carefully scrutinized Monet's *Rouen Cathedral* and I thought 'fibrous vertical structure.' . . . One can say that Cézanne is typically *lamellar*." Burliuk's text is entitled "Faktura." Bois also quotes numerous references to the phenomenon of *faktura* in the writings of Malevich, for example, where he calls Cézanne the inventor of a "new faktura of the pictorial surface," or when he juxtaposes the *linear* with the *textural* in painting. The concern for *faktura* seems still to have been central in 1919, as is evident from Popova's statement that "the content of pictorial surfaces is *faktura*." Even writers who were not predominantly concerned with visual and plastic phenomena were engaged in a discussion of *faktura*, as is the case of Roman Jakobson in his essay "Futurism," identifying it as

But the specifically Russian qualities of *faktura* are nonetheless challenged by other details of this production. For the religio-transcendental function assigned by Markov to the term *faktura* is just too close to the essential pursuit of collage aesthetics as defined in 1914 by, for example, Georges Braque. Braque argued, "That was the great adventure: color and shape operated simultaneously, but they were completely independent of each other." Similarly, Tatlin's request in 1913 that "the eye should be put under the control of touch" is too close to Duchamp's famous statement that he wanted to abolish the supremacy of the retinal principle in art. And, in the contemporaneous discussions of the term, any references to specifically Russian or religious functions are too rapidly jettisoned to maintain the credibility of Markov's argument. Already in 1916 Tarabukin wrote a definition of *faktura* that would essentially remain valid for the entire period of Laboratory constructivism to follow. "The form of a work of art," he declared, "derives from two fundamental premises: the *material* or medium (colors, sounds, words) and the *construction*, through which the material is organized in a coherent whole, acquiring its artistic logic and its profound meaning."[7]

What qualifies the concern for *faktura* as a paradigmatic feature (differentiating it at the same time from previous concerns for facture in the works of the cubists and futurists in western Europe) is the quasi-scientific, systematic manner in which the constructivists now pursued their investigation of pictorial and sculptural constructs, *as well as* the perceptual interaction with the viewer they generate. The equation between colors, sounds, and words established by Tarabukin was no longer the neoromantic call for *synaesthesia* that one could still hear at this time from Kandinsky and Kupka. Running parallel with the formation of structural linguistics in the Moscow Linguistic Circle and the Opoyaz Group in Petersburg in 1915 and 1916 respectively, the constructivists developed the first systematic phenomenological grammar of painting and

---

one of the many strategies of the new poets and painters who were concerned with the "unveiling of the procedure: therefore the increased concern for *faktura*; it no longer needs any justification, it becomes autonomous, it requires new methods of formation and new materials."

Quite unlike the traditional idea of *fattura* or *facture* in painting, where the masterful facture of a painter's hand spiritualizes the *mere* materiality of the pictorial production, and where the hand becomes at the same time the substitute or the totalization of the identifying signature (as the guarantee of authenticity, it justifies the painting's exchange value and maintains its commodity existence), the new concern for *faktura* in the Soviet avant-garde emphasizes precisely the mechanical quality, the materiality, and the anonimity of the painterly procedure from a perspective of empirico-critical positivism. It demystifies and devalidates not only the claims for the authenticity of the spiritual and the transcendental in the painterly execution but, as well, the authenticity of the exchange value of the work of art that is bestowed on it by the first.

For the discussion of the Markov statement and a generally important essay on the phenomenon of *faktura*, see also Margit Rowell, "Vladimir Tatlin: Form/Faktura," *October*, no. 7 (Winter 1978), pp. 94ff.

7.   Nikolai Tarabukin, *Le dernier tableau*, Paris, Editions Le Champ Libre, 1972, p. 102, cited in Rowell, p. 91.

Alexander Rodchenko. Oval Hanging Construction
(Surfaces Reflecting Light). *1921.*

sculpture. They attempted to define the separate material and procedural qualities by which such constructs are constituted with the same analytic accuracy used to analyze the *interrelationships* of their various functions—what Saussure would call the syntagmatic axis—which are equally relevant for the constitution of a perceptual phenomenon. Furthermore, they addressed the apparatus of visual sign production, that is, production procedures as well as the tools of these procedures. It was precisely the systematic nature of this investigation that led Barr in 1927 to see "an appalling variety of things" in Rodchenko's work.

When, in 1920–21, Rodchenko arrived more or less simultaneously at his sculptural series *Hanging Construction* (a series subtitled *Surfaces Reflecting Light*) and at the triptych *Pure Colors: Red, Yellow, Blue*, he had developed to its logical conclusion that separation of color and line and that integration of shape and plane that the cubists had initiated with such excitement. With some justification he declared, "This is the end of painting. These are the primary colors. Every plane is a plane and there will be no more representation."[8]

8.   Alexander Rodchenko, "Working with Maiakovsky," manuscript 1939, published in excerpts in *From Painting to Design*, exhibition catalogue, Cologne, Galerie Gmurzynska, 1981, pp. 190–191.

Even at this point in Rodchenko's development *faktura* already meant more than a rigorous and programmatic separation of line and drawing from painting and color, more than the congruence of planes with their actual support surface, more than emphasizing the necessary self-referentiality of pictorial signifiers and their contiguity with all other syntagmatic functions. It already meant, as well, more than just the object's shift from virtual pictorial/sculptural space into actual space. We should not take the reference to *Surfaces Reflecting Light* as anything less than an indication of the potential involvement of these artists with materials and objects in actual space and the social processes that occur within it.

Faktura also meant at this point, and not for Rodchenko alone, incorporating the technical means of construction into the work itself and linking them with existing standards of the development of the means of production in society at large. At first this happened on the seemingly banal level of the tools and materials that the painter employs — shifts that still caused considerable shock thirty years later with regard to Pollock's work. In 1917 Rodchenko explained his reasons for abandoning the traditional tools of painting and his sense of the need to mechanize its craft:

> Thenceforth the picture ceased being a picture and became a painting or an object. The brush gave way to new instruments with which it was convenient and easy and more expedient to work the surface. The brush which had been so indispensable in painting which transmitted the object and its subtleties became an inadequate and imprecise instrument in the new non-objective painting and the press, the roller, the drawing pen, the compass replaced it.[9]

The very same conviction about laboratory technology is concretized in Rodchenko's systematic experimentation with pictorial surfaces as *traces* or immediate results of specific procedures and materials: metallic and reflective paint are juxtaposed with matte gouaches; varnishes and oil colors are combined with highly textured surfaces.

It is this techno-logic of Rodchenko's experimental approach that seems to have prevented aesthetic comprehension for even longer than did Duchamp's most advanced work of 1913, such as his *Three Standard Stoppages* or his readymades. With its emphasis on the material congruence of the sign with its signifying practice, on the causal relationship between the sign and its referent, and its focus on the *indexical* status of the sign, Rodchenko's work has defied a secondary level of meaning/reading.[10]

9.   Alexander Rodchenko, exhibition pamphlet at the exhibition of the Leftist Federation in Moscow, 1917, cited in German Karginov, *Rodchenko*, London, Thames and Hudson, 1975, p. 64.
10.   The terminological distinction is of course that of C. S. Peirce as Rosalind Krauss has first

Further, this emphasis on the *process qualities* of painting was linked to a serially organized configuration, a structure that resulted as much from the commitment to systematic investigation as from the aspiration toward science with which artists wanted to associate their production. It is this nexus of relationships that tied these essential features of the modernist paradigm eventually to the socially dominant modes of control and management of time and perceptual experience in the Soviet Union's rapidly accelerating process of industrialization.

Faktura is therefore the historically logical aesthetic correlative to the introduction of industrialization and social engineering that was imminent in the Soviet Union after the revolution of 1917. For that reason *faktura* also became the necessary intermediary step within the transformation of the modernist paradigm as we witness it around 1920. When in 1921 A. V. Babichev, the leader of the Working Group for Objective Analysis (of which Rodchenko and Stepanova were members), gives a definition of art production, his statement is strikingly close to ideas of Taylorism, social engineering, and organized consumption, as they became operative at that time in both western European and American society. "Art," he wrote, "is an informed analysis of the concrete tasks which social life poses. . . . If art becomes public property it will organize the consciousness and psyche of the masses by organizing objects and ideas."[11]

Finally, the notion of *faktura* already implied a reference to the *placement* of the constructivist object and its interaction with the spectator. To emphasize spatial and perceptual contiguity by mirror reflection — as hinted in Rodchenko's project for constructions whose reflective surfaces would mirror their surroundings — means, once again, to reduce the process of representation to purely *indexical* signs:[12] matter seemingly generates its own representation without mediation (the old positivist's dream, as it was, of course, that of the early photographers). Contiguity is also incorporated in the *kinetic* potential of Rodchenko's *Hanging Constructions*, since their movement by air currents or touch literally involves the viewer in an endless phenomenological loop made of his or her own movements in the time/space continuum.

In the discussions of the Group for Objective Analysis from 1921, *construction* was defined as the organization of the kinetic life of objects and materials which would create new movement. As such it had been juxtaposed with the traditional notion of *composition*, as Varvara Stepanova defines it:

> Composition is the contemplative approach of the artist in his work. Technique and industry have confronted art with the problem of

---

applied it to Duchamp's work in her essay "Notes on the Index," *October*, nos. 3 and 4 (Summer and Fall 1977).

11.   A. V. Babichev, cited in Hubertus Gassner, "Analytical Sequences," in *Alexander Rodchenko*, ed. David Elliott, Oxford, Museum of Modern Art, 1979, p. 110.

12.   Krauss, "Notes," *passim*.

construction as an active process, and not a contemplative reflection. The "sanctity" of a work as a single entity is destroyed. The museum which was a treasury of this entity is now transformed into an archive.[13]

If these lines sound familiar today it is not because Stepanova's text had considerable impact on the thinking and practice of her peers, but rather because, more than ten years later, precisely the same historical phenomenon is described and analyzed in a text that is by now rightfully considered one of the most important contributions to twentieth-century aesthetic theory. I am speaking, of course, of Walter Benjamin's 1935 essay "The Work of Art in the Age of Mechanical Reproduction," and the following excerpt might be compared with Stepanova's 1921 statement:

> What they [the dadaists] intended and achieved was a relentless destruction of the aura of their creations, which they branded as reproductions with the very means of production. . . . In the decline of middle-class society, contemplation became a school for asocial behavior; it was countered by distraction as a variant of social conduct. . . . .[Dada] hit the spectator like a bullet, it happened to him, thus acquiring a tactile quality. . . . (Thus the dada work restores the quality of tactility to the art of the present day, a quality which is important to the art of all periods in their stages of transformation.)[14]

The historical observations by Stepanova and their subsequent theorization by Benjamin have another correlative in the work of Lissitzky from the period 1925–27. Already in 1923 in his *Prounenraum* for the Grosse Berliner Kunstausstellung, Lissitzky had transformed tactility and perceptual movement — still latent in Rodchenko's *Hanging Construction* — into a full-scale architectural relief construction. For the first time, Lissitzky's earlier claim for his *Proun-Paintings*, to operate as transfer stations from art to architecture, had been fulfilled.

It was, however, not until 1926, when he designed and installed in Dresden and Hannover what he called his *Demonstration Rooms* — room-sized cabinets for the display and installation of the nonrepresentational art of his time — that one finds Stepanova's analysis fully confirmed in Lissitzky's practice. The vertical lattice relief-construction that covers the display surfaces of the cabinet and that changes value from white, through gray, to black according to the viewer's

---

13.   Varvara Stepanova, quoted in Camilla Grey, *The Russian Experiment*, New York, Thames and Hudson, 1971, pp. 250–251.
14.   Walter Benjamin, "The Work of Art in the Age of Mechanical Reproduction," in *Illuminations*, trans. Harry Zohn, New York, Schocken Books, 1969, p. 238. The last sentence of this quotation, set into parenthesis, is taken from the second version of Benjamin's essay (my translation).

El Lissitzky. Cabinet of Abstract Art. *Hannoversches Landesmuseum, Hannover. 1926. Installation view shows aluminum relief walls and corner cabinet with movable panel. Works on display by Lissitzky, Schlemmer, and Marcoussis.*

position clearly engages the viewer in a phenomenological exercise that defies traditional contemplative behavior in front of the work of art. And the moveable wall panels, carrying or covering easel panels on display, to be shifted by the viewers themselves according to their momentary needs and interests, already incorporate into the display system of the museum the function of the archive that Stepanova predicted as its social destiny. In the late '20s Lissitzky wrote a retrospective analysis of his *Demonstration Rooms,* and once again it is crucial to compare his ideas with those of both Stepanova and Benjamin in order to realize how developed and current these concerns actually were in the various contexts:

> . . . traditionally the viewer was lulled into passivity by the paintings on the walls. Our construction/design shall make the man active. This is the function of our room. . . . With each movement of the viewer in space the perception of the wall changes; what was white becomes

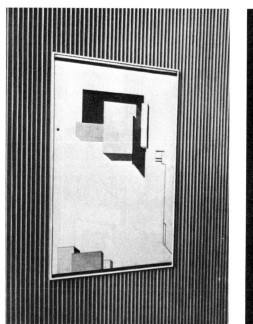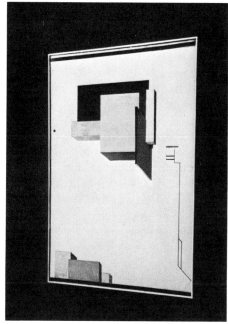

El Lissitzky. Floating Volume. *1919. Installed in El Lissitzky's* Cabinet of Abstract Art. *The two views indicate change from white to black depending on viewer's position.*

black, and vice versa. Thus, as a result of human bodily motion, a perceptual dynamic is achieved. This play makes the viewer active. . . . The viewer is physically engaged in an interaction with the object on display.[15]

The paradox and historical irony of Lissitzky's work was, of course, that it had introduced a revolution of the perceptual apparatus into an otherwise totally unchanged social institution, one that constantly reaffirms both the contemplative behavior and the sanctity of historically rooted works of art.

This paradox complemented the contradiction that had become apparent several years earlier when Lissitzky had placed a suprematist painting, enlarged

15.   El Lissitzky, "Demonstrationsräume," in *El Lissitzky*, ed. Sophie Lissitzky-Küppers, Dresden, VEB-Verlag der Kunst, 1967, p. 362.

to the size of an agitational billboard, in front of a factory entrance in Vitebsk. This utopian radicalism in the formal sphere—what the conservative Soviet critics later would pejoratively allude to as formalism—in its failure to communicate with and address the new audiences of industrialized urban society in the Soviet Union, became increasingly problematic in the eyes of the very groups that had developed constructivist strategies to expand the framework of modernism. It had become clear that the new society following the socialist revolution (in many respects a social organization that was comparable to the advanced industrial nations of western Europe and the United States at that time) required systems of representation/production/distribution which would recognize the collective participation in the actual processes of production of social wealth, systems which, like architecture in the past or cinema in the present, had established conditions of *simultaneous collective reception.* In order to make art "an informed analysis of the concrete tasks which social life poses," as Babichev had requested, and in order to "fill the gulf between art and the masses that the bourgeois traditions had established," as Meyerhold had called for, entirely new forms of audience address and distribution had to be considered. But around 1920 even the most advanced works among the nonutilitarian object-constructions—by Rodchenko, the Stenberg brothers, Tatlin, and Medunetsky—did not depart much further from the modernist framework of bourgeois aesthetics than the point of establishing models of epistemological and semiotic critique. No matter how radical, these were at best no more than a negation of the perceptual conventions by which art had previously been produced and received.

With sufficient historical distance it becomes clearer that this fundamental crisis within the modernist paradigm was not only a crisis of representation (one that had reached its penultimate status of self-reflexive verification and epistemological critique). It was also, importantly, a crisis of audience relationships, a moment in which the historical institutionalization of the avant-garde had reached its peak of credibility, from which legitimation was only to be obtained by a redefinition of its relationship with the new urban masses and their cultural demands. The Western avant-garde experienced the same crisis with the same intensity. It generally responded with entrenchment in traditional models—the "Rappel à l'ordre"—and the subsequent alignment of many of its artists with the aesthetic needs of the fascists in Italy and Germany. Or, other factions of the Paris avant-garde responded to the same crisis with an increased affirmation of the unique status of a high-art avant-garde, trying to resolve the contradictions of their practice by reaffirming blatantly obsolete conventions of pictorial representation. In the early '20s the Soviet avant-garde (as well as some members of the de Stijl group, the Bauhaus, and Berlin dada) developed different strategies to transcend the historical limitations of modernism. They recognized that the crisis of representation could not be resolved without at the same time addressing questions of distribution and audience. Architecture, utilitarian product design, and photographic factography were some of the practices that the Soviet avant-garde considered capable of establishing these new modes of simultaneous collective reception.[16] Arvatov gives a vivid account of the gradual transition from the modernist position in the Russian avant-garde to the factographic and utilitarian aesthetic:

> The first to retire were the expressionists, headed by Kandinsky, who could not endure extremist pressure. Then the suprematists, headed by Malevich, protested against the murder of the sanctity of art, since they were convinced of the complete self-sufficiency of art. They could not comprehend any other form of art production but that of the easel. . . . In 1921 the Institute for Artistic Culture, which had once united all the Left artists, broke up. Shortly thereafter the Institute started to work under the banner of productivism. After a long process of selection, after an obstinate fight, the group of non-representational constructivists crystallized within the group of the Left (Tatlin, Rodchenko, and the Obmochu-Group), who based their practice on the investigation and treatment of real materials as a transition to the constructive activity of the engineer. During one of the most important meetings of the Inchuk a resolution was passed unanimously to finish off with the self-sufficient constructions and to take all measures necessary in order to engage immediately with the industrial revolution.[17]

Photomontage: Between Faktura and Factography

The relatively late discovery of photocollage and montage techniques seems to have functioned as a transitional phase, operating between the fully developed modernist critique of the conventions of representation, which one sees in constructivism, and an emerging awareness of the new need to construct *iconic* representations for a new mass audience. Neither Lissitzky nor Rodchenko produced any photocollage work before 1922; and only as late as 1919 — when these artists had already pushed other aspects of postcubist pictorial and sculptural problems further than anyone else in Europe (except, of course, for Duchamp) — did the collage technique proper enter their work at all. It seems credible that in fact Gustav Klucis, a disciple of Malevich and a collaborator with Lissitzky, was the first artist to transcend the purity of suprematist painting by introducing iconic photographic fragments into his suprematist

16. The problem of the creation of conditions of simultaneous collective reception is dealt with in an essay by Wolfgang Kemp, "Quantität und Qualität: Formbestimmtheit und Format der Fotografie," *Foto-Essays zur Geschichte und Theorie der Fotografie*, Munich, Schirmer/Mosel, 1978, pp. 10ff.
17. Arvatov, *Kunst*, p. 43.

work in 1919, the very date that Heartfield and Grosz, Hausmann and Höch have claimed as the moment of their invention of photomontage.

Since by 1919 photomontage was widespread and commonly used in both advertising and commercial photography, the question of who actually introduced the technique into the transformation of the modernist paradigm is unimportant.[18] What is far more crucial is in what way the artists (who might very well have simultaneously "discovered" the technique for their own purposes quite independently of one another) related to the inherent potential and consequences of the reintroduction of (photographic) iconic imagery at precisely the moment when mimetic representation had seemingly been dismantled and definitively abandoned.

Announcing his claims to priority, Klucis also underlines the essential difference between the Soviet type of photomontage and that of the Berlin dadaists when he writes in 1931:

> There are two general tendencies in the development of photomontage: one comes from American publicity and is exploited by the

18.   The two essays that trace the history of photomontage in the context of the history of photography and the history of emerging advertising technology are Robert Sobieszek, "Composite Imagery and the Origins of Photomontage," Part I and II, *Artforum*, September/October 1978, pp. 58–65, and pp. 40–45. Much more specifically addressing the origins of photomontage in advertising techniques is Sally Stein's important essay, "The Composite Photographic Image and the Composition of Consumer Ideology," *Art Journal*, Spring 1981, pp. 39–45.

Gustav Klucis.
The Dynamic City. *1919.*

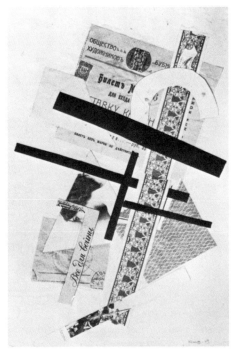

Alexander Rodchenko.
Ticket No. 1. *1919.*

Alexander Rodchenko.
Photomontage for Pro Eto. *1923.*

Dadaists and Expressionists—the so called photomontage of form; the second tendency, that of militant and political photomontage, was created on the soil of the Soviet Union. Photomontage appeared in the USSR under the banner of LEF when non-objective art was already finished. . . . Photomontage as a new method of art dates from 1919 to 1920.[19]

The hybrids that Klucis, Lissitzky, and Rodchenko created with their first attempts at collage and photomontage reveal the difficulty of the paradigmatic transformation that is inherent in that procedure, and the concomitant search, in the period 1919–23, for a solution to the crisis of representation. But beyond this, they suggest where the answer to these questions would have to be found, and they define the qualities and functions which the new procedures that legitimize iconic representation would have to offer. At the same time, it would seem that these artists did not want, on the one hand, to sacrifice any of the supreme modernist virtues they had achieved in their pictorial and sculptural

19. Gustav Klucis, Preface to the exhibition catalogue *Fotomontage*, Berlin, 1931, cited in Dawn Ades, *Photomontage*, London/New York, Pantheon, 1976, p. 15.

work: the transparency of construction procedures; the self-referentiality of the pictorial signifying devices; the reflexive spatial organization; and the general emphasis on the tactility, that is, the constructed nature of their representations. But, on the other hand, photocollage and photomontage reintroduced into the aesthetic construct—at a moment when its modernist self-reflexivity and purification had semiotically reduced all formal and material operations to purely indexical signs—unlimited sources for a new *iconicity* of representation, one that was mechanically produced and reproduced, and therefore—to a generation of media utopians—the most reliable. Looking at the photomontage work of 1923, such as Rodchenko's series *Pro Eto*, or Hausmann's work, one might well wonder whether the exuberance, willfulness, and quantity of the photographic quotations and their juxtapositions were not in part motivated by their authors' relief at having finally broken the modernist ban on iconic representation. This, in extreme contrast to the Parisian vanguard's collage work, in which iconic representation ultimately reappeared, but which never made use of photographic or mechanically reproduced iconic images.

But the rediscovery of a need to construct iconic representations did not, of course, result primarily from the need to overcome the strictures of modernism. Rather it was a necessary strategy to implement the transformation of audiences that the artists of the Soviet avant-garde wanted to achieve at that time. "Photomontage," an anonymous text (attributed by some scholars to Rodchenko) published in *Lef* in 1924, not only traces the historic affiliation of photomontage's conglomerate image with the strategies of advertising, juxtaposing photomontage's technique and its iconic dimension with the traditional techniques of modernist representation, but also introduces the necessity of *documentary* representation in order to reach the new mass audience:

> By photomontage we understand the usage of the photographic prints as tools of representation. The combination of photographs replaces the composition of graphic representations. The reason for this substitution resides in the fact that the photographic print is not the sketch of a visual fact, but its precise fixation. The precision and the documentary character give photography an impact on the spectator that the graphic representation can never claim to achieve. . . . An advertisement with a photograph of the object that is being advertised is more efficient than a drawing of the same subject.[20]

Unlike the Berlin dadaists who claimed to have invented photomontage, the author of this *Lef* text does not disavow the technique's intrinsic affiliation (and competitive engagement) with the dominant practices of advertising.

---

20.   Anonymous, *Lef*, no. 4 (1924), reprinted in *Art et Poésie Russes*, Paris, Musée national d'art moderne, 1979, pp. 221ff (my translation).

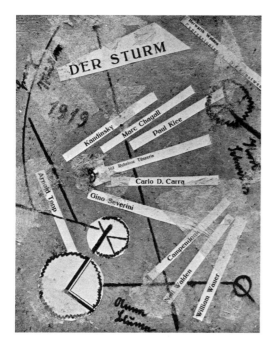

Kurt Schwitters. Untitled (Der Sturm). *1919.*

El Lissitzky. Photomontage for catalogue accompanying Soviet Pavilion at Pressa Exhibition, *Cologne. 1928.*

Quite the contrary, the author seems to invite that competition by defining photomontage from the start as an agitational tool that addresses the Soviet Union's urban masses. It is with this aspect in mind that the practitioners of photomontage could not accept the confinement of the medium to the forms of distribution they had inherited from collage: forms limited by the single, rectangular sheet of paper, its format, scale, and size of edition entirely determined by the most traditional studio notions of unique, auratic works of art.

While (with the exception of the work of John Heartfield) most western European photomontage remains on the level of the unique, fabricated image — paradoxically folding into the singularity of this object fragments of a multitude of technically reproduced photographic images from mass-cultural sources — the strategies of the Soviet avant-garde seem rather rapidly to have shifted away from a reenactment of that historical paradox. The productivist artists realized that in order to address a new audience not only did the techniques of production have to be changed, but the forms of distribution and institutions of dissemination and reception had to be transformed as well. The photomontage technique, as an artistic procedure that supposedly carries transformative potential *qua* procedure, as the Berlin dadaists seem to have believed, therefore, in the work of Rodchenko and Lissitzky, becomes integrated as only *one* among several techniques — typography, advertising, propaganda — that attempted to redefine the representational systems of the new society.

In 1926 Lissitzky developed a theory of contemporary art production that not only associated aesthetic practice with the needs of audience and patron class as prime determinants of the forms that production would assume, but also linked standards of modernist practice to distribution developments occurring in other communications media: books, graphic design, film. Although his beliefs were buoyed by the same naive optimism towards the enlightening power of technology and the media that would ten years later limit the ultimate relevance of Walter Benjamin's essay, Lissitzky's is not a mere "machine aesthetic." Rather, it is an attempt to establish an operative aesthetic framework that could focus attention simultaneously on the existing needs of mass audiences and on the available techniques and standards of the means of artistic production. Like Benjamin in his later essay, Lissitzky considers aesthetic forms and their procedures of production in the light of history rather than in terms of universal categories. Yet unlike Benjamin, he perceives the ensuing transformations as a product of needs and functions rather than as a result of technological changes. The text is important for the clarification of Lissitzky's motivation in the following years, as he decided to abandon almost all traditional forms of graphic and photographic, let alone painterly or sculptural, production, and to concentrate exclusively on those practices that establish the new "monumentality"—the conditions of simultaneous collective reception:

> It is shortsighted to suppose that machines, *i.e.*, the displacement of manual by mechanical processes, are basic to the development of the form and the figure of an artifact. In the first place it is the consumers' demand that determines the development, *i.e.*, the demand of the social strata that provide the "commissions." Today this is not a narrow circle anymore, a thin cream, but everybody, the masses. . . . What conclusions does this imply in our field? The most important thing here is that the mode of production of words and pictures is included in the same process: photography. . . . [In America] they began to modify the relation of word and illustration in exposition in the direct opposite of the European style. The highly developed technique of facsimile electrotype (half-tone blocks) was especially important for this development; thus photomontage was born. . . . With our work the Revolution has achieved a colossal labor of propaganda and enlightenment. We ripped up the traditional book into single pages, magnified these a hundred times, . . . and stuck them up as posters in the streets. . . . The innovation of easel painting made great works of art possible, but it has now lost its power. The cinema and the illustrated weekly have succeeded it. . . . The book is the most monumental art form today; no longer is it fondled by the delicate hands of a bibliophile, but seized by a hundred thousand hands.

. . . We shall be satisfied if we can conceptualize the epic and the lyric developments of our times in our form of the book.[21]

The degree to which Lissitzky focused at that time on the question of audience as a determinant of form, and on the perspective of creating conditions for simultaneous collective reception, becomes even more obvious in the essay's at-first surprising equation between the reading space of the printed page and the space of dramatic experience in the theater. According to Lissitzky the page (and its traditional layout and typography) shares conventions of confinement with the theater — the peep-show as he calls it — where the spectator is separated from the performers, and the spectator's gaze is contained — as in traditional easel painting — in the central perspective of the proscenium stage. The revolutionary transformation of book design ran parallel in Lissitzky's work to the revolution of the theatrical space, for example, as he would produce it in 1929 for Meyerhold's theater and its central, open-stage construction. Already in his 1922 book *Of Two Squares* (reading lessons for children, as he called it), he said that "the action unrolls like a film" and the method of typographical montage generates the tactility of experiencing the reader's movement through time and space.[22]

This integration of the dramatic experience of theatrical/cinematographic space and the perceptual experience of static signs of graphic/photographic montage and typography is successfully achieved in 1928 in Lissitzky's first major exhibition project for the International Press Exhibition, *Pressa*, in Cologne. Not surprisingly, we find on the first page of the catalogue that Lissitzky created to accompany the design of the USSR Pavilion the announcement, "Here you see in a typographic kino-show the passage of the contents of the Soviet Pavilion."[23]

Rather than thinking of Lissitzky's involvement with the design of exhibitions merely as a task-oriented activity that remains marginal to the central concerns of his work (as have most authors considering these projects), it seems more adequate to see them, along with Lissitzky's subsequent involvement with the propaganda journal *USSR in Construction*, as a logical next step in the development of his own work, as well as in the radical transformation of modernist aesthetics and art production as it had been occurring within the Soviet avant-garde since 1921 and the rise of productivism. We have no reason to doubt the sincerity of one of the last texts Lissitzky wrote, shortly before his death in 1941, a table of autobiographical dates and activities, where the entry

21. El Lissitzky, "Unser Buch," in *El Lissitzky*, pp. 357–360.
22. Yve-Alain Bois, "El Lissitzky: Reading Lessons," *October*, no. 11 (Winter 1979), pp. 77–96.
23. Lissitzky, *Katalog des Sowjet Pavillons auf der Internationalen Presse-Ausstellung*, Cologne, Dumont Verlag, 1928, p. 16.

under the year 1926 reads, "In 1926 my most important work as an artist began: the design of exhibitions."[24]

In 1927 Lissitzky had been commissioned to install his first "commercial" exhibition design in the Soviet Union, the exhibition of the Polygraphic Union, a relatively modest project in Moscow's Gorky Park. Unlike the 1926 design for the *International Contemporary Art Exhibition* in Dresden, or the cabinet design for the Hannover Landesmuseum in 1927, this project was conceived and produced as a set for a trade show rather than an exhibition of contemporary art; furthermore, it was the result of the collaboration of a group of artists.

Klucis, the "inventor" of photomontage, Lissitzky's colleague and disciple from Vitebsk, where both had struggled to come to terms with the legacy of Malevich's suprematism in 1919–20, was one of the collaborators in the project, as was Salomon Telingater, later to emerge as one of the major figures in the revolution of Soviet typographic design. It is in the catalogue of this exhibition — a book design project that was jointly produced by Lissitzky and Telingater — that we find Lissitzky's essay "The Artist in Production."

This text is not only Lissitzky's own productivist manifesto (Rodchenko and Stepanova's text, officially entitled "Productivist Manifesto," had appeared already in 1921, and Ossip Brik's manifesto "Into Production" had appeared in *Lef* in 1923), but it is also the text in which Lissitzky develops most succinctly his ideas about the uses of photography in general and the functions of photomontage in particular:

> As a result of the social needs of our epoch and the fact that artists acquainted themselves with new techniques, *photomontage* emerged in the years following the Revolution and flourished thereafter. Even though this technique had been used in America much earlier for advertising, and the dadaists in Europe had used it to shake up official bourgeois art, it only served political goals in Germany. But only here, with us, photomontage acquired a clearly socially determined and aesthetic form. Like all other great art, it created its own laws of formation. The power of its expression made the workers and the Komsomol circles enthusiastic for the visual arts and it had great influence on the billboards and newspapers. Photomontage at its present stage of development uses finished, entire photographs as elements from which it constructs a totality.[25]

Lissitzky's 1927 text not only traces an astonishingly clear history of the technique of photomontage and its origins in advertising technology, but it also gives us a clear view of his awareness that the functions of the technique within

24.   Lissitzky, *Proun und Wolkenbügel*, Dresden, VEB Verlag der Kunst, 1977, p. 115.
25.   Lissitzky, "Der Künstler in der Produktion," *Proun*, pp. 113ff.

the historical context of the Soviet avant-garde are entirely different from that of the Berlin dadaists, that the technique is only valid if it is bound into the particular needs of a social group. That is to say, he disavows photomontage as a new artistic strategy that has value *qua* artistic operation and innovational mode of representation/production. The nucleus of the inherent potential of photomontage, that is, the production of iconic, documentary information, already addressed in the anonymous text from *Lef* of 1924, is fully developed in Lissitzky's definition of the functions of the technique in 1927: the morphology of the products of that technique has changed substantially by comparison with its original manifestations in 1919–23. Those features that the technique of photomontage had inherited from its origins in collage and the cubist critique of representation were gradually abandoned. Also abandoned was the overlap of photomontage with the techniques of modern advertising. These techniques seemed to have generated, in the dada context, the extreme procedures of juxtaposition and fragmentation by which the origins in advertising were inverted and where the constructed artificiality of the artifact destroyed the mythical nature of the commodity. This shift became apparent in the gradual return to the *iconic* functions of the photograph, deleting altogether the *indexical* potential of the photograph (as still visible in Lissitzky's photograms of the '20s) as well as the actual indexical structure of the agglomerated fragments of the photomontage itself, where the network of cuts and lines of jutting edges and unmediated transitions from fragment to fragment was as important, if not more so, as the actual iconic representation contained within the fragment itself.

Thus *faktura*, an essential feature of the modernist paradigm that underlay the production of the Soviet avant-garde until 1923, was replaced by a new concern for the *factographic* capacity of the photograph, supposedly rendering aspects of reality visible without interference or mediation. It was at this moment — in 1924 — that Rodchenko decided to abandon photomontage altogether and to engage in single-frame still photography, which transforms montage through the explicit choice of camera angle, the framing of vision, the determinants of the filmic apparatus, and the camera's superiority over the conventions of human perception. In Lissitzky's essay this change is clearly indicated in the phrase arguing that "photomontage in its present stage of development uses finished entire photographs as elements from which it constructs a totality." From this we see that homogeneity in the single print is favored over fragmentation, iconic representation of an absent referent is favored over the indexical materiality of the trace of a verifiable process, tactility of the construction of incoherent surfaces and spatial references is exchanged for the monumentality of the camera-angle's awesome visions and the technological media optimism that it conveys. Yet while it is evident that at this moment the premises of the modernist paradigm were vacated, and that a programmatic commitment to new audiences entirely changed the nature of artistic production, it seems no more appropriate to neglect or condemn as *propaganda* Lissitzky's or Rodchenko's work from this period (nor their subsequent involvement with Stalin's State Publishing House in the 1930s) than it would be to condemn certain surrealist artists (those in particular who developed what Max Ernst was to call the technique of the "painted collage") as being responsible for providing advertising's visual and textual strategies, operative to this very day.

Between Photomontage and Propaganda: The Pressa

Partially as a response to his first successful exhibition design in Moscow in 1927, a committee chaired by Anatoly Lunacharsky decided to ask Lissitzky (together with Rabinowich, who later withdrew from participation) to design the Soviet Pavilion at the forthcoming *International Exhibition of Newspaper and Book Publishing* in Cologne, the first exhibition of its kind. Since the decision of the committee was made on December 23, 1927, and the exhibition was to begin in the first week of May 1928, Lissitzky and his collaborators had four months to plan and produce the design of the exhibition. Apparently just two days after the committee had appointed him, Lissitzky submitted a first general outline that foresaw the formation of a "collective of creators" with himself as the general coordinator of the design. Among the approximately thirty-eight members of the collective, only a few, among them the stage designer Naumova, had previously participated in exhibition design and the decoration of revolutionary pageants.[26] The largest group within the collective consisted of agitprop graphic designers, shortly thereafter to become some of the most important graphic designers of the Soviet avant-garde. The majority of the 227 exhibits were produced and assembled in the workshops for stage design in the Lenin Hills in Moscow. The other elements were designed in Moscow as well, but produced and assembled in Cologne under the supervision of Lissitzky and Sergei Senkin, who had traveled to the site of the exhibition to supervise and install the Soviet Pavilion.

The centerpiece of the exhibition was in fact the large-scale photomontage that Lissitzky had designed with Senkin's assistance. This *photofresco*, as Senkin called it, measured approximately seventy-two by eleven feet and depicted, in constant alternation of camera angles, of close-ups and long-shots, the history and importance of the publishing industry in the Soviet Union since the Revolution and its role in the education of the illiterate masses of the newly industrialized state. Thus the photofresco, *The Task of the Press Is the Education of the Masses* (its official title), functioned as the centerpiece of an exhibition that was devoted to documenting the achievements of the Revolution in the educational field for a skeptical, if not hostile western European public.

26.   For a detailed description of the history and the procedures of the work for the *Pressa* exhibition design, see Igor W. Rjasanzew, "El Lissitzky und die *Pressa* in Köln 1928," in *El Lissitzky*, exhibition catalogue, Halle (GDR), Staatliche Galerie Moritzburg, 1982, pp. 72–81.

El Lissitzky (in collaboration with Sergei Senkin).
Photofresco in Pressa Exhibition. *1928.*

The actual structure of the photofresco followed the strategies that Lissitzky had laid out in the essay that accompanied the catalogue of his first exhibition design in 1927. Large-scale photographic prints were assembled in an irregular grid formation and the visual dynamic of the montage resulted from the juxtaposition of the various camera angles and positions, but no longer from a jagged linear network of seams and edges of heterogeneous photographic fragments.

While the scale and size of the photomontage — it was installed on the wall at a considerable height — aligned the work with a tradition of architectural decoration and mural painting, the sequencing of the images and their emphatic dependence on camera technology and movement related the work to the experience of cinematic viewing, such as that of the newsreel. In their mostly enthusiastic reviews, many visitors to the *Pressa* exhibition actually discussed the theatrical and cinematic aspects of the photofresco. One critic reminisces that one went through "a drama that unfolded in time and space. One went through expositions, climaxes, retardations, and finales."[27] Reviewing both the Dresden *Hygiene Exhibition* design by Lissitzky and the Cologne *Pressa* design, a less well-disposed critic still had to admit the design's affiliation with the most advanced forms of cinematic production:

> The first impression is brilliant. Excellent the technique, the arrangement, the organization, the modern way it has been constructed. . . . Propaganda, propaganda, that is the keynote of Soviet Russian exhibitions, whether they be in Cologne or in Dresden. And how well the Russians know how to achieve the visual effects their films have been showing us for years![28]

Even though Lissitzky did not meet Dziga Vertov until 1929 (inaugurating a friendship that lasted until Lissitzky's death in 1941), it is very likely that in 1927–28 he was drawing not only upon the collage and montage sources of cubism, dadaism, and constructivism, but equally upon the cinematic montage techniques that Vertov had used in the first *Kino-Pravda* films, and used still more daringly and systematically in his work after 1923.

In his manifesto "We," published in *kinofot* in 1922 and illustrated by a compass and ruler drawing by Rodchenko from 1915, Vertov had called film "an art of movement, its central aim being the organization of the movements of objects in space." Hubertus Gassner speculates that this manifesto had considerable influence on Rodchenko, as well as the constructivists, and led him away from drawing and painting into the photographic montage production that Rodchenko published two issues later in the same journal.[29] It seems, however, that Vertov only voiced a concern that, as we saw above in several

27.   Rjasanzew, p. 78.
28.   Cited in Rjasanzew, p. 79.
29.   Hubertus Gassner, *Rodchenko Fotografien*, Munich, Schirmer/Mosel, 1982, p. 121.

instances, was very much at the center of the constructivist debate itself, to make "construction" and "montage" the procedures that would transform the passive, contemplative modes of seeing. Sophie Küppers argues that it was Vertov who learned the montage technique from Lissitzky's earliest experiments with the photogram and the photomontage, and that it was primarily Lissitzky's transparency technique and the double exposure as photographic montage technique that left a particularly strong impression on Vertov's own work in the mid-1920s. Only in the later work produced by Lissitzky for the magazine *USSR in Construction* can we recognize, according to Küppers, the influence of Vertov's *Kino-Pravda*.

In spite of the obvious parallels between the cinematographic montage and the photomontage, and leaving aside the question of historical priority and influence, it is important to clarify in this context the specific differences that existed between the mural-sized photomontages and exhibition designs of Lissitzky and the montage of Vertov's *Kino-Pravda*. Clearly the still photograph and the new photomontage, as Lissitzky defined it, offered features that the moving imagery of the film lacked: aspects of the same subject could be compared and contrasted and could be offered for extensive reading and viewing; complicated processes of construction and social transformation could be analyzed in detailed accounts that ran parallel with statistics and other written information; and the same subject could, as Rodchenko argued, be represented "at different times and in different circumstances." This practice of "realistic constructivism" as the critic Gus called Lissitzky's exhibition design, had in fact wrought a substantial change within collage and photomontage aesthetics. What in collage had been the strategy of *contingency*, by which material had been juxtaposed, emphasizing the divergence of the fragments, had now become the *stringency* of a conscious construction of documentary factographic information.

In an excellent recent study of Russian constructivism, Christina Lodder has argued that it was the failure of the constructivists actually to implement their productivist program (due to shortage of materials, lack of access to industrial facilities, disinterest on the part of the engineers and administrators of the State manufacturing companies) that drove these artists into the field of typography, publication and poster design, agitational propaganda and exhibition design.[30] The emergence of a strong antimodernism, backed by the Party as a result of Lenin's New Economic Policy in 1921, required the return to traditional values in art and laid the foundations for the rise of socialist realism. Lodder argues that it was as a result of these changes and as an attempt at competition with these reactionary forces that Lissitzky's and Rodchenko's work at that time employed iconic, photographic representation and abandoned

30.   Christina Lodder, *Russian Constructivism*, New Haven and London, Yale University Press, 1983.

the radical syntax of the montage aesthetic. The problem with this criticism, however — as with all previous rejections of the later work of Rodchenko and Lissitzky — is that criteria of judgment that were originally developed within the framework of modernism are now applied to a practice of representation that had deliberately and systematically disassociated itself from that framework in order to lay the foundations of an art production that would correspond to the needs of a newly industrialized collective society. Because, as we have seen, these conditions required radically different production procedures and modes of presentation and distribution, any historical critique or evaluation will have to develop its criteria from *within* the actual intentions and conditions at the origin of these practices.

Lissitzky's exhibition design does overcome the traditional limitations of the avant-garde practice of photomontage and reconstitutes it within the necessary conditions of simultaneous collective reception that were given in the cinema and in architecture. Further, in his new practice of montage, Lissitzky incorporated the method of "systematic analytical sequence," as Tretyakov was to define it shortly afterwards. Tretyakov wrote in 1931 that the photographer/ artist should move from the single-image aesthetic to the systematic photographic sequence and the long-term observation:

> If a more or less random snapshot is like an infinitely fine scale that has been scratched from the surface of reality with the tip of the finger, then in comparison the photoseries or the photomontage lets us experience the extended massiveness of reality, its authentic meaning. We build systematically. We must also photograph systematically. Sequence and long-term photographic observation — that is the method.[31]

Modernism's Aftermath

In spite of the fact that even the most conservative international newspapers reported enthusiastically on Lissitzky's *Pressa* design, and that he received a medal from the Soviet government in recognition of the success of this project as well as having been named an honorary member of the Moscow town Soviet, he seems to have been personally dissatisfied with the results. This is evident in a letter that he wrote on December 26, 1928, to his Dutch friend, the de Stijl architect J. J. P. Oud. "It was a big success for us," he mused, "but aesthetically there is something of a poisoned satisfaction. The extreme hurry

---

31.   Sergei Tretyakov, "From the Photoseries to the Long-Term Photographic Observation," in *Proletarskoje Foto*, IV (1931), 20, reprinted in German translation in *Zwischen Revolutionskunst und Sozialistischem Realismus*, ed. Hubertus Gassner and Eckhart Gillen, Cologne, Dumont Verlag, 1979, pp. 222ff.

and the shortage of time violated my intentions and the necessary completion of the form—so it ended up being basically a theater decoration."[32]

We will, however, find in neither Lissitzky's letters nor his diary entries any private or public disavowal of or signs of regret about having abandoned the role of the modernist artist for that of the producer of political propaganda in the service of the new Communist state. Quite the opposite: the letters we know Lissitzky to have written during the years of his subsequent involvement with both the design of exhibitions for the government and his employment by Stalin's State Publishing House on the magazine *USSR in Construction* clearly indicate that he was as enthusiastically at work in fashioning the propaganda for Stalin's regime as were Rodchenko and Stepanova, who were at that time involved in similar tasks. Clearly Lissitzky shared the naive utopianism that also characterizes Walter Benjamin's later essay, an optimism that Adorno criticized in his response to the text, saying,

> Both the dialectic of the highest and the lowest [modernism and mass-culture] bear the stigmata of capitalism, both contain elements of change. . . . Both are torn halves of an integral freedom, to which however they do not add up. It would be romantic to sacrifice one to the other, either as the bourgeois romanticism of the conservation of personality and all that stuff, or as the anarchistic romanticism of blind confidence in the spontaneous power of the proletariat in the historical process—a proletariat which is itself a product of bourgeois society.[33]

But it is also clear by now that both Lissitzky's and Benjamin's media optimism prevented them from recognizing that the attempt to create conditions of a simultaneous collective reception for the new audiences of the industrialized state would very soon issue into the preparation of an arsenal of totalitarian, Stalinist propaganda in the Soviet Union. What is worse, it would deliver the aesthetics and technology of propaganda to the Italian Fascist and German Nazi regimes. And only a little later we see the immediate consequences of Lissitzky's new montage techniques and photofrescoes in their successful adaptation for the ideological needs of American politics and the campaigns for the acceleration of capitalist development through consumption. Thus, what in Lissitzky's hands had been a tool of instruction, political education, and the raising of consciousness was rapidly transformed into an instrument for prescribing the silence of conformity and obedience. The "consequent inrush of barbarism" of which Adorno speaks in the letter to Benjamin as one possible result of the un-

32.   Lissitzky, *Proun*, p. 135.
33.   Theodor W. Adorno, Letter to Walter Benjamin, London, March 18, 1936, reprinted in *Aesthetics and Politics*, London, New Left Books, 1977, pp. 120ff.

Gustav Klucis. Photomontage poster (two versions). 1930.

dialectical abandonment of modernism was soon to become a historical reality. As early as 1932 we see the immediate impact of the *Pressa* project in its adaption for the propaganda needs of the Fascist government in Italy. Informed by the members of the Italian League of Rational Architecture, in particular Bardi and Paladini (who was an expert on the art of the Soviet avant-garde), the architect Giuseppe Terragni constructed an enormous mural-sized photomontage for the *Exposition of the Fascist Revolution*.[34] It would require a detailed formal and structural analysis to identify the transformations that took place within photomontage aesthetics once they were put to the service of Fascist politics. It may suffice here to bring only one detail to the attention of the reader, a detail in which that inversion of meaning under an apparent continuity of a formal principle becomes apparent, proving that it is by no means simply the case of an available formal strategy being refurbished with a new political and ideological content.

34.   Herta Wescher wrote in 1968 in her history of collage that P. M. Bardi's work *Tavola degli orrori* had been modeled upon Lissitzky's montage work published in Western journals. For Paladini, Wescher argues, the relationship was even more direct since he had been born in Moscow of Italian parents and had developed a strong interest in the Soviet avant-garde. In response to the exhibition of the Soviet Pavilion at the Venice Bienale in 1924, he published a study *Art in the Soviet Union* (1925). See Wescher, *Collage*, Cologne, Dumont Verlag, 1968, pp. 76ff.

John Heartfield. All fists have been clenched as one, *photomontage cover for special issue against fascism of* Arbeiter Illustrierte Zeitung, *vol. XIII, no. 40, 1934.*

The detail in question is the representation of the masses in Terragni's photomural, where a crowd of people is contained in the outlines of a relief shaped like the propeller of a turbine or a ship. Clearly it was one of the most difficult tasks, in constructing representations for new mass audiences, not only to establish conditions of simultaneous collective viewing, but further, actually to construct representations of the masses themselves, to depict the collectivity. One of the most prominent examples of this necessity is an early photomontage poster by Klucis, which in fact seems to have been so successful that Klucis used the same visual configuration for two different purposes.[35] The subject of

35.   Gustav Klucis's first version of the photomontage poster in 1930 reads, "Let us fulfill the plan of the great projects," and it was an encouragement to participate in the five-year plan of 1930. The second version of the poster is identical in its image of an outstretched hand which in itself contains a large number of outstretched hands and an even larger number of photographic portraits, but this time the inscription exhorts the women of the Soviet Union to participate in the election and decision-making process of their local soviets. This poster seems to have also had an influence on John Heartfield, who transformed Klucis's outstretched hand into an outstretched arm with a fist, giving the salute of the Communist International under the slogan, "All fists have been clenched as one," on the cover of the *AIZ*, no. 40 (1934). Here, as well as in Klucis's and Terragni's work, the image of the masses is contained in the synecdochic representation. In Klucis's and Heartfield's photomontages it is, however, the synecdoche of the human body as a sign of active participation, whereas in the Terragni montage it is the synecdoche of the machine that subjugates the mass of individuals. The inscription in Terragni's photomontage mural reads

the poster in both versions is the representation of political participation in the decision-making processes of the new Soviet State. In Klucis's poster participation is encouraged by an outstretched hand within which hundreds of faces are contained: thus the individuation resulting from the participation in political decisions and subordination under the political needs of the collectivity seem to be successfully integrated into one image. In Terragni's photomural the same structure has been deployed; this time, however, the overall form of the outstretched hand of the voting individual is replaced by the outlines of the machine (the propeller, the turbine) which contains the image of the masses of people. And it is clear that the Fascist image means what it unknowingly conveys: that the subordination of the masses under the state apparatus in the service of the continued dominance of the political and economic interests of the industrial ruling class has to be masked behind the image of technological progress and mastery. Abstracted as it is, however, from the interests of those who are being mastered, it appears as an image of anonymity and subjugation rather than one of individual participation in the construction of a new collective.

It is significant that the principles of photomontage are completely abandoned once the technique of the photomural is employed for the propaganda purposes of the German fascists. In the same manner that they had discovered Eisenstein's films as a model to be copied for their purposes (Leni Riefenstahl studied his work thoroughly for the preparation of her own propaganda movies), they had also recognized that the achievements of the Russian artists in the field of exhibition design could be employed to serve their needs to manipulate the urban and rural masses of Germany during the crisis of the post-Weimar period. When the German Werkbund, which had just been turned into a fascist organization, put together a popular photography show in 1933 called *The Camera*, the organizers explicitly compared their exhibition design with that of the Russians (without, of course, mentioning Lissitzky's name):

> If you compare this exhibition with the propaganda rooms of the Russians that received so much attention during the last years, you will instantly become aware of the direct, unproblematic, and truly grandiose nature of the representation of reality in this room. These pictures address the spectator in a much more direct manner than the confusion of typography, photomontage, and drawings. . . . This hall of honor is so calm and grand that one is almost embarrassed to talk any longer about propaganda in this context.[36]

To erase even the last remnant of modernist practice in photomontage, the seams and the margins where the constructed nature of reality could become

---

accordingly, "See how the inflammatory words of Mussolini attract the people of Italy with the violent power of turbines and convert them to Fascism."
36.   Kemp, *Foto-Essays*, p. 14.

Giuseppe Terragni. Photomontage mural for the
Exposition of the Fascist Revolution. *1932.*

*Photomural at the German Werkbund
Exhibition* Die Kamera, *Berlin. 1933.*

apparent — and therefore its potential for change obvious — had now become a standard practice in totalitarian propaganda, and construction was replaced by the awe-inspiring monumentality of the gigantic, single-image panorama. What had once been the visual and formal incorporation of dialectics in the structure of the montage — in its simultaneity of opposing views, its rapidly changing angles, its unmediated transitions from part to whole — and had as such embodied the relationship between individual and collectivity as one that is constantly to be redefined, we now find displaced by the unified spatial perspective (often the bird's-eye-view) that travels over uninterrupted expanses (land, fields, water, masses) and thus naturalizes the perspective of governance and control, of the surveillance of the rulers' omnipresent eye in the metaphor of nature as an image of a pacified social collective without history or conflict.

It remains to be determined at what point, historically as well as structurally, this reversal takes place within the practices of photomontage during the 1930s. Unification of the image and its concomitant monumentalization were — as we saw — already operative in Lissitzky's work for the *Pressa* exhibition. These tendencies were of considerable importance for the success of his enterprise. And according to Stepanova's own text, Rodchenko abandoned photomontage principles as early as 1924, replacing them by single-frame images and/or series of single-frame images with highly informative documentary qualities. At what point these factographic dimensions turned into the sheer adulation of totalitarian power, however, is a question that requires future investigation. That this point occurs within Rodchenko's work, if not also in Lissitzky's, for the journal *USSR in Construction* is a problem that modernist art historians have tried to avoid by styling these artists as purist heroes and martyrs who had to sacrifice their commitment to the spiritual realm of abstract art by their enforced involvement with the state. A revision of this comforting distortion of history is long overdue. It is a distortion that deprives these artists — if nothing else — of their actual political identity (their commitment to the cause of Stalinist politics was enthusiastic and sincere and came unforced, as is evident from the fact that an artist such as Tatlin, who did not work for the state agencies, continued to live his private, if economically miserable existence without harassment), as it deprives us of the understanding of one of the most profound conflicts inherent in modernism itself: that of the historical dialectic between individual autonomy and the representation of a collectivity through visual constructs. Clearly the history of photomontage is one of the terrains in which this dialectic was raised to the highest degree of its contradictory forces. Thus it is not surprising that we find the first signs of a new authoritarian monumental aesthetic defined through the very rejection of the legacy of photomontage in favor of a new unified imagery. In 1928 Stepanova could still trace this terrain's development through an apparently neutral political terminology in characterizing the climax of the productivist factographic position:

Within its short life, photomontage has passed through many phases of development. Its first stage was characterized by the integration of large numbers of photographs into a single composition, which helped bring into relief individual photo images. Contrasts in photographs of various sizes and, to a lesser extent, the graphic surface itself formed the connective medium. One might say that this kind of montage had the character of a planar montage superimposed on white paper ground. The subsequent development of photomontage has confirmed the possibility of using photographs as such . . . the individual snapshots are not fragmented and have all the characteristics of a real document. The artist himself must take up photography. . . . The value of the photograph itself came to assume primary importance; the photograph is no longer raw material for montage or for some kind of illustrated composition but has an independent and complete totality.[37]

But two years later, from within the Soviet Russian reflection upon the purposes and functions of the technique of photomontage itself we witness the rise of that concern for the new monumentality and heroic pathos that was the prime feature of the German fascist attack on the legacy of photomontage quoted above. In 1930, in his text "The Social Meaning of Photomontage," the critic O. L. Kusakov writes,

. . . the solution to the problem of the proletarian, dynamic photomontage is inherently connected to the simultaneous solution of the question for a monumental style, since the monumentality of the tasks of the construction of socialism requires a heroic pathos for the organization of the consciousness of the spectators. Only in a successful synthesis of dynamics and monumentality — in conjunction with the constitution of a dialectical relationship between the levels of life — can photography fulfill the functions of an art that organizes and leads life.[38]

Thus it seems that Babichev's original, utopian quest and prognosis for the future functions of a postmodernist factographic art to become "an informed analysis of the concrete tasks which social life poses," one that will "organize the consciousness and psyche of the masses by organizing objects and ideas," had become true within ten years' time, although in a manner that was perhaps quite different from what he had actually hoped for. Or we could say that the latent

37. Stepanova, "Photomontage" (1928), English translation in *Alexander Rodenchenko*, ed. Elliott, pp. 91ff.
38. O. L. Kusakov, "Die soziale Bedeutung der Fotomontage," *Sovetskoe Foto*, Moscow, 1930, no. 5, p. 130. Quoted from the German translation in *Zwischen Revolutionskunst und Sozialistischem Realismus*, pp. 230ff.

Alexander Rodchenko. Two pages from the magazine USSR in Construction, *no. 12, December 1933. (Special issue on the construction of the Stalin Canal.)*

Overprinted caption in photograph reads: In the course of 20 months almost 20,000 skilled workmen were trained in 40 trades. They were all ex-thieves, bandits, kulaks, wreckers, murderers. For the first time they became conscious of the poetry of labor, the romance of construction work. They worked to the music of their own orchestras.

element of social engineering, inherent in the notion of social progress as a result of technological development which art could mediate, had finally caught up with modernism's orientation toward science and technology as its underlying paradigms for a cognitively and perceptually emancipatory practice.

This historical dialectic seems to have come full circle in Rodchenko's career. In 1931 he worked as artist-in-residence on the site of the construction of the White Sea Canal in order to document the heroic technological achievements of the Stalin government and to produce a volume of photographic records. But apparently in the first year alone of his stay more than 100,000 workers lost their lives due to inhuman working conditions. While it is unimaginable that Rodchenko would not have been aware of the conditions that he photographed for almost two years, his subsequent publications on the subject only project a grandiose vision of nature harnassed by technology and the criminal and hedonistic impulses of the prerevolutionary and counterrevolutionary personality mastered through the process of reeducation in the forced labor camps of the White Sea Canal.[39]

While it is undoubtedly clear that at this time Rodchenko did not have any other choice than to comply with the interest of the State Publishing House if he wanted to maintain his role as an artist who participated actively in the construction of the new Soviet society (and we have no reason to doubt this to be his primary motive), we have to say at least that by 1931 the goals of factography had clearly been abandoned.

However, the contempt meted out from a Western perspective at the fate of modernist photomontage and factographic practice in the Soviet Union during the 1930s or at its transformation into totalitarian propaganda in fascist Italy and Germany seems historically inappropriate. For the technique was adapted to the specifically American needs of ideological deployment at the very same moment. Once again, the tradition of photomontage itself had first to be attacked in order to clear the ground for the new needs of the monumental propaganda machines. Here is Edward Steichen's American variation on the theme of an antimodernist backlash in favor of his version of a "productivist" integration of art and commerce in 1931:

> The modern European photographer has not liberated himself as definitely [as the American commercial photographer]. He still imitated his friend, the painter, with the so-called photomontage. He

---

39.   Gassner makes a first attempt at assessing these facts with regard to Rodchenko's career at large in his doctoral thesis on the artist, *Rodchenko-Fotografien*, especially pp. 104ff, and n. 475. The problem is, however, that he seems to base his information on the working conditions at the White Sea Canal and the number of victims on the "testimony" of Alexander Solzhnytsyn's writings, clearly a source that would have to be quoted with extreme caution in a historical study. The main work on Lissitzky's, Rodchenko's, and Stepanova's collaboration with Stalin's State Publishing House remains to be done.

has merely chosen the *modern* painter as his prototype. We have gone well past the painful period of combining and tricking the banal commercial photograph. . . . It is logical therefore that we find many modern photographers lined up with architects and designers instead of with painters or photographic art salons.[40]

Ten years later Steichen staged his first project at the Museum of Modern Art, the exhibition *Road to Victory.* Once again its propagandistic success depended almost entirely, as Christopher Phillips has shown, on a debased and falsified version of Lissitzky's exhibition designs.[41] In this case it was Herbert Bayer who provided American industry and ideology with what *he* thought Lissitzky's ideas and practice had attempted to achieve. Bayer was well suited to this task, having already prepared an elaborate photomontage brochure for the National Socialists' *Deutschland Ausstellung* of 1936, staged to coincide with the Berlin Olympics. When asked by Christopher Phillips about his contribution to this project for the Nazis, Bayer's only comment was, "This is an interesting booklet insofar as it was done exclusively with photography and photomontage, and was printed in a duotone technique."[42] Thus, at the cross-section of politically emancipatory productivist aesthetics and the transformation of modernist montage aesthetics into an instrument of mass education and enlightenment, we find not only its imminent transformation into totalitarian propaganda, but also its successful adaptation for the needs of the ideological apparatus of the culture industry of Western capitalism.

40.   Edward Steichen, "Commercial Photography," *Annual of American Design*, New York, 1931, p. 159.
41.   Christopher Phillips, "The Judgment Seat of Photography," *October*, no. 22 (Fall 1982), pp. 27ff, provides detailed information on Steichen's history and practice of exhibition design at the Museum of Modern Art in New York. Allan Sekula's essay, "The Traffic in Photographs" (reprinted in *Modernism and Modernity*, Halifax, The Press of the Nova Scotia College of Art and Design, 1983), gives us the best discussion of the *Family of Man* exhibition by Steichen and also touches upon the issues of exhibition design in general.
42.   I am grateful to Christopher Phillips for providing me with this information and for his permission to quote from his private correspondence with Herbert Bayer, as well as for his lending me the brochure itself. *Deutschland Ausstellung 1936* was also published as an insert in the design magazine *Gebrauchsgraphik*, April 1936.

Herbert Bayer. Photomural for Edward
Steichen's exhibition Road to Victory *at the
Museum of Modern Art, New York. 1942.*

Herbert Bayer. Photomontage for brochure
accompanying the exhibition Deutschland
Ausstellung, *Berlin. 1936.*

Eisenstein with Le Corbusier and Andrei Burov,
Moscow, 1928

Notes for a Film
of *Capital*

SERGEI EISENSTEIN

TRANSLATED BY MACIEJ SLIWOWSKI, JAY LEYDA, AND ANNETTE MICHELSON

October 12, 1927.

It's settled: we're going to film CAPITAL, on Marx's scenario—the only logical solution.

N.B. Additions . . . those are clips pasted to the wall of montage.[1]

October 13, 1927.

. . . To extend the line (and to explicate it, step by step) of dialectical development in my work. Let us recall:

1. STRIKE. The order—educational and methodological film on the methods and processes of class and of underground work. Whence—serial film structure and detachment from a specific place (in the project there's a whole series of escapes, prison life, rebellion, body-searches, *etc.*).

2. POTEMKIN. I'm emphasizing, just as the film's direction does, the dialectical result: a pathos of the ordinary and the psychological concrete: tarpaulin: mourning—*par excellence*. "Suddenly" . . .[2] the abstract emotion of the lions:[3] a [leap] from representation of ordinary life to abstract and generalized imagery.

3. OCTOBER Harnessed lions—speeches of Mensheviks, the bicycles, (N.B. the second derived from the car and motorcycle races that were cut into the mowing sequence of our GENERAL) led to a complete departure from the factual and anecdotal—the events of OCTOBER (in that section) are accepted, **not as**

---

1.   The image is that of the news bulletin affixed to walls of factories and other public places.

2.   "Suddenly . . .": the single word of the intertitle immediately preceding the opening shot of that section of Eisenstein's *Potemkin* known as "the Odessa Steps sequence."

3.   The sequence in *October* to which Eisenstein here refers is described by him as follows in the essay "A Dialectic Approach to Film Form," in *Film Form, Essays in Film Theory*, edited and translated by Jay Leyda, New York, Harcourt Brace and World, Inc.: "In the thunder of the Potemkin's guns, a marble lion leaps up, in protest against the blood-shed on the Odessa steps. Composed of three shots of three stationary marble lions at the Aluoka Palace in the Crimea: a sleeping lion, an awakening lion, a rising lion. The effect is achieved by a correct calculation of the length of the second shot. Its superimposition on the first shot produces the first action. This establishes time to impress the second position on the mind. Superimposition of the third position on the second produces the second action: the lion finally rises."

events, but as the conclusion of a series of theses; not the fact that the Mensheviks are 'singing' while the battle is in progress (a purely cinematic method of intercutting), but the historical nearsightedness of Menshevism. Not that a sailor finds himself in the bedroom of A[lexandra] F[yodorovna], but rather the "execution of the petite bourgeoisie and that which it represents," *etc.* Not an anecdote about the Wild Division, but "methodology, of propaganda." "In God's Name" becomes a treatise on deity.

After the drama, poem, ballad in film, OCTOBER presents a new form of cinema: a collection of essays on a series of themes which constitute OCTOBER. Assuming that in any film work, certain salient phrases are given importance, the form of a **discursive** film provides, apart from its unique renewal of strategies, their rationalization which takes these strategies into account. Here's a point of contact already with completely new film perspectives and with the glimmers of possibilities to be realized in CAPITAL, a new work on a libretto by Karl Marx. A film treatise.

Nov. 4, evening.

In America even cemeteries are private. 100% Competition. Bribing of doctors, *etc.* The dying receive prospectuses: "Only with us will you find eternal peace in the shade of trees and the murmur of streams," *etc.* (For C[APITAL].)

Stills from
STRIKE,
1924

Nov. 23, 1927.

We must consider as a basic principle of film-making that which is all-penetrating, down to the smallest detail, a principle no less for the purely technical elements of the general, overall shape.

Such was the case for POTEMKIN in the sequence of double attack "ta-ra" in which whole emotional structures as well as 'untrimmed' montage pieces redoubled themselves in intensity. (This is all explained in detail somewhere.) An example of the first type: the waiting scene on the quarterdeck and the scene when the ship awaits the encounter with the fleet.

The de-anecdotalization principle is (**clearly**) fundamental to OCTOBER. The working theory of 'overtones'[4] can literally be reduced to a single proposition. Didactically, in explaining the principles of OCTOBER, it's useful and essential, as a development of those principles, to explain the groping stage as well; for OCTOBER remains essentially a model of a two-level solution: de-anecdotalization is, in fact, a 'fragment of tomorrow', that is, the premise of the work to follow: C[APITAL].

That is, the very principle of logical reduction *ad limitum* of one fundamental detail.

N.B. Explain this in detail in connection with theme, treatment, *etc.*

Here are Pudovkin's observations on the technique and 'mastery' of OC-

TOBER. Thus: the "non-ordinary, life-like details" (as he puts it), manipulation of detail in montage; *i.e.*: the door opens before Kerensky "eight" times. (In untrimmed shots.)[5]

Together with the 'profit' of this device, he also cites the distributor's trick of 'getting' an audience—the so-called Boitler[6] trick: THE THIEF OF BAGDAD fills the cash register for a month; next month [receipts] decline. He holds the film in an almost empty house for a third month, and the audience then starts to pour in again for six consecutive months.

He describes, in similar terms, his perception (or more exactly—the audience's subconscious perception): a normal perception occurs, and then there's a break in the perception of something outside the logic of the ordinary. This moment is held, and then, at a given moment, a restructuring of ordinary perception takes place—and this is particularly powerful in its effect. *Voyez!* From a technical cut, through social interpretation, to the distribution trick, everything's part of the same. *Fabelhaft!*

For C[APITAL], a puppet theater must be shot, but only (God help us!) in

4.   The use of the notion of the overtone develops at a particular stage in the extension and radicalization of Eisenstein's theory and practice of montage, that of work on *The General Line* (retitled *The old and the New*), described in Eisenstein's essay, "The Filmic Fourth Dimension" as "the first film edited on the principle of the visual overtone. The montage of *Old and New* is constructed with this particular method. This montage is built, not on particular dominants, but takes as its guide the total stimulation through all stimuli. That is the original montage complex within the shot, arising from the colision and combination of the individual stimuli inherent in it.

"These stimuli are heterogeneous as regards their 'external natures,' but their reflex-physiological essence binds them together in an iron unity. Physiological in so far as they are 'psychic' in perception, this is merely the physiological process of a *higher nervous activity.*

"In this way, behind the general indication of the shot, the physiological summary of its vibrations as a *whole*, as a complex unity of the manifestations of all its stimuli, is present. This is the peculiar 'feeling' of the shot, produced by the shot as a whole. . . . As in that music which builds its works on a two-fold use of overtones." (The musical references cited elsewhere in this same text are to Debussy and Scriabin.)

5.   Pudovkin is citing a fragment of a major sequence in Eisentein's *October*, known as "The Ascent of Kerensky" in which the shape and dynamics of the Menshevik leader's career are epitomized. This sequence, brilliant in its use of temporal and spatial distension, constitutes a visual trope of extreme irony, sharply comic in effect. Eisenstein will refer to it from time to time in these journal entries. Here is his description of it, drawn from "A Dialectic Approach to Film Form," as an example of intellectual cinema: ". . . Kerensky's rise to power and dictatorship after July uprising of 1917. A comic effect was gained by sub-titles indicating regular ascending ranks ("Dictator"—"Generalissimo"—"Minister of Navy—and of Army"—*etc.*) climbing higher and higher, cut into five or six shots of Kerensky, climbing the stairs of the Winter Palace, all with exactly the same pace. Here a conflict between the flummery of the ascending ranks and the 'hero's' trotting up the same unchanging flight of stairs yields an intellectual result: Kerensky's essential nonentity is shown satirically. We have the counterpoint of a literally expressed conventional idea with the pictured action of a particular person who is unequal to his swiftly increasing duties. The incongruence of these two factors results in the spectator's purely intellectual decision at the expense of this particular person. Intellectual dynamisation."

6.   Mikhail Boitler was a former comic film actor, strongly influenced by Chaplin. Forced into retirement by the importation of Chaplin's films into the Soviet Union, he became director of a theatre specializing in the presentation of American films.

the manner which first comes to mind (as in a Daumier lithograph: Louis Philippe and the parliament—*Le capitaliste et ses jouets*). Exclusively through parallelism or a **device that fits the circumstances.**

Jan. 2, 1928.

For CAPITAL. Stock exchange to be rendered not as 'a Stock Exchange' (MABUSE, ST. PETERSBURG), but as thousands of 'tiny details'. Like a genre painting. For this, see Zola (*L'argent*). *Curé*—the main 'broker' for the whole area. The concierge—the negotiator of loans. The pressure of concierges like these in the problem of the Sov[iet] Union's acknowledgement of debts.

The very same audience held together by a patriotic theme. The idea of Revenge is Krupp's idea through the newspaper, *Le Figaro*, financed by him. In general, France *ausschlaggebend* for petit-bourgeois, philistine material. (On Krupp—following the lecture on French press by Charles Rappoport reported in *Vecherka*.[7]

March 8.

Yesterday thought a lot about CAPITAL. About the structure of the work which will derive from the methodology of film-word, film-image, film-phrase, as now discovered (after the sequence of "the gods").

The working draft.

Take a trivial progressive chain of development of some action . . . For instance: one day in a man's life. *Minutieusement* set forth as an outline which makes us aware of departure from it. For that purpose only. Only as the critique of the development of associative order of social conventions, generalizations and theses of CAPITAL.

Generalizations, from given cases to ideas (this will be completely primitive, especially if we move in a line from bread shortages to the grain shortage [and] the mechanics of speculation. And here, from a button to the theme of overproduction, but more clearly and neatly.)

In Joyce's ULYSSES there is a remarkable chapter of this kind, written in the manner of a scholastic catechism. Questions are asked and answers given.

The subject of the questions is how to light a Bunsen burner.

The answers, however, are metaphysical. (Read this chapter. It might be methodologically useful.) Thanks to Ivy Valterovna Litvinova.

March 9, 1928.

Yesterday's writing for CAPITAL very good. Still must find an adequate triviality for the 'spinal' theme.

Dreams about emperor. *Le Figaro* describes an interesting episode clearly illustrating the way in which the French bourgeoisie yearns for a king. The

7.   *VECHERNAYA MOSKVA,* an evening newspaper.

newspaper draws a striking picture of the "evening ball of the First Empire" organized a few weeks ago at Baron Pichon's splendid residence on the *Quai d'Anjou*. Guns of Austerlitz roared, attracting mobs of passers-by. Torches burned. Antique coaches, conveying famous historic personalities, rolled up the driveway. At nine in the evening Napoleon arrived with his entourage. He was met in the court by the imperial guard. The Austrian envoy presented himself. Napoleon and his spouse ascended the stairs. The ball, which was also attended by Prince Joachim Murat, the Count and Countess de Massa, Albufer and other historic figures, began. The newspaper mentions bitterly that the splendor of that evening was all a show, and that the Emperor and his suite were only Pichon's friends and acquaintances in make-up. (*Vecherka*, March 8, 1928.)

March 17, 1928.

On the level of 'historical materialism', current equivalents of historical turning points with a contemporary orientation must be sought. In CAPITAL, for example, the themes of textile machines and machine-wreckers should collide: electric streetcar in Shanghai and thousands of coolies thereby deprived of bread, lying down on the tracks—to die.

On deity: Agha Khan—irreplaceable material—cynicism of shamanism carried to the extreme. God—a graduate of Oxford University. Playing rugby and ping-pong and accepting the prayers of the faithful. And in the background, adding machines click away in 'divine' bookkeeping, entering sacrifices and donations. The best exposure of the theme of clergy and cult.

An economic invasion and construction of new cities. *Hansa-Bund*. To be interestingly demonstrated, perhaps, through the *makhnovshchina* episode.[8] Guliai-Pole, a lost hole, setting up jewelry stores within a week, hiding the filth of its streets with carpets and becoming, if not a little Paris, then at least a miniature Vienna. Influx of emigrants and predatory elements (from the book on Makhno). Cortezian and Pisarresque soldiery[9] is also linked. (Or for conveying the idea from another point of view.)

March 24, 1928.

A great episode, from Paris. A war victim. Legless man on a cart commits suicide—he throws himself into the water. Told by Max,[10] as recounted by some newspaper.

8.   The reference is to the counter-revolutionary episodes in the Ukraine under the leadership of Makhno.
9.   This would indicate an already existing interest in Eisentein's part in the history of the Mexican Conquest. This was to flower two years later in the major, uncompleted film project known as *Che Viva Mexico*, undertaken after Eisenstein's sojourn in Hollywood and preceding his return, in 1931, to the Soviet Union.
10.   Maxim Straukh, the actor, a childhood friend and frequent co-worker. Their collaboration began at the time of Eisenstein's early theatrical productions for the Proletkult Theater.

The bridge sequence from OCTOBER

The most important thing 'in life' now is to draw **conclusions** from formal aspects of OCTOBER.

It is very interesting that "gods" and "Kerensky's ascent" are structurally one and the same: the latter—identity of fragments and semantic *crescendo* of the intertitles; and the first—identity (implied) of the intertitles "God," "God," "God," and semantic *diminuendo* from the material. Series of meanings. These are surely some kind of first indications of the method's devices. It is interesting that these things can have no existence outside the meaning, the theme (unlike, for instance, the lifting 'bridge' which can function *überhaupt*). An abstract formal experiment is **inconceivable** here. As in montage in general.

Experiment external to the thesis is impossible. (Take this into consideration.)

March 31, 1928. 1 a.m.

School and church are obligatory in CAPITAL. *Voyez Barbusse: Faits divers, l'Instituteur.* On the whole, an amazing book. I am ready to take back all [my] wicked remarks on Barbusse. Read for three hours on end, and at night, too. A lot of things indispensable for CAPITAL.

The form of *faits divers* or collections of short film-essays is fully appropriate for replacement of 'whole' works . . . Something that's in STRIKE has the vats episode as a wedging of pure American comedy into a great, dark work. I remember how I reasoned that after four dark sections [the audience] would be tired and one would have to offer a comic *détention des nerfs* [sic] to intensify perception of the final sections.

April 2–3, 1928, night.

Somewhere in the West. A factory where it is possible to pinch parts and tools. No search of workers made. Instead, the exit gate is a **magnetic** check point. No comment needed. (Max read this somewhere. Will go into CAPITAL.)

April 4, 1928.

"... The ironic part outweighs the pathetic one. The German romantics already knew the advantage of irony over pathos. For purposes of intensification, **pathos had to be made fantastic and hyperbolic**. The living historical material did not allow that, however. The picture therefore revealed a split." (Leningrad newspaper *Kino*, discussion on OCTOBER, article by M. Bleiman.)

In connection with CAPITAL, 'stimuli', that is, suggestive materials, should be introduced. So, for instance, that excerpt from Bleiman suggests elements for pathos in CAPITAL (Say, for the last 'chapter'—dialectical method in practical class struggle).

In those 'great days' I noted on a scrap of paper that in the new cinema, the established place of eternal themes (academic themes of LOVE AND DUTY, FATHERS AND SONS, TRIUMPH OF VIRTUES, *etc.*) will be taken by a series of pictures on the subjects of 'basic methods'. The content of CAPITAL (its aim) is now formulated: **to teach the worker to think dialectically**.

To show the **method** of dialectics. This would mean (roughly) five-nonfigurative chapters. (Or six, seven, *etc.*) Dialectical analysis of historical events. Dialectics in scientific problems. Dialectics of class struggle (the last chapter).

"An analysis of a centimeter of silk stocking." (About the silk stocking **as such**, Grisha[11] copied out from somewhere—the silk manufacturers' fight for the short skirt. I added the competitors—the textile masters' for long skirts. Morality. Clergy, *etc.*)

Still very complicated to think 'somehow' in 'extra-thematic' imagery. But no problem ... *ça viendra*!

---

11.   G.V. Alexandrov, friend and collaborator of Eisenstein, listed as co-scenarist for *October, The General Line* and *Que Viva Mexico*. Their collaboration ceased after their return to the Soviet Union from the United States. and Alexandrov turned to the direction of film, specializing in comedy.

It's very interesting—about size. Perfectly new inter-relation between quantity and diversity of material in relation to the footage. "Overloading of the footage." (In answer to Grisha's apprehension—"What? China and America, too?" *etc., etc.*) The same in B. Gusman's text:

"The nature of cinematic language is such that effective presentation of a **brief** and consequently **insignificant** event requires, more than in any other art form, a great number of visual devices. **What in literature can be indicated by a few words, is conveyed on screen by a whole series of scenes and sometimes, even, of episodes, occupying a large section of the picture.** That's why BATTLESHIP "POTEMKIN" makes a much greater impression than OCTOBER . . . Indeed, what lingers in one's memory after seeing OCTOBER? One should probably acknowledge the depiction of the raising of the bridge as one of the most brilliant passages. Why? Because film language is completely revealed. And, to be exact, because the space Eisenstein allots to the showing of the bridges is disproportionately large (and Eisenstein could not have done otherwise, the very essence of cinema demanded it), he lacks footage to 'cinematize' the entirety of the October Revolution's series of extremely significant and vital aspects."

That statement about 'kilo'-footage of forceful representation of the trivial event is absolutely right. One might call them factual **units**. This is fully applicable to the **methods** of 'yesterday's' cinema.

From the point of view of **language**!! We are, after all, primarily after **economy of means** (by no means beyond our means). Where, if not in **directness**, shall we find it?)

Footage goes into effective presentation of **event unit**. Just as it will be used for disclosure ('giving shape') of the unit of **thought**. Which in terms of 'plot' corresponds to an event as unit in old cinema.

If POTEMKIN . . . was allowed one half or one whole event to each part (*i.e.*, mourning—meeting, flag; '*paskha*' [12]—the steps; pause—tarpaulin—mutiny,

12. A traditional Easter delicacy in the form of a cake.

etc.), then, for this project, **one idea** (and this means 'impressing', not 'chewing over' the event *entre parenthèses*—'mourning', 'pause', 'battle readiness', 'panic', *etc.*) to each part as there is one feeling to one whole or one half part, is just fine. The difference lies in the attractions[13] directed towards stimulating one concept, condensed (in this case) in terms of class, and the attractions directed towards arousing one's class-oriented emotion, (as in the previous case).

The difference (confusing in a comparison) is that of the **area** in which the attractions (that is, the montage elements) must produce the given **single effect**.

Sensuous attractions are assembled on the principle of a single emotion ("a sad old man," + "a sail being lowered," + "a forward tendency," + "fingers play-ing with a hat," + "tears in the eyes," *etc.*) There is a distinct 'similarity'.

The 'similarity' of intellectual attractions which go into a single piece of montage is not of a sensual kind. That is to say, it's definitely not one of appearance, either. Those fragments 'resemble' each other in terms of conditioned reflexes, *i.e.*, in terms of their meanings: baroque Christ and wooden idol do not resemble each other at all, but they do have the same **meaning**. A *balalaika* and a Menshevik 'resemble' each other not physically but abstractly.

China, pyramids, New York, all that frightened Grisha, are not really **themes**, but montage fragments for forming **thoughts**. They correspond to close-ups and medium shots of a single event.

13.   The genesis of Eisenstein's theory and style of montage is presented in "Through Theater to Cinema." "I think that first and foremost we must give the credit to the basic principles of the circus and the music-hall—for which I had had a passionate love since childhood Under the influence of the French comedians, and of Chaplin (of whom we had only heard), and the first news of the fox-trot and jazz, this early love thrived.

"The music-hall clement was obviously needed at the time for the emergence of a 'montage form of thought.' Harlequin's parti-coloured costume grew and spread, first over the structure of the program, and finally into the method of the whole production." Another popular source, cited by Eisenstein and his companions of the early years, was the form of the amusement park 'attraction', whose intensity of physical stimulus he assimilated into his aesthetic of dynamic conflict, drawing theoretical support from Pavlovian reflexology.

(N.B. *Abgesehen* from rules of 'spelling', that is of the montage ABC: a single fragment of meaning = *minimum* of two in montage. One fragment is **not**, **after all**, **visible**; the first is used for surprise, the second for perception.)

We say, one shot, "China," corresponds to the 'central' shot[14] of the horse on the bridge. Naturally, this will be five shots (or more). But one must remember that these are (taken) not to **explain China** but to explain one's main idea, Egypt, by use of this one shot in conjunction with the others, like those of New York: Egypt.

That shot is as unequivocal in this place as the shot of the sad old man is emotionally unequivocal.

This new outlook on things and events revealed itself with utmost clarity during a 'local' discussion:

Grisha: We will be in New York, in China, in Egypt (will expand in all directions). Mountains of material, *etc.*

I objected that we will not, after all, be seeking a **sensuous re-creation** of China or whatever, as we came to do in the case of the **battleship**, **factory**, **midday**, *etc.*

A sensuous re-creation calls for 'footage' (here Gusman is correct, but barbarically ascribes to it the concept of 'language').

N.B. I recall how I talked about OCTOBER at *Glavrepertkom*,[15] saying that Sovkino had not given 8,000 meters for additional shooting of the village and countryside. They expressed doubt: if it did not 'fit' into 500,000, how could it be done for [the other] 8? I said, the footage is not used for **meaning**. The footage is used for an emotional priming.

The only principle derived from past experience and now applicable as the general rule:

"That picture is cinematic whose story can be told in two words."

14.   The sequence to which the cited shot is central constitutes the supreme example of spatio-temporal distension and synthesis developed in *October*. It is analyzed and discussed at length in my "Camera Lucida/Camera Obscura," *Artforum*, XII (January, 1973).
15.   The governmental agency responsible for resolution of practical problems in film production.

 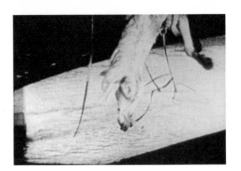

If the picture 'articulates' one or two thoughts, cinematizes 'a method', then this corresponds to the whole part placed 'under' the dominant of grief; that is, to brilliant film-conditioning. So, having China, India and the devil knows what else is not really so terrible.

Furthermore, one realizes that without even chasing around after the flavor of Egypt, the whole of CAPITAL could be 'constructed' on a set. *Schuftan*.[16] Glass. Model. It could be shot at the **Third Factory** [of Goskino]!!!![17]

N.B. This is obviously exaggeration to the point of paradox. *Walkenkratzer aus Vogelschau* and, on the whole, a terrific attraction of the **frame in itself** (sensuous attraction) that is, of the frame apart from its burden of meaning (intellectual attraction), is absolutely mandatory in this case. Why then, emotionalize we will; we must, *quand même*, mustn't we?

Non-fictional, then; not educational but absorbing and propagandistic.

To "Kerensky"—a maximal reaction: applause, laughter.

The Gods: perhaps the most sophisticated [structure] and the material which produces an effect with the most impressive image. Their formal selection (that is *abgesehen* from the 'philosophical' burden of meaning) and the formal parallelism constitute the academically brilliant, sensuously attractive montage.

Revenons à nos moutons. Film language is not **terrifying as far as footage is concerned**. On the contrary, it is the maximally succinct expressive mode; within fifteen meters the idea of Deity disqualifies itself;[18] it requires, at least, much less effort to make it physiologically persuasive.

16.   The Schuftan Effect, invented in 1925 by Eugene Schuftan, cameraman, is an illusionistic process designed to perfect, through the use of reduced models drawn on glass, the integration of *décor* into film. It thereby reduced the necessity of shooting on location.

17.   A small and ill-equipped film studio in Moscow.

18.   This celebrated sequence of *October* was conceived and is frequently cited by Eisenstein as the structural model for "intellectual montage." An account of it is given in "A Dialectic Approach to Film Form:" "Kornilov's march on Petrograd was under the banner of 'In the Name of God and Country.' Here we attempted to reveal the religious significance of this episode in a rationalistic way. A number of religious images, from a magnificent Baroque Christ to an Eskimo idol, were cut together.

April 6, 1928.

The first, preliminary **structural** draft of CAPITAL would mean taking a banal development of a perfectly unrelated event. Say, "A day in a man's life," or something perhaps even more banal.[19] And the elements of this chain serve as points of departure for the forming of associations through which alone the play of concepts becomes possible. The idea of this banal intrigue was arrived at in a truly constructive manner.

Association presupposes a stimulus. Give a series of these, without which there is 'nothing' to associate. The maximum abstractness of an expanding idea appears particularly bold when presented as an offshoot from extreme concreteness—the banality of life. Something suggested in ULYSSES provides additional support for the same formulation:

"... *Nicht genug! Ein anderen Kapitel ist im Stil der Bücher für junge Mädchen geschrieben, ein anderes besteht, nach dem Vorbild der scholastischen Traktate, nur aus Frage und Antwort: Die Fragen beziehen sich auf die Art, wie Mann einen Teekessel zum Kochen bringt, und die Antworten schwifen ins grosse Kosmische und Philosophische ab ...*" (Ivan Goll, *Literarische Welt*, Berlin: taken from a prospectus on ULYSSES [Rhein Verlag]).[20]

Joyce may be helpful for my purpose: from a bowl of soup to the British vessels sunk by England.

The conflict in this case was between the concept and the symbolisation of God. While idea and image appear to accord completely in the first statue shown, the two elements move further from each other with each successive image. Maintaining the denotation of 'God', the images increasingly disagree with our concept of God, inevitably leading to individual conclusions about the true nature of all deities. In this case, too, a chain of images attempted to achieve a purely intellectual resolution, resulting from a conflict between a preconception and a gradual discrediting of it in purposeful steps."

19.   This theme was, at the time of Eisenstein's writing, entering the tradition of film. Its supreme and most complex exemplification, Vertov's *The Man With the Movie Camera* was, in fact, in the stage of completion.

20.   "... Not enough! Another chapter is written in the style of books for young girls, another in the form of scholarly tracts, composed only of questions and answers; the questions are of the sort, how to bring a teakettle to the boiling point, and the answers digress into great cosmic and philosophical ..."

As a further intention: the setting of CAPITAL develops as visual instruction in the dialectical method.

Stylistically, this closed plot line, whose every moment serves as a point of departure towards materials that are both ideologically defined and physically dissociated, provides maximum contrast as well.

The final chapter should certainly produce a **dialectical decoding** of the very same story **irrespective** of the real theme. *Der grössten Speisung!* By means of which the 'beautiful' stylistic organicity of the work as a whole is accomplished.

Of course, this is quite conceivable even without a series of this kind (not through plot at all, but simply connected). Paradoxically, however, a deliberate 'small step back' from the final form always emphasizes brilliance of construction. Thus, it was good that THE WISE MAN was not simply a *revue*, but revised **Ostrovsky!**

The sequential arranging of the 'distancing elements' could eventually proceed quite differently as well. The final chapter is on the class struggle; the little story should therefore be constructed to gain maximum advantage from its dialectical disclosure.

The elements of the *historiette* itself are thus chiefly those which, in the form of puns, provide the impulse towards abstraction and generalization (mechanical spring-boards for patterns of dialectical attitudes towards events). The *historiette* as a whole: the material for a dialectical disclosure through an overwhelmingly passionate final section. This, too, [should be built up] in as gray and banal a manner as possible.

I.e., just as the 'house-wifely virtues' of a German worker's wife constitute the greatest evil, the strongest obstacle to a revolutionary uprising, given the German context. A German worker's wife will always have something warm for her husband, will never let him go **completely** hungry. And there is the root of her negative role which slows the pace of social development. In the plot, this could take the form of **'hot slop'**, and the meaning of this on 'a world scale'. One great danger: not to succumb to *niaiserie* through excessive 'oversimplification': "it's in the bag" . . .

April 7,

Today, with a banal relapse into the circular composition of Scheherezade, Tūt-nāmeh,[21] tales of Hauff. I explained to Grisha the mechanics of the CAPITAL project in outline while in the 'A' streetcar between Strasnaia and Petrovsky Gate (or perhaps after Nikitsky—I don't remember . . .). While riding home from Shub's[22] where we'd had chocolate with *paskha* and cake . . .

Voici:

Throughout the entire picture the wife cooks soup for her returning husband. N.B. Could be two themes intercut for association: the soup-cooking wife and the home-returning husband. Completely idiotic (all right in the first stages of a working hypothesis): in the third part (for instance), association moves from the pepper with which she seasons food. Pepper. Cayenne. Devil's Island. Dreyfus. French chauvinism. *Figaro* in Krupp's hands. War. Ships sunk in the port. (Obviously, not in such quantity!!) N.B. Good in its non-banality—transition: **pepper—Dreyfus—***Figaro*. It would be good to cover the sunken English ships (according to Kushner, 103 DAYS ABROAD) with the lid of a saucepan. It could even be not pepper—but kerosene for a stove and transition into *oil.*[23]

Chapter 4 (5, *etc.*; but the **next to the last**—comic, farcical):

Woman's stocking full of holes and a silk one in a newspaper advertisement. It starts with a jerky movement, to multiply into 50 pairs of legs—Revue. Silk. Art. The fight for the centimeter of silk stocking. The aesthetes are for it. The Bishops and morality are against. *Mais ces pantins* dance on strings pulled by the silk manufacturers and the garment peddlers who fight each other. Art. Holy art. Morality. Holy morality.

In the final section, soup is ready. A thin soup. The husband arrives. 'Socially' embittered. The hot, watery liquid—compromisingly washes away the pathos. Prospects of bloody skirmishes. And most horrifying of all—social indifference [equal] to social betrayal. Blood, the world in the flames of cataclysm. The Salvation Army. The Church Militant, *etc.* The man embraces his wife's skeleton. A neatly darned quilt is pulled over. A 'Surprise' (for sincere lyricism)—she gives him a cheap cigarette. Sentimentality that is much more awful in the context of that final horror. The quilt pulled over. Under the bed—a pot. With the handle broken off. But a pot, all the same . . .

For the time being, after Tūt-nāmeh, this may be revolting. Here and there, though—not bad. Diversify the parts with the **material** as sharply as is appropriate

21.   Translated as *Tales of the Parrot,* these are Persian texts in the Moghul style, School of Akbar (1556-1605).
22.   Esther Shub, the distinguished documentary film-maker, virtually the inventor of the compilation film. A long-time friend of Eisenstein she had, in fact, given his his very first employment in the re-editing of Lang's *Mabuse der Spieler,* for distribution in the Soviet Union. His apprenticeship under this accomplished editor was extremely important for the development of his own work.
23.   Eisenstein here suggests the depiction of a process of production in reverse, adding to his store of tropes the *hysteron proteron,* so frequently and successfully employed by Vertov.

and bring them to conclusion. Of a class nature.

Problem of volume of material which can fit in. To be solved by an incredible **succinctness** and by treating each part entirely **in its own way**. Perhaps one part even 'acted' with two characters—*ganz fein*. Another one, all from newsreels. *Etc.*

The character of the material presented calls for economy. The 'ancient' cinema was shooting **one event from many points of view**. The new one assembles **one point** of view from many events.

N.B. What will it be like in practice?—*qui vivra verra*!

After all, "the Gods" were condensed into something like 15 meters!

N.B. Everything has been written in **monstrous** doubt. It is still very reactionary! And it may be stylistically suitable only for an individual case. Cases far more 'to the left' (like the "Gods") are needed.

April 7, 1:30 a.m.

There must be one chapter on the materialist interpretation of the 'soul'. The chapter on reflexes. The whole of it could be built around that woman and the

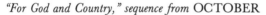

"For God and Country," sequence from OCTOBER

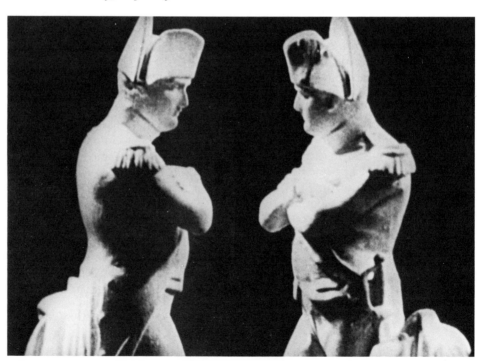

series of reflexes. Motor ones. Erotic. Purely mechanical. A complex series of conditioned reflexes. With a demonstration of the mechanisms of associative thinking, *etc.*

To expose the mechanisms of the states of a soul with, say, emotions evoked by a funeral procession. The loss of the male. The loss of the bread-winner. The heirs, *etc.* And all this cynicism is assembled in reverse to form a touching mourners' procession.

Provoke a head-on collision between **a stimulus and the final link** of a complex chain of conditioned reflexes. There no longer seems to be any interconnection. Terribly crude, physical stimulus (particularly bad—the erotic one!)— and, as the final link, some act of an extremely elevated (resp[ectively] sacrificial) spirituality.

N.B. It would be really funny to cast Khokhlova [24] as that woman. She might

24.   Alexandra Khokhlova was a leading film actress of the Soviet cinema. Her exceptional talent, intelligence and versatility illuminate, in particular, the films of her husband, Lev Kuleshov, the director and theorist of montage, the consideration of whose work is, in turn, important for a thorough understanding of Eisenstein's own development.

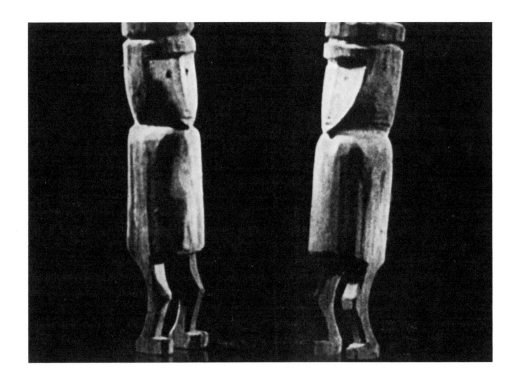

be very amusing as someone ugly becoming a beauty.

And then, in a gathering of momentum, reproduce the mechanics of irritation. Then guide the audience through a series of film stimuli to a definite emotional effect, and then give the intertitle:

Well then, now you have reached the state . . . , *etc.*, *etc.* To each chapter—its own principles of film adaptation. (1:45 a.m.)

April 7 evening.

In PROJECTOR No. 14 (132), Grosz's autobiography:

"I already had a disturbing feeling at that time that I should try to express and render in painting something similar to that which Zola was expressing in his work. . . .

"I want to start a whole cycle of pictures of this sort, which, as a delightful phrase of artists' slang has it, **one would like to try with one's tongue** . . ."

And here, from the same source, for CAPITAL:

". . . it was a delightful time, when everything was saturated in the symbolism of war, when every jar of artificial honey was decorated with an 'iron cross,

second class'; when 'God Punish England!' was pasted on the back of every letter ... **When old leather suitcases were made into soldiers' boots and army 'mousse' was so corrosive that it made holes in the tablecloth. Only the human stomach could withstand all that! . . ."**

N.B. It would be good to show kids guzzling the 'mousse' and its droplets eating away the tablecloth.

Here, too, (according to Ermler's stories about Berlin)—the coasters for beer mugs which read, "Germany cannot survive without colonies. Rice, pepper, *etc.*— we get everything from the colonies. England took the colonies away from us, *etc.*"

April 8.

CAPITAL will be dedicated—officially—to The Second International! They're sure to be 'overjoyed'! For it is hard to conceive of any more devastating attack against social democracy in all its aspects than CAPITAL.

The formal side is dedicated to Joyce.

The outline of events in historical order. For instance, in the farcical section, a dissolve from contemporary bishopric to Boccacciesque and La Fontainesque-Rabelaisian clergy. By no means 'sequentially' but *durcheinander*. The mannequins and costuming of the church are, after all, still sluggishly medieval, like all their teaching.

The continuity of a series should by no means be 'sequential' as in a plot—unfolding in a logically progressive manner, *etc*. An **associative unfolding**. Then the footage not frightening. Sometimes *les débris d'action* deliberately plot-like and continuous. Only not "the silk manufacturer plying a bishop with drink." Fie!!

Along the Dreyfus line. The trial shown as Daumier's *ventre législatif*. All the cardinal sins in judicial *typage*.[25] Or, even better, a single one, ten-fold, all-

25.   The concept complementary to that of montage in Eisenstein's theory and practice. Typage refers to the parameter of acting, and, by extension, to the pro-filmic aspect of cinema. "I want to point out that 'typage' must be understood as broader than merely a face without make-up, or a substitution

embracing. Then, it all **turns out** to be hanging by strings. The hand of the General Staff or something of that sort *fait sauter les pantins*. (In *Chambre constitutionnelle* and *Louis Philippe* by Daumier!)

In a scheme of this sort, parallelisms—parallel currents—have been **transformed** into a progressively associative series. **Very important**.

It would be good to move from the marionettes to a puppet theater for children (many **fine** kinds) with chauvinistic puppets—training in chauvinism from the cradle—and then to the *Gott-strafe-England* herd-like movement.

There are endlessly possible themes for filming in CAPITAL ('price', 'income', 'rent')—for us, the theme is **Marx's method**.

CAPITAL, in these rough drafts, **does not exhaust all new possibilities**. Must

of 'naturally expressive' types for actors. In my opinion, 'typage' included a specific approach to the events embraced by the content of the film. Here again was the method of east interference with the natural course and the combination of events. In concept, from beginning to end, *October* is pure 'typage'.

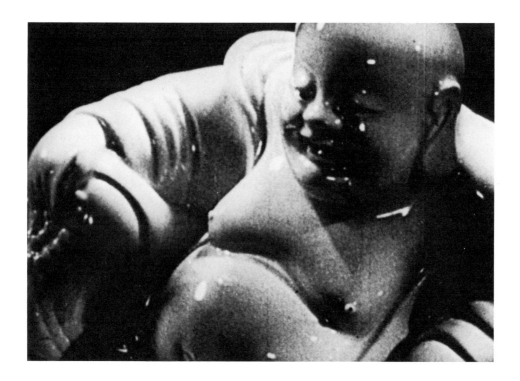

remember that very firmly. Perhaps, though, it should be explicated **at this stage**. Grisha says that our draft is still **generally accessible** in its 'virginal' state. We are therefore beginning to convert it into something accessible only *pour les raffinés*. It might therefore be reasonable not to invert everything to the very end. This should be done later, instead.

. . . A proper structure for the OCTOBER stage—in part, a newsreel along with two or three 'emotional' concentrations within the limits of that footage ('the bridge' and 'ascent'). Also think **about the emotional concentrations** within the sections of CAPITAL. But try, nevertheless, to make them *à la* ascent of Kerensky—using those principles and not ancient ones of the bridge.

Absolutely special will be the problem of the image and frame composition for CAPITAL. The ideology of the unequivocal frame must be thoroughly reconsidered. How, I can't yet tell. Experimental work is needed. For that, it's 'madly' necessary first to make THE GLASS HOUSE,[26] in which the (usual) idea of the **frame** is what happens to the **structure of things** in the fragments of OCTOBER and in CAPTIAL's entire structure.

There is still another variant instead of **soup**—in case CAPITAL is restricted (in its basic 'intrigue') to the 'world scale' and the Second International to the 'pedagogic' framework of USSR boundaries. Show the way in which our slovenliness (absenteeism, hooliganism, *etc.*) is a social betrayal of the working class as a whole. True, this is very harsh and less monumental. It's therefore more important, socially, to strike the traitorous front in its entirety.

April 11.

On repetition.
In terms of dialectical analysis, that is, analysis in contradictions, a procedure of this sort is very good. We had it to some extent in "The offensive of June 18" (*nach meinem Kompositionsvorschlag*):

June 18—the victorious regiments; June 18—the horror of exploding shells; June 18—Plekhanov's patriotic demonstration at Kazan Cathedral; June 18—relentless armored cars pursue the X regiment in an attack; June 18—innumerable protest demonstrations leave the factories; June 18—the shock battalions prance, *etc., etc., etc.*; June 18—a body hanging, suspended on [telegraph?] wire.

This is obviously a model of dialectical demonstration. Not realized. Very sorry.

Notez once again the unity of the intertitles!!! Just as in "The Gods" and (in

26.   *The Glass House* was a project of Eisenstein's, conceived in 1926 and developed parallel to the filming of *October* and the planning of *Capital*. The action of this satire on bourgeois society was to have taken place in a building whose walls, ceilings and floors were made of glass. In this text, one experimental possibility of the project is considered: the inclusion within one frame of several actions.

reverse) in Kerensky.

On this level, one could solve:

Ein Paar seidene Strumpfe—art.

Ein Paar seidene Strumpfe—morality.

Ein Paar seidene Strumpfe—commerce and competition.

Ein Paar seidene Strumpfe—Indian women forced to incubate the silk cocoon by carrying them in **their armpits!**

April 20, 1928.

What happens to the 'immaculate maidens' *du moment* I start to speak about CAPITAL and intellectual attraction! The secretary of the Artistic Council of Sovkino *d'un côte* (komsomol) and an old Polish underground activist *de l'autre*. They both dissuade. Both—absolutely capable of ecstasy. They support emotionalism in my work. They speak about 'warmth which must be preserved in my work. To create . . . *Très drôle.* Those 'pure in heart'—do they speak truth?

I think that intellectual attraction by no means excludes 'emotionality'. After all, a reflex action is perceived as the so-called presence of an affect. The question of paths of influence and perspective of *des zur Offenbarung Möglichen*—possibilities in the area of the expressible—thanks to those specifically new paths. **Preservation** of the evolutionary effect is **mandatory** and not at all excluded in practice: *i.e.,* Kerensky *steigt* has its own *Lachsalven*!

April 22.

Ogonek No. 17, April 22, 1928 brought out for C[APITAL] and in general:

A mailbox for foundlings. In Athens on a street near an orphanage, a box has been placed in which mothers can leave their babies. The baby immediately finds himself on a little mattress. Every two hours the box is checked and the contents are taken to the orphanage. This perfected abandonment of babies has, in addition to its originality, certain drawbacks. Just imagine, for instance, that three babies are abandoned within two hours. The first one is not going to feel too good. [Drawing of the box.]

Absolutely brilliant material, 'compressible' to the point of 'bloody irony'. Bourgeois culture and philanthropy.

"In the domain of culture, the professional and technological achievements of bourgeois art are great. Particularly important for the proletariat are the achievements of recent decades, in which methods of planned and constructive approach to artistic creation, lost to artists as representatives of the petite bourgeoisie, have been restored and raised to the level of scientific analysis and synthesis. The process then instituting the penetration of the creative process by dialectical and materialist principles, as yet unrealized by artists, constitutes the raw stuff of a future proletarian art."

This was a major contribution to an analysis of the arts.

The tragedy of today's 'leftists' consists in the fact that the still incomplete analytic process finds itself in a situation in which synthesis is demanded . . .

On new themes. It was actually important to show **tactics** in OCTOBER, and not the events. The most important tasks in a cultural revolution are not only **dialectical demonstrations but instruction in the dialectical method,** as well.

Given the available data on cinema, such tasks are not yet permissible. Cinema does not possess those means of expression, since there has been, until now, no demand for tasks of that sort; only now do they begin to be defined.

Pasolini: Murder of a Dissident*

MARIA-ANTONIETTA MACCIOCCHI

translated by THOMAS REPENSEK

Pasolini was killed November 1, 1975. Several days later I spoke out in *Le Monde:* "Crime is political. Pasolini was assassinated by society in a savage act of self-defense, a society which could not bear his defiance (of sexual, political, and artistic prohibitions), his undisguised equation of commitment and life. The hatred unleashed against him was expressed in the staging of the crime: a public execution, at high noon, so that everyone might see and learn." These remarks provoked anger from the church, from moralists, and from defenders of the established order, as well as the condemnation of the Italian Communist Party, of course. He couldn't have ended any other way, they claimed. He "sought," "willed" his death, almost ordered it, or, in the language of analysis, "acted in complicity with death." For two years everyone was content with this "explanation."

It wasn't until 1977 that Moravia, in the preface to his book, *Cronaca giudizia, persecuzione, morte,*[1] could write, "Pelosi and the others [the murderers] were the arm that killed Pasolini, but those who authorized the act are legion, in fact, all of Italian society."

This is why I must explore, in its obscurity, complexity, and subtlety, the dark political dimension of the crime, the collusion of those institutions which seek to establish an omnipresent social order and which, one year before the murder, took the form of a coalition between the Italian Communist Party (ICP) and the Christian Democrats (CD) known as the historic compromise. The sinister belief that Pasolini not only could but should be killed grew secretly in the same atmosphere that assigned the ICP the responsibility of maintaining moral order, of disinfecting a "horribly filthy country" (as Pasolini called it). Pasolini was Communist and homosexual. The Italian bourgeoisie hates Communists, yet respects them as the guardians of private morality, of "national" and "civic" virtues, which have been sacrificed to the profit of industry. Pasolini was hated,

---

*   This essay was originally delivered at a conference, "Dissidence and Authority," in Paris, February 1978, and was published in *Tel Quel,* no. 76.
1.   *Pasolini: cronaca giudizia, persecuzione, morte,* Milan, Garzanti, 1977.

therefore, not because he identified himself as a Communist, but because he attacked sexual prohibitions as a Communist, assuming the identity of artistic and political commitment, of art and life. The servile hypocrisy, the fascism of a conformist intelligentsia was outraged: in Italy, thinking has again become heresy. Hatred was not unleashed against Pasolini as a carrier of an assumed sexual aberration, but against "the dissident of dissidents" who ignored sexual and political taboos, publicly identified himself as a Communist, a homosexual, a mystic, as well as a poet and writer, filmmaker, literary critic, and novelist: the all-around artist. This was an intolerable breach of faith. The provocateur had become dangerous, and Italian society, under the banner of Communist morality, demanded revenge upon Pasolini for transgressing the limits of the established moral order—not middle class mores but official Communist ones: a crime more infamous than offense against the moral code of a bourgeoisie implicated in the fascism of Salò. The increasingly political and moral totalitarianism of the "historic compromise" effaces the endless dialectic between power and opposition. The death of the opposition sexualizes intensely the life of an entire society, from the dark bowels of fascism to the violence whose language is expressed—in the reality of the repression of the sexual nature of social relations—by the deadly call to aphasia. Is the social link paranoiac? At the time, Sollers wrote, "Affirming the perversity of social exchange, that is, *the intrinsically homosexual nature of social union*, he [Pasolini] became the Italian most threatened, because the least homosexual. The paradox even has its logic. Pasolini was killed so that the repressed homosexual center of society would remain so, sealed by the blood of someone able to *speak* of it. A ruthless sentence of aphasia."[2]

The history of recent art begins with a rape. In October 1949, with Zhdanov, the cultural czar, Pasolini's death sentence was foreshadowed at the age of twenty-seven by the Tribunal of the State and the Party. The first knot of the historic compromise was petit-bourgeois conformism to the moral order; its first spectacle, the condemnation of Pier Paolo Pasolini by both institutions, the first representing for him the enemy of class, the other the Red Spring. (He became a party member in 1947 and served as secretary of the Casarsa section in Friuli). He posted his *dazibaos* on the walls of his village, his own accounts of political events handwritten in slang or dialect—to disrupt the conventions of Italian lyric language—or diatribes against local Christian Democrats, or the parables in *Dialogue between Poor Communist and Unscrupulous Christian Democrat*. His fellow party members were suspicious of his hatred of the CD, of its ethical underpinnings, which they saw as an obstacle to political harmony. They suspected as well his appeal in his writings to the unconscious, to the irrational, to Freud, the interpretation of dreams, to psychoanalysis—modernist references that could only isolate him further. We are talking about the Zhdanov

2.   Philippe Sollers, paper delivered at the "Congress on Sexuality and Politics," Milan, November 1975, and published in *Tel Quel*, no. 65.

era, when Fadeiev, an apostle of socialist realism and prophet of cultural decadence, called Sartre a "hyena with a typewriter." A cold war was launched against "decadent intellectuals" at the Congress of Wroclaw, where the Soviet delegation stated that "Monopolistic enterprise needs wild men to realize their goal of global domination: writers, philosophers, reactionary artists are ready to work for their pay. Schizophrenics, morphine addicts, sadists, and pimps are placed on pedestals along with agitators, spies, and gangsters. The pages of novels, poetry, paintings, films are populated by these bestial characters. They are the 'heroes' to imitate and follow."[3]

Togliatti, in turn, wanted a party purged of "artistic decadence," and after the Communists' defeat by the CD on April 18, 1948, wanted his "new party" to be able to provide a moral guarantee to the Roman Church: "the proletarian ethic." At the same time he wanted to support the Russian church's condemnation of "degenerate intellectuals." What has never been analyzed—at least from a psychoanalytic perspective—is the myth of virility incarnated by the Communist party ever since the International, Marx, Lenin, and Stalin. Party, Patriarch, Power: Pasolini's initials, which he habitually used (P.P.P.). A party of males, for males. A party that therefore marginalizes all deviation, all singularity; which outlaws difference: women, homosexuals, the subproletariat.

The Male party, the self-constituted grey State of order. And Pasolini's battle against sexual taboos and moral violence is registered *everywhere* as a battle against the tyranny of the State. "The greyness of the State . . . a state of pure hypocrisy," founded on ". . . property secured/the horrible, animal greyness/that triumphs over light and shadow." In the name of this Moral/State, Togliatti wrote of Gide in *Rinascita* in 1949, "[He] would have done better to write about pederasty, his professional field." Pasolini's expulsion from the party for "moral turpitude" can be explained thanks to a letter he sent to a comrade by the name of Carlino and published posthumously, twenty-eight years later. It reveals his intense and unwonted despair. A simple story involving threatened blackmail by a priest: either renounce communism or his teaching career would be over. From pure "odium theologicum," according to Pasolini, the CD sent the Casarsa police to spy on him until a scandal developed and he was accused of "sexual aggression" upon his students. (In 1952 he was acquitted of this accusation by the courts,

3.   This may sound like familiar Stalinism from the fifties, but it is not as quaint as it appears. I encountered this language again today in an account of a meeting that took place in Moscow on December 21, 1977 in the great hall of the Central Writers' Bureau. It was interesting in part for its anti-Semitic speeches authorized by old Michael Suslov, inveterate ideological high priest, who in the fifties insisted on "snatching Mayakovsky from the clutches of the Jews." The triumphant return of the repressed spirit of Wroclaw was verified in the "neo-Stalinist" speech of the "principal speaker of the evening," as he was described in *Le Monde*: "The principal speaker of the evening was Piotr Palievski, assistant director of the Gorky Institute of World Literature and editor of *Foreign Literature*. Palievski, who in 1975 in his book *The Art of Realism* still inveighed against artists like Picasso, Stravinsky, and Khlebnikov, calling them no better than swindlers and frauds, condemned once again the art of the avant-garde."

but never by the party.) The school relieved him of his job, and soon after the party relieved him of his card. "I'm out of work," he wrote to Carlino. "In other words, reduced to begging. Simply because I am a Communist. The treachery of the Christian Democrats doesn't surprise me; your inhumanity does. It's stupid to talk about ideological deviation. In spite of you I am and will remain a Communist. Someone else in my position might have killed himself, but I unfortunately have to live for my mother." A shamed, embarrassed homosexual, P.P.P. had solicited from the party a defense of his *normality*. His membership card was the symbol of his innocence/virility. Like a poet or child he appealed to the "religion of his time" to deliver him from anxiety. But the party, which claims for itself the right of masculine sexuality, publicly withdrew its certification of virility from P.P.P., the twenty-seven-year-old poet. It declared him homosexual, hence unworthy of the ICP. It identified him as the Other. An ab-normal, il-legal, in-organic intellectual, he was cast into the hell of sexuality. *Innocence is impossible* for the Moloch Party/State. Pasolini, officially accused of sin, was forced publicly to take responsibility for his abnormal sexuality, to carry it to frenzy, provocation, rage. The rage of a grand accuser, the indicter of the scientific rationalism of Marxism, of its "religious senility." And *rage* is the last word of "Wisteria,"[4] the epigraph he uses to initial the course of his heretical experience:

> I've lost my strength;
> I've lost the sense of *rational*;
> cast off, silting up
> —in your religious senility—
> my life, sorry that the world
> is only fierce, and my soul rage.

He no longer referred to his isolation after '49. A penniless exile, he went to Rome with his mother, and, in a bleak suburb on the bleak Tiber, found, "as in a novel," a teaching position in a private school. Violent, working-class Rome, first locus of his inspiration as a writer and director, accepted him. "Poor, magnificent city/you taught me what cruel and playful men teach children."[5] He quickly became known, but we, his Communist friends, knew nothing about what he had endured, about the wounds that would never heal, his relentless love/hate of the Male party, his enthusiasm for the promise of political revolution and distaste for obscurantist tactics, expressed in his poem "Le ceneri di Gramsci,"[6] written in 1954. "The shame of self-contradiction, to be/with you and against you in visceral darkness."

But during that period everyone, including the Communists, who alone knew the facts, began to praise the poetic imagination of Pier Paolo.

Yet it was as a poet that Pasolini was excluded. The October 28, 1949

4.   "Il glicine," in *La Religione del mio tempo*, previously unpublished.
5.   "The Ditchdigger's Tears," *Poems 1953–1954.*
6.   "The Ashes of Gramsci," *ibid.*

headline of *L'Unità* announced: "The poet Pasolini has been expelled from the party." The term *poet*, used to mean irresponsible, extravagant, facile, corrupt, suggests the relationship between culture and the Communist movement better than a hundred abstract metaphors. "Consider the origin of the facts leading to this serious measure against the poet Pasolini," the article continued. "To condemn once again the negative influence of the philosophical thinking of Gide, Sartre, and other writers who wish to be considered progressive but who in fact assimilate the most sinister aspects of a degenerate bourgeoisie." The power of Zhdanovism, which is perhaps contained in Marxism and its negation of the irrational. In opposition to Marxism, Pasolini continually insisted on the "right of the irrational": "The chain has in effect been broken: the chain of free systems, since *Rimbaud*, since *Pound*, even the delicious dialectal poets. . . . Yet something of that Dionysiac intellectual drunkenness remains: it tends to be identified with *the pure irrational, the inalienable substance of poetic form*, so that in all poetry, however distilled, there remains a certain quantity of unattributable, indefinable expressiveness. *Marx* did not consider the irrational. I say *Marx* to mean Marxism" (*Ulisse*, September 1960).

Pasolini was the first heretic of the Marxist religion. He wrote not only against power, but also against those who, opposing power, represent the power of the future, "the powers that kill" in their schizoid manifestations: "archaic power . . . which dissolves the self's other, strips it of its essential freedom, freedom of the body." Freedom to think. The spirit of a Gramsci dominates his political life, "the more cut off from the world, the freer he was, . . . reduced to pure, heroic thought" (*Officina*, June 1957). Pasolini can be placed then within the opposition's opposition, continually displaced in a permanently critical state, inviting dissidence, appealing to heresy. He was committed, but as a criminal; his last collection of political articles is called *Pirate Writings*. He feared that every revolution, like 1968, would bring about the restoration of the Left. "We watch, terrified / in admiration and hatred of / whoever dares say something to oppose / the oppositional Establishment."

As years went by, the Left recognized him but continued to treat him with primitive tolerance. In 1960, I invited him to write a column of "dialogues" with readers for *Vie Nuove*—the weekly paper of the CC of the ICP, which I edited. His book *Le Ragazzi* had just been condemned for obscenity. The most distinguished Communist literary critic, Salinari, agreed once again with the official verdict, writing that the novel took "unhealthy interest in abasement, filth, decay, ambiguity." "What was immoral," Pasolini later wrote, "was of course the portrayal of the subproletariat whose existence was at the time universally denied."

His column at *Vie Nuove*,[7] which could have been titled "And you Com-

---

7.   These columns were collected in a volume published under the title *The Beautiful Banner* by the party's publisher. Editori Riuniti, in 1977. The exchange of letters between Pasolini and myself at the beginning was censored.

munists, comrades/non-comrades," created a scandal, but the party wanted to show that it "welcomed well-known intellectuals." I tried to protect him from surveillance by the Party Supervisory Committee and from my editors, who amused themselves by calling him a queer, an anarchist, a madman, and so forth, as soon as he turned his back. Pasolini had chosen to attack Marxist orthodoxy and morality from within the columns of the party paper. I agreed with him, as a woman and thus, within the Communist party, also marginal, excluded or always susceptible to exclusion, different, other.

His first answer to a *Vie Nuove* reader addressed the unexplained question of his exclusion from the party in '49. He criticized the prudery, "the old-maid prohibitionist anxiety . . . of the Italian Communist press," that is to say, of Marxism. "The sexual problem is obviously not a moral one; but since the Catholic middle class is hypocritically used to considering it one, so do middle-level Communist authorities, how should I say it, out of laziness. . . . We need an 'irrationalist' Marxist offensive, yet Marxists equate the irrational with literary, artistic decadence. Irrationality (within which the sexual problem is inscribed) is a category of the human soul, and it is therefore always a current, pressing problem."

The trial against Pasolini continued: in photographs we see him, time and again, seated before judges seated beneath a crucifix, always the defendant, accused for his books, his films, his life. Even after his death, when Sartre wrote to the judges: "We hope the court will not be influenced by the prejudices of Italian male society, and that the murder trial does not become Pasolini's trial." Psychiatrists and psychoanalysts were called to deliver their diagnostic opinions during his trials and after his death: he was mad because he was homosexual, homosexual because he was mad. Even madder for calling himself an artist-Communist-mystic-inquisitor. The verdict gradually became the judgment of an entire society in search of moral order, and of political organizations of intellectuals who hated Pasolini's freedom. The case against him grew stronger every day, strengthening the justification of repression; little wonder that one day someone felt authorized to kill him.

After one of Pasolini's first appearances in court, on the charge of attracting boys on the beach at Anzio to "wrestle with him, and paying them for it" (July 9, 1960; he was later acquitted), Togliatti forced me to cancel Pasolini's column, since "responsible comrades" considered it intolerable that a homosexual write for a newspaper read by working-class families. Togliatti's "party-of-the-masses" ethic reflected the deeply rooted and dominant ideas of a country that, within a few centuries, had given birth to two counter-revolutions: the Counter-Reformation and fascism. The contemporary press describes Togliatti's fury: "Moreover, [he] didn't consider Pasolini a great writer; on the contrary, his judgment in the matter was rather harsh." In the party memo to cultural section heads, Togliatti reaffirmed that Pasolini was not to be considered one of the party's "fellow travelers," and that his eventual ruin could not be construed as a loss. The dispute between Togliatti and myself over Pasolini began with a letter to me expressing his objection to Pasolini's analysis of D'Annunzianism in *Vie Nuove* as a rhetorical cancer of the Italian language, and insisting that I publish a critical reply from a reader/professor in Fiume. I published it. Pasolini replied. What was really at issue was Pasolini's quiet dismissal, the end of his column. I refused. Several months later I was no longer the editor of *Vie Nuove.*

My former editors at *Vie Nuove* and the head of the Cultural Commission at the time now deny that disciplinary action was taken, arguing that Pasolini continued to write his column after I left, until 1965, which is typical procedure. The dissident is eliminated from within while the appearance of tolerance is preserved. And afterwards, well, you die. The Communists are always looking for a corpse; they build a mausoleum over it and put a mummy inside, which they treat like a benevolent god. The concept of the mausoleum in Marxism should be studied. Every religion has its simoniacs. Now posters of Pasolini's tragic head are sold at the Festival of *Unità*, and films of "our comrade Pasolini" are shown at party meetings. The card taken from him in 1949 was returned with proper solemnity, with seniority, during the funeral rites over his swollen corpse. . . . Superb elegies transformed indomitable enemies on all sides into psalm-singing priests. In 1961, aware of what was going on and refusing to resign out of so-called solidarity, Pasolini used *Vie Nouve* to launch his most violent political attack against the Marxologists; he even included the scripts of films like the satirical and epic saga, *Uccellacci e uccellini.* There is an ironic dimension to political discourse, which was a valuable lesson to me. With saturation comes satire. The wise crow, instructing two derelicts, speaks with the voice of the master Marxist, the voice of Togliatti. Bored with hearing him rattle on, they wring his neck and eat him. "Masters are made to be eaten with relish," Pasolini wrote sweetly in *Vie Nuove.* First murder of the Great Thinkers. And through the character of Toto, Pasolini explains that he also wants "to talk about free love in the early years of communism, about the renunciation of that theoretical position, about Marxist morality, Stalinism, and the crisis of Marxism in the 1960s."

Eighteen years ago Pasolini was the first dissident to welcome the "crisis of Marxism," who wanted it to continue in spite of its own institutionalization, who expected from it a "courageous vision of disorder." He believed there was a genuine crisis of "Marxist cultural politics":

Realism is dead and Italian and non-Italian Marxism has invented nothing to replace it.

To see Marx quoted, as we face the continuing evolution of the world, is annoying . . . while the base is left unexplored for fear of allowing the critical function to consume too much.

In socialist countries, the Marxist vision is authoritarian: the revolution is over. . . . The contradiction between Marxism in the embrace of authority, between culture and power, is reduced to a painfully vacant exchange of words (1962).

Again, in 1963, "The ICP has earned its distinguished reputation; nevertheless, I sense the presence of ghosts: conformity, Stalinism, party patriotism, absence of criticism, self-criticism that is merely verbal."

In the "grey half-light of tolerance," as Foucault has called the sixties, Pasolini denounced Italy as a middle-class country, a Fascist state called consumer society, a shark, a pig: "A barracks, a seminary, a nude beach, a brothel populated by millions of circumspect bourgeois who discover they are pigs." This first detonation against the establishment was repeated almost verbatim by the revolutionary Italian "Automata" on Radio Alice, as Foucault, writing about Pasolini, recognized: "It was also around 1963 in Europe and the United States that people began once again to question the multiple forms of power, which judicious minds call fashionable. . . . So it is: a fashion that may last a while, as it was then in Bologna" (*Le Monde*, March 23, 1977).

The Fascists stalked Pasolini as long as he lived, waited for him around every corner, ready for a fight. Ten years after our "pirating" of the column in *Vie Nuove*—I had become a deputy in Naples in 1970—I invited him to Castellamare, a working-class town outside of Naples, for a screening of *Medea*.

He took this opportunity to speak of the "sexual nature of the social bond." As Pleynet writes,

> The nature of this bond, which Pasolini clarified for a vast public that only half understood him, preyed on the imagination of the twentieth-century mind. Obsession and fear occupy the ground abandoned by religion, and where religion relinquishes its control, women take their stand. When religion relents, repression escapes from reality, and the law is unable to ignore it because it represents at least half of humanity: women.[8]

The Fascists descended on the little town that night, calling for Pasolini's death. He was sheltered from the mob in a working-class hostel. The next day I was severely reprimanded by the Naples federation of the ICP, and the conservative *Il Mattino* castigated me in similar terms. An old story. In *Salò*, Pasolini concludes that the violence of power is pervasive, and that society, grounded in that power, accepts its laws only in a fundamentally perverse, immoral exchange. In this sense his aesthetic (heretical) experience corresponds to that of all the great dissidents of the last two centuries.

The last time I saw Pasolini was in Paris, at Vincennes, in November 1975, at a screening of Naldini's film *Fascista*. In the audience was a group of kids who threatened to beat him up. They objected to his poem "May 68" (where he had said that although "daddy's boys" were allowed to "play" at revolution, this wasn't the case for a farmer's son turned policeman). But what he really feared was that every rebellion would be followed by the reestablishment of the Left, that

---

8.   Marcelin Pleynet, "Le tombeau de Pasolini," *Art et Littérature*, Paris, Seuil, 1977.

the act of recovery would be the last act of revolt, a theme he developed in three poems the year following '68.

> The classic Left began its revival
> . . .
> Children discovered their first wrinkle and life
> claimed from them its first victory.[9]

> The party still broods us like a mother hen
> . . .
> So, the tail a little between the legs
> after running free, boys come home to the CLN
> to fight the repression, they say, of a wicked power:
> every alliance conceals deferment, and so a weakness . . .[10]

> In 1961, 1962 in New York
> appeared the first challengers of Power
> and its Past,
> called "beats," a fanciful, dated name;
> the invisible Masters saw with satisfaction
> that THEIR Past was beginning to be destroyed by animal sounds
> . . .
> The Communist parties and the unions waited,
> then their turn came,
> the vacuum was filled and now bosses and workers
> are positioned a little further distant face to face.[11]

His heretical rage against inevitable restoration continues today in our exhilaration in the slogan "'68 good, '77 better." He spoke to students with that soft anger and naked courage that for him was worth more than aggression. No one knew that he had dedicated a poem to Rudi Dutschke: "It's clear/I am a father after you." That he had made a film to raise money for *Lotta Continua.* Nor that he had assumed the editorship of that daily when Pannella was sent to jail. That he had signed the radicals' referendum on abortion, although irritated by feminist extremists who failed to understand that men are also controlled by it. He told students what he thought about their terrorist violence, extinguished intelligence—bored with consumption and perhaps tired of their own violent rhetoric. There was no violence in him. He once explained: "I have never in my

9. "The Restoration of the Left," 1969.
10. "More on the Left Establishment," 1969.
11. "The Restoration of the Left and Who," 1969.

life performed a violent act, physical or moral; not because I am fanatically nonviolent, which, if it is a form of ideological self-restraint, is of course violence . . . but simply because I have let my nature or more likely my culture take over." But he saw violence rising around him, and in his last political articles, the word *lynching* often appears. When Maurizio Ferrara, the editor of *L'Unità*, accused him of "irresponsible remarks," Pasolini agreed that his ideas had been "caricatural and reductive. It's more appropriate to call it a lynching. . . . You lynch someone when you take one of his ideas, alter it to suit you, and make it an obvious target of public contempt and ridicule." *La Stampa* was accused in almost the same words: "Without thinking, he objected to *lynching* and didn't realize what he had done" (1974, in *Pirate Writings*).

Pasolini found himself at the intersection of three great protests against State power: political, sexual, and mystic, that is, the protest of the unconscious itself, which is perhaps "heresy without a goal, for its own sake." "But who ever loved heresy/in a disinterested way? heresy without end: for the sake of itself?/No, no, everyone looks for ORTHODOX TRUTH/it's this that first creates unrest,/then revolt against power . . . The struggle has always been between the old orthodoxy and the new/That's what takes my spirit away, and makes me want to refuse to play" ("Reworking of 'orthodoxy,'" April 15, 1970).

What could he do politically? He voted Communist, but he felt alienated, a dis-organic intellectual, dis-organic in function in order to have organic reality. His "Testament," so called because it was written several hours before he was murdered, is a political agenda which was to be presented at the Radical Party Congress in Florence, November 2, 1975. It ends with these words: "Quickly forget successes and continue about your business in a stubborn, contradictory, demanding, willful way, undistinguished, setting snares, speaking evil. . . ."

I don't know how to conclude. I know that this poet of the apocalypse, who slipped through consumer society, received from that same society a funeral like a Roman circus. Italian intellectuals—the noisy puppets who hated him—the ruling class, the Left, and the ICP outdid themselves in the oratorical stylishness of the form known as "funeral elegy." But who is alive and who is dead? What is death? Pasolini wrote in his last book of poems:

> I am like a cat that's been burned alive
> Run over by a truck
> Hung from a tree by the kids in the street
> But with still at least six
> Of its seven lives . . . Death isn't
> Not being able to communicate
> But no longer being understood.
> I see with the eye of an image
> lynching officials
> watching my own extermination
> with a still scientific heart.

In the appeal in the sentence passed upon Pelosi, the fundamental
question remains. Was he alone? Or was he used as bait, an accomplice
in a planned, ruthless attack? The Juvenile Court, sentencing him to
nine years in jail, concluded that Pelosi had committed the crime "with
the help of other unidentified persons" . . . The conviction was influenced by medical/legal testimony to the effect that the young man
showed no evidence of injury, although he said he had been attacked
and had struggled with the victim for a long time. His hands were
clean, as were his clothes, which should have been stained with blood.

—*Repubblica*, November 2, 1977

The Fine Art of Gentrification

ROSALYN DEUTSCHE and CARA GENDEL RYAN

> *One day I walked with one of these middle-class gentlemen into Manchester. I spoke to him about the disgraceful unhealthy slums and drew his attention to the disgusting conditions of that part of town in which the factory workers lived. I declared that I had never seen so badly built a town in my life. He listened patiently and at the corner of the street at which we parted company he remarked: "And yet there is a good deal of money made here. Good morning, Sir."*
>
> — Friedrich Engels, *The Condition of the Working Class in England*

New York's Lower East Side is valuable property for today's art and real-estate markets, and speculators have every reason to feel optimistic. A working-class neighborhood for 160 years, the area has become in the 1980s the scene of a new art "phenomenon": over forty commercial galleries displaying their wares to a clientele of corporate art consultants and wealthy international collectors. In the fall of 1981 Fun Gallery and 51X opened. "When we started," explained Bill Stelling of Fun, "we didn't want to be considered a little podunk gallery in the East Village. We wanted people to see that we were as serious as any gallery on 57th Street."[1] By the spring of 1982 Nature Morte, Civilian Warfare, and Gracie Mansion were also ready for serious business. During the 1983 art season the number of galleries escalated to twenty-five. Scattered throughout an area of twelve square blocks, these galleries coalesced into

---

1.   All quoted statements, unless otherwise specified, are taken from interviews conducted by the authors in October and November 1984.

"Manhattan's third art district, after Uptown and Soho."[2] Most observers attribute the flurry of activity to a mystical vitality electrifying the Lower East Side and thus refuse to account for the interests operating to create the scene: "*Unaccountably*, at different times certain places — Paris's Left Bank, New York's Tenth Street — have an aura of art that attracts painters and sculptors."[3] Far from the natural development that words such as *phenomenon* and *aura* suggest, however, Art District Three has been constructed with the aid of the entire apparatus of the art establishment. This role was uncritically applauded in a brochure accompanying one of the first exhibitions devoted exclusively to art from the Lower East Side galleries: "[The galleries] have been enthusiastically embraced by the full complement of the art world — public and private institutions, journalists, collectors and artists. . . . This development affirms the perpetual renewal of the artists' community."[4]

When articles on East Village art as a new collective entity began to appear in the major art publications in September 1982, there were only the original five galleries. Four months later these "pioneer" enterprises were lauded in the *Village Voice* as the "heroes" of the art world for their dealings on the "Neo-Frontier."[5] In 1983, as an outpouring of articles on the new scene appeared in the *Voice*, *Arts*, *Artnews*, the *New York Times*, *Flash Art*, and *Artforum*, galleries began to proliferate. By May 1984 the *Wall Street Journal* announced that the art scene had moved to the East Village, and that summer *Art in America* published a lengthy round-up in a special section entitled "Report from the East Village."

An aura of fascination suffuses all of these accounts. The adulatory tone was engendered by a group of writers who continue to build their careers on regular updates of East Village art developments. These "East Village critics" — who are, in fact, not critics but apologists — celebrate the scene with an inflated and aggressive rhetoric of "liberation," "renewal," "ecstasy." Nicolas Moufarrege, one of the most prolific and rhapsodic of these propagandists, sums up the local zeitgeist as a savage and invigorating explosion of repressed energies. "It's the law of the jungle and the fittest survive . . . ultimately quality prevails," is his glib explanation for the scene's success.[6] Bill Stelling attributes the "turning point" in Fun Gallery's own success story to an *Artforum* article by Rene Ricard revealingly entitled "The Pledge of Allegiance." Using a militaristic language

2.   Grace Glueck, "A Gallery Scene That Pioneers in New Territories," *New York Times*, June 26, 1983, p. 27.
3.   Irving Sandler, "Tenth Street Then and Now," in *The East Village Scene*, Philadelphia, Institute of Contemporary Art, University of Pennsylvania, 1984, p. 10 (emphasis added).
4.   Helene Winer, *New Galleries of the Lower East Side* (exhibition brochure), New York, Artists Space, n.d. [January 1984], n.p.
5.   Kim Levin, "The Neo-Frontier," in Richard Goldstein and Robert Massa, eds., "Heroes and Villains in the Arts," *Village Voice*, January 4, 1983.
6.   Nicolas A. Moufarrege, "The Year After," *Flash Art*, no. 118 (Summer 1984), p. 51.

imbued with a dangerous romanticism, Ricard spells out his notion of the ideal artist — an East Village artist: "I want my soldiers, I mean artists, to be young and strong, with tireless energy performing impossible feats of cunning and bravura. . . ."[7] Like Ronald Reagan's campaign optimism, these writers' enthusiasm knows no bounds, and, also like that optimism, ignores hard social realities and complex political questions: questions, in the first case, about what is being done to other people's countries and, in the second case, to other people's neighborhoods.

For unlike other recent art developments, this time New York's two-billion-dollar art business has invaded one of the city's poorest neighborhoods. As an integral element of "a major phenomenon of the early-80s art scene,"[8] essential to its packaging, the Lower East Side has been described in the art press as a "unique blend of poverty, punk rock, drugs, arson, Hell's Angels, winos, prostitutes and dilapidated housing that adds up to an adventurous avant-garde setting of considerable cachet."[9] The area is hyperbolically compared with Montmartre — ". . . we may be witnessing a kind of American Bateau Lavoir, eighties-style. It is perhaps too soon to predict which of the artists is our Picasso or Stravinsky."[10] A recent novel about the racy adventures of a young East Village painter is entitled *It was gonna be like Paris*.

The representation of the Lower East Side as an "adventurous avant-garde setting," however, conceals a brutal reality. For the site of this brave new art scene is also a strategic urban arena where the city, financed by big capital, wages its war of position against an impoverished and increasingly isolated local population. The city's strategy is twofold. The immediate aim is to dislodge a largely redundant working-class community by wresting control of neighborhood property and housing and turning it over to real-estate developers. The second step is to encourage the full-scale development of appropriate conditions to house and maintain late capitalism's labor force, a professional white middle class groomed to serve the center of America's "postindustrial" society.[11] "We are so close to the Twin Towers and the financial district. They

---

7.   Rene Ricard, "The Pledge of Allegiance," *Artforum*, vol. XXI, no. 3 (November 1982), p. 49.
8.   Winer, n.p.
9.   Walter Robinson and Carlo McCormick, "Slouching Toward Avenue D," *Art in America*, vol. 72, no. 6 (Summer 1984), p. 135.
10.   Janet Kardon, "The East Village Scene," in *The East Village Scene*, p. 8.
11.   The Panglossian notion of a "postindustrial society" has entered political discourse at all levels. Used by its main theoretician Daniel Bell and other neoconservatives to describe a social order evolved from an economy that produces services rather than goods, the concept "postindustrial society" holds the promise of a "communal society wherein public mechanism rather than the market becomes the allocator of goods, and public choice, rather than individual demand becomes the arbiter of services" (Daniel Bell, as cited in Michael Harrington, *The Twilight of Capitalism*, New York, Simon & Schuster, 1976, p. 221). As Ernest Mandel points out, however, "far from representing a 'postindustrial society', late capitalism . . . constitutes generalized universal industrialization for the first time in history. Mechanization, standardization, over-

are both within walking distance from here," explains Father Joaquin Beaumont, the vicar for the Lower East Side, "and there are so many people who work there. I'm sure they would love to live closer instead of commuting to the suburbs every day. I think the plan is for the middle class and upper class to return to Manhattan. That's the gentrification process. It's so unjust. Those with a lot of money are playing with the lives and futures of people who have so little hope."

*

It is of critical importance to understand the gentrification process — and the art world's crucial role within it — if we are to avoid aligning ourselves with the forces behind this destruction. Definitions of gentrification — most generally issuing from the gentrifying classes — describe moments in the process, not the process itself. For the "urbanologist" gentrification is the "transfer of places from one class to another, with or without concomitant physical changes taking place."[12] For the mass media it is a "renaissance in New York City."[13] For one member of an urban minority, however, "gentrification is the process of white people 'reclaiming' the inner cities by moving into Black and Latin American communities. . . ."[14] But none of these definitions adequately sets out the reasons for this "transfer" of property, for this "renaissance." Nor do they explain the resettling of a white population in neighborhoods where until recently they would never have dared to venture. For gentrification cannot be defined unless we first isolate the economic forces that are destroying, neighborhood by neighborhood, city by city, the traditional laboring classes.

Between March 1977 and March 1984, over 215,000 jobs were added to New York City's economy. Most of these were created either in the business service sector or in the financial industries. During the same period over 100,000 blue-collar jobs disappeared from the city's industrial base. This shift from blue-collar to white-collar industries makes the economy of the city, according to the *New York Times*, "even more incompatible with its labor force."[15] Such an incompatibility between the work force and the economy is by no means specific to New York City; it is, rather, a national trend that began in the 1950s. In 1929, fifty-nine percent of the labor force was blue-collar; in 1957

specialization and parcellization of labour, which in the past determined only the realm of commodity production in actual industry, now penetrate into all sectors of social life" (Ernest Mandel, *Late Capitalism*, trans. Joris De Bres, London, Verso, 1978, p. 387).

12. Peter D. Salins, "The Limits of Gentrification," *New York Affairs*, vol. 5 (Fall 1979), p. 3.
13. Blake Fleetwood, "The New Elite and an Urban Renaissance," *New York Times Magazine*, January 14, 1979, p. 16.
14. "'Gentrification' or Genocide?" *Breakthrough*, vol. 5, no. 1 (Spring 1981), p. 32.
15. William R. Greer, "Business-Services Industries Pace Growth in Jobs in New York City," *New York Times*, December 3, 1984, p. 4.

the percentage slipped to forty-seven. By 1980 less than one-third of the total work force in the United States consisted of blue-collar workers.[16]

These percentages do not, however, reveal the profound nature of the "incompatibility." For the period between the end of the Second World War and the late '50s witnessed the "third industrial revolution," the increasing automatization of labor power. While between 1945 and 1961 the number of blue-collar workers increased by fourteen million, only two and a half million new jobs were created in the industrial sector. As the rate of unemployment increased, the rate of surplus value and profit also increased, in part because of the reduction of wages implicit in the ever-growing number of unemployed workers. The result of the relentless substitution of machines for men was, according to Ernest Mandel, "the very rapid reappearance of the industrial reserve army which had disappeared in the course of the Second World War." As long as the presence of this reserve army allowed the rate of surplus value to grow, there were no obstacles to unlimited capitalist expansion. Thus the years between 1951 and 1965 comprised, in the United States, a "genuine halcyon period for late capitalism."[17]

The economic and social policies of the Reagan administration reflect the nostalgia of the present capitalist classes for those "halcyon" days. It is, then, not surprising that these policies have had a disastrous effect on every stratum of the laboring classes, from the skilled "middle-class" blue-collar worker to the poor unskilled worker at the margins of the labor force. During the past four years this immiseration of the working classes has taken two forms. On the one hand, high interest rates, ballooning deficits, and an intractable dollar have swelled the ranks of the industrial reserve army with unemployment figures that have duplicated post-Depression records. During the first six months of 1984 the economy surged ahead with a growth rate of 8.6 percent, leaving in its wake eight million skilled and semi-skilled laborers out of work.[18] On the other hand, the second prong of Reagan's domestic policies, directed against those who will never serve the interests of "postindustrial" society, as either workers or consumers, carries the full vengeance of two hundred years of capitalism. These people, dwelling in the lower strata of what Marx identified as capital's surplus population, are victims "chiefly" of their own "incapacity for adaptation, an incapacity which results from the division of labor."[19] Thus, by tightening eligibility requirements for welfare programs, the Reagan administration has pushed some five and a half million working poor into official poverty. Then, by slashing funds from human resources programs, the government has

16.   Michael Harrington, *The Other America: Poverty in the United States*, Middlesex, Penguin Books, 1981, p. 32.
17.   Mandel, pp. 177, 178.
18.   Jonathan Fuerbringer, "Jobless Rate Held Steady in October," *New York Times*, November 3, 1984, p. 46.
19.   Karl Marx, *Capital*, trans. Ben Fowkes, New York, Vintage Books, 1977, vol. 1, p. 797.

insured that both the new and the old poor, who now number thirty-five million, will remain — if they survive at all — the "underclass" well into the next century.[20]

Gentrification is an important aspect of this strategy of impoverishment. By creating neighborhoods and housing that only the white-collar labor force can afford, the cities are systematically destroying the material conditions for the survival of millions of people. Expelled from the economy by Reaganomics, turned out of their homes by state legislation, these cast-offs of late capitalism are fast losing the right to survive in society at all.

The process of gentrification in New York City takes various forms. On the Lower East Side these have included abandoning buildings, harassing and evicting tenants, and rapidly turning over neighborhood property in order to escalate real-estate values. Generating a crisis of survival for the displaced class, this process contributes substantially to the plight of homeless people, who are now estimated to number at least 60,000 in New York City. Referring to these growing numbers of displaced families, an attorney for the Coalition for the Homeless recently stated, "We're talking about survival needs. They need a bed or a crib to sleep in. They need a blanket. They need milk."[21] A position paper issued by the Lower East Side Catholic Area Conference in response to the city's newest housing plan for the Lower East Side — the Cross-Subsidy program — states that "displacement is one of the most serious and socially disorganizing processes at work on the Lower East Side," and that the "need for low and moderate income housing for the people of our community cannot be left to the marketplace." Through gentrification, "low and moderate income people with few options . . . become the powerless victims of dynamic economic forces that are beyond their control."[22]

20.   The term *underclass* is used with predictable contempt and callousness by neoconservatives to characterize the lower classes. Their explanations for the existence of such a category run the gamut from the biological to the cultural, from the economic to the social, but, in the final analysis, they believe that many members of this class are socially and economically irredeemable because of their inability to assimilate bourgeois values and behavior. Edward Banfield presents the most distorted version of this view of the underlying conditions of poverty: "Most of those caught up in this culture are unable or unwilling to plan for the future, or to sacrifice immediate gratifications in favor of future ones, or to accept the disciplines that are required in order to get and to spend. . . . Lower-class poverty is 'inwardly' caused (by psychological inability to provide for the future and all that this inability implies)" (Edward Banfield, *The Unheavenly City*, cited in Murray Hausknecht, "Caliban's Abode," in Lewis A. Coser and Irving Howe, eds., *The New Conservatives*, New York, New American Library, 1976, p. 196).
21.   Quoted in Sara Rimer, "Homeless Spend Nights in City Welfare Office," *New York Times*, November 19, 1984, p. B4.
22.   Statement issued by Lower East Side Catholic Area Conference on the Cross-Subsidy Plan, November 5, 1984. Cross-subsidy is, according to a mayor's office press release of July 1984, an "innovative financing technique . . . to restore and create low and moderate income housing on the Lower East Side." It is, in reality, the old technique of turning over city-owned property to developers who will be "encouraged" to create twenty percent lower income housing. Supposedly the proceeds of the sale of city property will be used to rehabilitate over 1,000 housing

As one agent of these economic forces, the city — which owns sixty percent of the neighborhood's property through tax defaults and abandonment of buildings by landlords — employs well-tested tactics to facilitate the transformation of the Lower East Side. The first of these is to do nothing at all, to allow the neighborhood to deteriorate of its own accord. Through a strategy of urban neglect, the city has been biding its time until enough contiguous lots can be put together to form what is known in the real-estate business as "assemblages." These are sold for large sums of money at municipal auctions to developers who thus amass entire blocks for the construction of large-scale upper-income housing. Another tactic of the city is the 421-a tax abatement program. Since 1971, 421-a — which provides tax exemptions to developers of luxury housing — has been instrumental in converting entire areas of Manhattan from middle- and low-income neighborhoods into neighborhoods that only the rich can afford. Recently the city council approved a bill that restricts from further tax-exempted development the area between 96th and 14th Streets, an area already saturated with the results of this program. The new bill now leaves the Lower East Side even more vulnerable to what amounts to subsidized housing for the rich. As President Nixon's Council of Economic Advisors discovered fifteen years ago, "Investing in new housing for low-income families — particularly in big cities — is usually a losing proposition. Indeed the *most profitable investment* is often one that demolishes homes of low-income families to make room for business and high-income families."[23]

The 421-a program makes clear the city's choice of succession to the Lower East Side. The rights of the beneficiaries are being contested, however, by those whose claim is more legitimate. "The basic issue," in the words of Carol Watson, Director of the Catholic Charities' Housing Leverage Fund, "is who owns that land. By 'own' I mean in the very real sense, morally. And we believe that that land belongs to the poor, literally, in every way, legally, morally. It belongs to the people. Because they were the people who struggled when nobody else wanted the Lower East Side."

While it might be tempting to view this current situation as merely the latest development in an unchanging immigrant history of the Lower East Side, there are fundamental differences between the past and the present. The experience of European immigrants was one of gradual assimilation; for today's minorities it is one of attrition. Any attempt to equate these experiences would result in profound distortions. The immigrants admitted to this country from

---

units in the area, "many of which will eventually be sold to tenants at low cost." In Carol Watson's view, "Three years ago the mayor wouldn't have proposed such a program because the development community wouldn't have been interested. But the development community is now coming in on a large scale on the Lower East Side. The Cross-Subsidy program was born of that interest and the mayor's need to satisfy that interest."

23.   Cited in Harrington, *The Twilight of Capitalism*, p. 224. For analysis of the 421-a tax abatement program, see Maria Laurino, "Trickle-Down Real Estate," *Village Voice*, December 4, 1984, p. 5.

the mid-nineteenth century to the close of the First World War belonged to a displaced, "floating" labor force following capital, which had itself emigrated to the New World.[24] Because most of these European immigrants were allowed a niche either in the closed circuitry of the immigrant economy or in the city's burgeoning manufacturing industry, there were opportunities for many eventually to move out of the tenements and beyond the borders of the Lower East Side. The present inhabitants of the area have no equivalent role to play in today's economy, and therefore "upward mobility" is not the reason that fifteen percent of the residents left the neighborhood between 1970 and 1980. The exodus was due instead to arson and the wholesale abandonment of buildings by landlords. In many ways the demographic and economic transformations that have overtaken the Lower East Side coincide with what Michael Harrington described in 1962 as the evolution of the old ethnic slums into new slums for the "rejects of the affluent society." As Harrington stated it, "Where the ethnic slum once stood, in the 'old' slum neighborhood, there is a new type of slum. Its citizens are the internal migrants, the Negroes, the poor whites from the farms, the Puerto Ricans. They join the failures from the old ethnic culture and form an entirely different kind of neighborhood. For many of them, the crucial problem is color, and this makes the ghetto walls higher than they have ever been."[25] But the "new slum" of the Lower East Side is itself being radically transformed as the affluent classes invest millions to live there themselves at the expense of displacing a population that has nowhere else to go. It is this process of displacement that is often termed "renewal" or "revitalization." A cover story about gentrification in the *New York Times Magazine,* for example, featured a glittering New York skyline with the stripped-in caption: "Rediscovering the City: The New Elite Spark an Urban Renaissance."

*

The concurrence of the two Lower East Side "renewals" — the process of gentrification and the unfolding of the art scene — is rarely remarked in the art press. The possible interrelationship is treated in two ways: either it is ignored altogether or it is raised only as a side issue to be quickly dispensed with. Although they give the neighborhood a central role in their promotion of the scene, Moufarrege and Ricard never mention the word *gentrification.* Carlo McCormick and Walter Robinson, two other apologists for East Village art, concede in passing that artists affect gentrification, but that done, they immediately return to the business at hand: a lavishly illustrated, empirical categorization of the art and a paean to the pleasures of the scene. "Early coverage," they

24.   Marx, p. 794.
25.   Harrington, *The Other America,* p. 151.

write, "came in the form of 'human interest' stories and pseudo-sociological examination of shifts in neighborhood population. More serious attention came from the area's own critics — Nicholas [*sic*] Moufarrege, for example."[26] Hidden within the reportorial style of these two sentences is a strategic maneuver that dictates the focus of art-world attention. It is, of course, gentrification that causes these shifts in neighborhood population so casually dismissed by the authors. We, however, are encouraged to make a shift of our own, to direct our attention away from "pseudosociological" concerns to the "more serious" matter of art criticism. The reality of gentrification is in this way severed from what are deemed to be proper cultural concerns. Artists' relationship to gentrification may be a controversial issue for the Lower East Side community, but for the art world it is of marginal interest at best. Thus, Irving Sandler, in his essay "Tenth Street Then and Now," keeps his social commentary safely within the limits of parenthetical statement: "(Ironically, the emergence of the East Village art scene is a major cause of the gentrification or Sohoization of the neighborhood). . . . Be all that as it may, at the moment there are a number of lively artists identified with the East Village . . . and that's the bottom line."[27] And at the end of an article which poses a number of questions about the problematic nature of the East Village galleries, Kim Levin concludes succinctly, "in the end, who cares, as long as they are trying to show good art."[28]

Such a closure having been effected at the level of the aesthetic, it has been perpetuated by writers who claim to reorient earlier texts in a more rigorous direction, sobering up the intoxicated assessments of the "East Village critics." Among these is Roberta Smith, who in her *Village Voice* piece entitled "The East Village Art Wars" responded to the special East Village section in *Art in America*. In that section, a brief commentary by Craig Owens follows the long article by Robinson and McCormick. Owens's essay is, to date, the only attempt in the art press at an economic and social analysis. He indicts the East Village scene as a "surrender . . . to the means-end rationality of the marketplace" and as a "culture-industry outpost" where "subcultural" forms are fed to that marketplace as products of consumption, their vital resistance to dominant culture thereby defeated. The implication of Owens's argument is that, by advertising and validating the products of the East Village scene, preceding press coverage forms part of that scene's alliance with the market and its leveling of meaning and difference. By drawing attention to the economic and social functioning of the East Village scene, which has been suppressed by previous commentators, Owens's article clears the way for a meaningful inquiry into the implication of that scene in the process of gentrification.[29]

26.   Robinson and McCormick, p. 141.
27.   Sandler, p. 19.
28.   Kim Levin, "The East Village," *Village Voice*, October 18, 1983, p. 79.
29.   Craig Owens, "Commentary: The Problem with Puerilism," *Art in America*, vol. 72, no. 6 (Summer 1984), pp. 162–163.

Roberta Smith assumes a liberal posture toward the two *Art in America* texts, positioning herself as mediator between extremists. "To denounce or embrace the proceedings absolutely is simplistic," she writes, and then castigates Owens for what she terms his "unworldly and not-a-little repressive ·brilliance."[30] It would be a study in the workings of distortion to explain why the author of the single article on the East Village scene that addresses the material operations of power in the real world is called "unworldly," why the author of the only two critical pages amidst a deluge of celebratory articles is considered "repressive." This is yet another example of an increasing tendency in the art world for critics who are themselves steeped in prejudices to characterize as authoritarian anyone who raises difficult questions about the oppressive workings of the cultural apparatus. Smith has missed the point of Owens's article entirely. Owens is not functioning as the other side of the promotional enthusiasm for East Village art by becoming its censor; rather he explores the ways in which the East Village scene participates in the dominant culture even as it poses as "subcultural." To adopt what Smith sees as the correct thing to do—to decide whether any given East Village artist's work is "good" or "bad"—is once again to preclude questions about the scene's complex relation to the concrete conditions of contemporary life. Smith, then, is not a mediator at all; she has placed herself squarely within the dominant camp. Similarly, writers who pose "critical" questions about whether or not artists can survive early success, and whether or not the galleries can survive economically, keep the discussion well within the limits of art-world self-interest, bolstering the scene they purport to criticize. Is it, after all, the *galleries'* survival that is in question? What of the survival of the people of the Lower East Side?

*

Although the new East Village art scene and its legitimators in the press ignore the workings of gentrification, they have, in fact, allowed themselves to become enmeshed in its mechanism. Galleries and artists drive up rents and displace the poor. Artists have placed their housing needs above those of residents who cannot choose where to live. The alignment of art-world interests with those of the city government and the real-estate industry became explicit to many residents on the Lower East Side during the ultimately successful battle which community groups waged to defeat Mayor Koch's Artist Homeownership Program (AHOP). "The Artist Homeownership Program was like the discovery of our power," as Father Beaumont put it. "We never thought that we would win, but we won, and then we discovered our own strength." In August 1981 the city, acting through its Department of Housing Preservation and Development, issued a Request for Proposals for the development of AHOP.

30.   Roberta Smith, "The East Village Art Wars," *Village Voice*, July 17, 1984, p. 79.

The request solicited "creative proposals to develop cooperative or condominium loft-type units for artists through the rehabilitation of properties owned by the city." The goal, according to the city administration, was "to provide artists with an opportunity for homeownership to meet their special work requirements, to encourage them to continue to live and work in New York City and to stimulate unique alternatives for the reuse and rehabilitation of city-owned property."[31] By May 1982 the mayor's office announced that five groups of artists and two developers had been selected to rehabilitate sixteen vacant tenement buildings on the south side of East 8th Street between Avenues C and B, and on the east side of Forsyth Street between Rivington and Stanton Streets. The seven buildings to be rehabilitated by artists would eventually yield fifty-one units ranging in size from 1,500 to 3,000 square feet, at an estimated purchase price of $50,000 and a monthly carrying charge of $500. After three years these original owners would be free to sell their spaces to other artists at market rates. The nine buildings designated for rehabilitation by developers were first to be converted into sixty-nine units and then sold to "moderate income artists." The cost of AHOP, calculated by the city to total seven million dollars, was to be partially financed through the Participation Loan Program. This program consists of twenty-five million dollars in federal funds designated for low and moderate income people to help them secure mortgages at below market rates. The city's eagerness to allocate three million dollars of these public funds for the housing needs of white, middle-class artists was seen as a clear indication of the city's attitudes toward the housing needs of the poor. "It's like taking food out of the mouth of someone who is hungry and giving it to someone who is eating everyday," commented one community worker.[32]

For the fifty-one artist participants in AHOP, however, it was "vital to the cultural community that this program be approved by the City's Board of Estimate because it may offer an ongoing solution to the housing problems faced by artists in our City."[33] Various art institutions also wrote in support of the program:

> — Artists are "working-class" individuals who often hold two jobs in order to support their families and art-making activities. It is fitting that the people of the City of New York support them in their effort to lead less "nomadic" lives.[34]

31.   The New York City Artist Homeownership Program, Request for Proposals, p. 1.
32.   Nilda Pimentel, as cited in Richard Goldstein, "Portrait of the Artist as a Good Use," *Village Voice*, December 14, 1982, p. 20.
33.   Open letter to artists and art organizations requesting letters of support for Artists Homeownership Program issued by the fifty-one participants, January 27, 1983.
34.   Martha Willson and Barbara Quinn, Franklin Furnace, letter in support of AHOP, October 19, 1982.

— Before all our artists are forced out of Manhattan, [it is sincerely hoped that] the City will look into this problem with sensitivity and foresight. It should be recognized by the City that artists have very special housing needs.[35]

— An art city does not exist without a thriving community of committed, working artists. Without this community and the manifold peripheral activities it generates, New York will lose a great deal — not only intellectually but economically as well as collectors and tourists go elsewhere to buy and be stimulated by new art forms [sic]. The Artist Homeowners [sic] Program now being proposed is a means to combat this dilemma.[36]

Despite the fact that members of the art community lobbied hard to have AHOP implemented, it was defeated in February 1983. Considerable pressure brought to bear by various community groups forced many supporters in the art world and members of the Board of Estimate to change their minds.

No matter how thoroughly obscured by the art world, the role that artists and galleries play in the gentrification of the Lower East Side is clear to those who are threatened with displacement, as well as to the community workers who are trying to save the neighborhood for its residents. "I think that artists are going to find themselves in a very unfortunate situation in the coming year," says Carol Watson. "There is going to be a real political struggle, a very serious struggle on the Lower East Side. And those who line up on the side of profit are going to find themselves on the enemy list. It's just that simple. Certainly the gallery artists, new artists, white artists." It is not a case of mistaken class identity for the people of the Lower East Side to place artists and professionals in the same social category. Nor is it simplistic, as many apologists for the scene would like to claim, to include the new wave of artists among the neighborhood's enemies. For despite their bohemian posturing, the artists and dealers who created the East Village art scene, and the critics and museum curators who legitimize its existence, are complicit with gentrification on the Lower East Side. To deny this complicity is to perpetuate one of the most enduring, self-serving myths in bourgeois thought, the myth that, as Antonio Gramsci wrote, intellectuals form a category that is "autonomous and independent from the dominant social group. This self-assessment is not without consequences in the ideological and political field, consequences of wide-ranging import."[37]

The influx of artists in the late '70s and the opening of galleries in the early '80s constituted the first moment in the sustained process of the Lower East

35. Linda Shearer, Artists Space, letter in support of AHOP, October 19, 1982.
36. Barbara Haskell, Whitney Museum of American Art, letter in support of AHOP, October 20, 1982.
37. Antonio Gramsci, *Selections from the Prison Notebooks of Antonio Gramsci*, ed. and trans. Quintin Hoare and Geoffrey Nowell-Smith, New York, International Publishers, 1980, p. 7.

Side's gentrification. It is not surprising that young artists, as well as more established ones priced out of the loft market in Soho and Tribeca, found the neighborhood attractive. The median rent was $172, and space, a precious commodity everywhere else in Manhattan, was being squandered by the city in a display of calculated neglect. According to the Census of 1980, well over half the area's housing stock was built before 1939, including old-law tenements dating back to the days of Jacob Riis. "This neighborhood was always like starting over," recalls Marisa Cardinale of Civilian Warfare. "I've lived here a long time and there was nothing here." This attitude, common among many art-world "pioneers," is reminiscent of the late nineteenth-century Zionist slogan, "a land without a people for a people without a land."[38] And like the existence of the Palestinian people, the existence of the original residents of the Lower East Side is in the eye of the beholder. There were, in fact, over 150,000 people living in the area, thirty-seven percent Hispanic and eleven percent black. The median income for a family of four living in the neighborhood in the 1980s is $10,727, while that of an individual is $5,139.[39] The fact that more than forty percent of the total population lives in official poverty might account for their high rate of invisibility.

The second moment in the process of gentrification is contingent upon the success of the first. As one "urban expert" discovered, "For all the manifest political and 'social' liberalism of the gentrifying classes, its members display the same anxieties with respect to living among or near racial minorities as everyone else."[40] On the Lower East Side it was not until artists, the middle class's own avant-garde, had established secure enclaves that the rear guard made its first forays into the "wilderness." The success of these forays can best be measured by the rapid escalation in real-estate activity. According to a December 1982 article in the *Village Voice*, Helmsley-Spear, Century Management, Sol Goldman, and Alex DiLorenzo III had all invested in empty lots, apartment houses, and abandoned buildings. Rents in the last two years have risen sharply. A small one-bedroom apartment rents for approximately $1,000 a month, and storefront space that once rented for $6.00 a square foot now costs as much as $35.[41]

"I get irritated," says Dean Savard of Civilian Warfare, "when people point their finger at a gallery and say 'that's the reason why.' I know damn well that I'm not the reason why. It's a city plan that has been in existence for over twenty years." Gracie Mansion agrees that it is too "easy to point a finger at art galleries and say 'that's the problem.' Because if all the galleries got up and moved it would not stop gentrification. Or if the galleries hadn't opened at all it

38. Edward W. Said, *The Question of Palestine*, New York, Vintage Books, 1980, p. 9.
39. Income and Poverty Status, 1980 Census.
40. Salins, p. 6.
41. Ann-Byrd Platt, "The Art Scene Moves to the East Village," *Wall Street Journal*, May 2, 1984, p. 28.

wouldn't have made any difference. You see, the area was marked for gentrification way before a single gallery opened up." Peter Nagy of Nature Morte admits that he feels guilty. "I mean, what is this monster we created? — a monster that may end up causing more harm than good. The good angle is that more younger artists will have spaces to exhibit their work. The bad angle is that it is certainly going to gentrify the neighborhood by turning it into something like Soho. But I also think that it would have happened whether the galleries had been here or not. I also can't help but feel that in some ways the battle against gentrification is a provincialist attitude toward Manhattan."

Common threads of denial and rationalization run through these responses from East Village dealers to questions about their role in gentrification. Attitudes range from aggressiveness through puzzlement to the genuine concern expressed by Jack Waters and Peter Cramer of the alternative space ABC No Rio. "I don't see how [the galleries] can't be implicated," says Jack Waters. "We fall into that area of implication because we've got the best deal in town. We've got a low rent and minimal pressure. And the reason that we're here is because we're attractive, because we represent an art organization. Whether or not that's a save-face for the city, allowing it to say it's not involved in gross speculation . . . 'Look we gave the building to ABC No Rio' . . . it's really complex and for that reason I don't want to project an image of purity."

ABC No Rio is an exception, however. Similarly, certain artists and artists' groups who are not part of the commercial scene have taken a public position against gentrification. Most gallery dealers and artists, however, are all too eager to avoid the implications of their place in the neighborhood's recent history and to present themselves as potential victims of gentrification. This is the trap that Craig Owens falls into when he claims that "Artists are not, of course, responsible for 'gentrification'; they are often its victims, as the closing of any number of the East Village galleries, forced out of the area by rents they helped to inflate, will sooner or later demonstrate."[42] To portray artists as the victims of gentrification is to mock the plight of the neighborhood's real victims. This is made especially clear by the visible contrast between the area's obvious poverty and the art scene's conspicuous display of wealth. At this moment in history artists cannot be exempted from responsibility. According to Carol Watson, the best thing the artists of this city can do for the people of the Lower East Side is to go elsewhere. She realizes, however, that the hardest thing to ask individuals is not to act in their own best interest. Nonetheless, they need to decide whether or not they want to be part of a process that destroys people's lives. "People with choices," she says, "should choose not to move to the Lower East Side."

In addition to the economic impact of artists and galleries, the art world functions ideologically to exploit the neighborhood for its bohemian or sen-

42.   Owens, p. 163.

sationalist connotations while deflecting attention away from underlying social, economic, and political processes. The attitudes that permit this exploitation are the same as those that allow the city and its affluent residents to remain indifferent to the fate of the displaced poor: assessments of poverty as natural and gentrification as inevitable and in some ways even desirable. Armed with these attitudes and received notions of artists' exemption from social responsibility, together with more recent cultural trends — crass commercialism and the neoexpressionist ideology whereby subjective expression obfuscates concrete social reality — the participants in the new East Village scene arrive on the Lower East Side prepared to make it over in their own image. Consciously or unconsciously, they approach the neighborhood with dominating and possessive attitudes that transform it into an imaginary site. Art journals, the mass media, galleries, established alternative spaces, and museums manipulate and exploit the neighborhood, thereby serving as conduits for the dominant ideology that facilitates gentrification. Myriad verbal and visual representations of the neighborhood circulate in exhibition catalogues, brochures, and magazines. Through such representations a neighborhood whose residents are fighting for survival metamorphoses into a place "that encourages one to be the person he is with greater ease than other parts of the city."[43] Inevitably, concrete reality evaporates into thin air: "One must realize that the East Village or the Lower East Side is more than a geographical location — it is a state of mind."[44]

*

Why have exploitative representations of the Lower East Side and its residents met with so little resistance from today's art-world audience? What is responsible for this acquiescence in power and for the ease with which social considerations about the Lower East Side are pushed into the background? Would this cooperation between the art scene and a process like gentrification have been so easily achieved in the past? Throughout the '60s and '70s significant art, beginning with minimalism, was oriented toward an awareness of context. Among the radical results of this orientation were art practices that intervened directly in their institutional and social environments. While a number of artists today continue contextualist practices that demonstrate an understanding of the material bases of cultural production, they are a minority in a period of reaction. The specific form this reaction takes in the art world is an unapologetic embrace of commercialism, opportunism, and a concomitant rejection of the radical art practices of the past twenty years. The art establishment has resurrected the doctrine that aestheticism and self-expression are the proper

43.   Nicolas A. Moufarrege, "Another Wave, Still More Savagely Than the First: Lower East Side, 1982," *Arts*, vol. 57, no. 1 (September 1982), p. 69.
44.   *Ibid.*, p. 73.

concerns of art and that they constitute realms of experience divorced from the social. This doctrine is embodied in a dominant neoexpressionism which, despite its pretentions to pluralism, must be understood as a system of rigid and restrictive beliefs: in the primacy of the self existing prior to and independently of society; in an eternal conflict, outside of history, between the individual and society; in the efficacy of individualized, subjective protest. The participants in the East Village scene serve this triumphant reaction. But the victory of neoexpressionism and its East Village variant, like the victory of all reactions, depends on a lie in order to validate itself, in this case the lie that neoexpressionism is exciting, new, and liberating. Such a lie obstructs critical thinking by obscuring the social subjugation and oppression that such "liberation" ignores and thereby assists.

The rule of the neoexpressionist regime and its culmination in the legitimation of the East Village scene depend on yet another lie — the falsification of art's recent history with the purpose of concealing its radical basis and presenting it as, instead, oppressive. This enables the new scene to congratulate itself for breaking the bonds of tyranny. The specific content of this revision of history authorizes the current rejection of politics and the prevailing false definitions of liberation that justify both art-world support for the East Village scene and its blindness to the social struggle on the Lower East Side. For it is not "energy" that has produced the East Village scene, but history, and that history is being rewritten from the distorted perspective of neoexpressionism. Since this rewriting occurs within our most prestigious art institutions, it is not surprising that they are also extending their approval to the East Village phenomenon.

One of the clearest instances of this reconstruction of recent art history in the name of neoexpressionism is the Whitney Museum's 1983 exhibition *Minimalism to Expressionism*, which attempted to supplant earlier views of minimal art. Originally understood as a materialist critique of the artwork's autonomy, minimalism demanded a consideration of the work's spatial and temporal contexts, a consideration which led to a recognition of the contingency of perception. In contrast to this initial assessment of the radicality of minimalism, the Whitney presented the movement as conservative, thereby setting it up as a foil for neoexpressionism's pretense to liberation. To effect this, the museum guided the viewer through the exhibition with wall labels and a brochure that contained such deceptive judgments of minimalism as the following:

- Art adopted inflexible and authoritarian qualities.
- In Minimalism individual personality was repressed.
- Cool precise icons of formalism filled pristine, white-walled, and artificially lit exhibition spaces.
- In Minimalism life and art were compartmentalized.[45]

45.   Patterson Sims, *Minimalism to Expressionism* (exhibition brochure), New York, Whitney Museum of American Art, n.p.

Inflexible, authoritarian, repressive, cold, formalist, life-denying — these words have grown increasingly familiar. They are the simplistic charges leveled against any critical questioning of received idealist notions of art. An art practice that challenged the prevailing authority of formalism and entrenched ideas of individual creation is now called authoritarian and formalist; art that made context part of the work through attention to real time and space now becomes divorced from life or simply cold. The hidden agenda of the Whitney's exhibition was to bolster the pretensions of neoexpressionism to a radicality purported to reside in its excessive emotion. According to the exhibition's curator Patterson Sims, this emotion *contrasts* with our conservative era, while minimalism's "coldness" was at odds with the radical society of its day: "The heightened realities of the Neo-Expressionists seem as contrary to their numbed, impoverished, and conservative times as Minimalism's denial of the eccentricities and energy of the 1960s. Now, at a time of cutbacks and retrenchment, artistic excess has taken over." Within the terms of this inverted view, *radical* and *conservative* are depoliticized into synonyms for *emotional* and *intellectual*, *hot* and *cold*. It is only within the restricting confines of such an argument that neoexpressionism's retreat from political art practice into the expression of solipsistic feelings can be heralded as a significant development.

But this is exactly what is being done by the artists, dealers, and critics of the East Village scene:

- The art world has done it again. . . . A new avant-garde has been launched.[46]
- Art too long repressed, exploded with savage energy.[47]
- One finds here a sophisticated sense of current issues and trends, unrestrained by any stylistic borders.[48]
- Politically and socially relevant, a reaction to the reckoning severity of the '70s, lives in the art itself. . . .[49]
- . . . the East Village is greatly a reaction against intellectualization. . . . If there is indeed nothing new in the East Village, it is because its basis of individuality does not rely on such measures. Artists seek only to express themselves.[50]

While it might seem that this last passage is intended as criticism of the scene, Carlo McCormick actually supports the notion of individual liberation embodied in an expressive painting. This program of individual, as opposed to social or political liberation is so unthreatening to the status quo that Fun Gallery does fifty percent of its selling to art consultants. The graffiti art that Fun spe-

46.   Robinson and McCormick, p. 135.
47.   Moufarrege, "The Year After," p. 51.
48.   Kardon, p. 8.
49.   Moufarrege, "Another Wave," p. 69.
50.   Carlo McCormick, "The Periphery of Pluralism," in *The East Village Scene*, p. 47.

cializes in is now largely indistinguishable from standard neoexpressionism, with its gestural painting, mythological motifs, and apocalyptic themes. "Art consultants," says Bill Stelling, "obviously like the art that is less controversial. This is why this kind of art works in corporate headquarters. . . . It's not something that would offend someone in the Moral Majority."

Individual liberation is yet another element of the dominant ideology that determines the way in which the art world represents the neighborhood. East Village scene makers view the Lower East Side as a liberating place that offers "a choice which allows one to be oneself."[51] But who has such choices? To characterize the neighborhood as a place of choices is to base one's assessment on nonpolitical concepts of freedom, and is therefore to be unconscious of the crippling lack of options that is the real condition of Lower East Side residents. The limitations on these people's lives are not at all a result of emotional repression but of the formidable economic forces arrayed against them.

*

Last fall the Institute of Contemporary Art at the University of Pennsylvania mounted the first museum exhibition of East Village art. It took only three years from the opening of the first East Village galleries for the most prestigious of art-world institutions — the museum — to authorize the new system. The University of California at Santa Barbara quickly followed suit with *Neo-York*, an exhibition augmented by a "public forum," film and video about the Lower East Side, as well as a "street party" featuring "East Village food and drink." The ICA show was more modest, accompanied only by an illustrated catalogue containing three essays. The exhibition was motivated, according to its curator Janet Kardon, by the museum's mandate to be on the "cutting edge of the newest art issues," and the catalogue's introductory essay, written in a matter-of-fact, informative manner, expressed the hope that the show would inspire a critical discourse. The catalogue itself, however, offered not a single critical assessment. Filled instead with clichés about the freedom, spirit, and diversity of the East Village scene, Kardon's introduction refers to gentrification in terms of the appearance of new restaurants and boutiques. One essay notes that there has been a "youthful restoration of the inner city."[52] With these museum exhibitions, the neighborhood has once again been exploited for its promotional value.

The Lower East Side enters the space of the ICA catalogue in three forms: mythologized in the texts as an exciting bohemian environment, objectified in a map delimiting its boundaries, and aestheticized in a full-page photograph of a

51.   Nicolas Moufarrege, "East Village," *Flash Art*, no. 111 (March 1983), p. 37.
52.   McCormick, p. 33.

Lower East Side "street scene." All three are familiar strategies for the domination and possession of others. The photograph, alone, is a blatant example of
the aestheticization of poverty and suffering that has become a staple of visual
imagery. At the lower edge of the photograph a bum sits in a doorway surrounded by his shopping bags, a liquor bottle, and the remnants of a meal. He
is apparently oblivious of the photographer, unaware of the composition in
which he is forced to play a major role. Abundant graffiti covers the wall
behind him, while at the left the wall is pasted over with layers of posters, the
topmost of which is an advertisement for the Pierpont Morgan Library's Holbein exhibition. The poster features a large reproduction of a Holbein portrait
of a figure facing in the direction of the bum in the doorway. High art mingles
with the "subculture" of graffiti and the "low-life" represented by the bum in a
photograph which is given a title, like an artwork: *First Street and Second Avenue
(Holbein and the Bum)*. The photograph displays familiar elements of an easily
produced artfulness: the "rightness" of the image, its "meaningful" juxtaposition
of high culture and low life, and the compositional unity achieved through the
figure's placement at the bottom of the graffitied spiral and the manner in
which the bum and portrait in similar dress appear to face each other. While its
street subject has long been popular among art photographers, this photograph
is inserted into the pages of a museum catalogue for the purpose of advertising
the pleasures and unique ambience of this particular art scene. Only an art
world steeped in the protective and transformative values of aestheticism and
the blindness to suffering that such an ideology sanctions could tolerate, let
alone applaud, such an event. For this picture functions as a tourist shot, introducing the viewer to the local color of an exotic and dangerous locale. It is,
however, ironic that the site of this photograph is also the place where a very
different kind of photograph was first produced in the United States. At the
turn of the century, Jacob Riis published texts illustrated with photographs of
the Lower East Side in books such as *How the Other Half Lives* in order to
stimulate social reform. Whatever the manifold failings of this mode of liberal
social documentary, they pale beside the photograph in the ICA catalogue,
which is untroubled by any social conscience whatsoever. Whereas Riis's
muckraking attempted to force attention on unpleasant realities that people
would rather have ignored, *Holbein and the Bum* exemplifies a completely de-
graded, aestheticized documentary which Martha Rosler has described as "the
documentary of the present, the petted darling of the monied, a shiver-
provoking, slyly decadent, lip-smacking appreciation of alien vitality or a fragmented vision of psychological alienation in city and town."[53] This is the docu-
mentary-cum-art-photograph that, like *Holbein and the Bum*, is intended not to

---

53.   Martha Rosler, "In, Around, and Afterthoughts (On Documentary Photography)," in
Martha Rosler, 3 Works, Halifax, The Press of the Nova Scotia College of Art and Design, 1981,
p. 80.

call attention to the plight of the homeless but to fit comfortably into the pages of an art catalogue, unveiling to art lovers the special pleasures of the East Village as a spectacle for the slumming delectation of those collectors who cruise the area in limousines.

To such missions a dazed bum presents no barriers. He is, rather, a consummate lure, since his presence forecloses complex thoughts about the reality or social causes underlying "ambience." The figure of a bum is laden with connotations of the eternally and deservedly poor. It thus holds historical analysis at bay. A recognition of the entrenched bourgeois social codes in images of bums lies behind another work that deals with Lower East Side subject matter, *The Bowery in Two Inadequate Descriptive Systems* by Martha Rosler. Rosler's *Bowery* is notable for its *absence* of bums, for its refusal to perpetuate the codes and thereby serve the workings of power. "The buried text of photographs of drunks," Rosler writes, "is not a treatise on political economy."[54] Rather, as a member of that group which Marx referred to as the "refuse of all classes,"[55] the bum is poor but avoids placement in class struggle. Insofar as he signifies laziness and a conscious refusal to earn his own living, he provides an alibi for revelers in the East Village scene to indulge in the most callous attitudes toward poverty, and like the gentrifiers on the Lower East Side they remain indifferent to the miseries surrounding them. This is the indifference that the young Engels described with such amazement in 1844, after his first trip to the industrial city of Manchester. Even in his horror, Engels could point to the reasons, engendered by capitalism, for such callousness: "The middle classes have a truly extraordinary conception of society. They really believe that all human beings . . . have real existence only if they make money or help to make it."[56] The beggar in middle-class society is therefore "stamped forever as one who has lost all claim to be regarded as a human being."[57] Yet, because the bum also signifies a decision not to work, he has been commandeered by the art world for another purpose — as a metaphor for the artist's own purported refusal of bourgeois convention. In this way, the figure of the bum provides the requisite identification with marginal figures and social outcasts by which avant-garde and bohemian glamour accrues to the East Village scene despite its embrace of conventional values.

In the image of the bum, the problems of the homeless poor, existing on all sides of the East Village art scene, are mythologized, exploited, and finally ignored. Once the poor become aestheticized, poverty itself moves out of our

54.   *Ibid.*, p. 79.
55.   Karl Marx, *The Eighteenth Brumaire of Louis Bonaparte*, Moscow, Progress Publishers, 1954, p. 63.
56.   Friedrich Engels, *The Condition of the Working Class in England*, New York, Macmillan, 1958, p. 311.
57.   *Ibid.*, p. 314.

field of vision. Images like *Holbein and the Bum* disguise the literal existence of thousands of displaced and homeless people who are not only produced by late capitalism but constitute its very conditions. As a process of dispersing a "useless" class, gentrification is aided and abetted by an "artistic" process whereby poverty and homelessness are served up for aesthetic pleasure.

Critique of Institutions

A Conversation with Hans Haacke

YVE-ALAIN BOIS, DOUGLAS CRIMP,
and ROSALIND KRAUSS

Krauss: Since your work has, from the beginning, resisted painting, implicitly criticizing painting as incapable of supporting any serious critique of its own assumptions, what made you decide that your work for your Tate Gallery exhibition last spring would be a painting?

Haacke: That wasn't the first time I did a painting.

Crimp: Right. There's the portrait of Reagan that formed part of *Oelgemaelde, Hommage à Marcel Broodthaers*, the work for Documenta 7. But it is true, isn't it, that the portrait of Margaret Thatcher is the first instance in which you've used a painting by itself?

Haacke: No, there's another precedent, aside from the paintings I did before I turned to three-dimensional work in the early '60s. For a show in Montreal in 1983, I made what I called a *Painting for the Boardroom*, an industrial landscape. It is a somewhat impressionistic aerial view of the Alcan aluminum smelter in Arvida, Quebec. I painted it after a photograph that I found in an Alcan P.R. pamphlet. It is a cheerful, sunny picture. Into the bright sky I painted a short caption which announces, in a tone of pride, that the workers at Arvida have an opportunity to contract bone fibrosis, respiratory diseases, and cancer. The painting is framed in aluminum siding. Obviously, in all three cases, I chose to paint because the medium as such has a particular meaning. It is almost synonymous with what is popularly viewed as Art — art with a capital A — with all the glory, the piety, and the authority that it commands. Since politicians and businesses alike present themselves to the folks as if they were surrounded by halos, there are similarities between the medium and my subjects. When I planned the Reagan painting, I was also inspired by the thinking of Marcel Broodthaers. In the catalogue preface to his *Musée d'art moderne, Département des aigles, Section des figures* (1972), he pointed to the parallelism between the mythic powers of the eagle, the symbol of empire, and the mythic powers of art. Contrary to popular belief, eagles are really not courageous birds; they are even afraid of bicycles, as Broodthaers wrote. Their power is due to projection. The same is true for art — and political power. They need the red carpet, the gold frame, the aura of the office/museum — the paraphernalia of a seeming immortality and divine origin.

Krauss: But in the case of the Broodthaers work, the medium, we could say, is a standard iconographical emblem, rather than oil paint's being the medium.

Haacke: It is important that the Thatcher portrait is an oil painting. Acrylic paint doesn't have an aura. I was also deliberate in the choice of the Victorian frame. I had it built especially. For the design, I followed the example of frames around paintings by Frederick Leighton and Burne-Jones at the Tate. In effect, these frames elevate their contents to the status of altarpieces, endow the paintings with religious connotations. I don't have to tell you what gold represents. As with the frame, I tried to mimic, as best I could, the love for genre detail and the paint style of the Victorian era. And so all the details are Victorian, the interior with its furniture, the curtain with its tassles, the Tate Gallery's own sculpture of Pandora by Harry Bates, the typeface on the bookspines, and so on. I thought I should place Margaret Thatcher into the world that she represents. As you know, she expressly promotes Victorian values, nineteenth-century conservative policies at the end of the twentieth century.

Krauss: Most of the information in the painting, as well as its title, *Taking Stock (unfinished)*, refers to the Saatchis. Do you mean for the Saatchis to be understood as Victorian figures as well?

Haacke: Of course, in their own way, the Saatchis are also Victorians. They match the young bourgeois entrepreneurs of the nineteenth century, relatively unfettered by tradition, without roots in the aristocracy, and out to prove themselves to the world. Their conquests are the brash takeovers of advertising companies around the world. After successful forays in the U.K., a few years ago they gobbled up Compton, a big Madison Avenue agency with an international network. And last year it was the turn of McCaffrey & McCall, another New York agency. By now the Saatchi empire has grown to be the eighth largest peddler of brands and attitudes in the world. Naturally, they align themselves with the powers that promise to be most sympathetic to their own fortunes. So they ran the election campaign for Margaret Thatcher in 1979, and again last year. They also had the Tory account for the European Parliamentary elections this year. Heseltine, the Tory minister, who has an interest in *Campaign*, the British advertising trade journal, has been a good friend of the Saatchis since the days when Maurice Saatchi worked for the journal. Everyone in London assumes that, as a reward for their services during Margaret Thatcher's first election campaign, the Saatchis got the account of British Airways. Not to be outdone, the Saatchis' South African subsidiary took it upon itself to run the promotion of the constitutional change that was presented in a referendum to the white voters by the South African government's National Party. Foes of apartheid think that this change, in effect, cemented the system which reserves political power in South Africa *exclusively* for the white minority, which constitutes sixteen percent of the population.

Crimp: Both the Reagan and Thatcher paintings were also presumably intended to comment on the relationship between these people's reactionary politics and the current revival of painting in a reactionary art-world situation. The Reagan portrait appeared in a Documenta exhibition that everyone knew would lend its authority to the painting revival, while the Thatcher portrait contains information about the power of the Saatchis, who are active promoters of the new painting. Why then did you choose a hyper-realist, or perhaps a late nineteenth-century academic style for these paintings, rather than a style that might more directly comment upon the neoexpressionism which is the dominant mode of the return to painting?

Bois: The iconological mode you've used is indeed quite remote from what is going on in contemporary painting.

Crimp: It's true, of course, that what is going on now involves historical references, and I can see that you would want to make the connection between these political personalities and Victorian values, but that choice also reduces the work's pungency with regard to current painting.

Haacke: But if I had concentrated on the style of current painting, the political content would have been left out. I would have been dealing exclusively with an art-world affair. The art world is not *that* important. Moreover, the attitudes associated with much of the retro type of painting favored by the Saatchis amounts to a gold-frame celebration of a romantic individualism of a bygone era, which clearly predates and differs essentially from the attitudes of the original expressionists. Much of the current painting is coy naughtiness.

Krauss: I'd like to explore further what you said about the kind of image politicians like Reagan and Thatcher wish to elaborate for themselves. It's true that the oil portrait, because of its aura, its air of nobility, is important for this image, yet connecting the Saatchis and Thatcher also brings into play something which involves the opposite of this aura, something which is very much of the twentieth century—the public relations selling of politicians through the media. I'm interested to think about an act which restores a traditional aura to Thatcher and Reagan, who have been sold by television, who most often have their images conveyed through the medium of video.

Hans Haacke. Taking Stock (unfinished).
1983–84. First shown in the exhibition
Hans Haacke, *Tate Gallery, London,*
January 25–March 4, 1984.

Inscriptions:
On the foot of the column, left: ES SAATCHI TRUS/
ITECHAPEL GAL/TRONS OF NEW/ART
COMMITTEE/HE TATE/GALLER.
On the top shelf of the bookcase: MS, CS.
On the spines of the books in the bookcase: Allied Lyons,
Avis, BL, Black & Decker, Blue Nun, British
Airways, British Arts Council, British Crafts
Council, British Museum, British Rail, Campbell
Soup, Central Office of Information, Conservatives
British Elections, Conservatives European
Elections, Cunard, Daily Mail, Dunlop (acc.
lost), DuPont, Gilette, Great Universal Stores,
Johnson & Johnson, IBM, Massey-Ferguson,
Max Factor, National Gallery, National Portrait
Gallery, Nestle, Playtex, Proctor & Gamble,
Rank Organization, Rowntree Mackintosh,
Royal Academy, South Africa Nationalist Party,
Serpentine Gallery, Tottenham Hotspurs,
TV-am, United Buscuits, Victoria & Albert
Museum, Wales Gas, Walt Disney, Wimpey,
Wrangler.
On the paper hanging over the edge of the table: In the
year ended March 31st 1978 Brogan Developers
Ltd. (Saatchi Investment Ltd.) sold art works
valued at £380,319.
On the paper lying at Thatcher's foot: Saatchi & Saatchi
Company PLC/The year ended September 1982/
Furniture, equipment, works of art and motor
vehicles/Gross current £15,095,000/replacement
cost/Depreciation £7,036,000/Net current
£8,059,000/replacement cost. Tangible net assets
are stated at historical cost or valuation less
accumulated depreciation. The cost and valuation
of tangible fixed assets is written off by equal
annual installments over the expected useful lives
of the assets: for furniture and equipment between
6 and 10 years. No depreciation provided for
works of art.

The initials MS and CS on the rims of the broken
plates on the top shelf of the bookcase refer to the
brothers Maurice and Charles Saatchi, whose
portraits appear in the center of the plates. In
1982 Julian Schnabel, known for his paintings
with broken plates, had an exhibition in the same
space at the Tate Gallery where the Haacke show
was later installed. Nine of the eleven paintings
by Schnabel were owned by Doris and Charles
Saatchi. At the time, Charles Saatchi was a
member of the Patrons of New Art Committee of
the Tate. The museum is a public institution
operated by the British government. While the
Patrons are a private association with the goal of
acquiring and donating contemporary works to
the Tate, they also appear to have influence on the
museum's exhibition policies. Among its members
are collectors and nearly all London art dealers,
as well as the New York dealer Leo Castelli. There
have been complaints that the Saatchis have never
donated a work to the Tate Gallery.

Charles Saatchi was also a member of the Board
of Trustees of the Whitechapel Gallery, another
public institution in London. It is suspected that
he profited from inside information about
exhibition plans of the Gallery, which allowed
him to buy works, notably by Francesco Clemente
and Malcolm Morley, at a favorable moment.

Doris Saatchi, a Smith College graduate and
ex-copywriter for Ogilvy & Mather, and her
husband Charles began collecting art in the
early '70s. Initially interested in photorealism,
they shifted their attention to minimalism and
neoexpressionism. When the Museum of
Contemporary Art in Los Angeles opened in
1983, it invited eight collectors to present
selections from their holdings. The Saatchis chose
works by Baselitz, Chia, Clemente, Guston,
Kiefer, Morley, Schnabel, and Stella. In a further
attempt to exert control over the art world,
Saatchi & Saatchi made a bid to buy *Art in America*
when Whitney Communications offered it for sale.

The financial base for such ventures is the income
from the advertising agency Saatchi & Saatchi
Company PLC, which has been built by the
Saatchi brothers, through mergers, into the largest
British advertising agency and the eighth largest
worldwide. In 1982 they acquired Compton
Communications, a large New York agency with
a worldwide network, and in 1983, McCaffrey &
McCall, also of New York. Shares of Saatchi &
Saatchi are traded on the stock exchanges in
New York and London.

Doris and Charles Saatchi are soon to open a
private museum in the north of London, to be
designed by Max Gordon, a friend and former
colleague at the Tate. A catalogue of the Saatchi
collection with contributions from well-known art
critics and historians is being prepared by Doris
Saatchi, who also writes for the *World of Interiors*,
Artscribe, and *Architectural Review*.

In February 1984, one month after the opening of
the Haacke exhibition at the Tate Gallery, Charles
Saatchi resigned his position on the Patrons of
New Art Committee of the museum. He also
resigned his trusteeship of the Whitechapel
Gallery.

Haacke: Margaret Thatcher's public relations advisors evidently told her that she should style herself after the Queen, including her taste in clothing. She also took voice training lessons to get rid of her shrillness. Her entire image has been transformed over the past few years to fit the media better. It pays politically to look like the Queen rather than like the nation's headmistress. I therefore thought I should paint her in a haughty, regal pose. In order to accentuate her rivalry with Queen Elizabeth and also to strengthen the period look, I seated her on a chair with the image of Queen Victoria on its back. It is a chair that I found in the collection of the Victoria & Albert Museum. Thatcher would like to rule an Imperial Britain. The Falklands War was typical of this mentality.

Bois: So that is why you used the emblematic tradition, the iconographic symbols?

Haacke: Yes. I hope everybody understood that this was done tongue-in-cheek.

Crimp: It also seems that there is a strategic aspect to this, insofar as you are using a painting style that even the most naive museum goer can read. It's possible in this way to capture a broader audience, and interestingly enough there was a very large media response to the Tate Gallery work. By resorting to this auratic art form, you get press coverage that you probably wouldn't get if you were to use a more avant-garde kind of object. I'd like to ask you something related to the question of strategies, because I was struck by the fact that two of your most recent works are, on the one hand, a portrait painting, which makes all kinds of concessions to being a traditional work of art, and, on the other hand, the *Isolation Box, Grenada*, which makes no pretense to being a work of art.

Bois: Except that, in a way, it becomes a bad piece of minimal sculpture.

Haacke: Indeed, there, too, there is a subtext. When I read about the isolation boxes in the *New York Times*, I immediately recognized their striking similarity to the standard minimal cube. As you see, one can recycle "minimalism" and put it to a contemporary use. I admit that I have always been sympathetic to so-called minimal art. That does not keep me from criticizing its determined aloofness, which, of course, was also one of its greatest strengths. As to the implied incompatibility between a political statement/information and a work of art, I don't think there are generally accepted criteria for what constitutes a work of art. At least since Duchamp and the constructivists, this has been a moving target. On a more popular level, of course, there are strong feelings about what does or does not look like a work of art. Minimal cubes obviously don't qualify, whereas anything painted on canvas is unquestionably accepted. The argument rages only about whether or not it is a good work.

Hans Haacke. U.S. Isolation Box, Grenada, 1983. *1984.*
First shown in conjunction with Artists Call Against U.S. Intervention in Central America *in the public mall of the Graduate School and University Center of the City University of New York, January 1984.*

David Shribman reported in the *New York Times*, November 17, 1983, that the U.S. troops that had invaded Grenada detained prisoners in boxlike isolation chambers at the Point Salines airport. The wooden boxes measured approximately eight by eight feet, had four small windows so high that one could see neither in nor out, and had a number of ventilation holes with a radius of half an inch. Inside one box a prisoner had written, "It's hot in here." The prisoners were forced to enter these boxes by crawling through a hatch that extended from the floor to about knee level.

Shortly after the exhibition opened, the administration of the Graduate School moved the sculpture into a dark corner of the mall and turned it in such a way that the inscription was hardly visible. Only after strenuous protests was the work restored to its original position.

An editorial in the *Wall Street Journal*, February 21, 1984, attacked this work and a gravelike mound of earth in memory of Maurice Bishop, the slain prime minister of Grenada, by the New York artist Thomas Woodruff. The *Journal* found these two works to be "in proper company" with "America's greatest collection of obscenity and pornography" a few blocks down 42nd Street. The writer of the editorial also called the Isolation Box "the most remarkable work of imagination in the show."

Artists Call Against U.S. Intervention in Central America, an ad hoc coalition of artists in the U.S. and Canada, staged numerous exhibitions, performances, and other events in over twenty cities from January to March 1984. They were organized in protest against U.S. policy in Central America and in solidarity with the victims of that policy. Claes Oldenburg designed the poster. In New York, more than 700 artists of all ages and styles participated, among them both internationally renowned and totally unknown artists. Established commercial galleries such as Leo Castelli, Paula Cooper, and Barbara Gladstone, as well as alternative galleries, made their spaces available. *Artists Call* took out a three-quarter-page advertisement in the Sunday edition of the *New York Times*. Most art journals reported the events extensively. *Arts Magazine* carried the Oldenburg poster on its cover.

Hans Haacke. But I think you question my motives. *1978–79.*
First shown in a one-man exhibition at the Stedelijk van Abbemuseum, Eindhoven, January 1979.

Krauss: One of the things that struck me when I saw the Philips piece [*But I think you question my motives, 1978–79*] was that the blown-up, rather dramatic, high chiaroscuro photographs of black youths seemed to make reference to the works of Gilbert and George from the same period. So it seems to me that there is always a component of your work that reveals certain formal moves made within the art world and the contents to which those forms can be exceedingly porous.

Haacke: I didn't think of Gilbert and George. Those are photos from a South African business magazine. They were probably supplied by the Philips P.R. department. But it is true that I often play on the modes of the contemporary art world; and I try to make something that is accessible to a larger public, which does not care for the histrionics of the art world. As Douglas pointed out, it helps that these pieces do not have the look of hermetic "avant-garde" art.

Translations:
Left Panel: We are businessmen and we look for business opportunities, which is the only factor governing our decisions. Political considerations don't come into it. Nobody is going to help South Africa unless he is paid for it, and obviously you need know-how from abroad. We are here to stay. — Jan Timmer, Managing Director of Philips in South Africa.
Center Panel: But I think you question my motives. You see me just as a man of capital. However, above all I really would like to help people to have the freedom to develop themselves as much as possible, to create opportunities for themselves, to take initiatives and carry the responsibility for them. — Frits Philips, in his autobiography, *45 Years with Philips.*
Right Panel: The Employee Councils are advisory bodies. They are precluded from negotiating minimum wages or conditions of employment; and in fact wages are rarely discussed. The average black worker earns 229 rand a month. Blacks are excluded from apprentice training for radio and TV technicians by the *Job Reservations Act.* — *Financial Mail,* Johannesburg, July 22, 1977, supplement on Philips.

Philips investments in South Africa amount to approximately $83 million. In a work force of more than 1900, blacks, coloreds, and Indians predominantly occupy jobs for untrained or low-skilled workers. Responding to the wishes of the South African government, Philips established lamp manufacturing facilities in Rosslyn, at the border of a Bantustan ("homeland"). Philips dominates the South African market for lightbulbs, radios, hi-fi equipment, tape recorders, and electrical appliances, and has a sizeable share of the market for television sets. Moreover, Philips is active in telecommunications and sophisticated electronics. Because of the low personal income of the black majority population and the widespread lack of electricity in black residential areas, the possibility for an expansion of the market in consumer electronics is limited.

The Mirage fighter planes of the South African airforce as well as its Alouette, Gazelle, Puma, and Super Frelon helicopters are guided by radio-altimeters and/or radar equipment from Philips. Such fighter planes and helicopters were loaned or sold to Ian Smith's white government of Rhodesia (now Zimbabwe) by South Africa. Philips also supplies the South African police with radio equipment in spite of a U.N. military embargo, and Philips radio-altimeters guide the Exocet missiles which have been supplied to South Africa.

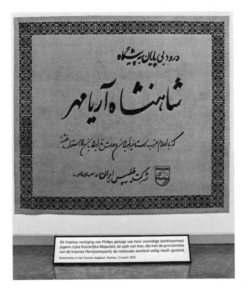

Hans Haacke. Everlasting Gratitude. *1978.*
First shown in a one-man exhibition at the
Stedelijk van Abbemuseum, Eindhoven, 1979
(The exhibition opened one week after the Shah's
final departure from Iran).

Translation: Philips of Iran expresses its everlasting
gratitude to His Imperial Majesty, the Shah of
Iran, who secured national unity by founding the
Iranian Resurgence Party. — Advertisement in
the Iranian newspaper, *Kayhan*, March 5, 1975.

In terms of sales, Philips is the fifth largest
non-American multinational industrial
corporation. With 383,900 employees (as of 1977)
it ranks with companies such as General Motors,
Ford, and ITT. Corporate headquarters are
located in Eindhoven, Holland. In spite of the
decline in the number of employees from 99,000
(1971) to 85,700 (1977), the company remains
the largest private employer in Holland (during
the same period the number of Philips employees
in low-wage countries, notably in the Third World,
rose significantly).

In Iran, Philips maintains facilities and a sales
organization. During the Shah's regime, the
Iranian military received, among other material,
210 Tiger and Phantom fighter planes, sixteen
Super Frelon helicopters, and 1500 Chieftain
heavy tanks, all equipped with radio-altimeters,
UHF radios, and/or night vision equipment from
Philips. When the Shah left the country in January
1979, twelve vessels of the *Kaman* class, with
guided missile firepower, were under construction
for the Iranian navy. Their missile guidance
systems were produced by a Dutch subsidiary of
Philips, Hollandse Signaalapparaten BV, in
Hengelo.

Bois: But there is an important difference between this kind of work and the Thatcher and Reagan paintings. Until now, your work has involved a minimal transformation of the material. There was not an elaborate coding through art. I'm thinking of another Philips piece [*Everlasting Gratitude*, 1978], in which the transformation involved only the addition of the Philips logo.

Haacke: Actually, I didn't add anything. It is a facsimile of a Philips ad that appeared in a Teheran newspaper in 1975.

Bois: That's exactly my point. Before, the context was the signifier. Only a change of context was required for a change of meaning to take place. But now there seems to be a much greater mediation through art-historical codes.

Haacke: Only in part. Obviously, had I only made a photocopy of the newspaper ad, it would have remained at the level of documentation. The shift to another material and its inherited connotations changes it radically. Tapestry is something we know from art history. And the panel underneath the Philips tapestry—that's the way things are displayed in museums.

Crimp: If I understand what Yve-Alain is getting at, it is more that in the Thatcher work, for example, you are *creating* an image as opposed to taking an advertisement and making a facsimile of it and adding information.

Haacke: Some of the ads I invented myself, emulating contemporary corporate style. The quotations about what's good about art for business [*On Social Grease*, 1975] I took from books and newspapers. I made commemorative plaques of them so that they look as if they would be at home in the lobby of corporate headquarters or in the boardroom. Transplanting them from that imagined context into an art gallery can be devastating. That's where the context Yve-Alain is referring to plays an important role.

Bois: In a way, the Thatcher piece refers to a history of satirical portraiture, whereas when you transform a quotation from a business into an advertisement format, there is no mediation through art history. The context or the medium is immediate for the viewer because of this abrupt transformation. But in the Thatcher painting, the transformation is far more complicated.

Haacke: Maybe there are more layers. Indeed, I use context as a material.

Bois: Your earlier work reminds me of the strategies of the situationists, which involved the simple robbery of codes. For example, they released films whose soundtracks had been removed and replaced with others. They made a film that was simply a porno-Kung-Fu film from Hong Kong to which they added a soundtrack that was a shouting-match between Maoists and Trotskyists. The reason they were called situationists is because they changed strategies for each new situation, and because they invented situations, disruptive events within the apparently smooth flow of "reality." I have felt that your work was very much connected with that of the situationists, because they too wanted to show the connections between investment, advertising, and the culture industry. But with your paintings, there is no longer the same brilliant economy of means. What I found extraordinarily provocative in your works was their efficiency in revealing so much meaning through such slight transformation. But with a painting, you have to start from scratch and make the object.

Krauss: You're talking about the economy of means in the readymade principle; but if the readymade in this case is Victorian painting, then in a way it's the same economy. Was it difficult to do?

Haacke: Yes. I did a lot of painting in art school and for a while afterwards. But I never learned this kind of painting, with figures, perspective, and so forth. So I listened around, looked into painting manuals, and went to museums to study how such paintings are done. I have no delusions about having produced a masterwork in the traditional sense of the craft. I hope it is good enough for a passing grade. For my purpose, this is all it needs. But it was fascinating, and I had fun doing it. Another reason for making a painting was that I had been stamped a conceptualist, a photomontagist, that sort of thing. This was a way to mess up the labels. There were, in fact, a good number of people who thought that my portrait of Reagan was a photograph, or that I'd paid somebody to paint it for me. It was therefore very important that I painted it myself. Normally, I have no qualms about paying someone to execute something I can't do, as long as I can afford it.

Crimp: Again, it seems to me that it is a question of strategies, of devising a work which is appropriate to the problem at hand. That's why I was interested to ask about the differences between the Thatcher portrait and the *Isolation Box, Grenada.* It seems to me that one of the problems of making politically engaged art today is to devise something that won't simply be assimilated because it has accepted the conventional aesthetic codes. For example, if at this moment there is a great deal of attention paid to Leon Golub's work, attention that certainly was not given to him in the past, it's because he makes figurative paintings, and figurative painting has returned as a sanctioned style.

Haacke: Not exclusively.

Crimp: Perhaps not exclusively. But the generalization of Golub's imagery makes it possible for the Saatchis to collect his work, or for his paintings to be seen in the context of the Whitney Biennial, for example, and not to disturb the situation, because they fit into the predominant painting mode. So it seems that the problem one faces is to invent a style for each work which allows one to enter the art context but which is not lacking in specificity in such a way that the political thrust vanishes into the dominant aesthetic of the present.

Haacke: Concerning the Grenada piece, aside from the minimal art reference, I used dada strategies—the readymade, challenge to cultural norms, and so on. While it looks like a dumb box and nothing else, it is, I believe, perfectly within the range of twentieth-century art theory as we know it. But you are right, it was the political specificity that caused the amazing hoopla around the piece. I thought it would take more to get the *Wall Street Journal* to foam at the mouth and commit three factual errors in one editorial.

Crimp: Do you feel that you must always make a specific aesthetic choice, that you have to invent a form that can be understood in aesthetic as well as political terms?

Haacke: It seems to work that way.

Crimp: What I mean is, do you think this is necessary in a strategic sense, something that will continue to make it possible for you to function within the art context? I'm curious about this because it seems to me that artists of your generation were able to achieve a certain degree of success in the more liberal climate of the late '60s and early '70s, and having achieved that success, you can, to some extent, continue to function. But for an artist beginning right now, it would be much more difficult to enter the art scene as a politicized artist. Therefore the problem for such an artist would be to devise a strategy that would result in some visibility for his or her work.

Haacke: Yes, I already had a foot in the door when I moved towards politically engaged work. It got stepped on, but I didn't lose the foot. For young artists today it may be more difficult. They will have to invent their own tricks for survival. I can't tell them what to do.

Bois: I was interested to read in your recent interview [*Arts Magazine*, April 1984] that you thought that if your Guggenheim piece had been censored in 1975, rather than in 1971, it would not have had the same impact.

Haacke: I think I wouldn't have received as much support. As soon as the Vietnam War was over and the draft abolished, everyone relaxed and thought, "Well, now we can go home, the fight is over." People withdrew into their private worlds. This is the political vacuum which was then filled by the Right. We have to live with it today.

Bois: The way you define context as part of your material is also taking such political shifts into consideration. If you change strategies, it's presumably because the larger context has changed as well. Knowing your past work, I would never have expected the painting of Thatcher, but apparently you thought of it as a way of adapting to a different situation.

Haacke: I remember saying, some time in the '70s, that I might do a painting when the right context presented itself.

Krauss: You could feel painting coming on. . . . Speaking of painting, I was tremendously moved by the two works about painting, the Manet [*Manet-PROJECT '74*, 1974] and the Seurat [*Seurat's "Les Poseuses" (small version), 1888–1975*, 1975]. I find that the history of ownership of the Manet is very touching: the experience of the European avant-garde supported by well-to-do Jewish intellectual fellow-travelers, which then runs into the stone wall of Hermann Abs and the postwar German industrial machine. But what about the Seurat? Its history of ownership took place mainly in the U.S., after it was bought by De Zayas and then John Quinn. Did you intend that to be revealing of the formation of a taste for the avant-garde in this country?

Haacke: No. What triggered the Manet piece was the context of its exhibition. I was invited to participate in a show in Cologne which was to celebrate the hundredth anniversary of the Wallraf-Richartz Museum. For this occasion, the museum published a golden brochure with reproductions of paintings that had recently been acquired. Particular attention was given to Manet's *Bunch of Asparagus*. Aside from a reproduction of the painting, there was a photograph of Abs delivering a speech celebrating the painting, which was sitting on a studio easel behind him during the ceremonies of its donation. Of course, I knew who Abs was; any newspaper reader in postwar Germany is more or less aware of the role he played and still plays today.

Krauss: Played during the war?

Haacke: During the Nazi period and after.

Crimp: What is revealed about Hermann Abs in the piece is the perfectly smooth transition between his work for the Reich and his work for the reconstruction.

Haacke: So this was the hook on which I could, so to speak, hang the painting — a typical example of *l'art pour l'art*. Naturally, when I started I didn't know anything about the history of the painting's ownership. On the one hand, there is the telling role of Abs — as you say, the smooth transition from the Nazi period to postwar Germany—but of equal interest is the history of culture, how culture is always part of social and political history. That is fascinating—and moving. And then there is also the art historian's custom to trace the provenance of a work, usually restricted to the authentication of the object, which, of course, also establishes its monetary value. I took it a step further in my "tombstones," with the C.V.s of the painting's owners. The documented increase in value and the circumstances under which the painting changed hands serve as headlines for the panels. As you know, the museum officials did not care to have their patron's past displayed on the walls of the museum; the piece was censored.

As for the Seurat piece, I was interested in the phenomenon of art investment. In the course of the research I discovered that this painting by Seurat had been acquired by a newly formed international art investment company with the beautiful name Artemis. I then followed its history in the same way as I had with the Manet, and I discovered a number of interesting things. The painting leads you to anarchist circles in Paris and their friends in established galleries, and to wealthy Parisian art groupies. Eventually it is sold across the Atlantic, where there is the Stieglitz circle, John Quinn, representing the legal establishment of New York, and again socialites dabbling in art. During the Depression, the painting was picked up as a bargain by someone whose family fortune apparently was immune to the financial chaos of the time. He eventually offered it up on the auction block, because he needed money to add a period ballroom to his house on Rittenhouse Square in Philadelphia. Artemis is indirectly linked to the fortunes that were made in the Belgian colonies. By way of a company director, there is also a presence at the Museum of Modern Art. It is an incredible story. I have learned a lot about the underpinnings of high culture from it.

Krauss: Since part of your medium is research, it has a side aspect of calling attention to the support system for the art industry. One of the things that you point out about Peter Ludwig [*The Chocolate Master*, 1981], for example, is that he increases the value of his works by putting them in museums where research will be done on them, through which they gain a certain historical density, and thus their monetary value rises. So your research and the research typical of art history mirror each other. Of course, one of the things that happens with research is fortuitousness. Just as the history of the Jewish patrons of the avant-garde emerges from the Manet piece, another story, slightly more sinister, emerges from the Seurat work—the story of the very wealthy patrons of the American avant-garde, the Blisses, the Rockefellers. McIlhenny is an example, as was De Zayas, and John Quinn. In a way all these people were already proto-big-art-investment types. What I'm saying is that those seemed to me remarkably different cases.

Haacke: A footnote to your remark about Manet and the Jewish intellectual pa-

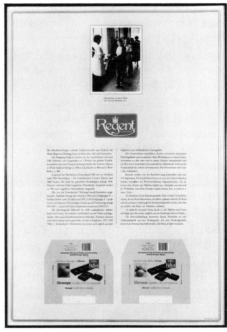

Hans Haacke. The Chocolate Master.
*1981. (1 of 7 diptychs.) First shown in
one-man exhibition, Paul Maenz Gallery,
Cologne, during* Westkunst, *a major survey
of art since 1939, May 1981.*

Translations:
*Left Panel: Art Objects on Permanent Loan Are Exempt
from Property Taxes.* Peter Ludwig was born in 1925
in Koblenz, the son of the industrialist Fritz
Ludwig (Cement Factory Ludwig) and
Mrs. Helene Ludwig (née Klöckner).

After his military service (1943–45), he
studied law and art history. In 1950 he received
a doctorate with a dissertation on "Picasso's Image
of Man as an Expression of his Generation's
Outlook on Life." The dissertation focuses on
relations between contemporary literature and
the work of Picasso. Historical events get little
attention.

In 1951 Peter Ludwig married a fellow
student, Irene Monheim, and joined Leonard
Monheim KG, Aachen, his father-in-law's
business. In 1952 he became managing partner,
in 1969, president, and in 1978, chairman of the
Leonard Monheim AG, Aachen.

Peter Ludwig is represented on the boards of
directors of Agrippina Versicherungs-Gesellschaft
and Waggonfabrik Uerdingen. He is the chairman
of the regional council of the Deutsche Bank AG

for the district Cologne-Aachen-Siegen.

Since the beginning of the 1950s, Peter and
Irene Ludwig have been collecting art. At first
they collected old art. Since 1966 they have been
concentrating on modern art: pop art,
photorealism, pattern painting, art from East
Germany, and neoexpressionism. Since 1972
Peter Ludwig has been an adjunct professor at the
University of Cologne and holds seminars in art
history at the Museum Ludwig.

Permanent loans of modern art are located
at the Museum Ludwig, Cologne, the Neue
Galerie-Sammlung Ludwig and the Suermondt-
Ludwig Museum in Aachen, the national galleries
in West and East Berlin, the Kunstmuseum Basel,
the Centre Pompidou in Paris, and the state
museums in Saarbrücken and Mainz. Medieval
works are housed at the Schnütgen Museum in
Cologne, the Couven Museum in Aachen, and the
Bavarian National Gallery. The Rautenstrauch-
Joest Museum in Cologne has pre-Columbian and
African objects, as well as works from Oceania.

In 1976 the Wallraf-Richartz Museum of
Cologne (now Museum Ludwig) received a
donation of pop art. The Suermondt Museum in
Aachen (now Suermondt-Ludwig Museum) was
given a collection of medieval art in 1977. A
collection of Greek and Roman art, which includes
permanent loans located in Kassel, Aachen, and

Würzburg, was donated to the Antikenmuseum Basel (now Antikenmuseum Basel and Museum Ludwig). In 1981 a collection of modern art was given to the "Austrian Ludwig Foundation for Art and Science."

Peter Ludwig is a member of the Acquisitions Committee of the State Gallery in Düsseldorf, of the International Council of the Museum of Modern Art, New York, and of the Advisory Council of the Museum of Contemporary Art, Los Angeles.

Right panel: Regent. Under the Regent label the Monheim Group distributes milk chocolate and assorted chocolates, mainly through the low-priced Aldi chain stores and vending machines.

The production takes place in Aachen, where the company employs 2500 people in two factories. It also has its administrative headquarters there. About 1300 employees work in the Saarlouis plant, some 400 in Quickborn, and approximately 800 in West Berlin.

The labor union Nahrung-Genuss-Gaststätten negotiated wages ranging from DM 6.02 (scale E = assembly-line work, under eighteen years) per hour to DM 12.30 (scale S = highly skilled work). According to the union contract, the lowest salary amounts to DM 1097. — per month, and the highest salary scale stipulates a minimum of DM 3214. —.

The overwhelming majority of the 2500 foreign workers are women. They come predominantly from Turkey and Yugoslavia. However, foreign workers are also hired by agents in Morocco, Tunisia, Spain, and Greece (price "per head": DM 1000. — in 1973). Another contingent of foreign workers crosses the border daily from nearby Belgium and Holland.

The company maintains hostels for its female foreign workers on its fenced-in factory compound in Aachen, as well as at other locations. Three or four women share a room (the building of hostels for foreign workers is subsidized by the Federal Labor Agency). The rent is automatically withheld from the worker's wages.

The company keeps a check on visitors to these hostels and, in fact, turns some away. The press office of the Aachen Diocese and the Caritas Association judged the living conditions as follows: "Since most of the women and girls can have social contacts only at the workplace and in the hostel, they are practically living in a ghetto."

Female foreign workers who give birth reportedly have to leave the hostel or they must find a foster home for the child at a price they can hardly afford. Another option would be to offer their child for adoption. "It should be no problem for a big company which employs so many girls and women to set up a day care center."

The personnel department retorted that Monheim is "a chocolate factory and not a kindergarten." It would be impossible to hire kindergarten teachers. The company is not a welfare agency.

Der Pralinenmeister (The Chocolate Master) is the promotional catchword with which Trumpf chocolate products are marketed. Trumpf is one of seven brand names of the West German Leonard Monheim AG, which maintains production facilities in Germany, Belgium, Canada, and the United States. Sales in 1982 amounted to approximately $660 million (46% outside Germany). Peter Ludwig is the chairman of the chocolate empire with headquarters in Aachen. Together with his wife Irene, he holds the majority of shares.

Through donations from their art collection, through hints about possible future donations, as well as through loans, they have gained considerable influence in a large number of European museums. When the city of Cologne accepted a donation of pop art in 1976, it agreed to build a museum for twentieth-century art, which was to be completed for the donor's sixtieth birthday and to be named after him. The construction thus far is estimated to have cost in excess of $100 million. The contract also stipulates that the Ludwigs must be consulted when curators and the director of the museum (all city civil servants) are appointed and that the donor is to be given a detailed report on the museum's operations twice a year.

The Neue Galerie-Sammlung Ludwig, a municipal museum in Aachen, regularly serves as the first public showcase and promoter of Ludwig's new acquisitions. Among the shows in Aachen have been presentations of photorealism, pattern painting, neoexpressionism, art from East Germany and the Soviet Union, and recently art from New York's Lower East Side.

A plan promoted by Ludwig to establish a German Ludwig Foundation, to be financed by the city of Cologne, the state of North Rhine-Westphalia, and the federal government and to hold unspecified works from the collector, was vigorously opposed by the entire museum profession. It was feared that the foundation, which was to organize exhibitions, purchase works, and administer a collection, would drain scarce funds from currently decentralized museum activities, and that, with Ludwig as chairman, it would exert an overpowering and dangerous influence on the entire art world. The plan collapsed when Ludwig angrily withdrew his proposal, although the public agencies were ready to finance the scheme.

trons. Some Jews thought my work was anti-Semitic. I had to insist that they read all the way through to the end of the story. Only then did they concede that I was not anti-Semitic. My insistent mention of the owners' religions reminded them of Nazi practices. Obviously, it was essential for my piece that Abs, who managed so well under the Nazis, appeared in the context of their victims.

Crimp: There is a specificity to all of your works in relation to where they are first shown, including even a language specificity—that is, if you make a work for a Dutch museum, the language will be Dutch. So I wonder about your reasons for showing works again in other places where they don't have that degree of specificity, or for selling them, which assumes they continue to have value according to the notion of the universal nature of the work of art. Take, for example, the Alcan work [*Voici Alcan*, 1983]. People living in Quebec know the public relations strategies of Alcan the way people living in the U.S. know the public relations strategies of, say, Mobil. But taken out of the context of Montreal, where your Alcan work was shown, the work's meaning is reduced to a kind of generality which compromises its value.

Hans Haacke. Voici Alcan. *1983.*
First shown in one-man exhibition, Galerie France Morin, Montreal, February 1983.

Translations:
Left panel: LUCIA DI LAMMERMOOR, produced by the Montreal Opera Company with funding from Alcan. Alcan's South African affiliate is the most important producer of aluminum and the only fabricator of aluminum sheet in South Africa. From a nonwhite work force of 2300, the company has trained eight skilled workers.
Center panel: STEPHEN BIKO, black leader, died from head wounds received during his detention by the South African police. Alcan's South African affiliate sells to the South African government semifinished products which can be used in police and military equipment. The company does not recognize the trade union of its black workers.
Right panel: NORMA, produced by the Montreal Opera Company with funding from Alcan. Alcan's South African affiliate has been designated a "key point industry" by the South African government. The company's black workers went on strike in 1981.

Alcan Aluminum Ltd., through its subsidiaries and affiliates, is one of the largest producers of aluminum ingot in the world and operates large aluminum fabrication facilities in some thirty-five countries. Throughout the world it has approximately 66,000 employees. It is the largest manufacturing employer in Quebec. The head office of the totally integrated multinational company is in Montreal. On December 31, 1981, 48% of the common shares were held by residents of Canada, 45% by residents of the U.S. The Chairman of the Board, Nathaniel V. Davis, a U.S. citizen, is reputed to control a considerable block of shares. While the largest single shareholder is the Caisse de Dépot et de Placement, which administers the pension funds of the province of Quebec, it is not represented on the Board of Directors.

Alcan has marketed aluminum in South Africa since 1930. In 1949 it started production at its plant in Pietermaritzburg near Durban. Major new investments occurred between 1969 and 1972. When Alcan sold a block of its shares in 1973 to the South African Huletts Corporation it stressed that this was not a political move. Duncan Campbell, a vice-president of Alcan, explained, "The decision was made purely for commercial and financial reasons. It doesn't mean we're pulling out of South Africa." The increase in South African ownership in Alcan's South African affiliate allows the company to borrow locally and

thereby to circumvent restrictions imposed by the South African government. The chairman of Huletts Aluminum was represented on the Defense Advisory Board of the prime minister of South Africa. In the early '70s Alcan was accused by church groups of having paid its black workers wages below the poverty datum line. In 1982 representatives of the United Church of Canada, the Canadian Conference of Catholic Bishops, the Redemptorist Fathers, and the Anglican Church of Canada filed a proxy resolution at Alcan's annual meeting requesting the board of directors to establish a South African review committee to "examine the company's activities in South Africa, including the sale of its products to the South African military, the status of Huletts' chairman on the Defense Advisory Board, and the storage of weapons on company premises, as well as the training of militia units of Huletts employees." Speaking for the board, Nathaniel Davis, its chairman, opposed the resolution. He explained that all security regulations of South Africa are binding on Alcan's affiliate. "While it is entirely normal and indeed inevitable," he said, that Alcan products are used by the South African military, Alcan was not permitted, under South African law, to disclose the nature of sales for military use.

Stephen Biko was the cofounder and central figure in the Black People's Convention, the South African black consciousness movement. He was arrested without charges by the Special Branch of the South African Police on August 18, 1977, and detained in Port Elizabeth. The police admitted having forced Biko to spend nineteen days naked in a cell before he was interrogated around the clock for fifty hours while shackled in handcuffs and leg irons. During his detention he suffered severe head injuries. In a semiconscious state he was taken naked in a Land Rover to a hospital in Pretoria, about fourteen hours away from Port Elizabeth. He died from his injuries on September 12.

Alcan has been sponsoring cultural programs, ranging from the Théâtre Alcan and the production of the popular TV series *Les Ploufs* to architectural conferences and an art collection in the company's headquarters. Cosponsorship of two productions of the Opéra de Montréal with Hydro-Quebec linked Alcan in a highly visible way with the provincially owned utility company. Cheap hydro-electric power is the main asset of Alcan's aluminum production in Quebec. In the recent past Alcan has been threatened with nationalization of the electric power generating plants it owns in the province.

"Voici Alcan" is the title of a glossy brochure which was published by Alcan in 1979.

Haacke: Specificity does limit a work somewhat to the occasion for which it is produced. But there is more to it. Let's look at the practical side. If I'm invited for a show, which doesn't happen every day, I cannot make ten or fifteen works for it, because it always takes me a long time to complete just one piece. So I have to show earlier works, too. As long as there is one new work, I think an intelligent viewer understands that the other works once played an equally topical role. In fact, they provide a useful foil for the new piece. So the situation is not quite as restrictive as it sounds in your question. Many of the corporate strategies referred to in my pieces are not unique to the company I happen to focus on. As you say, Alcan, as much as Mobil, uses culture to further the fortunes of its shareholders. Both have recognized that, in order to succeed, they have to shape public opinion. Both are multinationals. No matter where you go in the capitalist world, you stumble across the Mobil logo. Alcan happens to be overshadowed in the U.S. by Reynolds and Alcoa, which used to be a sister company, but Alcan is well known in Europe, in Africa, India, Brazil, and Australia. Even though *Voici Alcan* was made for an exhibition in Quebec, the Tate Gallery audience in London could relate to it, particularly because, due to the historical and close trade relations between the U.K. and South Africa, apartheid is a hot topic in London. Naturally, I had to provide translations of the French captions, as I always translate texts into the language of the country where the works are exhibited, if they were not done in that country's language. Also, the Ludwig piece got a lot of attention in London. As I suspected, viewers drew parallels to the Saatchis' attempts to gain a controlling foothold in public museums. And the public learned, through the Ludwig example, what that could entail. The Saatchis, like Ludwig, run a multinational company. Both have ambitions to influence cultural policies outside their home countries. And both are household names in the inner circles of the international art world.

There are other works that are specific and still have general relevance, such as the confrontation between Reagan and antinuclear protests across my red carpet. People in Kassel, as much as in London and New York, thought that this concerned them directly. So, in a way, many of my pieces are "multinational." There is, maybe, still another reason to exhibit works that do not retain their bite when transplanted from their original contexts. I think it is important to build up and display a record of this kind of work in order to enrich the critical discourse. I am often told that an array of examples demonstrates that socially engaged work need not be one-dimensional and tied to a single medium or a single approach. So the exhibition of the methodology can serve a useful purpose, too. As to selling the works, let's not forget that we are not living in an ideal society. One has to make adjustments to the world as it is. In order to reach a public, in order to insert one's ideas into the public discourse, one has to enter the institutions where this discourse takes place. Under present circumstances, that is easier if an exchange value comes along with use value. As you know, more often than not it is by way of commercial galleries that one eventually gets invited to shows that attract larger audiences. Documenta, museum exhibitions, and so forth rarely present works that have not been, at least marginally, sanctioned by the art trading posts. The same is true for the art press. I am sure we would not be discussing this here today if I had not shown in commercial galleries. You would probably not know my work, and it might be very different or totally nonexistent. One more practical point: my work, like that of many artists, is expensive to produce. We have an overhead. So an occasional sale helps to underwrite the production. But I am far from being able to live off the sale of my work, nor do I have the ambition to do so. That would make me dependent of the fortunes of the market. So, all in all, it is a messy situation, full of compromises. But I think one has to be pragmatic. Otherwise, one is completely paralyzed. If I had not made adjustments, by now I would be consumed by bitterness and nothing would have been achieved.

Bois: How did you present the Thatcher painting? just by itself? or with a long caption? Was there any information about the Saatchis, for example?

Haacke: No. That is unnecessary in London, because, since the Thatcher election campaign, Saatchi & Saatchi is a household name. Everybody knows them. What the general public doesn't know is their involvement with art. When I show the piece elsewhere, I will have to provide some background information.

Crimp: In addition to the information the painting contains, though, there is much more about the Saatchis' art manipulations that is not there—for example, the fact that Doris and Charles Saatchi bought works by Malcolm Morley after Charles Saatchi learned in a Whitechapel Gallery trustees meeting that the gallery planned to stage a Morley exhibition. Did you try to make such information available?

Haacke: It's not there for a simple reason. I just couldn't think of a good way to get this in without a breach of style and without overburdening the painting with text. However, the interviews generated by the Thatcher/Saatchi piece have allowed me to elaborate on such items. This fallout, at the secondary level is, in a way, part of the piece. By the way, I was told that not only in the case of the Morley purchases did Saatchi profit from inside information and positions within public institutions. And it was also the talk of the London art world that the Saatchis owned nine of the eleven paintings in the Schnabel show at the Tate Gallery. In any case, it might be worth stating precisely what is in the painting: that Charles Saatchi is a trustee of the Whitechapel Gallery is inscribed in the column behind Margaret Thatcher, as is the fact that he is on the Patrons of New Art Committee of the Tate Gallery. The Saatchi advertising accounts of venerable British art institutions, including the Tate, are listed together with other big accounts as book titles on the Victorian bookshelf. And you can read about the company's art investment in the papers on the little table and at Maggie's foot. From all of this one can draw conclusions about the connections between the Saatchis, the current British government, and the conflicts of interest that arise out of their positions on public institution boards and their private interests in the art world. By the way, I just heard that Charles Saatchi has resigned from the Board of the Whitechapel and from the Patrons Committee of the Tate. I have no idea whether that had anything to do with my *Taking Stock.*

Crimp: Can we talk more generally about the tenor of the current situation? Now that it has become clear that a concerted effort is being made to suppress politicized art activity, an effort on the part of neoconservatives both directly and indirectly involved in policy making at the government level, what strategies do you see as possible for artists?

Haacke: It is necessary to make clear that someone like Hilton Kramer is not disinterested, as he claims to be. When he talks about high art and good writing, and so forth, he follows a hidden political agenda, for which these terms serve as a smokescreen. I recently reread Kramer's "Turning Back the Clock: Art and Politics in 1984" [*New Criterion*, April 1984]. It is quite amazing how he presents himself there as the impartial arbiter, beyond ideology. Strategically, this makes a lot of sense. The moment one knows that, for all practical purposes, he is in charge of the art section in the neoconservative shadow cabinet, his credibility is shot. His denial that high art is as much affected by and influences its sociopolitical environment as other products of the consciousness industry is, of course, as much an ideological position as its opposite.

Krauss: One of the most astonishing things Kramer says in that article is that the very idea that art has a political basis is totalitarian, that it is a Stalinist position.

Haacke: He suggests, in barely veiled form, that art works, and the accompanying critical writing, that question current U.S. policies and the tenets of capitalism are leading us down the road to the Gulag. According to this point of view, several of the current presidential candidates and senators and congressmen are suspect. As you know, this is the classic neoconservative doctrine as propounded by its godfather, Irving Kristol, who calls Kramer a friend and was probably instrumental in securing funds for launching the *New Criterion.* It is not surprising to find the historian Gertrude Himmelfarb, who is Kristol's wife, among the regular contributors to Kramer's *Kampfblatt.* Kramer's publisher, Samuel Lipman, doubles as a music critic for Norman Podhoretz's *Commentary*, another neoconservative periodical. As a Reagan appointee, Lipman also pushes the "social agenda" on the National Council on the Arts, which governs the NEA. All of these nice people see one another regularly as members of the Committee for the Free World under the leadership of Midge Decter, Podhoretz's wife. And their activities are funded by the same group of conservative foundations.

Where the Left is sometimes unnecessarily vulnerable — and Kramer exploits this weakness wherever he can — is in its tendency to make mechanical attributions of ideology. In that respect, it mirrors the Right. We should recognize that things need to be evaluated within their respective historical contexts. Taken out of context, they are likely to be misread and can play the opposite role from that of their original settings. For instance, if my Grenada box were reproduced in *Soldier of Fortune*, it would have changed its meaning totally, even at this moment.

Krauss: That is also the best argument against idealist claims for art.

Haacke: Yes. Meaning and value are contingent. Threatening his readers with the specter of the "Stalinist ethos," Kramer is, in effect, out to undermine the First Amendment. This echoes arguments by Lawrence Silberman, his fellow member on the Committee for the Free World. Silberman urged his friends at a recent conference to shake off the fear of being charged with McCarthyism. Kramer's suggestion that arts activities which incorporate criticism of this administration's policies and question the sanctity of the capitalist system should not receive money from the NEA makes partisan politics a "new criterion" for government funding. Quite a remarkable position for someone who claims to fight for freedom! Under this formula, government agencies would be restructured to serve as censors and to perform the task of the reelection committee of whoever happens to occupy the White House. In Britain, like on the Continent, museums are public institutions, totally paid for by the taxpayers. There, even more than in the U.S., one can argue that they are constitutionally obliged to show art irrespective of its relative allegiance to a particular government's ideological coloration.

Crimp: But you can make the same argument for American museums, because in the end we as taxpayers support them. Museums are tax-exempt institutions; all donations to them are tax-deductible. The ordinary taxpayer has to make up for donations to museums, whether by private individuals or corporations.

Haacke: Absolutely. The same can be said of the *New Criterion*. The conservative foundations that fund Kramer's publication are tax-exempt. Consequently we taxpayers are chipping in to cover for their exemptions; and Kramer's sponsors were very generous. As start-up money, he got $375,000 from the Smith Richardson Foundation, $200,000 from the Carthage Foundation of Richard

Mellon Scaife, and $100,000 from the John M. Olin Foundation.* In the beginning, the editorial offices shared an address with the Olin Foundation on Park Avenue. According to the *New York Times*, the Scaife Family Charitable Trust also contributed, but because the Trust does not have to make its records public, we don't know how much came from there. Richard Mellon Scaife is known to be the bankroller of the New Right. Among numerous other organizations, he also helped the Heritage Foundation, which, by the way, advertises in the *New Criterion*. In the opinion of a writer in an article in the *Washington Post* on the Scaife funded groups, it is clear that their "collective effect has been to help shape the way Americans think about themselves and their nation's problems." This is also the goal of Hilton Kramer's publication. Any doubts about this are dispelled by his introduction to the first issue. A far cry from his claim to disinterestedness!

Crimp: One of the things that your work has revealed is the specific "interestedness" of corporate sponsorship of the arts. Not only do corporations use their support of culture to clean up their dirty images, but they are able to effect a self-censorship on the part of the institutions they fund. And within the contemporary art world, the force of the marketplace has become so total that one has the sense that the kind of interventionist work that you and a few other artists make can hardly make a dent in the monolithic monster that the art world has become.

Bois: In your text ["Museums, Managers of Consciousness," *Art in America*, February 1984], you make a distinction between the old-style dealer and the new, between the Castelli generation and the Mary Boone.

Haacke: In principle, I think, things were not all that different in the past. But now, with the arrival of multinational conglomerates, it has taken on a new dimension, both in terms of market and ideological control. Ten years ago, corporations did not have so much influence on the art world, nor could the gallery/museum/collector complex exert as much pressure internationally.

Crimp: Certainly one change took place after the recession of the early '70s, which precipitated a crisis for art institutions. That crisis was met by corporate support, so that now museums are virtually prisoners to corporations. Few museums can now do a major exhibition without corporate sponsorship, which drastically reduces the kind of exhibitions that can and will be organized.

---

*   These figures are a matter of public record, as all tax-exempt foundations must file financial reports, which are made available at the Foundation Center in New York.

Haacke: The younger people working in galleries and museums no longer know a different kind of art world. They assume that this is the natural state of affairs. And so they all become little entrepreneurs.

Krauss: What seems to me especially brilliant about your work is that you identified style as one of the enemies; you understood style as a category born of idealism, as a fundamentally nonhistorical way of thinking. And therefore your willingness to change depending upon the situation became a way of avoiding the situation that Douglas referred to before regarding Leon Golub, in which Golub's paintings can be recuperated and made chic once figuration has become fashionable. You seem to have been consistently aware of this problem.

Haacke: I'm not sure whether I was aware of it. Now, of course, I am. It helped that I was primarily what you might call job-oriented. Even in the '60s, I wanted things to function, in a very literal, physical sense. I carried this approach over to the more recent work. For example, in order to conduct a poll of the art public, one has to devise certain social situations, and for the presentation of the results, one has to use particular graphic means. Whether they happen to conform to the period style or not is irrelevant.

Krauss: But you have always had a certain parodic relationship to style and to formal aspects of the art of the time when you were working.

Crimp: It seems to have to do with utility, as you say. One of the problems with much recent political art is that artists seem to be trying to achieve a fixed style for political work. This is what I find somewhat problematic about Barbara Kruger's work, for example. There are various stylistic signifiers in her work—the black, white, red of Russian constructivism; the photomontage of Heartfield; the generic images of the '40s and '50s, a time when ideology seemed perhaps more naked in the photographic image. All of this tends to reduce the work to a generalized political statement, rather than one of real specificity. This may be one of the reasons that Barbara's work has been so well received, this and the fact that the work's graphic beauty is its most obvious characteristic.

Bois: There is a difference in your work, which is that you have always been wary of the possibility of recuperation, which was at the core of the thinking of the situationists also. So each time the possibility arose, you would just shift your position.

Haacke: Yes, one needs to be aware of the potential for recuperation. But this should not reach paranoid proportions. If I had been too concerned about co-optation, I would probably not have been able to do the things I've done. It can have a paralyzing effect. I saw this with some colleagues and students in the

'60s and '70s. They either stopped working altogether or went through tremendous personal crises, from which some eventually emerged as cynical entrepreneurs. In either case, that amounted to a capitulation to the powers that be. It takes stamina and shrewdness to survive in this mess.

Bois: One of the reasons I was always so impressed by what I've called your economy of means is that your work simply provides information, and information can't be obliterated. So even if the work is recuperated and transformed into a meaningless object in a museum, it still carries that information. This quality of immediacy, of simply adding information, is the way your work will always resist complete co-optation.

Crimp: Except insofar as one gets further away from what is referred to historically. After all, Heartfield can be recuperated now, even though his work includes real information.

Bois: But Heartfield is recuperated mainly on stylistic grounds, as a dadaist photomonteur; but I don't think Hans's work could be recuperated in this way.

Haacke: Nothing can escape eventual absorption. But you are right; the informational aspect probably makes it immune, at least for a while. We just have to reconcile ourselves to the historical contingency of things. Otherwise, we fall into the idealist trap of believing in universal meanings and values. But if the dissenting voices become the mainstream chorus, as it happened, for example, toward the end of the Vietnam War, what more can one hope for?

The Function of the Studio*

DANIEL BUREN

translated by THOMAS REPENSEK

Of all the frames, envelopes, and limits—usually not perceived and certainly never questioned—which enclose and constitute the work of art (picture frame, niche, pedestal, palace, church, gallery, museum, art history, economics, power, etc.), there is one rarely even mentioned today that remains of primary importance: *the artist's studio.* Less dispensable to the artist than either the gallery or the museum, it precedes both. Moreover, as we shall see, the museum and gallery on the one hand and the studio on the other are linked to form the foundation of the same edifice and the same system. To question one while leaving the other intact accomplishes nothing. Analysis of the art system must inevitably be carried on in terms of the studio as the *unique space* of production and the museum as the *unique space* of exposition. Both must be investigated as customs, the ossifying customs of art.

What is the function of the studio?

1. It is the place where the work originates.
2. It is generally a private place, an ivory tower perhaps.
3. It is a *stationary* place where *portable* objects are produced.

The importance of the studio should by now be apparent; it is the first frame, the first limit, upon which all subsequent frames/limits will depend.

What does it look like, physically, architecturally? The studio is not just any hideaway, any room.[1] Two specific types may be distinguished:

1. The European type, modelled upon the Parisian studio of the turn of the century. This type is usually rather large and is characterized

*   This essay, written in 1971 and published here for the first time, is one of three texts dealing with the art system. The others were "Function of the Museum," published first by the Museum of Modern Art, Oxford, and subsequently in *Artforum*, September 1973; and "Function of an Exhibition," *Studio International*, December 1973.

1.   I am well aware that, at least at the beginnings of and sometimes throughout their careers, all artists must be content with squalid hovels or ridiculously tiny rooms; but I am describing the studio as an archetype. Artists who maintain ramshackle work spaces despite their drawbacks are obviously artists for whom the *idea* of possessing a studio is a necessity. Thus they often dream of possessing a studio very similar to the archetype described here.

primarily by its high ceilings (a minimum of 4 meters). Sometimes there is a balcony, to increase the distance between viewer and work. The door allows large works to enter and to exit. Sculptor's studios are on the ground floor, painters' on the top floor. In the latter, the lighting is natural, usually diffused by windows oriented toward the north so as to receive the most even and subdued illumination.[2]

2. The American type,[3] of more recent origin. This type is rarely built according to specification, but, located as it is in reclaimed lofts, is generally much larger than its European counterpart, not necessarily higher, but longer and wider. Wall and floor space are abundant. Natural illumination plays a negligible role, since the studio is lit by electricity both night and day if necessary. There is thus equivalence between the products of these lofts and their placement on the walls and floors of modern museums, which are also illuminated day and night by electricity.

This second type of studio has influenced the European studio of today, whether it be in an old country barn or an abandoned urban warehouse. In both cases, the architectural relationship of studio and museum—one inspiring the other and vice versa—is apparent.[4] (We will not discuss those artists who transform part of their studios into exhibition spaces, nor those curators who conceive of the museum as a permanent studio.)

These are some of the studio's architectural characteristics; let us move on to what usually happens there. A private place, the studio is presided over by the artist-resident, since only that work which he desires and allows to leave his studio will do so. Nevertheless, other operations, indispensable to the functioning of galleries and museums, occur in this private place. For example, it is here that the art critic, the exhibition organizer, or the museum director or curator may calmly choose among the works presented by the artist those to be included in this or that exhibition, this or that collection, this or that gallery. The studio is thus a convenience for the organizer: he may compose his exhibition according to his own desire (and not that of the artist, although the artist is usually perfectly content to leave well enough alone, satisfied with the prospect of an exhibition).

2.   Thus the architect must pay more attention to the lighting, orientation, etc., of the studio than most artists ever pay to the exhibition of their works once they leave the studio!
3.   We are speaking of New York, since the United States, in its desire to rival and to supplant the long lamented "School of Paris," actually reproduced all its defects, including the insane centralization which, while ridiculous on the scale of France or even Europe, is absolutely grotesque on the scale of the United States, and certainly antithetical to the development of art.
4.   The American museum with its electric illumination may be contrasted with its European counterpart, usually illuminated by natural light thanks to a profusion of skylights. Some see these as opposites, when in fact they merely represent a stylistic difference between European and American production.

Thus chance is minimized, since the organizer has not only selected the artist in advance, but also selects the works he desires in the studio itself. The studio is thus also a boutique where we find ready-to-wear art.

Before a work of art is publicly exhibited in a museum or gallery, the studio is also the place to which critics and other specialists may be invited in the hope that their visits will release certain works from this, their purgatory, so that they may accede to a state of grace on public (museum/gallery) or private (collection) walls. Thus the studio is a place of multiple activities: production, storage, and finally, if all goes well, distribution. It is a kind of commercial depot.

Thus the first frame, the studio, proves to be a filter which allows the artist to select his work screened from public view, and curators and dealers to select in turn that work to be seen by others. Work produced in this way makes its passage, in order to exist, from one refuge to another. It should therefore be portable, manipulable if possible, by whoever (except the artist himself) assumes the responsibility of removing it from its place of origin to its place of promotion. A work produced in the studio must be seen, therefore, as an object subject to infinite manipulation. In order for this to occur, from the moment of its production the work must be isolated from the real world. All the same, it is in the studio and only in the studio that it is closest to its own reality, a reality from which it will continue to distance itself. It may become what even its creator had not anticipated, serving instead, as is usually the case, the greater profit of financial interests and the dominant ideology. It is therefore only in the studio that the work may be said to belong.

The work thus falls victim to a mortal paradox from which it cannot escape, since its purpose implies a progressive removal from its own reality, from its origin. If the work of art remains in the studio, however, it is the artist that risks death . . . from starvation.

The work is thus totally foreign to the world into which it is welcomed (museum, gallery, collection). This gives rise to the ever-widening gap between the work and its place (and not its *placement*), an abyss which, were it to become apparent, as sooner or later it must, would hurl the entire parade of art (art as we know it today and, 99% of the time, as it is made) into historical oblivion. This gap is tentatively bridged, however, by the system which makes acceptable to ourselves as public, artist, historian, and critic, the convention that establishes the museum and the gallery as inevitable neutral frames, the unique and definitive locales of art. Eternal realms for eternal art!

The work is made in a specific place which it cannot take into account. All the same, it is there that it was ordered, forged, and only there may it be truly said to be in place. The following contradiction becomes apparent: it is impossible by definition for a work to be seen in place; still, the place where we see it influences the work even more than the place in which it was made and from which it has been cast out. Thus when the work is in place, it does not take place (for the public), while it takes place (for the public) only when not in place, that is, in the museum.

Expelled from the ivory tower of its production, the work ends up in another, which, while foreign, only reinforces the sense of comfort the work acquires by taking shelter in a citadel which insures that it will survive its passage. The work thus passes—and it can only exist in this way, predestined as it is by the imprint of its place of origin—from one enclosed place/frame, the world of the artist, to another, even more closely confined: the world of art. The alignment of works on museum walls gives the impression of a cemetery: whatever they say, wherever they come from, whatever their meanings may be, this is where they all arrive in the end, where they are lost. This loss is relative, however, compared to the total oblivion of the work that never emerges from the studio!

Thus, the unspeakable compromise of the portable work.

The status of the work that reaches the museum is unclear: it is at the same time in place and in *a* place which is never its own. Moreover, the place for which the work is destined is not defined by the work, nor is the work specifically intended for a place which preexists it and is, for all practical purposes, unknown.

For the work to be in place without being specially placed, it must either be identical to all other existing works, and those works in turn identical among themselves, in which case the work (and all other identical works) may travel and be placed at will; or the frame (museum/gallery) that receives the original work and all other original—that is, fundamentally heterogenous—works must be adjustable, adapting itself to each work perfectly, to the millimeter.

From these two extremes, we can only deduce such extreme, idealizing, yet interesting formulations as:

1. all works of art are absolutely the same, wherever and whenever produced, by whatever artist. This would explain their identical arrangement in thousands of museums around the world, subject to the vagaries of curatorial fashion;

2. all works of art are absolutely different, and if their differences are respected and hence both implicitly and explicitly legible, every museum, every room in every museum, every wall and every square meter of every wall, is perfectly adapted to every work.

The symmetry of these propositions is only apparent. If we cannot conclude logically that all works of art are the same, we must acknowledge at least that they are all installed in the same manner, according to the prevailing taste of a particular time. If on the other hand we accept the uniqueness of each work of art, we must also admit that no museum ever totally adapts itself to the work; pretending to defend the uniqueness of the work, the museum paradoxically acts as if this did not exist and handles the work as it pleases.

To edify ourselves with two examples among many, the administration of the Jeu de Paume in Paris has set impressionist paintings into the museum's painted walls, which thereby directly frame the paintings. Eight thousand kilometers away at the Art Institute of Chicago paintings from the same period and by the same artists are exhibited in elaborate carved frames, like onions in a row.

Does this mean that the works in question are absolutely identical, and that they acquire their specific meanings only from the intelligence of those who present them? That the "frame" exists precisely to vary the absolute neutrality of all works of art? Or does it mean that the museum adapts itself to the specific meaning of each work? Yet we may ask how it is that, seventy years after being painted, certain canvases by Monet, for example, should be recessed into a salmon-colored wall in a building in Paris, while others in Chicago are encased in enormous frames and juxtaposed with other impressionist works.

If we reject numbers 1 and 2 proposed above, we are still faced with a third, more common alternative that presupposes a necessary relationship between the studio and the museum such as we know it today. Since the work which remains in the studio is a nonentity, if the work is to be made, not to mention seen in another place, in any place whatsoever, either of two conditions must apply; either

1. the definitive place of the work must be the work itself. This belief or philosophy is widely held in artistic circles, even though it dispenses with all analysis of the physical space in which the work is viewed, and consequently of the system, the dominant ideology, that controls it as much as the specific ideology of art. A reactionary theory if ever there was one: while feigning indifference to the system, it reinforces it, without even having to justify itself, since by definition (the definition advanced by this theory's proponents) the space of the museum has no relation to the space of the work; or

2. the artist, imagining the place where his work will come to grief, is led to conceive all possible situations of every work (which is quite impossible), or a typical space (this he does). The result is the predictable cubic space, uniformly lit, neutralized to the extreme, which characterizes the museum/gallery of today. This state of affairs consciously or unconsciously compels the artist to banalize his own work in order to make it conform to the banality of the space that receives it.

By producing for a stereotype, one ends up of course fabricating a stereotype, which explains the rampant academicism of contemporary work, dissimulated as it is behind apparent formal diversity.

In conclusion, I would like to substantiate my distrust of the studio and its simultaneously idealizing and ossifying function with two examples that have influenced me. The first is personal, the second, historical.

1. While still very young—I was seventeen at the time—I undertook a study of Provençal painting from Cézanne to Picasso with particular attention given to

the influence of geography on works of art. To accomplish my study, I not only traveled throughout southeastern France but also visited a large number of artists, from the youngest to the oldest, from the obscure to the famous. My visits afforded me the opportunity to view their work in the context of their studios. What struck me about all their work was first its diversity, then its quality and richness, especially the sense of reality, that is, the "truth," that it possessed, whoever the artist and whatever his reputation. This "reality/truth" existed not only in terms of the artist and his work space but also in relation to the environment, the landscape.

It was when I later visited, one after the other, the exhibitions of these artists that my enthusiasm began to fade, and in some cases disappear, as if the works I had seen were not these, nor even produced by the same hands. Torn from their context, their "environment," they had lost their meaning and died, to be reborn as forgeries. I did not immediately understand what had happened, nor why I felt so disillusioned. One thing was clear, however: deception. More than once I revisited certain artists, and each time the gap between studio and gallery widened, finally making it impossible for me to continue my visits to either. Although the reasons were unclear, something had irrevocably come to an end for me.

I later experienced the same disillusion with friends of my own generation, whose work possessed a "reality/truth" that was clearly much closer to me. The loss of the object, the idea that the context of the work corrupts the interest that the work provokes, as if some energy essential to its existence escapes as it passes through the studio door, occupied all my thoughts. This sense that the main point of the work is lost somewhere between its place of production and place of consumption forced me to consider the problem and the significance of the work's *place*. What I later came to realize was that it was the reality of the work, its "truth," its relationship to its creator and place of creation, that was irretrievably lost in this transfer. In the studio we generally find finished work, work in progress, abandoned work, sketches—a collection of visible evidence viewed simultaneously that allows an understanding of process; it is this aspect of the work that is extinguished by the museum's desire to "install." Hasn't the term *installation* come to replace *exhibition*? In fact, isn't what is installed close to being established?

2. The only artist who has always seemed to me to exhibit real intelligence in his dealings with the museum system and its consequences, and who moreover sought to oppose it by not permitting his works to be fixed or even arranged according to the whim of some departmental curator, is Constantin Brancusi. By disposing of a large part of his work with the stipulation that it be preserved in the studio where it was produced, Brancusi thwarted any attempt to disperse his work, frustrated speculative ventures, and afforded every visitor the same perspective as himself at the moment of creation. He is the only artist who, in order to preserve the relationship between the work and its place of production, dared to present his work in the very place where it first saw light, thereby short-circuiting the

museum's desire to classify, to embellish, and to select. The work is seen, for better or worse, as it was conceived. Thus, Brancusi is also the only artist to preserve what the museum goes to great lengths to conceal: the banality of the work.

It might also be said—but this requires a lengthy study of its own—that the way in which the work is anchored in the studio has nothing whatsoever to do with the "anchorage" to which the museum submits every work it exhibits. Brancusi also demonstrates that the so-called purity of his works is no less beautiful or interesting when seen amidst the clutter of the studio—various tools; other works, some of them incomplete, others complete—than it is in the immaculate space of the sterilized museum.[5]

The art of yesterday and today is not only marked by the studio as an essential, often unique, place of production; it proceeds from it. All my work proceeds from its extinction.

---

5.   Had Brancusi's studio remained in the Impasse Ronsin, or even in the artist's house (even if removed to another location), Brancusi's argument would only have been strengthened. (This text was written in 1971 and refers to the reconstruction of Brancusi's studio in the Museum of Modern Art, Paris. Since then, the main buildings have been reconstructed in front of the Centre Baubourg, which renders the above observation obsolete—author's note.)

LOUISE LAWLER

Statue before painting, *Perseus with the Head of Medusa,* by Canova.

Rodin.

Arranged by Janelle Reiring.

Arranged by Claire Vincent at the Metropolitan Museum of Art, New York City.

Arranged by Carl Lobell at Weil, Gotshal, and Manges.

Arranged by Donald Marron, Susan Brundage, Cheryl Bishop at Paine Webber, Inc.

Peace by Pierre Puvis de Chavannes over Sheraton roll-top desk at the Hillstead Museum, Farmington, Connecticut.

Reception area.

The Hillstead Museum, Farmington, Connecticut, was formerly the home of Mr. and Mrs. Alfred Atmore Pope and their daughter, Theodate. It was designed for them by Stanford White, with the acknowledged assistance of Theodate, in 1899.

Mr. Pope was one of the first American collectors of European impressionism. He became acquainted with some of the artists and their work through Mary Cassatt, a friend of the family, and he purchased many paintings from the Parisian dealer, Durand Ruel. He also collected sculpture, prints, Ming vases, Majolica plates, Wedgwood services, but without exceeding his need to furnish his home.

Theodate Pope Riddle was the last resident of Hillstead. In her will she directed the executors to "maintain [it] the same forever as a museum in which the past would remain untouched and inviolate."

Photographs by August Sander, one by Ansel Adams, sculpture by Robert Smithson, desk light by Ernesto Gismondi; arranged by Barbara and Eugene Schwartz.

Sixteen etchings by Whistler, two by Seymour Hayden, three early impressions of engravings by Dürer, three scenes in Paris by Charles Meryon, and four views of Rome by Piranesi are hung in this entrance hall.

Vitrine.

Work by Allan McCollum arranged by the artist at the home of Mr. and Mrs. Robert Kaye, Rumford, New Jersey; art consultant, Jack Boulton.

Wright, Meier, Klein.

Roche, Dinkeloo, & Assoc., Metropolitan Museum of Art, André Meyer Gallery.

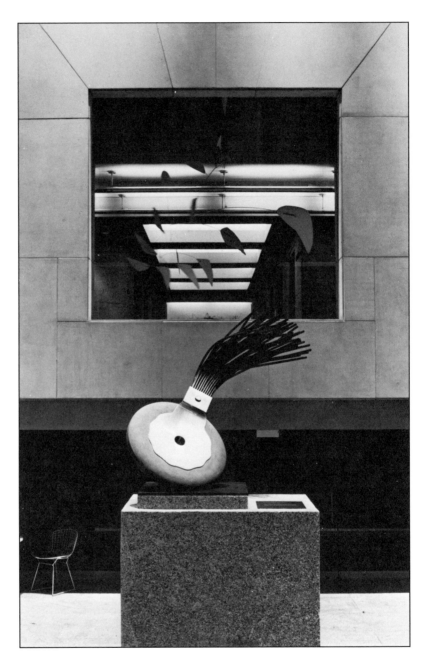

Calder, Franzen, Oldenburg.

The Art of Exhibition*

DOUGLAS CRIMP

> . . . *documenta 7.* Not a bad name because it suggests an attractive
> tradition of taste and discrimination. It is no doubt an honorable
> name. Therefore it may be followed by a subtitle as in those novels
> of long ago: *In which our heroes after a long and strenuous voyage through
> sinister valleys and dark forests finally arrive in the English Garden, and at the
> gate of a splendid palace.*[1]

So writes Artistic Director Rudi Fuchs in his introduction to the catalogue for
the Documenta exhibition of 1982. What one actually encountered, however,
at the gate of the splendid palace, the Museum Fridericianum in Kassel, were
not heroes at all, but rather a junky-looking construction workers' trailer displaying various objects for sale. The status of these things — whether works of
art or merely souvenirs — was not immediately apparent. Among the T-shirts,
multiples, and other wares to be found here and at other stands throughout the
English garden were sheets of stationery whose upper and lower margins were
printed with statements set in small typeface. At the top of one sheet, for example, one could read the following:

> If it is not met with respectful seriousness, the work of art will hardly
> or not at all be able to stand its ground in the environment: the world
> around it, customs and architecture, politics and cooking — they all
> have become hard and brutal. In constant noise one can easily miss
> hearing the soft sounds of Apollo's lyre. Art is gentle and discreet,
> she aims for depth and passion, clarity and warmth.

On the lower margin of the same sheet the source of this astonishing claim was
given: "Excerpts from a letter to the participating artists by the Director of
Documenta 7, R. H. Fuchs, edited and published by Louise Lawler."

---

* An earlier version of this essay was presented as a lecture in a series entitled "Situation de
l'art contemporain à travers les grandes manifestations internationales," at the Musée National
d'Art Moderne, Paris, on May 7, 1984.
1. Rudi Fuchs, "Introduction," in *Documenta 7*, Kassel, 1982, vol. 1, p. xv.

Not officially invited to participate in Documenta, Lawler was not a recipient of the letter from which her stationery quotes. She was, however, represented in the show in this marginal way through a subterfuge. Jenny Holzer, who had been invited, presented as part of her contribution a collaborative venture with Fashion Moda, the alternative gallery situated in the South Bronx. That is to say, Fashion Moda is located in the very heart of an environment that is hard and brutal indeed, the most notorious black and Hispanic slum in the United States; and it is there, not to stand its ground against its environment, but rather to engage with it constructively.

Though Lawler had not received Fuchs's letter, she had been interested to read it, as many of us had, for it had become the focus of art-world gossip about the forthcoming major contemporary art event. With its absurd title—"Documenta 7: A Story"—and its equally absurd opening sentence—"How can I describe the exhibition to you: the exhibition which floats in my mind like a star?" —this letter revealed Fuchs's fundamentally contradictory perspective. On the one hand, he claimed that he would restore to art its precious autonomy, while on the other hand, he made no secret his desire to manipulate the individual works of art in conformity with his inflated self-image as the master artist of the exhibition. Whether the artists intended it or not, Fuchs would insure that their works would in no way reflect upon their environment: the world around them, customs and architecture, politics and cooking.

I, too, had read the letter, circulated in the spring of 1982, and it made me curious to attend the press conference Fuchs was to give at Goethe House in New York as part of the promotional campaign for this most costly of international art exhibitions. I fully expected Fuchs to confirm there the rumors that his exhibition would constitute a complete return to conventional modes of painting and sculpture, thereby breaking with the earlier Documentas' inclusion of experimental work in other mediums such as video and performance, as well as of practices that openly criticized institutionalized forms of both production and reception. This, of course, Fuchs did, as he showed slide after slide of paintings and sculptures, mostly in the neoexpressionist style that had already come to dominate the art market in New York and elsewhere in the Western world. What I had not expected from the press conference, though, was that at least half of the artistic director's presentation would be not about art works but about work in progress to ready the exhibition spaces for the installation. "I feel," he said, "that the time one can show contemporary art in makeshift spaces, converted factories and so on, is over. Art is a noble achievement and it should be handled with dignity and respect. Therefore we have finally built real walls."[2]

---

2.   Quoted in Coosje van Bruggen, "In the Mist Things Appear Larger," in *Documenta 7*, vol. II, p. ix.

And it was these walls, together with the lighting design and other details of museological endeavor, that he took great pains to present to his listeners.[3]

In his preface to Documenta's catalogue Fuchs succinctly summarized his art of exhibition. "We practice this wonderful craft," he wrote, "we construct an exhibition after having made rooms for this exhibition. In the meantime artists attempt to do their best, as it should be."[4] Everything as it should be: the artistic director builds his walls—permanent now, since there will be no return to that time when temporary structures would suffice or even be necessary to meet the unconventional demands of unconventional art practices—and in the meantime the artists apply themselves to the creation of works of art appropriate to this hallowed setting.

No wonder, then, that the status of those objects in the Fashion Moda pavilions remains in question. Louise Lawler's stationery, Jenny Holzer's posters of streetwise provocations, the knickknacks produced by members of Colab, Christy Rupp's T-shirts silkscreened with the image of an attacking rat—whatever else these things may be, they are certainly not appropriate to the sacred precincts of art as reaffirmed by Rudi Fuchs. For these are deliberately marginal practices, works manufactured cheap and sold cheap, quite unlike the paintings and sculptures within the museum buildings, whose real but disguised condition is that of the international market for art, dominated increasingly by corporate speculation. Moreover, the Fashion Moda works intentionally confront, rather than deny, dissemble, or mystify the social bases of their production and circulation. Take, for example, Christy Rupp's rat image.

Rupp and I live in the same building in lower Manhattan, just a few blocks south of City Hall, where the most reactionary mayor in New York's recent history delivers the city over to powerful real estate developers while city services decline and our poorer citizens are further marginalized. The combination of the Reagan administration's cuts in federal programs to aid the poor and New York's cynically manipulated housing shortage has resulted in a reported 30,000 homeless people now living on the streets of the city.[5] The hard and

---

3. At one point, Fuchs showed a slide of a patch of white paint on a portion of a newly constructed wall. This, he said, was the color of whitewash he had chosen. The audience laughed, assuming that Fuchs was indulging in a moment of self-parody, but Fuchs became indignant at the laughter. For far too long, he argued, art has been subjected to the affront of walls carelessly covered with acrylic-base paints. A chemical concoction, acrylic paint evidently represented for Fuchs yet another aspect of that unnatural environment which in its hardness and brutality conspired to drown out the soft sound of Apollo's lyre.

4. Rudi Fuchs, "Forward," in *Documenta 7*, vol. II, p. vii.

5. The U.S. Department of Housing and Urban Development reported on May 1, 1984, that there were an estimated 28,000–30,000 homeless people in New York City. A spokesman for the Community of Creative Nonviolence, a private nonprofit group that works with the homeless, said, however, that the official government statistics were "utterly ridiculous," that the Reagan administration was vastly underestimating the scope of the problem for political reasons. Estimates of the number of homeless nationwide by nongovernment antipoverty groups are often ten

Christy Rupp. Rat Patrol. *1979.*

brutal conditions of these people's lives can be imagined by observing the few of them who spend every evening in the alleyway behind our building competing with rats for the garbage left there by McDonald's and Burger King. Mayor Koch was publicly embarrassed in the spring of 1979, when the media reported the story of a neighborhood office worker attacked by these rats as she left work. Such an event would certainly have been routine had it happened in one of the city's ghetto districts, but in this case the Health Department was called in, and their findings were rather sensational: the vacant lot adjoining the alleyway contained thirty-two tons of garbage and was home to an estimated 4,000 rodents.[6] But they also found something else, even more difficult to explain to the public. Pasted to the temporary wall barricading the vacant lot from the street were pictures of a huge, sinister attacking rat, reproductions of a photograph from

times the government's figures of 250,000–350,000. Cf. Robert Pear, "Homeless in U.S. Put at 250,000, Far Less Than Previous Estimates," *New York Times*, May 2, 1984, p. A1.
6.   See Andy Soltis and Chris Oliver, "Super Rats: They Never Say Die," *New York Post*, May 12, 1979, p. 6, in which an official of the Health Department's Pest Control Bureau is reported as saying, "You go into the South Bronx and this happens on an ongoing basis. It was highlighted here because of the woman who was bitten."

the Health Department's own files. And these pictures were not only there but everywhere else in the vicinity where the city's usual accumulations of rotting garbage might indeed attract rats. It was as if a Health Department guerrilla action had posted advance warnings of the incident that had now taken place. The coincidence of scandalous event and the pictures which seemed to foretell it was an aspect of the story the news media were eager to report, and so they tracked down the guerrilla herself, Christy Rupp. But who was this woman? Interviewed on TV, she clearly knew a considerable amount about the city's rat problems, more even than the bureaucrats from the Health Department. Why, then, did she call herself an artist? and why did she refer to those ugly pictures as her art? Surely a photograph of a rat borrowed from Health Department files and mechanically reproduced is not a creation of artistic imagination; it has no claim to universality; it would be unthinkable to see the picture on exhibition in a museum.

But that, of course, is part of its point. Rupp's *Rat Patrol*, as she called her activity, is one of those art practices, now fairly numerous, that makes no concessions to the institutions of exhibition, even deliberately confounds them. As a result, it cannot be understood by most people as art, for it is only the exhibition institutions that can, at this historical juncture, fully legitimate any practice as art. Our understanding of this fact has been intensified recently because, since the late '60s, it has been the subject of much of the most important work by artists themselves. And it is precisely this understanding that Rudi Fuchs sought to suppress through his exhibition strategies and rhetoric at Documenta 7. One can only assume that his attempts were fully calculated, since Fuchs, in his capacity as director of the van Abbemuseum in Eindhoven, had been one of the foremost proponents of art which revealed or criticized the conditions imposed on art by its modes of exhibition, or of art which broke with the notion of aesthetic autonomy by directly confronting social reality.

Needless to say, Fuchs was not entirely successful at Documenta in imposing his new view of art as merely gentle and discreet, standing its ground against the environment. Because he worked with four other curators, he was forced to include a number of artists who took it as their responsibility to unmask his art of exhibition. Thus at the approach to the Fridericianum in Kassel one was confronted with various disruptions of the decorum that Fuchs had wanted to insure. I have already mentioned the Fashion Moda stand, which the curator in charge of the American selection, Coosje van Bruggen, had insisted on accepting. Even more provocative perhaps was the work of Daniel Buren. This consisted of pennants of Buren's familiar striped material strung from high poles, which also carried loud speakers. From these were broadcast fragments of musical compositions in chronological order by composers ranging from Lully through Mozart and Beethoven to Verdi and Scott Joplin. The music was periodically interrupted by recitations of color names in fourteen languages. Buren thereby created at the entrance to the exhibition an atmo-

Daniel Buren. Les Guirlandes *at Documenta 7, with Johann August Nahl's* Monument to Frederick II *in foreground. (Photo-souvenir: Daniel Buren.)*

sphere that the critic Benjamin Buchloh described as "appropriate to a fun fair or the grand opening of a gas station."[7] Such an atmosphere is considerably more suitable to the self-promotion of the state of Hesse and the festive gathering of the international art community than would have been Fuchs's wished-for air of reverence. Moreover, Buren simultaneously parodied the show's simplistic notions of history (one volume of the catalogue, for example, arranged the entrants according to their birth dates) and of nationalism, a category newly revived to foster stronger market competition.

Inside the three museum buildings, the Fridericianum, the Orangerie, and the Neue Galerie, Fuchs willfully distributed works by any one artist throughout the galleries so that they would appear in perversely unlikely juxtaposition with works by various other artists. The result was to deny difference, dissemble meaning, and reduce everything to a potpourri of random style, although Fuchs liked to speak of this strategy as effecting dialogues between artists. The genuine significance of these groupings, however, was more accurately captured in Lawrence Wiener's phrase printed on the Fridericianum's frieze: "Viele farbige Dinge nebeneinander angeordnet bilden eine Reihe vieler farbiger Dinge." Translated for the wrapper which bound together the two hefty volume's of the show's catalogue, the statement reads in English: "Many colored objects placed side by side to form a row of many colored objects."

Within the precincts of the museum buildings it was considerably more difficult for artists to force an awareness of Fuchs's tactics. One work, however, strongly countered Fuchs's program to override art's involvement with significant public issues. This was Hans Haacke's *Oelgemaelde, Hommage à Marcel Broodthaers*, relegated to the Neue Galerie rather than given pride of place in the Fridericianum. Haacke's work consisted of a confrontation: on one wall was a meticulously painted oil portrait of President Reagan; on the opposite wall was a gigantic photomural of a peace demonstration. The portrait was surrounded by the museological devices traditionally used to enhance the art work's aura, to designate the work of art as separate, apart, inhabiting a world unto itself, in conformity with Fuchs's doctrine. Contained within its gold frame, illuminated in its own special glow by a small picture lamp, provided with a discreet wall label, protected by a velvet rope strung between two stanchions, the painting was kept, like the *Mona Lisa*, a safe distance from the admiring viewer. With this parodying of museological paraphernalia Haacke paid tribute to Broodthaers's museum fictions of the early '70s while simultaneously mocking Fuchs's desire to elevate and safeguard his masterpieces. From this little shrine of high art a red carpet led underfoot to the facing wall, where Haacke installed an en-

---

7.   Benjamin H. D. Buchloh, "Documenta 7: A Dictionary of Received Ideas," *October*, no. 22 (Fall 1982), p. 112. I am indebted to Buchloh's review for clarification of many of the issues of Documenta 7 discussed in this essay.

Hans Haacke. Oelgemaelde, Hommage à Marcel Broodthaers. *1982.*

larged photograph taken in Bonn just one week before the official opening of Documenta. This photo was shot at a demonstration, the largest held thus far in postwar Germany, to protest Reagan's arrival to lobby support in the Bundestag for deployment of American cruise and Pershing 2 missiles on German soil.

In its high degree of specificity, Haacke's work was able to do what the vast majority of paintings and sculptures in the exhibition could not. Not only did Haacke insert into this context a reminder of the real historical conditions which we now face, but he also reflected upon the relevant terms of current aesthetic debate. If not for Haacke's work, one would hardly have known that photography has recently become an important medium for artists attempting to resist the hegemony of the traditional beaux arts, that Walter Benjamin's classic essay on mechanical reproduction has become central to critical theories of contemporary visual culture. Nor would one have understood that this debate also encompasses a critique of the museum institution in its function of preserving the auratic status of art that was Benjamin's main target. All we learn of

this from Fuchs is that "our culture suffers from an illusion of the media," and that this is something to be overcome by the exhibition enterprise.[8]

But what is more important than these debates, Haacke's *Oelgemaelde* suggested to the viewer that the relevant history of the town of Kassel was nearer to us than the one to which Documenta's artistic director constantly made reference. Fuchs sought to locate his Documenta within the grand tradition of the eighteenth century, when the aristocrats of Hesse-Kassel built their splendid palace, one of the first museum buildings in Europe. The official postcard of Documenta 7 was a photograph of the neoclassical statue of the Landgrave Frederick II by Johann August Nahl, which stands in front of the Museum Fridericianum; in addition, each volume of the catalogue carries on its cover a photograph of one of the allegorical sculptures adorning the pediment of the museum, not surprisingly those representing the old beaux-arts categories of painting and sculpture.

8.   Fuchs, "Forward," p. vii.

Kassel has, however, as I have stated, a recent history that is far more relevant. If Fuchs had to build walls within the museum it was because the original ones had been destroyed by the Allied bombings of World War II. Kassel, once at the very center of Germany, was one of Hitler's strategic ammunition depots. But Kassel no longer lies at the center of Germany; it is now only a few miles from the border of that other Germany to the east. Haacke's work, then, might have evoked for Documenta's visitors not Kassel's glorious eighteenth-century past, but its precarious present, at a time when the tensions of the cold war have been dangerously escalated once again. Perhaps it is this hard and brutal fact above all that Fuchs would have us forget as we are lulled by the soft sounds of Apollo's lyre.

*

Fuchs's desire to reaffirm the autonomy of art against the incursion of urgent historical facts was far more thoroughly realized in another international exhibition staged later in 1982, also in Germany. Appropriately titling their show *Zeitgeist*, the organizers, Norman Rosenthal and Christos Joachimides, were much bolder than Fuchs in their denial of the realities of the political climate and in their exclusion of any art that might unsettle the mystificatory tendencies which they presented as exemplary of the spirit of the times. Once again the exhibition was mounted in a historic museum building, the Kunstgewerbemuseum in Berlin, now known as the Martin-Gropius-Bau, after its architect. Joachimides made reference to this building's history in the closing paragraph of his catalogue introduction:

> When Mario Merz came to Berlin a number of months ago and visited the Martin Gropius Building to discuss his contribution to the exhibition, he quite spontaneously remarked, "Che bell Palazzo!" [Here we are, again, in front of a splendid palace.] On another occasion, Norman Rosenthal spoke of the tension between the interior and the exterior, between the reality and the memory that the building evokes. Outside, an environment of horror, made up of the German past and present. Inside, the triumph of autonomy, the architectural "Gesamtkunstwerk" which in masterly and sovereign manner banishes reality from the building by creating its own. Even the wounds which reality has inflicted on it are part of its beauty. That is also — ZEITGEIST: the place, *this* place, *these* artists, at *this* moment. For us the question is how does an autonomous work of art relate to the equally autonomous architecture and to the sum of memories which are present today.[9]

9.   Christos Joachimides, "Achilles and Hector before the Walls of Troy," in *Zeitgeist*, New York, Braziller, 1983, p. 10.

Kunstgewerbemuseum, Berlin, c. 1946.

How indeed? But first, we might be a bit more specific about what those memories are and what that present reality is. The Martin-Gropius-Bau lay virtually in complete ruin after the war, since it was in direct proximity to the Gestapo headquarters, the SS office building, Ernst Sagebiel's Ministry of Aviation, and Albert Speer's Reichs Chancellery. Defended to the last, this administrative center of Nazi power came under the heaviest bombing and shelling of any area of the city. Throughout the period of reconstruction, the Kunstgewerbemuseum remained a neglected pile of rubble; not until the late '70s was restoration undertaken. Even now, much of the ornamentation is irreparably damaged. But perhaps even more relevant than these traces of shelling is the fact that one must enter the building from the rear, since the former front stands only a few yards from the Berlin Wall. This presumably is the environment of horror to which Rosenthal referred as he mused on the triumph of autonomy of this building and the works of art to be contained within it.

Had Rosenthal and Joachimides invited artists such as Hans Haacke to participate in *Zeitgeist*, their rhetorical question might have received some answers of real importance.[10] For it is part of the stated program of Haacke's

10.   This portion of the present essay was written prior to Haacke's work for the Neue Gesell-

enterprise, as well as that of other artists working with a similar approach, that the context of the exhibition dictates the nature of the intervention he will make. As Haacke put it, "The context in which a work is exhibited for the first time is a material for me like canvas and paint." This means, of course, that Haacke's work must relinquish its claim to autonomy and universality, as well as its status as an easily marketable commodity. And it is these latter aspects of art to which Rosenthal and Joachimides have shown themselves to be primarily devoted. Nevertheless, the idea of commissioning works specifically for the context of *Zeitgeist* did not entirely elude this pair. In order to give an impressive sense of uniformity to the grand atrium space of the museum, they asked eight of the participating artists each to paint especially for the exhibition four paintings with the dimensions of three by four meters. The artists dutifully complied, adjusting the size and format of their products to meet the demands of exhibition, just as a dress designer might alter the shape of one of his creations to suit the needs of an unusually portly client. The young American painter David Salle even took the daring step of foregoing his usual cryptic poetic titles and labeled his tailor-made creations *Zeitgeist Painting Nr. 1*, *Zeitgeist Painting Nr. 2*, *Zeitgeist Painting Nr. 3*, and *Zeitgeist Painting Nr. 4*. The prospective collectors would no doubt be very pleased to have acquired works thus stamped with the imprimatur of a prestigious international show.

For a description of the *zeitgeistig* art works, I will rely upon one of the American contributors to the catalogue, the eminent art historian Robert Rosenblum, whose agility in adapting to any new aesthetic fashion makes him especially qualified to speak for this one:

> The ivory towers where artists of an earlier decade painstakingly calculated hairbreadth geometries, semiotic theories, and various visual and intellectual purities have been invaded by an international army of new artists who want to shake everything up with their self-consciously bad manners. Everywhere, a sense of liberating eruption can be felt, as if a turbulent world of myths, of memory, of molten, ragged shapes and hues had been released from beneath the repres-

---

schaft für Bildende Kunst in West Berlin, a work which fully confirms my speculation. *Broadness and Diversity of the Ludwig Brigade*, presented elsewhere in this issue of *October*, does indeed use as its starting point the proximity of the Berlin Wall to the place of exhibition, the Künstlerhaus Bethanien. And it therefore takes as its subject German-German relations, relations which have again been much in the news due to the proposed visit of Erich Honecker to Bonn this fall, and its postponement under Soviet pressure.

One more example of the way in which Rosenthal and Joachimides might have received real answers to their question: Last winter in the *Art & Ideology* exhibition at the New Museum of Contemporary Art in New York, Allan Sekula showed *Sketch for a Geography Lesson*, a work consisting of photographs and accompanying text that, again, takes the effects of the renewal of cold war tensions in Germany as its subject, although in a manner quite different from Haacke's *Oelgemaelde*.

sive restraints of the intellect which reigned over the most potent art of the last decade. The objective territory of formal lucidity, of the impersonal, static surfaces of photographic imagery has been toppled by earthquakes which seem both personal and collective, outbursts of the artists' own fantasies culled, however, from the most public range of experience, whether from mythology, history, or the vast inventory of earlier works of art that constantly assail the contemporary eye and mind in every conceivable place, from magazines and postcards to subway stations and middle-class interiors.

From this Pandora's Box, a never-ending stream of legendary creatures is emerging, populating these new canvases in the most unexpected ways. This attack upon the traditional iconoclasm of abstract art and the empirical assumptions of photographic imagery has aggressively absorbed the wildest range of beings taken from the Bible, from comic strips, from historical legend, from literary pantheons, from classical lore. An anthology of works by the artists represented here might include images, for example, not only of Jesus (Fetting), Pegasus (LeBrun), Brünnhilde (Kiefer), Orion (Garouste), Prometheus (Lüpertz), Victor Hugo (Schnabel), and Picasso (Borofsky), but also of Bugs Bunny (Salle), and Lucky Luke (Polke). The result is a visual Tower of Babel that mixes its cultures — high and low, contemporary and prehistoric, classical and Christian, legendary and historical — with an exuberant irreverence that mirrors closely the confusing glut of encyclopedic data that fills our shared visual environment and provides us with the material of dreams and art.[11]

One could spend some time analyzing a text in which ivory towers are invaded by international armies, who then proceed to build, still within the ivory tower, a Tower of Babel; or again, a prose style whose vagaries of terminology can slide from "historical legend" to the binary opposition "legendary" versus "historical." It is, in any case, a peculiar view of history that sees one decade as ruled by an intellect that is called repressive and the next as liberated by an eruption of self-consciously bad manners. But this history is, after all, only *art* history, an institutionalized discipline of which Rosenblum is a reigning master. For him, the word *history* might well be replaced by *Zeitgeist*, for he can comprehend nothing more than changes in sensibility and style. Thus the art-historical shift that is chronicled by the exhibition *Zeitgeist* is merely another predictable swing of the pendulum of style from cool to hot, from abstract to figurative, from Apollonian to Dionysian. (We may note here that in this re-

11.   Robert Rosenblum, "Thoughts on the Origins of 'Zeitgeist,'" in *Zeitgeist*, pp. 11–12.

gard Rudi Fuchs had confused his terms when he invoked the soft sounds of Apollo's lyre, for at Documenta, too, the dominant mode of painting was the shrill bombast of neoexpressionism.)

Rosenblum's history as Zeitgeist was corroborated in the exhibition catalogue by his colleague Hilton Kramer, who reduced it finally to a simple matter of changing tastes. Kramer had hit upon this novel idea that new art could be explained as a change in taste in trying to come to grips in his *New York Times* column with the work of Julian Schnabel and Malcolm Morley. Clearly pleased that he had found the solution to the dilemma, he decided to quote himself in his *Zeitgeist* essay:

> Nothing is more incalculable in art—or more inevitable—than a genuine change in taste. . . . Although taste seems to operate by a sort of law of compensation, so that the denial of certain qualities in one period almost automatically prepares the ground for their triumphal return later, its timetable can never be accurately predicted. Its roots lie in something deeper and more mysterious than mere fashion. At the heart of every genuine change in taste there is, I suppose, a keen feeling of loss, an existential ache—a sense that something absolutely essential to the life of art has been allowed to fall into a state of unendurable atrophy. It is to the immediate repair of this perceived void that taste at its profoundest level addresses itself.[12]

Kramer goes on to explain that what had been lost from art during the '60s and '70s was poetry and fantasy, the drama of the self, the visionary and the irrational; these had been denied by the orthodoxies of pure, cerebral abstraction. Again, it is a question only of style and sensibility and the subject matter they can generate.

But what is left out of these descriptions of contemporary art? What is, in fact, repressed, denied? The hidden agenda of this version of recent history is the calculated exclusion of the truly significant developments of the art of the past two decades. By characterizing the art of this period as abstract, geometric, intellective, the real terms of art practice are elided. Where do we read in these texts of the critique of the institutions of power which seek to limit the meaning and function of art to the purely aesthetic? Where is a discussion of the attempted

---

12.   Hilton Kramer, "Signs of Passion," in *Zeitgeist*, p. 17. It is interesting that Kramer here speaks of changes in art as *compensatory* for a sense of loss inherent in a previous style, for it is precisely that sense of loss and its periodic *intensification* that Leo Steinberg proposed, in his "Contemporary Art and the Plight of Its Public" (in *Other Criteria*, New York, Oxford University Press, 1972), as the very condition of innovation within modernism. It was with this contrast between, on the one hand, Steinberg's understanding of modernism and, on the other hand, Kramer's resentment of it that Annette Michelson began her review of Hilton Kramer's *The Age of the Avant-Garde*; see Michelson, "Contemporary Art and the Plight of the Public: a View from the New York Hilton," *Artforum*, vol. XIII, no. 1 (September 1974), pp. 68–70.

dissolution of the beaux-arts mediums and their replacement with modes of production which could better resist those institutions? Where do we find an analysis of work by feminists and minorities whose marginalization by the art institutions became a significant point of departure for the creation of alternative practices? Where do we find mention of those direct interventions by artists in their local social environments? Where, in short, in these essays can we learn of the political critique which has been the real thrust of our recent art?

The answer is, of course: nowhere. For Rosenblum and Kramer, for Rosenthal and Joachimides, and for Fuchs, politics is what art must deny. For them art is gentle and discreet, it is autonomous, and it exists in an ivory tower. Art is, after all, only a matter of taste. To this endeavor politics is a threat. But what of *their* politics? Is there only an *art* of exhibition? Is there not also a politics of exhibition? Is it not a politics that chooses as the symbol of an exhibition the statue of an eighteenth-century imperial ruler? that invites only one woman to participate in an exhibition of forty-three artists? [13] Can we not recognize a politics that would limit a discussion of repression and liberation to matters of style? Is it not, assuredly, a politics that wants to confine art to a pure realm of the aesthetic?

Interestingly enough, Hilton Kramer's conversion to the aesthetic of neo-expressionism took place at about the same time that he underwent another, somewhat more concrete conversion. After sixteen years as art critic for the *New York Times*, arguably the most influential newspaper in America, Kramer resigned to found his own magazine. Generously financed by major conservative foundations, Kramer's *New Criterion* is now recognized, after two years of publication, as the principal intellectual organ of the Reagan administration's cultural policies. Under the guise of a return to established moral values and critical standards, these policies in fact include a defunding and further marginalization of all cultural activities seen as critical of the right-wing political agenda, and a gradual dismantling of government support for the arts and humanities, to be replaced by monies from the private sector. This latter term, a favorite of the present United States government, is best translated as corporate self-interest, which has already begun to tighten its grip on all aspects of American cultural activity, from television programming to art exhibitions. Kramer's efforts in this regard are well served by his publisher, Samuel Lipman, who sits on President Reagan's National Council on the Arts, the body that oversees the activities of the National Endowment for the Arts. The effectiveness of Kramer's new magazine may be discerned from the fact that within several months of his writing an article in the *New Criterion* condemning the Na-

---

13.   These are the figures for the *Zeitgeist* exhibition. *A New Spirit in Painting*, an earlier show organized in London by Rosenthal and Joachimides, together with Nicolas Serota, contained work by thirty-eight artists, not one of whom was a woman.

tional Endowment's art critics fellowships, the Chairman of the Endowment announced their cancellation.[14]

It is within this context that we must see Kramer's claims of a high-minded neutrality on aesthetic issues, his abhorrence of the politicization of art. In an article in the *New Criterion* entitled "Turning Back the Clock: Art and Politics in 1984," Kramer violently attacked a number of recent exhibitions which attempted to deal with the issue of art and politics. His central argument was that any attempt to see the workings of ideology within the aesthetic is a totalitarian, even Stalinist position, which leads inevitably to an acquiescence in tyranny. But what is tyranny if not that form of government that seeks to silence all criticism of or opposition to its policies? And what is the aesthetic production most acceptable to tyranny if not that which either directly affirms the status quo or contents itself with solipsistic exercises in so-called self-expression? Kramer's own acquiescence in the tyrannical suppression of opposition is most evident in his essay's implicit call for the defunding of those exhibition venues showing political art, which he reminds his readers time and time again are recipients of public financial support; or in his questioning the suitability for academic positions of those politically committed art critics who acted as curators for the shows. But these McCarthyite insinuations are hidden behind a veil of supposedly disinterested concern for the maintenance of aesthetic standards. In Kramer's estimation, not only is it virtually inconceivable that political art could be of high aesthetic quality, but what is worse, this art appears intentionally to negate aesthetic discourse altogether. To prove his point, Kramer singled out Hans Haacke's contribution to one of the exhibitions organized under the auspices of Artists Call Against U.S. Intervention in Central America. Here is his discussion of Haacke's work:

> In the show at the City University mall we were shown, among much else, a huge, square, unpainted box constructed of wood and

14.   See Hilton Kramer, "Criticism Endowed: Reflections on a Debacle," *New Criterion*, vol. 2, no. 3 (November 1983), pp. 1–5. Kramer's argument consisted of an accusation of conflict of interest, wherein "at the core of the program there was certainly a nucleus of friends and professional colleagues who were assiduous in looking after each other's interests" (p. 3). This is Kramer's characterization of what is otherwise known as the peer-panel system of judging, in which members of the profession are asked to judge the work of their fellow critics. Needless to say, the result will be a certain degree of overlap among grantees and jurors over a period of years. It seems highly likely, however, that Kramer's real opposition to the critics fellowships stems from his perception that "a great many of them went as a matter of course to people who were opposed to just about every policy of the United States government except one that put money in their own pockets or the pockets of their friends and political associates" (p. 4).

Frank Hodsell, Chairman of the National Endowment for the Arts, disavowed the influence of Kramer's article on the decision to cancel the fellowships. He did admit, though, that "doubts expressed by the National Council on the Arts" were a deciding factor, and it is said that Samuel Lipman personally provided each member of the Council with a copy of Kramer's article. See Grace Glueck, "Endowment Suspends Grants for Art Critics," *New York Times*, April 5, 1984, p. C16.

standing approximately eight feet high. On its upper side there were some small openings and further down some words stencilled in large letters. A parody of the Minimalist sculpture of Donald Judd, perhaps? Not at all. This was a solemn statement, and the words told us why: "Isolation Box As Used by U.S. Troops at Point Salines Prison Camp in Grenada." The creator of this inspired work was Hans Haacke, who was also represented in the "Art and Social Conscience" exhibition [this exhibition, also a target of Kramer's attack, was held at the Edith C. Blum Art Institute at Bard College] by a photographic lightbox poster attacking President Reagan. Such works are not only devoid of any discernible artistic quality, they are pretty much devoid of any discernible artistic existence. They cannot be experienced as art, and they are not intended to be. Yet where else but in an art exhibition would they be shown? Their purpose in being entered into the art context, however, is not only to score propaganda points but to undermine the very idea of art as a realm of aesthetic discourse. President Reagan and his policies may be the immediate object of attack, but the more fundamental one is the idea of art itself.[15]

But whose idea of art? Whose realm of aesthetic discourse? Whose artistic quality? Kramer speaks as if these were all decided matters, and that everyone would therefore agree that Haacke's work can be nothing other than propaganda, or, as was suggested in a *Wall Street Journal* editorial, pornography.[16] It seems to have escaped Kramer's attention that Haacke used the by now fully historical aesthetic strategy of appropriation in order to create a work of rigorous factual specificity. Haacke's *Isolation Box, Grenada* is a precise reconstruction of those used by the U.S. army only a few months before in blatant disregard of the Geneva Convention. As he read the description in the *New York Times* of the prison cells built expressly for the brutal humiliation of Grenadian and Cuban hostages,[17] Haacke did not fail to note their resemblance to the "minimalist

15. Hilton Kramer, "Turning Back the Clock: Art and Politics in 1984," *New Criterion*, April 1984, p. 71.
16. "Artists for Old Grenada," *Wall Street Journal*, February 21, 1984, p. 32. The passage in question reads: "To our knowledge the CCNY [sic] exhibition has not been reviewed yet by a prominent New York art critic. Perhaps critics have noticed that a few blocks down 42nd Street one can see what's maybe America's greatest collection of obscenity and pornography, and that in this respect, the CCNY artists' interpretation of what the U.S. did in Grenada is in proper company." For a reply to the editorial by Hans Haacke and Thomas Woodruff, see "Letters," *Wall Street Journal*, March 13, 1984.
17. See David Shribman, "U.S. Conducts Grenada Camp for Questioning," *New York Times*, November 14, 1983, pp. A1, A7. The passages describing the isolation boxes read as follows: "Beyond the control gate and barbed wire, and between two clusters of tents, are the most prominent features of the camp, two rows of newly constructed wooden chambers, each measuring about eight feet by eight feet." "Beside [the interrogation booths], however, were 10 isolation booths, each with four small windows and a number of ventilation holes with a radius of half an

sculpture of Donald Judd," and thus to recognize the possibility of appropriating that sculptural aesthetic for a work of contemporary political relevance. But
presumably for Kramer it is an acquiescence in tyranny to reclaim an aesthetic
position for the purpose of questioning a government that disregards international law to invade a tiny sovereign state, that mistakenly bombs a mental
asylum and kills scores of innocent people, and that exercises total press censor-
ship throughout the invasion.

*

Hilton Kramer's failure to recognize the historical avant-garde strategy in
Haacke's *Isolation Box, Grenada* is not simply governed by his desire to forestall
the hard political questions that Haacke's work raises. Kramer's purpose is more
sweeping: to suppress any discussion of the links between the artistic avant-
garde and radical politics, and thus to claim for modern art a continuous, unproblematic aesthetic history that is entirely severed from episodes of political
engagement. The lengths to which Kramer will go to fulfill this purpose can be
determined by reading, in the same "Art and Politics" essay, his attack on one
of the curators of the New Museum's *Art & Ideology* exhibition, the main target
of Kramer's rage:

> Benjamin H. D. Buchloh, . . . who teaches art history at the State
> University of New York at Westbury, defends the propaganda ma-
> terials he has selected for this exhibition by, among other things,
> attacking the late Alfred H. Barr, Jr., for his alleged failure to com-
> prehend "the radical change that [modern] artists and theoreticians
> introduced into the history of aesthetic theory and production in the
> twentieth century." What this means, apparently, is that Alfred Barr
> would never have accepted Professor Buchloh's Marxist analysis
> of the history of modern art, which appears to be based on Louis
> Althusser's *Lenin and Philosophy*. (Is this really what is taught as mod-
> ern art history at SUNY Westbury? Alas, one can believe it.)[18]

I will not dwell upon, but simply call attention to these parenthetical remarks,
should anyone doubt that Kramer's tactics now include red-baiting. More important in our context is the deliberate falsification achieved by the word *modern*,
which Kramer has placed in brackets. To accuse Alfred Barr of failing to comprehend *modern* artists and theoreticians is something that even the most ex-

---

inch. Prisoners must enter these booths by crawling through a hatch that extends from the floor of
the booths to about knee level."
18.   Kramer, "Turning Back the Clock," p. 71.

tremist enemies of Barr's positions would be hesitant to do, and it is not at all what Buchloh did. Here is a fuller portion of the passage from which Kramer quoted:

> When one of the founding fathers of American Modernism and the first director of the institution that taught the American Neo-avant-garde arrived in the Soviet Union in 1927 on a survey journey to take stock of international avant-garde activities for their possible import into the United States, he saw himself confronted with a situation of seemingly unmanageable conflicts. On the one hand, there was the extraordinary productivity of the modernist avant-garde in the Soviet Union (extraordinary by the numbers of its constituency, men and women, its modes of production, ranging from Malevich's late Suprematist work through the laboratory period of the Constructivists to the Lef Group and the Productivist Program, from Agit Prop-theater productions to avant-garde film production for mass audiences). On the other hand, there was the obvious general awareness among artists and cultural producers, critics and theorists that they were participating in a final transformation of the modernist aesthetic, which would irretrievably and irrevocably alter the conditions of production and reception as they had been inherited from bourgeois society and its institutions (from Kant's aesthetics and the modernist practices that had originated in them). Moreover, there was the growing fear that the process of that successful transformation might be aborted by the emergence of totalitarian repression from within the very system that had generated the foundations for a new socialist collective culture. Last of all and crucial, there was Alfred Barr's own disposition of interests and motivations of action within that situation: searching for the most advanced modernist avant-garde in a moment and place where that social group was just about to dismantle itself and its specialized activities in order to assume a new role and function in the newly-defined collective process of a social production of culture.
>
> The reasons why Alfred Barr, one of the first "modern" art historians, then just about to discover and establish the modern avant-garde in the United States, was determined (in the literal sense) to fail in comprehending the radical change that those artists and theoreticians introduced into the history of aesthetic theory and production in the twentieth century, are obviously too complex to be dealt with in this context. . . .[19]

19.   Benjamin H. D. Buchloh, "Since Realism There Was . . . (On the Current Conditions of Factographic Art)," in *Art & Ideology*, New York, The New Museum of Contemporary Art, 1984,

In spite of the fact that Buchloh devoted a lengthy paragraph to detailing the special historical circumstances of *those* artists and theoreticians that Barr failed fully to comprehend (again, as Buchloh says, for historically specific, or determined reasons), Kramer substituted the general term *modern* for Buchloh's *those* — those productivists who were at that moment in the late '20s on the brink of dissolving the autonomous modernist mediums in favor of a collective social production.

I have quoted Buchloh's essay at length not only to demonstrate the insidious, falsifying tactics of Hilton Kramer's neoconservative criticism, but also because it is of particular pertinence to the contemporary art of exhibition. For it is precisely the desire to dissemble the history of disruptions of the modernist aesthetic development that constitutes the present program of the museum that Alfred Barr helped to found. It was Buchloh's point that the Museum of Modern Art had presented the history of modern art to the American public, and more particularly to the artists within that public, that never fully articulated the true avant-garde position. For that position included the development of cultural practices that would critically reveal the constricting institutionalization of art within modern bourgeois society. At the same time, those practices were intended to function socially outside that institutionalized system. At MOMA, however, both in its earlier period and still more today, the works of the Soviet avant-garde, of Duchamp, and of the German dada artists have been tamed. They are presented, insofar as it is possible, as if they were conventional masterpieces of fine art. The radical implications of this work have been distorted by the institution so as not to allow interference with its portrayal of modern art as a steady development of abstract and abstracting styles.

Although it is perfectly clear that the current installation of the MOMA collections is intended to present not merely individual objects of modern art but rather a *history* of those objects — "These collections tell the story of modern art," proclaims a recent MOMA press release — it is also clear that the justification for the false construction of that history is connoisseurship; MOMA's primary responsibility, as they apparently see it, is to provide the public with a direct experience of great works of art unburdened by the weight of history.[20] This rationale is, in fact, spelled out in the new museum installation at the entrance to the Alfred H. Barr Jr. Galleries. On the dedicatory plaque, Barr is quoted as once having defined his task as "the conscientious, continuous, resolute distinction of quality from mediocrity."[21] To determine just how this con-

pp. 5–6. A slightly different version of this same discussion appears in Buchloh's essay "From Faktura to Factography," reprinted in this book. There Buchloh develops much further the precise circumstances to which Barr was witness on his journey to the Soviet Union, as well as later developments.

20.   This contradiction is, of course, deeply embedded in the history of modern museology and is therefore far from unique to the Museum of Modern Art.

21.   Hilton Kramer quotes Barr's connoisseurship goals approvingly in his "MOMA Reopened:

*Installation of Soviet avant-garde works at the Museum
of Modern Art, 1984. (Photo: Louise Lawler.)*

noisseurship principle is exercised in the interests of a biased history would require a detailed analysis of, among other things, the relative weight and density
given to particular artists and movements — of the prominence accorded Picasso
and Matisse, for example, as opposed to, say, Duchamp and Malevich; of the
special care taken with the installation of cubism as against that of the Soviet
avant-garde, now relegated to a cluttered stair hall; of the decisions to exhibit
certain works owned by the museum while others are banished to storage.

The Museum of Modern Art in the Postmodern Era," *New Criterion*, Summer 1984, p. 14. Indeed, his entire critique of the new MOMA installations and opening exhibition is based on what
he sees as a failure of the current museum officials to exercise connoisseurship as fully and wisely
as did Barr. For example, he condemns *An International Survey of Recent Painting and Sculpture* as "the
most incredible mess the museum has ever given us," which is due to the fact that "of anything resembling connoisseurship or critical acumen there is not a trace" ("MOMA Reopened," p. 41).

There is, however, a less complex but far more effective means by which MOMA imposes a partisan view of the objects in its possession. This is the rigid division of modern art practices into separate departments within the institution. By distributing the work of the avant-garde to various departments — to Painting and Sculpture, Architecture and Design, Photography, Film, Prints and Illustrated Books — that is, by stringently enforcing what appears to be a natural parceling of objects according to medium, MOMA automatically constructs a formalist history of modernism. Because of this simple and seemingly neutral fact, the museum goer can have no sense of the significance of, to give just one example, Rodchenko's abandonment of painting in favor of photography. That Rodchenko saw painting as a vestige of an outmoded culture and photography as possibly instrumental in the creation of a new one — the very situation that Alfred Barr witnessed during the trip to the Soviet Union to which Buchloh referred — this history cannot be articulated through the consignment of Rodchenko's various works to different fiefdoms within the museum. As it is, one experiences Rodchenko merely as an artist who worked in more than one medium, which is to say, as versatile, like many "great" artists. Seen within the Department of Photography, Rodchenko might seem to be an artist who increased the formal possibilities of photography, but he cannot be understood as one who saw photography as having a far greater potential for social utility than painting, if for no other reason than that photography readily lent itself to a wider system of distribution. Mounted and framed as individual auratic works of art, Rodchenko's photographs cannot even convey this most simple historical fact. Such a misrepresentation of modernism, inherent in the very structure of MOMA, was to have particular consequences for postwar American art — the point of Buchloh's discussion of this issue in his essay for the *Art & Ideology* show — and it is those consequences in their fuller contradictions which we are now experiencing in the contemporary art of exhibition, a point to which I shall return.

Hilton Kramer's summary dismissal of Buchloh's analysis of Barr's encounter with the Soviet avant-garde, effected simply by labeling it Althusserian,[22] can be more fully understood when placed alongside his own characterization of this crucial episode, one which transpired just before the founding of the museum in 1929. In a special issue of the *New Criterion* devoted entirely to an

---

22.   Buchloh's discussion of this very specific moment in the history of modern art does not, in fact, refer to Althusser's *Lenin and Philosophy*; rather his discussion of the contemporary politicized work of Allan Sekula and Fred Lonidier does. He notes, "If Althusser's argument is correct that the aesthetic constitutes itself only inside the ideological, what then is the nature of the practice of those artists who, as we are suggesting, are in fact trying to develop practice that is operative outside and inside the ideological apparatus? The first argument that will of course be leveled against this type of work is that it simply cannot be *'art'* . . ." ("Since Realism There Was," p. 8). This "first argument" is precisely the one Kramer used against Hans Haacke and the other political artists he attacked.

essay on the reopened museum, Kramer is again careful to separate aesthetics from politics:

> [Barr] had been to Germany and Russia in the Twenties, and had been deeply impressed with the art — and with the ideas governing the art — which he studied there. These ideas were radical in more than an aesthetic sense — although they were certainly that. They were radical, or at least were thought to be at the time, in their social implications as well. At the Bauhaus in Germany and in the councils of the Russian avant-garde in the early years of the Revolution, the very conception of what art was or should be was altered under the influence of a powerful utopian ideology. As a result, the boundary separating fine art from industrial art was, if not completely abandoned by everyone concerned, at least very much questioned and undermined. Henceforth, from this radical perspective, there were to be no aesthetic hierarchies. A poster might be equal to a painting, a factory or a housing project as much to be esteemed as a great work of sculpture.
>
> It is my impression that at no time in his life was Barr very much interested in politics. It was not, in any case, the political implications of this development that drew him to it. What deeply interested him were its aesthetic implications, and therefore, under his influence, what governed the museum's outlook from its earliest days was a vision that attempted to effect a kind of grand synthesis of modernist aesthetics and the technology of industrialism.[23]

Whether or not Kramer fairly appraises Barr's political interest, he attributes to him an understanding of the aesthetics of the avant-garde that fully deradicalizes them, though Kramer persists in using the term *radical*.[24] It is by no means the case that the early avant-garde was simply interested in giving to "architecture, industrial design, photography, and film a kind of parity with painting, sculpture, and the graphic arts," to elevate work in other mediums "to the realm of fine art."[25] On the contrary, the true radicalism of the early avant-garde was its abandonment of the very notion of fine art in the interests of social production, which meant, for one thing, destroying easel painting as a form. The orig-

---

23.   Kramer, "MOMA Reopened," p. 42.
24.   Ironically, Kramer's version of Barr's encounter with the Soviet avant-garde is virtually identical to Buchloh's, even to the point of noting that Barr severed the art from the politics that motivated that art. The difference, of course, is that Buchloh shows that this separation resulted, precisely, in Barr's failure to comprehend "the radical change that those artists and theoreticians introduced," while Kramer simply repeats Barr's failure.
25.   Kramer, "MOMA Reopened," p. 42.

*Entrance foyer of Architecture and Design Galleries,
Museum of Modern Art, 1984. (Photo: Louise Lawler.)*

inal avant-garde program did not consist of an aesthetics with social implications; it consisted of a politicized aesthetic, a socialist art.[26]

Kramer is, however, quite correct in his discussion of the historical results of the deradicalization of the avant-garde: "The aesthetic that originated at the Bauhaus and other avant-garde groups has been stripped of its social ideology and turned into the reigning taste of the cultural marketplace."[27] Indeed, the work of the avant-garde, severed from its political setting and presented as fine art, could serve as examples for product design and advertising. As if to illustrate this process of transforming agitprop into advertising,[28] the entrance to

26. For a detailed discussion of this question, see Buchloh, "From Faktura to Factography."
27. Kramer, "MOMA Reopened," pp. 42–43.
28. This process is, in fact, one of *re*transformation, since agitprop had originally transformed advertising techniques for political purposes. See Buchloh, "From Faktura to Factography," pp. 96–104.

MOMA's design galleries displays posters by members of the Soviet avant-garde juxtaposed with advertisements directly or indirectly influenced by them. Underneath Rodchenko's poster for the Theater of the Revolution is an ad for Martini designed by Alexei Brodovich, a Russian emigré who had clearly absorbed his design lessons early and directly. On the opposite wall Gustav Klucis and Sergei Senkin's agitprop "Let Us Carry Out the Plan of the Great Work" and El Lissitzky's "USSR Russische Ausstellung" announcement are hung next to a recent advertisement for Campari. To this deliberate blurring of important distinctions in use-value Kramer, of course, nods his approval, noting that in this regard MOMA has fulfilled its mission. But now that modernism has been fully assimilated into consumer culture, when we enter the current design department, "well, we suddenly find ourselves in something that looks vaguely reminiscent of Bloomingdale's furniture department," and so "it becomes more and more difficult to believe such an installation is necessary."[29] Mission accomplished, then, MOMA has come full circle. It can now get back to the business of art as it had been prior to Barr's "radical notion" of a broadened definition of aesthetic endeavor. "Today," Kramer concludes, "it is only as an institution specializing in high art that the new MOMA can claim to have a great and necessary purpose."[30]

In this, the official neoconservative view of the current purposes of the museum, it is one of the consequences of the distortion of the historical avant-garde that the museum should abandon altogether its task of presenting any practices which do not conform to the traditional view of fine art, to return, that is, to the prerogatives of painting and sculpture. And indeed, the inaugural exhibition at the reopened Museum of Modern Art, entitled *An International Survey of Recent Painting and Sculpture*, did just that. Specifically citing Documenta and *Zeitgeist* as precedents for the show, Kynaston McShine, the curator responsible for the selection, claimed to have looked at "everything, everywhere" because "it was important to have work from a lot of different places and to introduce a large public to a great deal of current activity. I wanted it to be an international cross-section of what is going on."[31] To limit "what is going on" to painting and sculpture, however, is to dissemble willfully the actual facts of artistic practice at this historical juncture. To look at "everything everywhere" and to see only painting and sculpture is to be blind—blind to every significant aesthetic endeavor to continue the work of the avant-garde. The scandal of the international survey—quite apart from its promiscuous inclusion of just about any trivial product of today's market culture and its chaotic, bargain-basement installation—is its refusal to take account of the wide variety of practices that

29.   Kramer, "MOMA Reopened," pp. 43–44.
30.   *Ibid.*, p. 44.
31.   Quoted in Michael Brenson, "A Living Artists Show at the Modern Museum," *New York Times*, April 21, 1984, p. 11.

question and propose an alternative to the hegemony of painting and sculpture. And the scandal is made all the more complete when one remembers that it was also Kynaston McShine who organized MOMA's last major international exhibition of contemporary art, the *Information* show of 1970, a broad survey of conceptual art and related developments. Like Rudi Fuchs, then, McShine cannot claim ignorance of that work of the late '60s that makes a return to painting and sculpture so historically problematic. Even within the absurd terms of McShine's stated principle of selection — that only those artists whose reputations were established after 1975 would be considered[32] — we are given no reason whatsoever for the exclusion of all the artists whose work continues and deepens the tendencies shown in *Information*. The short introduction to the catalogue, unsigned but presumably written by McShine, slides around the problem with the following pathetic statement:

> The exhibition does not encompass mediums other than painting and sculpture. However one cannot help but register the current tendency of painters and sculptors to cross the border into other disciplines such as photography, film, video, and even architecture. While these "crossovers" have become expected in recent years, less familiar to a general audience is the attraction to music and performance. Represented here are artists active not only in painting and sculpture but also in performance art. Inevitably, some of their theatrical concerns present themselves in their work, most often in a narrative or autobiographical form.[33]

32. *Ibid.* Even this stated criterion is entirely belied by the exhibition of some thirty artists whose reputations were well established by the mid-'70s; five of the artists in the show are listed in the catalogue documentation as having had one-person exhibitions at MOMA before 1977.

An International Survey of Recent Painting and Sculpture, like *Zeitgeist*, failed to take note of the achievements of women artists. Of 165 artists only fourteen were women. A protest demonstration staged by the Women's Caucus for Art failed to elicit any public response from the officials of the museum. This must be seen in contrast to the various demonstrations of the early '70s against unfair museum policies, when, at the very least, MOMA was responsive enough to enter into public dialogue over the grievances. But, of course, if women were very poorly represented in MOMA's reopening show, it is largely because women are centrally involved in the vanguard of alternative practices. To have admitted them would have been to acknowledge that traditional painting and sculpture are not the most important, and certainly not the only forms of current art practice.

33. "Introduction," in *An International Survey of Recent Painting and Sculpture*, New York, Museum of Modern Art, p. 12. That this introductory essay is both unsigned and only two pages long makes one wonder just how seriously contemporary art is being considered at MOMA. McShine was quoted in the *Times* as saying, "The show is a sign of hope. It is a sign that contemporary art is being taken as seriously as it should be, a sign that the museum will restore the balance between contemporary art and art history that is part of what makes the place unique" (quoted in Brenson, p. 11). But if this is the case, why does the curator of the show feel no obligation to provide a critical discussion of the artists chosen and the issues addressed in the contemporary art exhibition? By contrast, the first *historical* show to open at the museum, *Primitivism in Twentieth Century Art*, is accompanied by a two-volume catalogue containing nineteen lengthy essays by fifteen scholars and critics. Perhaps the answer is to be found in the final paragraph of the intro-

Embedded in a two-page compilation of clichés and banalities—

—The concerns expressed in the work are basic, universal.

—The artist as creator, dreamer, storyteller, narcissist, as the instrument of divine inspiration, is represented in many works.

—Inspiration ranges from underwater life to the structure of flora and fauna to the effects of light.

—. . . there is a liveliness in the current international art scene that stems from the freedom and diversity enjoyed by artists today.

—The artists demonstrate an integrity, imagination, and ambition that affirm the health of their profession.—

such a paragraph, in its deliberate weakness and vagueness, is designed to tell us nothing at all about the vociferous opposition that persists among current avant-garde practitioners to conventional painting and sculpture. By his choice of the term *crossover*, McShine once again resorts to the myth of artistic versatility to demean the significance of genuinely alternative and socially engaged art production. That the reactionary tradition represented in the international survey might be placed in jeopardy, shown to be historically bankrupt, by such production is completely ignored by McShine.

It is interesting in this regard to recall an interview given to *Artforum* ten years ago by William Rubin, then and now director of the Department of Painting and Sculpture. There Rubin stated what was at the time a fairly common view of contemporary aesthetic developments:

Perhaps, looking back 10 [which is to say now], 15, 30 years from now, it will appear that this modernist tradition really did come to an end within the last few years, as some critics suggest. If so, historians a century from now—whatever name they will give to the period we now call modern—will see it beginning shortly after the middle of the 19th century and ending in the 1960s. I'm not ruling this out; it may be the case, but I don't think so. Perhaps the dividing line will be seen as between those works which essentially continue an easel painting concept that grew up associated with bourgeois democratic life and was involved with the development of private collections as well as the museum concept—between this and, let us say, Earthworks, Conceptual works and related endeavors, which want another environment (or should want it) and, perhaps, another public.[34]

---

duction to the international survey: "Those who see this exhibition will, one trusts, understand that art is about looking and not about reading or listening."

34.   William Rubin, in Lawrence Alloway and John Coplans, "Talking with William Rubin: 'The Museum Concept Is Not Infinitely Expandable,'" *Artforum*, vol. XIII, no. 2 (October 1974),

Though Rubin states his own hesitation regarding the view he presents, he seems to have had a remarkably clear understanding of the actual facts of art history of the '60s and early '70s. It is therefore all the more astonishing that the museum department headed by Rubin should now mount an exhibition that unquestionably attempts to negate that understanding. What do Rubin and McShine believe transpired in the intervening decade? Were the endeavors that Rubin saw as having possibly created a rupture with modernism only "passing phenomena," as he suggested the coming years might tell? Judging not only from McShine's survey, but also from the installation of that part of the permanent collection comprising the art of the '60s and '70s, the answer must be in the affirmative, for there is no evidence of the "postmodern" art of which Rubin speaks. With the exception of a few works of minimal sculpture, there is no trace of the art of that period that led even Rubin to wonder if modern art, traditionally defined, had come to an end.

Yet anyone who has witnessed the art events of the past decade carefully might come to a very different conclusion. On the one hand, there has been an intensification of the critique of art's institutionalization, a deepening of the rupture with modernism. On the other hand, there has been a concerted effort to marginalize and suppress these facts and to reestablish the traditional fine arts categories by all conservative forces of society, from cultural bureaucracies to museum institutions, from corporate boardrooms to the marketplace for art. And this has been accomplished with the complicity of a new breed of entrepreneurial artists, utterly cynical in their disregard of both recent art history and present political reality. These newly heralded "geniuses" work for a parvenu class of collectors who want art with an insured resale value, which will at the same time fulfill their desire for mildly pornographic titillation, romantic cliché, easy reference to past "masterpieces," and good decor. The objects on view to celebrate the reopening of MOMA were made, with very few exceptions, to cater to this taste, to rest easily over the sofa in a Trump Tower living room or to languish in a bank vault while prices escalate. No wonder then that McShine ended his catalogue introduction with the very special hope "to encourage everyone to be in favor of the art of our time." Given what he has presented as the art of our time, his currying of our favor could hardly be at odds with that of the sponsors of the exhibition, the AT&T Corporation, who mounted a new advertising campaign to coincide with the show. "Some of the masterpieces of tomorrow are on exhibit today," reads the ad's banner headline, under which appears a reproduction of one of Robert Longo's recent glorifications of

---

p. 52. In this interview, Rubin attempts to defend the museum against the charge that it has become unresponsive to contemporary art. He insists that this art simply has no place in a museum, which he sees essentially as a temple of high art. This, of course, puts him in perfect accord with Kramer's position. What is never acknowledged, however, is that ignoring those forms of art that exceed the museum — whether the work of the historical avant-garde or that of the present — will necessarily give a distorted view of history.

AT&T advertisement, New York Times Magazine, *June 3, 1984.*

corporate style, now in MOMA's permanent collection. That corporate interests are in perfect accord with the art presented in MOMA's inaugural show is a point underscored in the catalogue preface written by the museum's director, whose long paragraph of praise and thanks to AT&T contains the following statement: "AT&T clearly recognizes that experiment and innovation, so highly prized in business and industry, must be equally valued and supported in the arts."[35]

Experiment and innovation are prized in business and industry, of course, because they result in ever-expanding consumer markets and higher profits. That this is also the motive of the works presented in *An International Survey of Recent Painting and Sculpture* is hardly less obvious. But if the thousands of visitors who flocked to the newly reopened museum failed to grasp this fact, MOMA confronted them with a still more persuasive demonstration of the corporate view of art, something which Hilton Kramer referred to as "the most audacious *coup de théâtre* anyone has ever attempted at MOMA." Our first glimpse of this was in a full-page photograph that appeared in the *New York Times Magazine* above the caption "While celebrating its permanent collection of masterworks from the modernist period, the museum will continue to exhibit the new." The "new" in question, the *coup de théâtre* was shown being installed in the dramatic two-story space over the escalator leading to the design galleries; the "new" is a helicopter. Here is how a museum press release described the new acquisition:

> A ubiquitous contemporary artifact, the Bell 47D-1 helicopter was acquired several months ago by the [Architecture and Design] Department, and will be suspended above visitors as they enter the fourth floor galleries. Utilitarian in appearance — it is the helicopter equivalent of the jeep — the model 47 went into production in 1947 and set an industry record by remaining in production for the next three decades. As an example of industrial mass production, it is, according to Department Director Arthur Drexler, "a peculiarly memorable object."

Just how memorable a helicopter may be was well illustrated last year in an exhibition at the Museo del Barrio presented in conjunction with Artists Call Against U.S. Intervention in Central America. The exhibition contained some fifty drawings by Salvadoran and Guatemalan refugee children living across the borders in Honduras and Nicaragua, and virtually every one of the drawings depicted this "ubiquitous contemporary artifact," ubiquitous indeed, since it is and has been the most essential instrument of counter-insurgency warfare

---

35.   Richard E. Oldenburg, "Preface," in *An International Survey of Recent Painting and Sculpture*, p. 9.

While celebrating its permanent collection
of masterworks from the modernist period,
the museum will continue to exhibit the new.

Illustration, New York Times Magazine, *April 15, 1984.*

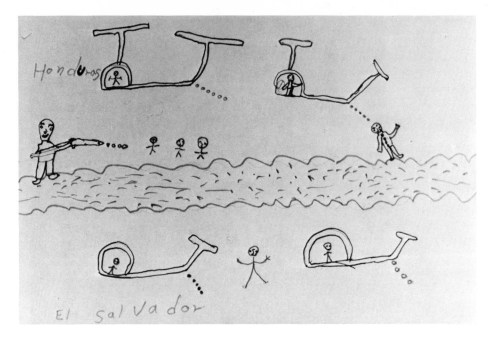

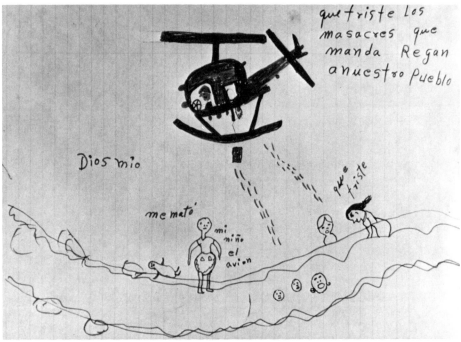

Drawings by Salvadoran children in the Mesa Grande refugee camp, Honduras, shown in
Children in Exile: Drawings by Refugee Children from Guatemala and El Salvador,
El Museo del Barrio, January 10–31, 1984.

since the Korean War. Even Francis Ford Coppola did not fail to understand the sinister symbolic value of this "memorable object" in his highly mythologized portrayal of Americans in Vietnam. But symbols aside, the hard facts are that Bell helicopters are manufactured by the Fort Worth corporation Textron, a major defense contractor, which supplies the Bell and Huey model helicopters that are right now in use in El Salvador, Honduras (which means, of course, against the Sandinista government of Nicaragua), and Guatemala.[36] But because the contemporary art of exhibition has taught us to distinguish between the political and the aesthetic, a *New York Times* editorial entitled "Marvelous MOMA" was able to say of MOMA's proud new art object:

> A helicopter, suspended from the ceiling, hovers over an escalator in the Museum of Modern Art. . . . The chopper is bright green, bug-eyed and beautiful. We know that it is beautiful because MOMA showed us the way to look at the 20th century.[37]

36.   In September, the *New York Times* reported that the U.S. government was planning to double the number of combat helicopters in the Salvadoran force by the end of this year: "In the last few weeks, 10 new Hueys have been sent to El Salvador and 10 to 15 more are expected by the end of the year. . . . Under that schedule, the Salvadoran fleet will have increased to 49 from 24 within six months" (James LeMoyne, "U.S. Is Bolstering Salvador Copters: Plans to Double Fleet by End of Year to Let Latins Use New Tactic on Rebels," *New York Times*, September 19, 1984, p. A1). The article went on to say that "such helicopter attacks were the mainstay of American operations in Vietnam. If the Salvadoran Army masters the tactic, it will have made a considerable advance from the often militarily inept force that has been unable to contain rebel offensives in the last two years."
       Reporting for the *Nation* in October, Scott Wallace described the effects of American helicopters on the people of El Salvador: "Although U.S. officials deny that the helicopter-borne assault teams will be used to terrorize civilians who back the guerrillas, government forces are already rehearsing the tactic. On August 30, around the time the shipment of Hueys arrived, army units launched helicopter assaults on the townships of Las Vueltas and San José Las Flores in rebel-controlled zones of Chalatenango province.
       "Journalists who arrived on the scene ten days later were told by local peasants that at least thirty-seven women, children and old people had been killed in the operation. According to the villagers, helicopters bearing Salvadoran troops, led by the U.S.-trained Atlacatl Battalion, stalked a group of several hundred peasants who were escorted by a small force of armed guerrillas. The peasants described their bewilderment and terror as they saw the helicopters land troops on hilltops all around them, cutting them off. When the soldiers closed in, some people panicked and plunged into the rapidly flowing Gualsinga River, where several drowned. Others were cut down by machine-gun fire or taken prisoner" ("Hueys in El Salvador: Preparing for a Stepped-Up War?" *Nation*, October 20, 1984, p. 337).
37.   "Marvelous MOMA," *New York Times*, May 13, 1984, Section 4, p. 22. I wish to thank Cara Ryan for pointing out this editorial and more generally for her advice and support during the writing of this essay.

The Judgment Seat
of Photography

CHRISTOPHER PHILLIPS

> *From a photographic print, for example, one*
> *can make any number of prints; to ask for the*
> *"authentic" print makes no sense.*
>
> —Walter Benjamin, "The Work of Art
> in the Age of Mechanical Reproduc-
> tion"
>
> *My ideal is to achieve the ability to produce*
> *numberless prints from each negative, prints*
> *all significantly alive, yet indistinguishably*
> *alike, and to be able to circulate them at a*
> *price no higher than that of a popular maga-*
> *zine or even a daily paper. To gain that ability*
> *there has been no choice but to follow the path*
> *that I have chosen.*
>
> —Alfred Stieglitz, catalogue preface to
> his exhibition at the Anderson Galleries,
> 1921

Photography, at least from the inception of Fox Talbot's negative/positive technique, would seem the very type of what Jean Baudrillard has recently called the "industrial simulacrum"—his designation for all of those products of modern industrial processes that can be said to issue in potentially endless chains of identical, equivalent objects.[1] Duplicability, seriality, "copies" that refer back to no "original": these are the hallmarks of Baudrillard's "order of simulacra." They are, as well, precisely those characteristics one might ascribe to photography as the principal source of the mass imagery that ceaselessly circulates throughout the global *société de consommation*.

---

1.   Jean Baudrillard, *L'Echange symbolique et la mort*, Paris, Editions Gallimard, 1976, pp. 85–88.

This perspective, needless to say, is considerably at odds with the institutional trends that have, in recent years, borne photography triumphantly into the museum, the auction house, and the corporate boardroom. A curious denial — or strategic avoidance — of the fact of photography's sheer multiplicity informs much of today's authoritative discussion of the medium. Consider the assertion of the present director of the Museum of Modern Art's Department of Photography that "a photographic print is a much less predictable product than a print from an engraving or an etching plate," or his assurance that the likelihood of a photographer's being "able truly to duplicate an earlier print is very slight."[2]

This passage from multiplicity, ubiquity, equivalence to singularity, rarity, and authenticity seems conveniently to account for the kind of closure effected by photography's gradual reconstitution as an art and as the museum's natural and special object of study. When we turn, however, to consider the institutional setting in which this transformation might be said principally to have taken place, we quickly discover the process to have been more complex and equivocal than suspected. I speak, of course, of the MoMA Department of Photography, which for nearly half a century, through its influential exhibitions and publications, has with increasing authority set our general "horizon of expectation" with respect to photography. MoMA's assimilation of photography has indeed proceeded, on the one hand, through an investing of photography with what Walter Benjamin called the "aura" of traditional art — accomplished, in this case, by revamping older notions of print connoisseurship, transposing the ordering categories of art history to a new register, and confirming the workaday photographer as creative artist. But equally important has been the museum's considerable effort to reappropriate, on its own terms, those very aspects of photographic reproducibility believed by Benjamin to signal the aura's demise.

The cultural transformation of photography into a museum art provides, and in no small degree, an ironic postscript to the thesis that Benjamin elaborated in his 1936 essay "The Work of Art in the Age of Mechanical Reproduction." And it is for that very reason that I shall retain, in the background of the discussion that follows, the pair of terms "cult value" and "exhibition value." Their opposition provides the basis for Benjamin's claim that "that which withers in the age of mechanical reproduction is the aura of the work of art."[3]

This oft-cited fragment compresses into aphorism a rich and ingenious argument, one by now sufficiently familiar to require no full-scale treatment here. In brief, Benjamin proceeded from what he saw as a historical distinction

2.   John Szarkowski, "Photography and the Private Collector," *Aperture*, vol. 15, no. 2 (Summer 1970), n.p.
3.   Walter Benjamin, "The Work of Art in the Age of Mechanical Reproduction," trans. Harry Zohn, in *Illuminations*, New York, Schocken Books, 1969, p. 223.

between two modes of reception of art. Cult value was rooted in art's origins in religious/magical ritual, whence the unique presence manifested in the aura of the work of art. Exhibition value involved the gradually changing function of the work of art as it became portable and (later) duplicable—thus, the passage from the fixed fresco or mosaic of the Renaissance to the mobile "public present-ability" of easel painting. Tracing these two modes to modern times, Benjamin described a secularized cult value that revealed itself in a preoccupation with the singularity and the physical authenticity of the treasured art object. Here, moreover, religious mystery was progressively displaced by the mysteries of creative genius and eternal value, mysteries whose meaning could be inter-preted to art's public only through the mediations of the art expert and the con-noisseur. In this view—and Benjamin is writing during his least ambiguously Marxist phase—the aura of the secular work of art, the "unique phenomenon of a distance however close it may be," is disclosed as a function of its embed-dedness in the constraining discourse that bourgeois society calls cultural tradi-tion.

But tracing the course of exhibition value in similar fashion to the present, Benjamin saw in the nineteenth century's perfection of technically precise reproduction media such as photography and film the opportunity not only to prise art from its cultural constraints, but to transform radically its traditional functions. As the singular original gave way to a plurality of increasingly precise copies, so would the previously unbridgeable gap between art and its audience give way to universal availability and accessibility. Hence, Benjamin anticipated a "dissolution" of the aura, a proliferation of meanings, in short a "tremendous shattering of tradition." It is here that the Marxist thread of his discourse emerges explicitly, for Benjamin welcomed the de-sacralization of the work of art, the "liquidation" of cultural tradition, as clearing the way for a radical critique of bourgeois society. In particular, he identified photography and film—forms conceived as inherently reproducible—as the indispensable instruments of such a critique, since they promised to introduce new modes of perception and analysis in ways immediately comprehensible to a mass public.

Now while the last decade has seen a remarkable renewal of interest in those facets of Benjamin's thought that I have so schematically outlined, there has been a notable absence (at least in America) of a corresponding reexamina-tion of the shrewdest criticism it originally received—that of Theodor Adorno. After reviewing what he called Benjamin's "extraordinary study," Adorno nonetheless voiced a strong skepticism in regard to its argument. By setting up an enabling opposition between cult value and exhibition value, privileging the latter, and representing it as an unequivocally positive agent of change, Adorno felt that Benjamin had lapsed into a technological determinism. The techniques of reproducibility, Adorno claimed, having arisen wholly within the framework of the capitalist order, were not to be so easily disentangled from their role in the functioning of that order. If the historical processes that

Benjamin condensed under the rubric exhibition value were not, in fact, incompatible with the values of bourgeois culture, they could not fulfil the conveniently one-sided role that Benjamin wished them to play. Of the relation between the traditional forms of high art and the new technical modes, Adorno insisted, "Both bear the scars of capitalism, both contain elements of change. . . . Both are torn halves of full freedom, to which however they do not add up."[4]

One can only share Adorno's belief that Benjamin's undeniably pioneering effort carries more than a trace of the social and technological romanticism so evident in Germany between the wars, evident in figures as diverse as Brecht and Moholy-Nagy. With this proviso, however, and aware of the utopian aspect of exhibition value, we can see Benjamin's two modes of reception as providing a useful starting point for the consideration of a remarkable process: the way in which photography — the medium believed by Benjamin to have effectively overthrown the "judgment seat" of traditional art[5] — has in turn been subjected to the transfiguring gaze of art's institutional guardian: the museum.

*

From the time of MoMA's opening in 1929, photography received the museum's nodding recognition as one branch of modernist practice, doubtless spurred by MoMA director Alfred H. Barr, Jr.'s awareness of the photographic activity of the European avant-garde. The first showings of photography at the museum resulted, however, from the intermittent enthusiasms of Lincoln Kirstein, then one of the most active members of the MoMA Junior Advisory Committee. It was Kirstein who, with Julian Levy, in 1932, arranged the first exhibition to feature photographs (in this case giant photomurals by Steichen and Berenice Abbott, among others) in "Murals by American Painters and Photographers." The next year, Kirstein sponsored the showing of photographs of American Victorian houses by his friend Walker Evans — a project Kirstein had conceived and personally financed. Until 1935, however, the date of Beaumont Newhall's arrival as librarian (replacing Iris Barry, who now headed the new Film Department), no MoMA staff member spoke with authority for photography's interests.[6]

4.   Quoted in Susan Buck-Morss, *The Origin of Negative Dialectics*, New York, Free Press, 1977, p. 149. The Adorno-Benjamin correspondence has been published in *Aesthetics and Politics*, London, New Left Books, 1977. A discussion of Benjamin's use of "cult value" and "exhibition value" can be found in Pierre V. Zima, "L'Ambivalence dialectique: Entre Benjamin et Bakhtine," *Revue d'Esthétique*, no. 1 (1981), 131–40. Benjamin's friend Brecht detected a lingering theological tone in the concept of the aura, calling it, in his *Arbeitsjournal*, "all mysticism, mysticism, in a form opposed to mysticism. . . . it is rather ghastly" (Buck-Morss, p. 149).
5.   Walter Benjamin, "A Short History of Photography," trans. Stanley Mitchell, *Screen*, vol. 13, no. 1 (Spring 1972), 6.
6.   Kirstein was the author of what was apparently the museum's first major statement on the subject, "Photography in the United States," in Holger Cahill and Alfred H. Barr, Jr., eds., *Art in*

Murals by American Painters and Photographers.
MoMA installation. 1932.

Newhall's exhibition, "Photography 1839–1937," is usually cited as a crucial step in the acceptance of photography as a full-fledged museum art. Considered from a slightly different perspective, it also emerges as an important link in the series of four great didactic exhibitions staged at MoMA during 1936–38; the others were Barr's "Cubism and Abstract Art" (1936) and "Fantastic Art, Dada, and Surrealism" (1936), and the retrospective "Bauhaus: 1919–1928" (1938). Together, these exhibitions demonstrated MoMA's influential modernization of what had come to be known among museum profes-

America in Modern Times, New York, Reynal and Hitchcock, 1934. The essay was based on a talk given as part of a series of MoMA-sponsored coast-to-coast broadcasts introducing the American radio audience to modern painting, sculpture, architecture, photography, and film.

sionals as the "aesthetic theory of museum management."[7] The central tenets had at first been spelled out in the dramatic reorientation of the Boston Museum of Fine Arts three decades earlier. At that time the educational role of art museums had been sharply distinguished from that of history or science museums. Rather than provide useful information or technical instruction, the art museum was increasingly directed toward the service of "joy not knowledge." That is, it began to serve as *vade mecum* to aesthetic appreciation; it became a treasure house of "eternal" monuments of art, the guarantor of art's continuous tradition. Like Barr, Newhall had been schooled in the essentials of this approach—connoisseurship and rigorous art-historical scholarship—in the famous museum seminars led by Paul Sachs at Harvard's Fogg Art Museum.[8] By the mid-'30s, MoMA's refinement of these methods—through the rationalization of collection building, the augmentation of the role of the research library, and the extension of scholarly commentary to exhibition catalogues— accounted in part for its reputation in museum circles. The four exhibitions of 1936-38—with their vast installations, exhaustive documentation, and ambitious catalogue essays—carried the process one step further. They sought to impart a convincing retrospective order to their heterogeneous domains, and, by so doing, to confirm MoMA's claim as the preeminent institutional interpreter of modern art and its allied movements.

Turning again to "Photography: 1839-1937," we can see that Newhall's exhibition is frankly uninterested in the old question of photography's status among the fine arts; rather, it signaled MoMA's recognition that implicit in photography's adoption by the European avant-garde was a new outlook on the whole spectrum of photographic applications. The approach of photography's centenary year provided reason enough to stage in America the kind of far-reaching examination that had been common in Germany, for example, for over a decade. Newhall's exhibition—comprising more than 800 catalogued items grouped according to technical processes (daguerreotypy, calotypy, wet-plate, and dry-plate periods) and their present-day applications (press photography, infra-red and X-ray photography, astronomical photography, "creative" photography)—clearly seems guided more by Moholy-Nagy's expansive notion

7.   Certainly a major factor in this movement was the proliferation of art reproductions. The issue of copies (public education) versus originals (aesthetic appreciation) came to a head at the Boston MFA over the purchase of plaster casts of original marbles, and ultimately led to the resignation of the museum's director, Edward Robinson. For a full account of that museum's subsequent formulation of the "religion" of art, see Benjamin Ives Gilman, *Museum Ideals*, Cambridge, Mass., 1918.
8.   Sachs, in addition to his incalculable influence on the emerging American museum profession, more particularly served as the principal academic presence on the committee convened by Mrs. John D. Rockefeller, Jr., in 1929 to draw up plans for a Museum of Modern Art. Sachs long remained an important member of MoMA's board.

of *fotokunst* than by Stieglitz's *kunstphotographie*.[9] Moholy was, indeed, one of Newhall's principal advisers and "teachers" before the exhibition. Stieglitz, on the other hand, who still insisted on the utter opposition of fine-art and applied photography, not only declined to cooperate with Newhall, but refused to allow his later photographs to be represented.[10]

Without resorting to devices as overtly didactic as Moholy's eight "varieties of photographic vision," Newhall nevertheless conceived the exhibition primarily as a lesson in the evolution and specialization of photographic techniques; the work of Muybridge, Atget, Stieglitz, and Anschutz, for instance, was presented under the rubric of dry-plate photography. The scope of the exhibition, its organization primarily along technical lines, and Newhall's refusal to make the expected pronouncement on photography's place among the fine arts — together these represented a notable departure from the usual practice of an American art museum. Lewis Mumford raised the question in the *New Yorker*:

> Perhaps it is a little ungrateful for me to suggest that the Museum of Modern Art has begun to overreach itself in the matter of documentation. . . . What is lacking in the present exhibition is a weighing and an assessment of photography in terms of pure aesthetic merit — such an evaluation as should distinguish a show in an art museum from one that might be held, say, in the Museum of Science and Industry. In shifting this function onto the spectator, the Museum seems to me to be adding unfairly to his burden. . . .[11]

Mumford notwithstanding, we need only to look more closely into Newhall's catalogue essay to locate the emerging signs of MoMA's reordering of photography along lines consistent indeed with the conventional aims of the art museum. In Newhall's long essay (the seed of his subsequent *History of Photography*), we find an explicitly articulated program for the isolation and expert judging of the "aesthetic merit" of photographs — virtually any photograph, regardless of derivation. Newhall's method here seems to me directly related to that of Alfred Barr in his *Cubism and Abstract Art*, published the previous year.

---

9.   Newhall's exhibition follows precisely along the lines of the series of large photography exhibitions held in Germany from 1925 until the early 1930s, as described by Ute Eskildsen, "Innovative Photography in Germany between the Wars," in *Avant-Garde Photography in Germany 1919–39*, San Francisco, San Francisco Museum of Modern Art, 1980. These joint showings of scientific, commercial, and creative "new vision" photography and film placed the camera at the center of the postwar technological aesthetic in Germany, and should be seen as forming part of the background of Walter Benjamin's writings during this period.

10.   For an indication of the position of Stieglitz's die-hard followers regarding photography outside the fine-art tradition, see R. Child Bayley's remarkably brief "Photography Before Stieglitz," in *America and Alfred Stieglitz*, New York, The Literary Guild, 1934, pp. 89–104.

11.   Lewis Mumford, "The Art Galleries," *The New Yorker*, April 3, 1937, p. 40.

Barr's famous flow charts of the various "currents" of modern painting depended on an admittedly formalist supposition: the existence of a self-enclosed, self-referential field of purely aesthetic factors, untouched by the influence of any larger social or historical forces. What is explicit in Barr (and what provoked, by way of rejoinder, Meyer Schapiro's "Nature of Abstract Art") reappears sub rosa in Newhall. Drawing on the earlier, overwhelmingly technical histories of photography (those of Eder and Potonniée, in particular), Newhall outlined photography's history primarily as a succession of technical innovations—independent, for all intents and purposes, of developments in the neighboring graphic arts or painting—that were to be assessed above all for their aesthetic consequences.

How were these aesthetic factors to be isolated? Newhall found the key in the purist/formalist appeal to those qualities somehow judged to be irreducibly intrinsic to a given medium or, in Newhall's words, "generic to photography."[12] In this case, "In order that . . . criticism of photography should be valid, photography should be examined in terms of the optical and chemical laws which govern its production."[13] On this basis, and taking his cue, I suspect, from Barr's well-known opposition (in *Cubism and Abstract Art*) of the "two main traditions of abstract art," Newhall likewise located two main traditions of aesthetic satisfaction in photography: from the optical side, the *detail*, and, from the chemical side, *tonal fidelity*. This "schism" is found "to run through the entire history of photography"[14] from the daguerreotype (detail) and calotype (tonal mass) to the modern high-resolution products of the view camera and the less precise but graphically more forceful images of the miniature camera. The creative application of these primary qualities consists, for Newhall, in the recognition of "significant" detail, and in the arrangement of "large simple masses" or a "fine range of shimmering tones."[15]

The aims of this method, as specified in the preface added to the next year's revised edition, were "to construct a foundation by which the significance of photography as an esthetic medium can be more fully grasped."[16] The limits and constraints of these aims are nowhere more clearly revealed than in Newhall's remarks on the nineteenth-century French photographer Charles Marville. Marville had, in the 1860s, documented the condemned sections of

12. Beaumont Newhall, *Photography: 1839–1937*, New York, Museum of Modern Art, 1937, p. 41.
13. *Ibid.*, p. 41.
14. *Ibid.*, p. 44.
15. *Ibid.*, pp. 43–44. This duality was already a commonplace in the 1850s, as evidenced in Gustave Le Gray's preface to his *Photographie: Traité nouveau* of 1852. For a contemporary "inquiry into the aesthetics of photography" along the same line, see James Borcoman, "Purism versus Pictorialism: The 135 Years War," in *Artscanada*, vol. 31, nos. 3–4 (December 1974).
16. Beaumont Newhall, *Photography: A Short Critical History*, New York, Museum of Modern Art, 1938, p. 9.

old Paris before they were razed to make way for Haussmann's boulevards. For Newhall, Marville's photographs can be considered "personal expressions" principally by virtue of the photographer's "subtle lighting and careful rendition of detail."[17] Having once established this priority, any social/historical residue can be unobtrusively rechanneled as nostalgia — in Newhall's words, "the melancholy beauty of the condemned and vanished past."[18]

The appearance at MoMA, three years before the founding of a full department of photography, of this rudimentary way of "looking at photographs," seems in retrospect the real point of interest in Newhall's 1937 exhibition. By carefully limiting his attention to what he later codified as the "relationship of technique to visualization,"[19] Newhall opened the door to a connoisseurship of photographs that might easily range beyond the confines of art photography, yet still avoid the nettlesome intermediary questions raised by the photographic medium's entanglement in the larger workings of the world.

Newhall never fully explored the implications of such a method; by 1940, when he was named the museum's curator of photography (the first time any museum had created such a post), he had already redirected his interests to what he conceived as photography's creative, rather than practical or applied, side. In his "Program of the Department," he now called for the study of photography to be modeled on that of literature, conventionally conceived: as the examination "under the most favorable conditions, of the best work that can be assembled."[20] In practice, this involved a new dependence on the connoisseur's cultivated, discriminating taste; on the singling out of the monuments of photography's past; on the elaboration of a canon of "masters of photography"; and on a historical approach that started from the supposition of creative expression — in short, an art history of photography. For the sources of this reinscription of photography within the traditional vocabulary of the fine arts, we must look not only to Newhall, but to the two others who presided with him over the inception of the department: the collector David Hunter McAlpin and the photographer Ansel Adams.

Signs of this reinscription were already clear in 1938, when Newhall's earlier essay reappeared, revised, as *Photography: A Short Critical History*. Where Moholy-Nagy might be seen as the guiding spirit of 1937, now Stieglitz was firmly installed as *genius loci*: a new dedication rendered homage to Stieglitz,

---

17. Newhall, *Photography: 1839–1937*, p. 48.
18. *Ibid.* Newhall was aware of the very different method at work in Gisèle Freund's *La Photographie en France au dix-neuvième siècle*, Paris, Monnier, 1936, which he cites. The validity of his own method must have seemed self-evident, for the possibility of alternative procedures is nowhere acknowledged.
19. Beaumont Newhall, "Program of the Department," *The Bulletin of the Museum of Modern Art*, vol. 8, no. 2 (December-January 1940–41), 4.
20. *Ibid.*

and one of his photographs was reproduced as frontispiece. More revealing was the disappearance of that section of the earlier essay in which Newhall (echoing Moholy) had scored the dependence of Stieglitz's Photo-Secession group on the models of genre painting, and pointed out that its members' production of prints had been "arbitrarily limited, in spite of the fact that an inherent characteristic of photography is its ability to yield infinite identical prints."[21] In its place there now appeared a paean to Stieglitz as visionary, which revolved around the claim that "the step to modern art was logical and direct, for Stieglitz and the group were alive to every type of revelation through pictures."[22]

Newhall's new alignment with such a transcendent claim of modernist photography, rather than with the more openly functionalist claims of the "new vision," can be seen as one means of attracting the support necessary to establish a full department at MoMA. The key step was the involvement—thanks to Newhall's friend Ansel Adams—of David Hunter McAlpin, a wealthy stockbroker related to the Rockefeller family, whom Stieglitz had groomed as a collector of photographs. It was McAlpin who initially agreed to provide funds for the museum to purchase photographs, and who was subsequently invited to join the MoMA board as the founding chairman of the Committee on Photography. In 1940, it was McAlpin who arranged to bring Ansel Adams to New York as vice-chairman of the new department, to join Newhall in organizing its first exhibitions.[23]

Looking at the first exhibition staged by Newhall and Adams, "60 Photographs: A Survey of Camera Esthetics," and reading the texts that accompanied it, one finds a number of markers set in place to delimit the kinds of photographs with which the new department would be concerned. Quick to appear are notions of rarity, authenticity, and personal expression—already the vocabulary of print connoisseurship is being brought into play. The collector David McAlpin introduced the theme of the rarity of the photographic original:

> The history of painting, sculpture, and the other arts . . . is widely accessible to all. By reason of the perishable nature of plates, films, and prints, original photographic material is scarce. Much of it has disappeared. What remains is scattered, its whereabouts unknown.[24]

Newhall, elaborating upon this idea, broached the possibility of a rarity of still greater degree:

21.   Newhall, *Photography: 1839–1937*, p. 64.
22.   Newhall, *Photography: A Short Critical History*, p. 64.
23.   Newhall's account can be found in the interview included in Paul Hill and Thomas Cooper, *Dialogue with Photography*, New York, Farrar, Straus and Giroux, 1979, pp. 389–390.
24.   David H. McAlpin, "The New Department of Photography," *The Bulletin of the Museum of Modern Art*, vol. 8, no. 2 (December-January 1940-41), 3.

From the prodigious output of the last hundred years relatively few great pictures have survived — pictures which are personal expressions of their makers' emotions, pictures which have made full use of the inherent characteristics of the medium of photography. These living photographs are, in the fullest sense of the word, works of art.[25]

Having indicated the narrowing scope of his interests, Newhall went on to imply a comparative system of classification of photographic prints, one ultimately enabling him to suggest the way in which the question of authenticity might be addressed. Physical authenticity could be referred back to considerations of technical process, which had figured so prominently in his 1937 essay; "60 Photographs" allowed Newhall to emphasize his expert familiarity with the special characteristics of calotypes, albumen prints, platinum prints, direct photogravures, palladio-types, chloride prints, bromide prints, and so on. But a more subtle test of authenticity was the degree to which a photograph might be enveloped, without incongruity, in the language and categories usually reserved for fine art. Thus Newhall called attention to the photographic interpretation of such traditional genres as landscape, portraiture, and architectural studies. Further, a way of placing photographs according to the degree and direction of visual stylization was suggested, along an axis bounded by the terminals of "objective" and "abstract" renderings.

But the chief claim made for the work presented in "60 Photographs" was this: "Each print is an individual personal expression."[26] As the ultimate guarantee against the charge that the photographic process was merely mechanical, this claim presents no special difficulty when made, as it was here, on behalf of photographers like Stieglitz, Strand, Weston, Sheeler, and Walker Evans — self-conscious modernists all. The stakes are somewhat different, however, when the same claim is extended to earlier photographs made in a variety of circumstances and for a variety of reasons. And it is here, I think, that we may look to Ansel Adams for the first flowering of a practice that reappears, in the tenure of John Szarkowski, as a crucial feature of MoMA's critical apparatus: the projection of the critical concerns of one's own day onto a wide range of photographs of the past that were not originally intended as art.

Not surprisingly, Adams undertook a modernist rereading of the work of the nineteenth-century wet-plate photographers of the American West in the light of the post-Stieglitz "straight" aesthetic. Just before his move to New York in 1940, Adams (with Newhall's help) organized a large exhibition in San Fran-

25. Newhall, "Program of the Department," p. 2.
26. Beaumont Newhall, "The Exhibition: Sixty Photographs," *The Bulletin of the Museum of Modern Art*, vol. 8, no. 2 (December-January 1940–41), 5.

cisco that highlighted such early western photographers as Timothy O'Sullivan, William Henry Jackson, Jack Hillers, and Carleton Watkins. By confining his attention to questions of photographic technique and the stylistics of landscape (and pushing to the margins the very different circumstances that had called these photographs into being), Adams was able to see in them "supreme examples of creative photography," belonging to one of the medium's "great traditions"[27]—needless to say, his own. The same pronounced shift in the "horizon of expectation" brought to earlier work is evident, as well, in the essay— "Photography as an Art"—that Newhall contributed to the same catalogue. In it he redrew the boundaries of art photography to accommodate the Civil War documentation of the Brady group. Admitting that the photographs had been made "without any implied esthetic intent," he claimed them for art on the grounds that they seemed, to him, undeniably "tragic and beautiful" and that they specifically prefigured the concerns of latter-day documentary stylists like Walker Evans and Berenice Abbott.[28] These Civil War and early western photographs were brought together at MoMA two years later, beginning their long rehabilitation as independent, self-contained aesthetic objects.

*

To a remarkable degree, the program of nearly thirty exhibitions mounted by the MoMA Department of Photography from 1940–47 anticipates what has emerged only in the last decade as the standard practice of other American museums.[29] The exhibitions centered on historical surveys ("French Photographs—Daguerre to Atget," 1945), the canonization of masters ("Paul Strand," 1945, and "Edward Weston," 1946), and the promotion of selected younger photographers (Helen Levitt and Eliot Porter, 1943; Henri Cartier-Bresson, 1947). Typically the photographs were presented in precisely the same manner as other prints or drawings—carefully matted, framed, and placed behind glass, and hung at eye level; they were given precisely the same status: that of objects of authorized admiration and delectation. In this museological mise-en-scène, the "outmoded" categories of artistic reception that Walter

27. "Above all, the work of these hardy and direct artists indicates the beauty and effectiveness of the straight photographic approach. No time or energy was available for inessentials in visualization or completion of their pictures. Their work has become one of the great traditions of photography" (Ansel Adams, introduction to *A Pageant of Photography*, San Francisco, San Francisco Bay Exposition Co., 1940, n.p.).
28. Beaumont Newhall, "Photography as an Art," in *A Pageant of Photography*, n.p.
29. Any assessment of Newhall's department must bear in mind the complicated comings and goings that marked the war years. On Newhall's departure for military service, his wife Nancy became acting curator. The next year saw Willard Morgan (husband of the photographer Barbara Morgan) named director of the department, an arrangement that lasted only one year. And in 1942 and 1945 Edward Steichen was brought in to stage spectacular patriotic exhibitions.

Benjamin had expected photography to brush aside — "creativity and genius, eternal value and mystery" — were displaced onto a new ground and given new life. Photography — an admittedly narrow range of it, initially — was laid out on an institutionalized interpretative grid and made the object of expert aesthetic judgment. Moreover, by extending the axes of this grid — formalist reading, the presupposition of creative intent, the announced preciousness of the photographic print — it was conceivable that a related order might eventually be imposed on the outlying regions of photography's past.

One may reasonably wonder, then, seeing that Newhall's curatorial policies so clearly anticipate today's uncontested norm, why, in the summer of 1947, did MoMA's trustees cancel their support for those policies, name the sixty-eight-year-old Edward Steichen as director of the photography department, and accept Newhall's sudden resignation?

Simply put, it seems clear that Newhall's exhibition program failed equally to retrieve photography from its marginal status among the fine arts and to attract what the museum could consider a substantial popular following. While Barr's exhibitions, "Cubism and Abstract Art" among them, were instrumental in creating a flourishing market for modern painting and sculpture, thereby

The Photographs of Edward Weston. *MoMA installation. 1946.*

confirming MoMA's status as an important art-world tastemaker, Newhall's photography exhibitions had no comparable effect. A striking index of photography's marginality can be found in a curious 1941 MoMA showing called "American Photographs at $10," which offered for sale limited-edition prints by the photographers who figured most prominently in Newhall's emerging canon — Stieglitz, Weston, and Adams, among them. The language in which the prints were presented all but confessed the absence of an audience attuned to the proclaimed transcendent aims of modernist art photography:

> The exhibition and sale is an experiment to encourage the collecting of photographs for decoration and pleasure. Once a photographer has worked out a suitable relationship between grade of paper, exposure and development to make one fine print, he can at the same time make many more of identical quality. Thus the unit cost can be lowered.[30]

More seriously, Newhall's insistent championing of photography as fine art drew the open hostility of that section of the photographic press that claimed to speak for the nation's millions of amateurs: the department was called "snobbish," "pontifical," and accused of being shrouded in "esoteric fogs."[31] In light of the museum's desire for funds for expansion in the mid-1940s, the declaration of John A. Abbot, vice-president of the museum's board, that MoMA intended actively to seek the "support of the photographic industry and photography's vast and devoted following"[32] clearly spelled trouble for Newhall. In Newhall's later recollection:

> Suddenly I was told by the director that the Trustees had decided to appoint Edward Steichen as the Director of Photography. I'd felt that I could not work with Steichen. I respected the man, I knew the man pretty well by this time. I just didn't see that we could be colleagues. It was as simple as that. My interests were increasingly in the art of photography; his were increasingly in the illustrative use of photography, particularly in the swaying of great masses of people.[33]

The approach that Newhall had mapped out at MoMA survived, of

---

30.   Wall label for "American Photographs at $10," visible in an installation view filed in the MoMA archive. As the history of the Julian Levy Gallery during the 1930s made evident, the market for original photographs was never strong enough to support even one gallery specializing in photography.

31.   Bruce Downes, "The Museum of Modern Art's Photography Center," *Popular Photography*, February 1944, p. 85.

32.   *Ibid.*, p. 86.

33.   Newhall interviewed by WXXI-TV, Rochester, 1979, transcript pages 27–28.

course: as an influential text (his *History of Photography*, first published in 1949[34])
and in an important institutional enclave (the George Eastman House, whose
first director he became). Nevertheless, the next fifteen years at MoMA were
marked by Steichen's inclination not to give a "hoot in hell"[35] for photography
conceived as an autonomous fine art.

*

In his 1947 study of the former Bauhaus artist/designer, Herbert Bayer,
Alexander Dorner offered this ironic conception of the classically conceived exhibition gallery:

> The gallery shows works of art containing eternal ideas and forms in
> an equally immutable framework of space which itself has grown out
> of the absolute immutability of the inner form. . . . The visitor . . .
> is supposed to visit a temple of the eternal spirit and listen to its
> oracle.[36]

Announcing to his American audience that the age of art forms such as these
was at an end, Dorner hailed the Bauhaus for its "explosive transformation of
the very idea *art*"; in language strikingly similar to Walter Benjamin's he described the situation brought about by the decline of traditional art forms as
one "bursting with energies which, once set to work in the practical context of
life, might well influence life on a tremendous practical scale."[37]

Bayer's own contrasting idea of the aims of the modern exhibition
descended from El Lissitzky's revolutionary use of repetitive photographic/
typographic clusters in the late 1920s, mediated by the Bauhaus's rationalization of Lissitzky's techniques in the 1930s. Bayer called on the modern exhibition to apply all of the techniques of the "new vision" in combination with color,

34.   In light of the increasing awareness of the problematic role played by narrative representa-
tion in historiography (see, for example, Hayden White's "Interpretation in History," *New Literary
History*, vol. 4, no. 2 [Winter 1973]), it deserves to be noted that the narrative strategy of
Newhall's 1949 *History* was devised with the aid of a Hollywood scriptwriter, Ferdinand Reyner.
See Hill and Cooper, *Dialogue with Photography*, pp. 407–408. In Newhall's words, "*The History of
Photography* was deliberately planned with the help of a storyteller."
35.   "When I first became interested in photography, I thought it was the whole cheese. My
idea was to have it recognized as one of the fine arts. Today I don't give a hoot in hell about that"
(Steichen on the occasion of his ninetieth birthday, as reported in the *New York Times*, March 19,
1969).
36.   Alexander Dorner, *The Way Beyond "Art": The Work of Herbert Bayer*, New York, Wittenborn,
Schultz, 1947, pp. 107–108. Dorner was the former director of the Landes Museum in Hanover,
Germany, for whom El Lissitzky had designed special rooms for the exhibition of abstract art in
1925. After emigrating to the U.S., he joined the faculty of the Rhode Island School of Design.
37.   Dorner, *The Way Beyond Art*, p. 15.

*El Lissitzky. Soviet Pavilion, International
Hygiene Exhibition, Dresden. 1930.*

*Herbert Bayer. Diagram of extended vision in
exhibition presentation. 1930.*

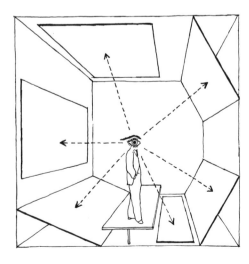

scale, elevation, and typography — all of these to serve, moreover, a decidedly instrumental end. The modern exhibition, he wrote,

> . . . should not retain its distance from the spectator, it should be brought close to him, penetrate and leave an impression on him, should explain, demonstrate, and even persuade and lead him to a planned and direct reaction. Therefore we may say that exhibition design runs parallel with the psychology of advertising.[38]

In the Germany of the 1920s and early '30s, this turn of emphasis could well be seen as essential to the rapid education of a backward public to the complexities of an emerging technological culture; such, of course, was one of the overriding themes of the entire Bauhaus project. But these principles, transported to the America of the postwar period, proved quite readily adaptable to very different ends — particularly when used to shape the extravagant thematic exhibitions that marked Steichen's years at MoMA.

Now it might seem that Steichen — one of the founders of the Photo-Secession and, with Stieglitz, one of the first promoters of European modernist art in America — was uniquely fitted to fulfill Newhall's efforts to consolidate a place for fine-art photography within the museum. But since the 1920s, Steichen's ambitions had carried him far beyond the confines of art photography: his portrait and fashion photography for *Vanity Fair* and *Vogue* brought him personal celebrity and fortune, and during his service in the U.S. Navy in World War II he learned the enormous power of quasi-documentary reportage aimed at the home-front audience. It was with this knowledge that, in 1942, he first came to MoMA:

> During the war I collected photographs and organized an exhibition called "Road to Victory," and it was that exhibition which gave ideas to the board of directors of the Museum. Here was something new in photography to them. Here were photographs that were not simply placed there for their aesthetic values. Here were photographs used as a force and people flocked to see it. People who ordinarily never visited the museum came to see this. So they passed the proposition on to me that I keep on along those lines.[39]

The impact of "Road to Victory" depended largely on the ingenious installation devised for Steichen by Herbert Bayer, who had left Germany in 1938. Spectators were guided along a twisting path of enormous, free-

38. Herbert Bayer, "Fundamentals of Exhibition Design," *PM*, December/January 1939/40, p. 17. *PM* (Production Manager) was the publication of New York's Laboratory School of Industrial Design.
39. Edward Steichen, "Photography and the Art Museum," in *Museum Service* (Bulletin of the Rochester Museum of Arts and Sciences), June 1948, p. 69.

Above: Road to Victory. *MoMA installation by Herbert Bayer. 1942. Below:* Power in the Pacific. *MoMA installation by George Kidder Smith. 1945.*

standing enlargements of documentary photographs — some as large as ten by forty feet. This arrangement was calculated to produce a visual narrative that combined the most dramatic devices of film and *Life*-style photojournalism. In *PM*, the photographer Ralph Steiner wrote, "The photographs are displayed by Bayer as photographs have never been displayed before. They don't sit quietly on the wall. They jut out from the walls and up from the floors to assault your vision. . . ."[40] The exhibition attracted immense crowds and critical plaudits, as did its 1945 successor, "Power in the Pacific."

It was in just this direction, and in this style, that Steichen was invited to continue at MoMA after the war: rather than contest the peripheral status of art photography, he was to capitalize on photography's demonstrably central role as a mass medium that dramatically "interpreted" the world for a national (and international) audience. That the museum harbored such an interest seems peculiar only if one ignores MoMA's extensive wartime program, in which the museum's prestige was directed towards the "educat[ion], inspir[ation], and strengthen[ing of] the hearts and wills of free men in defense of their own freedom."[41] Later — as Eva Cockcroft has shown — after carrying out a number of wartime cultural missions for Nelson Rockefeller's Office of Inter-American Affairs, MoMA emerged as one of the principal actors in the cultural Cold War.[42] In welcoming Steichen to MoMA in 1947, Rockefeller (then president of MoMA's board) served notice that the Department of Photography's concerns would no longer be confined to the aesthetic realm:

> Steichen, the young man who was so instrumental in bringing modern art to America, joins with the Museum of Modern Art to bring to as wide an audience as possible the best work being done throughout the world, and to employ it creatively as a means of interpretation in major Museum exhibitions where photography is *not the theme but the medium through which great achievements and great moments are graphically represented.*[43]

One can, with Allan Sekula, see productions like "The Family of Man" as

40.   Ralph Steiner, in *PM*, May 31, 1942. The Edward Steichen Archive, MoMA. A more complete account of the "Road to Victory" exhibition can be found in my "Steichen's 'Road to Victory,'" *Exposure*, vol. 18, no. 2 (Fall 1980).
41.   Quotation from John Hay Whitney, then president of MoMA's board, cited in Russell Lynes, *Good Old Modern*, New York, Athenaeum, 1973, p. 233.
42.   Eva Cockcroft, "Abstract Expressionism: Weapon of the Cold War," *Artforum*, vol. 12, no. 10 (June 1974), 39–41.
43.   "Edward Steichen Appointed Head of Photography at Museum of Modern Art," undated 1947 MoMA press release, The Edward Steichen Archive, MoMA, italics added. Rockefeller notes, in conclusion, "I am particularly pleased that the enlarged program for the Department, headed by Mr. Steichen, has the endorsement and support of the photographic industry."

exercises in sheer manipulation; but one can also see in their enthusiastic reception that familiar mass-cultural phenomenon whereby very real social and political anxieties are initially conjured up, only to be quickly transformed and furnished with positive (imaginary) resolutions.[44] From this standpoint, in "Korea: The Impact of War" (1951), doubts about dispatching American soldiers to distant regional battles are acknowledged (in a careful juxtaposition of the photographs of David Douglas Duncan), only to be neutralized in an exhibition setting that emphasized stirring images of American military might. In the same way, the global patriarchical family proposed as utopia in "The Family of Man" (1955) stands to gain considerably when set as the only opposing term to the nightmare image of atomic destruction. And "The Bitter Years" (1962) — coming at the height of the superpower war of nerves over Cuba and Berlin — consciously revived (for the first time in two decades) and reinterpreted the FSA's Depression-era photographs as an inspirational demonstration of the "fierce pride and courage which turned the struggle through those long bitter years into an American epic."[45]

While one could profitably examine such exhibitions as Barthesian "mythologies," ritual reenactments and carefully channeled resolutions of Cold War anxieties, I wish to call attention to the form in which they were conceived and circulated. For the underlying premise at work is that of the ultimate availability and duplicability of photographs — a notion believed to have revolutionary implications in the 1930s, but now reappropriated and domesticated in a later and very different set of circumstances. To prise photographs from their original contexts, to discard or alter their captions, to recrop their borders in the enforcement of a unitary meaning, to reprint them for dramatic impact, to redistribute them in new narrative chains consistent with a predetermined thesis — thus one might roughly summarize Steichen's operating procedure.[46] Furthermore, beginning as early as the 1942 "Road to Victory," each of these thematic exhibitions was conceived not as a single presentation, but as a set of multiple "editions" of varying physical dimensions intended to circulate — in the manner of motion pictures or magazines — throughout the United States and the world. Thus, by the mid-1950s, MoMA's initial press release anticipated that "The Family of Man" would open simultaneously in New

44.   See Allan Sekula, "The Traffic in Photographs," *Art Journal*, vol. 41, no. 1 (Spring 1981), 15–25. See also Fredric Jameson, "Reification and Utopia in Mass Culture," *Social Text*, no. 1 (1979), 130–148.

45.   "A Talk with Steichen," *WPAT Gaslight Revue*, vol. 8, no. 2 (October 1962), 40.

46.   In the 1942 "Road to Victory," for example, the dramatic turning point of the exhibition hinges on the juxtaposition of a photograph of the Pearl Harbor explosions with a Dorothea Lange photograph of a grim-visaged "Texas farmer" who is made to say, in caption, "War — they asked for it — now, by the living God, they'll get it!" Examining the original Lange photograph in the MoMA Archive, one finds this very different caption: "Industrialized agriculture. From Texas farmer to migratory worker in California. Kern County. November, 1938." For similar instances involving recropping, see Ulrich Keller, "Photographs in Context," *Image*, December 1976, pp. 1–12.

The Family of Man. *MoMA installation by Paul Rudolph. 1955.*

York, Europe, Asia, and Latin America, thereafter to travel globally for two years.[47]

The successful application of such techniques entailed, of course, two major factors: the all-but-total disappearance of the individual photographer within the larger fabric, and a disregard of the supposed personal-expressive qualities of the "fine print."[48] The photographers complied, for the most part, signing over to the museum the right to crop, print, and edit their images. In this way, the potential void left, at one level, by the abandonment of Newhall's main tenets—the photographer as autonomous artist, the original print as personal expression—was promptly filled at another by the museum's emergence as orchestrator of meaning. One would by no means be mistaken in seeing Steichen as MoMA's glorified picture editor, sifting through thousands of images from different sources and recombining them in forms reflecting the familiar mass-cultural mingling of popular entertainment and moral edification.[49]

This slippage of the photographer from the status of autonomous artist to that of illustrator of (another's) ideas marked the entire range of Steichen's exhibitions at MoMA; and it was not confined to the giant thematic shows that constituted its most visible aspect. The young photographers, however, who came of age just after World War II and looked to the mass-circulation magazines for their livelihood, generally understood illustration as the condition of photography. The most renowned artist-photographers at this time could expect to sell their work for no more than fifteen to twenty-five dollars per print.[50] Irving Penn was surely not alone in his insistence (at the 1950 MoMA symposium, "What Is Modern Photography?") that "for the modern photographer the end product of his efforts is the printed page, not the photo-

47.   "Museum of Modern Art Plans International Photography Exhibition," MoMA press release, January 31, 1954. The Edward Steichen Archive, MoMA.
48.   This was the point of Ansel Adams's main complaint. "The quality of the prints—of all his exhibits of this gross character—was very poor. . . . If a great Museum represented photography in such a style and quality, why bother about the subtle qualities of the image and the fine print?" (Ansel Adams, correspondence with this writer, January 30, 1980).
49.   "The Family of Man" can be seen to spring directly from the series of photo-essays supervised by picture editor John G. Morris for the *Ladies Home Journal* in 1947. "People Are People the World Over" used photojournalists like Robert Capa and Larry Burrows to present the everyday lives of families from twelve countries, on the premise that "the family is still the basic building block of society."
50.   At the MoMA Christmas print sale of 1951, one could buy photographs by Weston, Ansel Adams, Frederick Sommer, Charles Sheeler, and Berenice Abbott, among others, for $10–$25. At this particular sale, Harry Callahan (7), outsold Weston (5). The virtual nonexistence of a market for original photographs underlay the continuing difficulties of Helen Gee's Limelight Gallery, from 1954–61 the only New York gallery to regularly feature photography; see Barbara Lobron, "Limelight Lives," *Photograph*, vol. 1, no. 3 (1977), 1–3. As late as 1962, at the time of Steichen's retirement, Harry Callahan could expect to receive five dollars for each print purchased by the museum.

Forgotten Photographers. *MoMA installation. 1951.*

graphic print. . . . The modern photographer does not think of photography as an art or of his photograph as an art object."[51]

This view could only be reinforced by the presentation of photographs in the MoMA galleries. Under Steichen, the typical gallery installation resembled nothing so much as an oversized magazine layout, designed to reward rapid scanning rather than leisurely contemplation. Too frequently, the designer's hand appeared to greater advantage than the photographer's eye. Even in exhibitions of "creative" photography, the preciousness of the fine print was dramatically deemphasized. Prints were typically shown flush-mounted on thick (nonarchival) backing board, unmatted, and without benefit of protective glass. In addition, one could from time to time expect to encounter giant color transparencies, commercial press sheets, and inexpensive prints from color slides.

51.   Quoted in "What Is Modern Photography," *American Photography*, March 1951, p. 148. The symposium included statements by Penn, Margaret Bourke-White, Gjon Mili, Ben Shahn, Walker Evans, and Charles Sheeler, among others. Each participant, however, was limited to a five-minute statement, in order that the proceedings might be carried to a "Voice of America" radio audience.

It should not be thought that fine-art photography of the kind that Newhall had sponsored vanished entirely from the MoMA galleries—it did not. It was, however, acknowledged as a tiny band on the photographic spectrum, at a time when Steichen—an adept auto-publicist—encouraged a view of himself as the grandfatherly "dean" of *all* photography and MoMA as its institutional monitor. Soon after his arrival at the museum, for example, he let it be known that "he want[ed] to gather under his wing the 200,000 of America's amateurs . . . and teach them something about making pictures. Later on he want[ed] them to send the pictures to him for sorting and cataloguing. . . ."[52] He subsequently organized large survey exhibitions treating diverse special topics like news photography (1949), color photography (1950), and abstraction in photography (1951)—this last juxtaposing "creative" work with analogous scientific work. Such exhibitions never raised the question of the artistic status of any branch of photography. Rather, they demonstrated that all photography, if properly packaged, could be efficiently channeled into the currents of the mass media. Indeed, during this period magazine inserts and syndicated newspaper interviews largely replaced exhibition catalogues.

52.   Gilbert Bayley, "Photographer's America," *New York Times Magazine*, August 31, 1947, p. 39.

Abstraction in Photography. *MoMA installation. 1951.*

Two irregular series of smaller exhibitions clearly showed the limitations of Steichen's approach when applied to the handling of historical and serious contemporary photography. Photography's past was acknowledged in a number of so-called "flashback" exhibitions interspersed between the larger shows. These surveyed the work of the Photo-Secession (1948), nineteenth-century French photography from the Cromer Collection of the George Eastman House (1949), and the work of Stieglitz and Atget, shown together in 1950. But in the absence of extensive magazine coverage, exhibition catalogues, or critical writing, these exhibitions attracted little attention and left virtually no trace.[53]

More significant were the many small exhibitions organized to illustrate various photographers' treatments of a given theme — the theme was defined, of course, by Steichen. The best-known were the five installments of "Diogenes with a Camera" (1952–61), in which a great many photographers presented the

53. According to Newhall's count of selected publications on the history of photography from 1900–70, the 1950s saw fewer than half as many publications in this area than had the 1930s. The 1960s, on the other hand, witnessed a dramatic increase, more than doubling the number of publications of the 1930s. Newhall's compilation was made available at the Photographic Collectors' Symposium, George Eastman House, October 1978.

Postwar European Photography. *MoMA installation.*
1953.

results of their ostensible search for truth — the whole notion, one may suppose, a remnant of the claims previously made for art photography's incorporation of transcendent values. Gradually these exhibitions fell prey to Steichen's sentimental and moralizing tendencies; so much so that in 1962, when he wished to pair two of his favorites, Harry Callahan and Robert Frank, in a final "Diogenes," Frank flatly refused to exhibit under that title.[54]

The photographic values that Steichen consistently encouraged remained those of the glossy picture magazines: emotional immediacy, graphic inventiveness, avoidance of difficulty. Photographers who chose to explore what were defined as peripheral areas — whether of a social or an aesthetic nature — quickly faced loss of access to what had become (thanks in part to Steichen's proselytizing) a mass audience for photography. Callahan and Frank were typical of the ambitious younger photographers whose reputations benefited from their regular inclusion in MoMA exhibitions, but who nonetheless eventually chafed at the constraints of the mass-media model imposed on all of the work presented there. Callahan's rigorous formalist side was never shown to advantage, nor was his extensive work in color; as he later remarked of his exhibitions at MoMA during those years, "It was always a Steichen show. Always."[55] In the same way, the poignant, romantic Robert Frank whose work appeared at MoMA resembled only slightly the photographer whose corrosive social vision informed *The Americans* — a book that defined itself in opposition to the reigning norms of *Life* magazine and professionally "committed" photojournalism. ("I do not like the adoration of grand old men," was Frank's later, testy dismissal.[56])

At a time, then, when most American art museums still considered photography well beyond the pale of the fine arts, a peculiar set of circumstances allowed Steichen effectively to establish MoMA as the ultimate institutional arbiter of the entire range of photographic practice. In dissolving the categories by means of which Newhall had sought to separate fine-art photography from the medium's other applications, Steichen undermined the whole notion of the "cult value" of the fine print. In the process he attracted a wide popular following for photography as a medium, and won for it (and for himself) the regular

54.   Frank agreed to show his work minus the "Diogenes" label. But "Modern Art Museum officials were dismayed over the number of beatniks — about 80 of them — who crowded in the swank, private opening of Robert Frank's new photography exhibit. There wasn't much the museum could do about it, though. The beats were Frank's friends. . . ." *New York Daily News*, March 5, 1962. The Edward Steichen Archive, MoMA.
55.   Jacqueline Brody, "Harry Callahan: Questions," *Print Collectors' Newsletter*, January-February 1977, p. 174. A good discussion of Callahan's relation with Steichen can be found in Sally Stein, "Harry Callahan: Works in Color/ The Years 1946–1978" in the exhibition catalogue *Harry Callahan: Photographs in Color/The Years 1946–1978*, Center for Creative Photography, 1980.
56.   Robert Frank, "Letter from New York," *Creative Camera*, July 1969, p. 234.

attention of the mass press. The price exacted at MoMA was the eclipse of the individual photographer and the subordination of his or her work to the more or less overtly instrumental demands of illustration. This was the situation inherited by Steichen's successor in 1962.

*

A survey of the installation views of MoMA's photographic exhibitions from the early 1960s to the present induces a dizzying realization of the speed of photography's cultural repackaging. Steichen's hyperactive, chock-a-block displays metamorphose before one's eyes into the cool white spaces of sparsely hung galleries. Mural-sized enlargements shrink to conventional proportions, and the eccentric clustering of photographs of wildly assorted dimensions gives way to an orderly march of prints of utterly uniform size. The fine-art accoutrements of the Newhall years—standard white mattes, wooden frames, and covering glass—quickly reappear. With no knowledge of the particulars of John Szarkowski's program as director of MoMA's Department of Photography, one could easily surmise that the museum's claims for photography's "cult value" had been dusted off and urgently revived.[57] What one could not infer, of course, is the extent to which those claims resounded beyond the museum's walls to a rapidly proliferating network of galleries, collectors, critics, and arts administrators, all specializing, in one way or another, in photography.

The barbed title of his first exhibition, "Five Unrelated Photographers" (1962), announced that although Steichen had personally chosen him as his successor, Szarkowski was no acolyte. It gradually became apparent that Szarkowski, trained as an art historian, held no affection for Steichen's casting of photography in the role of social instrument and "universal language." Instead, he represented an aestheticizing reaction against Steichen's identification of photography with mass media. While deploring the "graphic gymnastics" of latter-day photojournalism, however, he showed equally little interest in the "artistic" alternatives at hand, in the photomysticism of Minor White or the expressive abstraction of Aaron Siskind. Szarkowski noted "incipient exhaustion" in the bulk of the photographs of the past decade, adding, "Their simplicity of meaning has—not to put too fine a point on it—often verged on vacuity."[58]

What Szarkowski sought, rather than a repetition of Newhall's attempt to cordon off a "high" art photography more or less independent of the medium's

57.   The MoMA Archive holds a full selection of installation views from the early 1930s to the present. These provide an invaluable record of the ways art has been presented to the public over the last half century.
58.   John Szarkowski, "Photography and Mass Media," *Aperture*, vol. 13, no. 3 (1967), n.p.

everyday uses, was the theoretical salvaging of photography in its entirety from the encroachments of mass culture. He wished, on this account, to redefine the medium's aesthetic nature in such a way as to set it on an irrevocably autonomous course. At a time when most excursions into photography's history still followed the narrow genetic-biographical path evidenced in Newhall's *Masters of Photography* (1958) and shared its emphasis on "the unmistakable authority of genius," Szarkowski turned to quick advantage the presumption (inherited from Steichen) that the MoMA Department of Photography might address any of the medium's multiple facets. From this institutional salient, he was able to set about reconstructing a resolutely modernist aesthetic for photography and remapping a "main tradition" in order to legitimize it.[59]

59.   Andreas Huyssen distinguishes modernism from avant-garde by means of the relation of each to artistic tradition, modernism, devising more and more hermetic strategies to preserve art's realm of autonomy, avant-garde as the embodiment of postauratic antitradition. See "The Search for Tradition: Avant-Garde and Postmodernism in the 1970s," *New German Critique*, no. 22 (Winter 1981), 23–40. In this light, see Hilton Kramer's uncomprehending "Anxiety about the Museumization of Photography," *New York Times*, July 4, 1976, in which he castigates Szarkowski for "providing a haven for the anti-art impulse."

Diogenes with a Camera *(Harry Callahan).*
MoMA installation. 1952.

Even before coming to MoMA Szarkowski had clearly indicated the direction his search for a usable tradition would take. In 1958, linking his own ambitions as a photographer to the precedents set in the previous century by Brady, O'Sullivan, and Jackson, he proclaimed, "I want to make pictures possessing the qualities of poise, clarity of purpose, and natural beauty, as these qualities were achieved in the work of the good wet-plate photographers."[60] In 1967, five years after arriving at MoMA, he elaborated on the same theme. In the essay "Photography and Mass Media," he sharply distinguished the work of these nineteenth-century photographers from the "flabbiness" of media-age photography and its ostensibly creative offshoots. These latter he faulted as "less and less interested in clear observation," which was what he felt photography's true vocation to be.

60.   John Szarkowski, *The Face of Minnesota*, Minneapolis, University of Minnesota, 1958. The book's format — short informal essays paired with single photographs — anticipated Szarkowski's MoMA productions. Two years earlier, Szarkowski had attracted attention with his Guggenheim-sponsored book *The Idea of Louis Sullivan*, featuring his own photographs of Sullivan's buildings and a short, lyrical essay. His photographs served as his initial point of contact with both Newhall and Steichen.

Harry Callahan, *MoMA installation. 1977.*

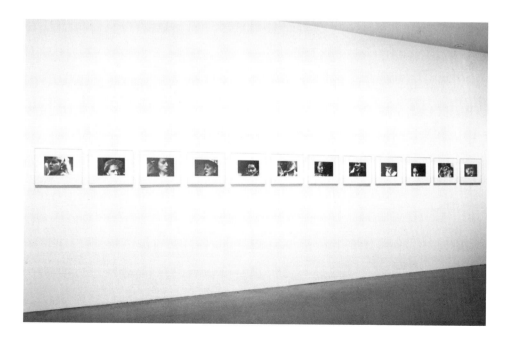

> During photography's first century it was generally understood . . .
> that what photography did best was to *describe* things: their shapes
> and textures and situations and relationships. The highest virtues of
> such photographs were clarity of statement and density of informa-
> tion. They could be read as well as seen; their value was literary and
> intellectual as well as visceral and visual.[61]

With such an agenda—realistic description without overt prescription—
Szarkowski could view with equanimity the impending collapse of photojournalism in the early 1970s. Assuming more and more the role of aesthetic
guide, he recommended as models to younger photographers the works of
Atget, Sander, and Frances Benjamin Johnston—all "deliberate and descriptive," and "constructed with the poise and stability which suggest Poussin or
Piero." Such pictures, he advised, "are not only good to look at, they are good
to contemplate."[62]

Szarkowski's ambitious program for establishing photography in its own
aesthetic realm has been set forth explicitly in no single work, but arrived at
piecemeal in a series of slender essays over the last twenty years. His project
has followed, I think, three main lines. These include: (1) the introduction of a
formalist vocabulary theoretically capable of comprehending the visual structure (the "carpentry") of any existing photograph; (2) the isolation of a modernist visual "poetics" supposedly inherent to the photographic image; and (3) the
routing of photography's "main tradition" away from the (exhausted) Stieglitz/
Weston line of high modernism and toward sources formerly seen as peripheral
to art photography.

The formalist theme first appeared in *The Photographer's Eye* (1964), in
which Szarkowski presented a selection of photographs—both celebrated and
anonymous—that epitomized for him the visual characteristics intrinsic to photography. Reworking John Kouwenhoven's thesis (outlined in the 1948 *Made*

61.   Szarkowski, "Photography and Mass Media."
62.   *Ibid.* It seems worthwhile to note that of the two illustrations introduced to underline his
point, only one (a carefully staged tableau by Frances Benjamin Johnston) is a photograph. The
other—connecting Szarkowski's pictorial concerns to an older, more prestigious tradition—is
Poussin's *The Arcadian Shepherds*. Using just this painting as his object of commentary, Louis Marin
has recently provided a remarkable analysis of the contemplative process in question here, as well
as a partial "history of reading" in the visual arts. What Marin calls the post-Renaissance classical
system of representation, founded on one-point linear perspective and the assumed transparency
of the picture plane, permits two simultaneous and contradictory readings: (1) as a duplication or
immediate mirroring of objects or scenes; or (2) as (someone's) representation of those scenes or
objects. As we will see, for Szarkowski the operation of these contradictory modes is a precondition for the emergence of what he calls the "narrative voice" in modernist art photography. See
Marin, "Toward a Theory of Reading in the Visual Arts: Poussin's *The Arcadian Shepherds*," in
Suleiman and Crosman, eds., *The Reader in the Text*, Princeton, Princeton University Press, 1980,
pp. 293-324. Also see Craig Owens's valuable commentary in "Representation, Appropriation,
and Power," in *Art in America*, May 1982, pp. 9-21.

in America) that the American artistic tradition could be conceived as the interplay of native ("vernacular") and European ("cultivated") strains, Szarkowski offered a list of photography's basic formal elements that drew equally on what Kouwenhoven had called the American "respect for optical reality" and the essentially European concern for coherent, self-sufficient form. His five characteristics — the detail, the thing itself, time, the frame, and the vantage point — provided not only a checklist that could be held up to any photograph for the cool appraisal of its organizing logic, but also a range of stylistic alternatives that were explicitly regarded as "artist's choices."

Interestingly, Szarkowski's concern with locating photography's formal properties signaled no incipient move toward abstraction. The formal characteristics he acknowledged were all modes of photographic *description*: instead of stressing (as had Clement Greenberg in his formalist essays on painting) the necessary role of the material support in determining the essential nature of the medium, Szarkowski wished to reserve unexamined for photography that classical system of representation that depends on the assumed transparency of the picture surface.[63] Thus the delimitation of formal elements could prove no end in itself, but only set the stage for a move to the iconographic level.

The central text in this regard is the curious *From the Picture Press* (1973), an investigation of the formal and iconographic properties of the "millions of profoundly radical pictures" that have filled the pages of the daily press. The enabling assumption here — one with important consequences for Szarkowski's whole aesthetic enterprise — is that of the "narrative poverty" of the photograph, a notion first broached in *The Photographer's Eye*. In essence, this entails the view that, considered strictly in terms of the visual descriptions inscribed within the picture frame, an individual photograph can, at best, give a "sense of the scene" but can never convey a larger narrative meaning. For Szarkowski, it does not follow that one ought to seek a supplement to the image beyond the frame. (What is at stake, after all, is the self-sufficiency of the photograph.) He recommends, instead, a particular mode of transformation of pictorial content: "If photographs could not be read as stories, they could be read as symbols."[64]

63. See Victor Burgin's commentary in "Photography, Phantasy, Function," in *Screen*, vol. 21, no. 1 (1980). As suggested by his emphasis on pure photographic description, Szarkowski has shown little interest in work in which the photographer's "hand" figures prominently, or work that explicitly calls photography's means of representation into question (as with Michael Snow or Jan Dibbets). As curator of the Department of Photography in the late 1960s and early 1970s, Peter Bunnell covered these areas to some extent in exhibitions like "Photography as Printmaking" (1968) and "Photography into Sculpture" (1970). Bunnell directed considerably more attention than Szarkowski to the connoisseurship of the "fine print," especially to the "subjective mannerisms, in part directed by techniques and materials, which render each print unique and which, in the last analysis, place man as the actual medium of expression" ("Photography as Printmaking," *Artist's Proof*, New York, Pratt Graphics, 1969, p. 24).
64. John Szarkowski, *The Photographer's Eye*, New York, MoMA, 1965, n.p. Benjamin, of

Selecting a number of press photographs from the files of the *Daily News* (with the help of Diane Arbus and Carole Kismaric), *From the Picture Press* provided an admittedly witty exercise in aesthetic reprocessing. Separated from their original contexts and their original captions, organized into iconographic categories ("ceremonies," "disasters," and the like), the images could now be savored for their surprising conjunctions of formal coherence and narrative ambiguity. They could be seen, in Szarkowski's words, as "short visual poems — they describe a simple perception out of context."[65] It is significant that the vocabulary of indeterminacy used thus to characterize the poetics of imagery duplicates that already familiar throughout the range of modernist art and literature: "As images, the photographs are shockingly direct, and at the same time mysterious, elliptical, and fragmentary, reproducing the texture of experience without explaining its meaning."[66] Moreover (as becomes clear in a later essay), Szarkowski finds these the essential qualities built into the images produced by the photographic medium; in this way photography can be claimed to produce its own, inherently modernist "new pictorial vocabulary, based on the specific, the fragmentary, the elliptical, the ephemeral, and the provisional."[67]

Szarkowski's distribution of emphases — falling, as I have indicated, on the transparency of photography's representational apparatus, the formal/stylistic elements peculiar to its descriptive system, and its ready-made modernist pictorial syntax — finally prepares the ground for the emergence of an aestheticized authorial "voice" proper to photography. In the work of Gary Winogrand, Diane Arbus, Lee Friedlander, and William Eggleston, for example — Szarkowski's "heirs of the documentary tradition"[68] — the adoption of the unmanipulated "in-

---

course, in "A Short History of Photography," cites Brecht on the necessity of constructing a supplement to the photographic image. And Dorothea Lange, in *An American Exodus*, conceives the documentary mode as depending on what she calls a "tripod" of meaning furnished by the relation of the image, the caption, and the text.

65.   John Szarkowski, *From the Picture Press*, New York, MoMA, 1973, p. 5.
66.   *Ibid.*, p. 6.
67.   John Szarkowski, *William Eggleston's Guide*, New York, MoMA, 1976, p. 6. Elsewhere Szarkowski links photography to the modern literary imagination. Writing of Crane's *The Red Badge of Courage*, he calls it a "profoundly photographic book," and speculates that Crane had "surely known" the Brady photographs. As Szarkowski describes the "thousands of Civil War photographs that survive," we see "only bits of machinery, records of destruction, a bit of a forest where a skirmish had occurred, and little knots of grey clad men, living or dead, waiting for a revelation of the larger meanings of the conflict." He describes Crane's book, similarly, as "the personal trial of one ignorant participant, seen from so close a perspective that large patterns are invisible" (Szarkowski, "American Photography and the Frontier Tradition"). Presumably Crane or Szarkowski might have found the same effect in Stendhal, writing well before the invention of photography.
68.   "The heirs of the documentary tradition have redirected that idea in the light of their own fascination with the snapshot: the most personal, reticent, and ambiguous of documents. These photographers have attempted to preserve the persuasiveness and mystery of these humble, intuitive camera records, while adding a sense of intention and visual logic" (John Szarkowski, wall

visible" style of documentary initially links their work to that aspect of the classical system of representation that posits (in Louis Marin's words) that "nobody is speaking; it is reality itself that speaks." But the new critic/connoisseur is on hand to certify the presence of the artist, and to provide expert guidance to the formal strategies of concealment through which the artist-photographer (to quote Marin on the reverse face of the classical paradigm) "inscribes himself as the center of the world and transforms himself into things by transforming things into *his* representations." These "contradictory axioms" of the classical system operate with considerable force in photography and, in Szarkowski's scheme, ultimately to the advantage of the artist-photographer. Thus his insistence that even though at first Winogrand's pictures may seem the uninflected "mechanical utterance of a machine,"

> As we study his photographs, we recognize that although in the conventional sense they may be impersonal, they are also consistently informed by what in a poem we would call a voice. This voice is, in turn, comic, harsh, ironic, delighted, and even cruel. But it is always active and distinct—always, in fact, a narrative voice.[69]

Admittedly, this postulation of a unitary authorial "voice" makes it possible to reckon critically with those contemporary artist-photographers who (proceeding along the familiar modernist route that Shklovsky called the "canonization of peripheral forms") have chosen to mimic the unperturbed stability of nineteenth-century topographic photographs, or to adopt the snapshot's seemingly unpremeditated jumbling of visual events as a metaphor for the fragmented, elusive quality of modern life. More subtly than Newhall's emphasis on "personal expression," it restores the presence of the artist through a reading method that makes it possible to see Eggleston's laconic photographs, for instance, primarily as "patterns of random fact in the service of an imagination—not the real world."[70] But whatever its value as a critical procedure for valorizing the work of one privileged sector of today's art photography, it provides at the same time a powerful rationale for the systematic rereading, along precisely the same lines, of the photographs of the past. Unfortunately, since photography has never been simply, or even primarily, an art medium—since it has operated both within and at the intersections of a variety of institutional discourses—when one projects a present-day art-critical method across the entire range of the photography of the past, the consequences are not incon-

label introducing "Photography: New Acquisitions," April 1970). Winogrand, Arbus, and Friedlander had already shown together in the exhibition "New Documents" (1967).
69.   John Szarkowski, "American Photography and the Frontier Tradition," *Symposion über Fotografie*, Graz, Austria, Forum Stadtpark, 1979, p. 107.
70.   Szarkowski, *William Eggleston's Guide*, p. 8.

siderable. Nor, given the prevailing winds of today's art market, are they likely to be disinterested. Thus, for example, the critic Ben Lifson's automatic reinterpretation of Robert Capa's politically committed Spanish Civil War reportage as a self-conscious "experimenting with photographic syntax." For Lifson, Capa's redemption for an aestheticized photographic tradition can proceed only by means of his transformation into an artist/author whose photographs can be safely read as a "fiction of his own creation."[71]

Such selective and reductive readings are, however, sanctioned by Szarkowski's conception of photography's past and its "central tradition." He writes: "Most of the meanings of any picture reside in its relationships to other and earlier pictures — to tradition."[72] But turning away from Newhall's lineage of successive individual "masters," he redirects attention to those photographers who "chose not to lead photography but to follow it, down those paths suggested by the medium's own eccentric and original genius."[73] Although echoing Eliot's insistence (in "Tradition and the Individual Talent") that the poet has not a personality but a medium to express, and that the medium's "main cur-

New Documents. *MoMA installation. 1967.*

rent . . . does not at all flow invariably through the most distinguished reputations," Szarkowski nonetheless goes far beyond Eliot's proposed "ideal order" of "existing monuments." His ideal order theoretically extends to *all* of photogra-

71.   Ben Lifson and Abigail Solomon-Godeau, "Photophilia: A Conversation about the Photography Scene," *October*, no. 16 (Spring 1981), 107. Describing the work of Robert Capa in the same language he might employ for that of, say, Gary Winogrand, Lifson brings to mind a 1970 MoMA exhibition called "Protest Photographs." Staged just after the mass protests that greeted the American invasion of Cambodia, the exhibition presented a number of prints push-pinned to the wall, as if they had just been rushed over from the photographers' darkrooms. One might have thought that here was a contemporary reflection of the concerns that animated photographers like Capa. On closer inspection, however, the photographs were revealed as exercises in virtuosity by Winogrand, Burk Uzzle, and Charles Harbutt — all using demonstration sites as an arena for what Szarkowski (writing elsewhere of Winogrand's formal bent) called "the recognition of coherence in the confluence of forms and signs."
72.   John Szarkowski, *New Japanese Photography*, New York, MoMA, 1974, p. 9.
73.   Szarkowski, "American Photography and the Frontier Tradition," p. 99.

phy: "Not only the great pictures by great photographers but *photography*—the great undifferentiated whole of it—has been teacher, library, and laboratory for those who have consciously used the camera as artist."[74] It would seem, then, that for Szarkowski historical practice should consist of the sifting of fragments and shards, and their reordering as a privileged representation of moments in the unfolding of photography's main tradition. If, as Edward Said has suggested, the proper vehicle for the display of such fragments is the chrestomathy, we can see in *Looking at Photographs* (1973), Szarkowski's most widely read book, a connoisseur's collection of photographic fragments ordered by and encased in his own richly allusive prose.

One further consideration remains. Szarkowski's comparison of the bulk of the photographic production of the nineteenth and early twentieth century to an "untended garden"[75] and a "genetic pool of possibilities"[76] hints that, indeed, he regards the development of photography as "something pretty close to an organic issue."[77] Reaching for a suitable analogy, he likens his search for photography's main tradition to "that line which makes the job of curator rather

The Work of Atget: Old France. *MoMA installation. 1982.*

similar to the job of a taxonomist in a natural history museum."[78] Can one say, then, that Szarkowski conceives of photography as endowed with an essential nature, determined by its origins and evident in what he calls an "evolutionary line of being"?[79]

Such would appear to be the case, at least on the basis of MoMA curator Peter Galassi's 1981 exhibition "Before Photography," which sought to give substance to Szarkowski's conjecture that photography was "like an organ-

74.   Szarkowski, *The Photographer's Eye*, n.p.
75.   Szarkowski, *Looking at Photographs*, New York, MoMA, 1973, p. 11.
76.   Quoted in Maren Stange, "Photography and the Institution: Szarkowski at the Modern," *Massachusetts Review*, vol. 19, no. 4 (Winter 1978), 701.
77.   *Ibid.*
78.   *Ibid.*, p. 698.
79.   *Ibid.*, p. 701.

ism . . . born whole."[80] Galassi's slim but ambitious catalogue had two aims: to portray photography as the legitimate (albeit eccentric) offspring of the Western pictorial tradition and to demonstrate that it was born with an inherent "pictorial syntax" that forced originality (and modernism) upon it. In stressing photography's claims as the heir to the system of one-point linear perspective, Galassi argued that the advent of photography in 1839 issued not from the juncture of multiple scientific, cultural, and economic determinations but from a minor tendency in late eighteenth-century painting. It was this tendency (evident primarily in hitherto-unremarked landscape sketches), notable for an embryonic pictorial syntax of "immediate synoptic perception and discontinuous forms," that somehow "catalyzed" photography into being. The larger point of this peculiar argument is that while photography incorporated what has been called here the classical paradigm of representation, the new medium was incapable of taking over painting's conventional pictorial language. For, according to Galassi, "the photographer was powerless to com-

80.   Szarkowski, *The Photographer's Eye*, n.p.

Before Photography. *MoMA installation. 1981.*

pose his picture. He could only . . . take it."[81] By reason of this "unavoidable condition," originality was forced, not simply on the photographer, but on the medium itself. In this way, what Szarkowski elsewhere referred to as the "monstrous and nearly shapeless experiment" of photography's first century can be seen as the unbidden working out of the "special formal potentials" of photography's inherent and singular syntax of the specific, the fragmentary, the elliptical, and so on. Incarnated in the work of "primitives" (Szarkowski's term) like Brady and O'Sullivan, this "new pictorial language" awaited its recognition and appropriation by self-conscious artist-photographers like Walker Evans, Lee Friedlander, or Robert Adams.

Thus endowed with a privileged origin — in painting — and an inherent nature that is modernist *avant la lettre*, photography is removed to its own aesthetic realm, free to get on with its vocation of producing "millions of profoundly radical pictures." As should be apparent, this version of photographic history is, in truth, a flight from history, from history's reversals, repudiations, and multiple determinations. The dual sentence spelled out here — the formal isolation and cultural legitimation of the "great undifferentiated whole" of photography — is the disquieting message handed down from the museum's judgment seat.

81.   Peter Galassi, *Before Photography*, New York, MoMA, 1981, p. 17. Three generally critical reactions to Galassi's argument are developed in S. Varnedoe's "Of Surface Similarities, Deeper Disparities, First Photographs, and the Function of Form: Photography and Painting after 1839," in *Arts Magazine*, September 1981; Joel Snyder's review in *Studies in Visual Communications*, vol. 8, no. 1 (1982); and Abigail Solomon-Godeau's "Tunnel Vision," in *Print Collectors' Newsletter*, vol. 12, no. 6 (January-February 1982). Only the last-cited attempted to establish the connection between Galassi's effort and Szarkowski's critical position.

Psychoanalysis

Iconographie Photographique de la Salpêtrière, *Vol. I,*
Attitudes Passionnelles: Extase. *1878.*

Flavit et Dissipati Sunt

JOAN COPJEC

Flavit et dissipati sunt: for those who do not "have" Latin, "he blew and they were scattered." The title is not mine, but Freud's, or possibly Freud's; that is, he entertained it as a possible title for the chapter he would write on therapy in his work on hysteria.[1] But doubtless he thought better of it, for he never did use it, but substituted instead "The Psychotherapy of Hysteria," which has none of the imaginative attraction of the rejected, impossible title. This essay, a discussion of the photographs of hysterics which appear in the three-volume *Iconographie Photographique de la Salpêtrière* (Service de J.-M. Charcot)[2] reinstates this title, a colophon of speculation on its rejection and on its relation to hysteria. Outside the question of the inappropriateness of the particular image in the title—of the Janet-like position in which it places the analyst with respect to "the poor little thing," the hysteric;[3] the hubris it reveals in the face of the doubts hysteria cast on scientific knowledge; and the Janus-like way it turns its back on the discovery of the resistances—there is the question of the inappropriateness of the image in general, of the image to scientific thought.

For some time Freud wanted to maintain a distance (as the particular image demonstrates) between himself, the analyst, and the hysteric, the analysand. The hysteric, in the very essay named by the substituted title, "The Psychotherapy of Hysteria," is characterized by him as being, as a rule, of a "visual" rather than a "thoughtful, verbal type." The psychotherapy consists in making a "picture" vanish "like a ghost that has been laid" to rest, in getting rid of it by turning it into words. The lines are clearly drawn: the analysand is on one side with images, the analyst on the other with thoughts. This notion of the inferiority of the image lingers even in Freud's obituary of Charcot, to whom he owed so much of his work on hysteria and whose picture hung always in Freud's office: Charcot, he summar-

1.   See Sigmund Freud, *The Interpretation of Dreams*, trans. James Strachey, New York, Avon, 1965, pp. 247–248, 508.
2.   D.M. Bourneville and P. Regnard, *Iconographie Photographique de la Salpêtrière*, Paris, Vol. I, 1877; Vol. II, 1878; Vol. III, 1879–80.
3.   See Pierre Janet, *The Major Symptoms of Hysteria*, New York, Macmillan, 1920.

ized, was not of the cognitive, reflective type, but (who can deny that the territory which abuts is not on the same, but an inferior, plane?) he had an artistic temperament; he was "a visuel, a seer." Our case rests here where Freud believes he rests this ghost. What we witness in this obituary (and Freud himself will develop in "Mourning and Melancholia" the concepts which allow us to say this) is a case of insufficient mourning. His thinking will not rid itself so easily of the image which will always haunt it from within. Although he will continue to reject images as imperfect, he will not cease to look for the appropriate ones, refusing at times to reject them even in their imperfections. At the conclusion of his attempt to explain the relation between memory and perception by way of the image of the photographic apparatus, he says, "I see no necessity to apologize for the imperfections of this or any other image."[4]

Perhaps the most vivid image of the psychotherapy of hysteria is one proposed not by Freud but by Anna O.: "chimney-sweeping," she named it in English. This is a particularly apt image for the song of innocence which psychoanalysis sang in its infancy. Breuer of Anna O.'s analysis: "I used to visit her in the evening when I knew I should find her in her hypnosis, and I then relieved her of the whole stock of imaginative products which she had accumulated since my last visit."[5] The studies of hysteria had only just left the uterus and could still be pictured as a dusting and cleaning, an easy job as long as the "period of incubation" (Charcot's term for that period which Freud later renamed "elaboration," the period between the trauma and the symptom) had not progressed too far. Images could be plucked from thoughts, symptoms from bodies, meanings from dreams:

> And by came an Angel who had a bright key,
> And he open'd the coffins and set them all free.

During this period of innocence it was indeed expected that "if all do their duty, they need not fear harm." But this period was not to last very long, for when Breuer thought he had finished his professional duty, it became clear that Anna O. had been shirking hers—she persisted in malingering, developed a hysterical pregnancy, and exposed the analyst to the harm of her imaginative production. Analysis, in short, had met the resistances which were to initiate it into the world of experience, that is, the psychoanalytic experience, or the transference. On the verge of recognizing this, Freud pronounced what would have served as a warning to Breuer if it had been spoken soon enough: "Treatment does not consist in extirpating a foreign body, but of melting resistances and thus enabling circulation to make its way into a region that has hitherto been cut off."[6] Would I be guilty of preformationism to suggest that in this germ of a narrative is encased the

4.   Freud, *The Interpretation of Dreams*, p. 575.
5.   Josef Breuer and Sigmund Freud, *Studies on Hysteria*, trans. James and Alix Strachey, London, Penguin, 1978, p. 83.
6.   *Ibid.*, p. 377.

whole of the argument of this essay? That what we see here in miniature is the whole of the movement from the concept of images that can be plucked from thoughts to that of images which initiate the circulation of a chain of thoughts? Perhaps. It is only the future developments of Freud's own, as well as others', thoughts/images that retrospectively lends such significance to this one moment. By my consciousness of the finality of the future perfect, I have, of course, concealed a whole history.

I will begin again, therefore, at a specific historical point, one just anterior to Freud's intervention, just anterior to the discovery of the resistances. As it is the historical/philosophical relation of images to thought which we are attempting to define; as the study of hysteria foregrounds the problematic of this relationship—the illness of the malingerer, the hysteric, first presenting itself as an image which menaced knowledge, confusing categories of real and unreal illness, true perceptions and false images, making the physician a potential victim of trickery and deception and casting doubt on his senses which were the foundation of his knowledge, the image, in brief, conflated with madness and presented as inimical to thought; and as one of the most thorough documentations of this relationship is around the work of Charcot—the three volumes of his *Clinical Lectures on the Diseases of the Nervous System*[7] in which he devotes over a third of his attention to hysteria, balancing, one might say, the three volumes of photographs of hysterics—the question of Freud's rejection of an image is reformulated around this material at hand: what is the relationship of the images of hysteria to the theory, the system of thought, of hysteria?

Illustrative. The reply is immediate and obvious. Seemly. The images were pedagogical props to be used to supplement Charcot's Tuesday and Friday Lectures. The biographers, including Freud, all offer support for this thesis: although Charcot's diction was remarkably clear, he was not a brilliant orator. (There is implied in this evaluation, this subordination and conjunction, a notion of rhetoric and of ornament which is not contemporary but of the era of Charcot). That is to say, he had a discursive failing which he made up for by the auxiliary of visual images. He instrumented his meanings with an array of illustrations that ranged from his own body, which mimicked the clinical symptoms (paralyses, contractures, muscular hyperexcitability, etc.); to projected images (he was one of the first to use projection equipment in a classroom); and charts, synoptic drawings, graphic diagrams, statuettes, and plaster casts. But all of these were only substitutes for the real image itself, the hysterical patient who was Charcot's primary illustration and whom he brought from the wards to the classroom. They usually obliged by imitating perfectly the major crises of hysteria. In return for this they were paid attention by the crowds who gathered in the Charcot amphitheater.

---

7. These were published in English by the New Sydenham Society, London, 1874–89. Freud obtained permission from Charcot to translate the lectures into German while he was studying with him in Paris. The lectures were published by Deuticke in Vienna in 1886.

To this amphitheater there was attached the "living pathological museum" (Charcot's term), that is, the infirmary wards; a studio for molding; a laboratory of pathological anatomy and physiology; an ophthalmological room; and, in 1876, a photographic laboratory. It was Duchenne de Boulogne who introduced Charcot to medical photography. Duchenne was a pioneer researcher in the field of electrophysiology. He experimented with the electrical excitation of muscles and wrote about the system of reflexes which produced physiognomic expressions. It was Albert Londe, however, who became director of the laboratory. Londe, it seems, was interested in photographing the "leading ladies" of hysteria, for he brought to Charcot three of the most famous, Louise Glaiz, Alphonsine Bar., and Blanche Wittmann. These women had the special talent of responding well to hypnotic suggestion and on this account they were used by hospitals, exchanged from one to the other throughout France for medical and legal experimentation.

We see in the photographs in the *Iconographie* the mark of these two men, or the mark, rather, of the historical concerns which they represented. We find in the

Iconographie, *Vol. II, Hallucinations:*
Repugnance *(far left),* Terreur *(left),*
Ironie *(right). 1878.*

three volumes a concentration on the physiognomies of the patients; that is, the facial expressions of the patients are the primary expressions of hysteria presented in the photographs. The mental conditions of the patients are their facio-somatizations. Anguish, surprise, disdain, irony, disgust, terror, repugnance—the inscriptions, unaided by any other "creative geography" (sometimes the backgrounds are scratched out; most often the face fills almost the entire frame), pretend to restate the physiognomic as fact, as though the image could reveal immediately what it was, as though existence and meaning were identical. Some of these inscriptions seem perfectly accurate. In volume I, for example, plate XXXV is a photograph of "repugnance," which appears to be a correct naming of the facial expression—lips pursed as though they had just closed over something foul. Sometimes they seem unquestionably inaccurate; plate XXXIV, for example, is a photograph of "terror," which looks decidedly more like anger or defiance. And sometimes they seem arbitrary, as in plate XXXII, which is a photograph of "irony." What should a photograph of irony look like? There is irony, surely, in the fact that these are photographs of hysterics, which means precisely that they are all under the sign of irony, of deception, that what seems, what appears, *is* not. It is not the emotional state but the disease which is the truth of these symptoms, these photographs.

We also find a concentration on, a privileging of the individual in these photographs. Augustine and Suzanne emerge as the "heroines" of the *Iconographie*. Which is also ironic, as the intention of the photographs is to mark out the identifiable, the repeatable characteristics of hysteria, which would entail, one also presumes, the effacing of the individuality of the hysteric. As these photographs of hysterics are at odds, then, on at least these two points, with the theory of hysteria, how can we say that they support the theory?

Lubricity, Charcot tells us over and over again in his lectures, is characteristic of hysteria, which is evanescent, mobile. There is a *carpe diem* theme throughout the lectures which offers the images as the rosebuds gathered by instantaneous photography. Volume III of the lectures reproduces part of a series of photographs, taken by Londe in the laboratory of the Salpêtrière, of a woman in the midst of an attack of rhythmical chorea, which Charcot is at pains to distinguish as specific to hysteria and thus different from the other tremors and choreiform movements which have an organic origin. The movements of rhythmical chorea include neither oscillations nor vibrations and are systematic. It is these traits which distinguish them from ordinary chorea. The photographs, then, trace these movements as a way of identifying the symptoms' difference from others, which would otherwise appear to be the same because the movements are executed too quickly and fluidly for the human eye to distinguish them. The images resemble and function similarly to those of Muybridge or the more physiologically oriented Marey, whose tambour was being used at this same time to register the muscular tremors of hysterics. The camera supplemented the eye which sought visual proof of the theory.

And yet it was not only lability which the photographs were to fix, but incompleteness as well. The most labile manifestation of the disease was the attack which Charcot carefully described in an effort to distinguish hysteria from epilepsy, a disease which was also accompanied by attacks and was often, for this reason, confused with hysteria. The hysteric crisis, as Charcot described it, was articulated in four phases: the epileptoid phase of convulsions; the phase of large movements of salutation, violence, arcs of circle; the hallucinatory phase of passionate attitudes; and the phase of terminal delirium. The syntagmatic progression of these crises became the paradigm of the disease—the Salpêtrièrian hysteric. The problem was, as Charcot statistically states, that one-third of the cases of hysteria never exhibited these attacks and not all of the other two-thirds exhibited the full attack. Many cases of hysteria were, then, according to Charcot, "incomplete." In one lecture, for example, Charcot uses two separate cases—that of Porz-, who had hysterogenic zones but no attacks, and that of Pin-, who had complete attacks but no hysterogenic zones—to supplement each other, fill in the hiatus in the clinical picture of the other, to produce one plenitudinous picture of hystero-traumatic monoplegia. The first volume of the *Iconographie* is devoted to this graphic form of hysteria, the attack in four phases. The graph is not continuous, however, as the images of chorea are. Instead what is presented are the repetitions of each phase in several different patients so that the various patients and photographs together make up a whole picture.

It is not to be supposed that all this means that there was a classification—hysteria, complete hysteria—which existed in some pure form and became embodied in varying degrees of incompletion in individual patients. We have not only Foucault's extensive analysis which tells us the difference between this classificatory approach in medicine, which historically preceded Charcot, and the anatomo-clinical approach with which he was contemporaneous, but we have also Charcot's own direct and indirect statements which suggest his adherence to the clinical method. The legend of Charcot includes the following repartee, quoted by Freud: a group of students, skeptical of Charcot's clinical observations, interrupted him by objecting that the observations he made contradicted the Young-Helmholtz theory which was then dominant. To these objections Charcot replied, "Theory is fine, but it doesn't stop things from existing."[8] Freud refers to this incident as an example of his teacher's "practicing nosology,"[9] a term Charcot himself uses to describe the clinical method of investigation which, it is implied, made possible the inauguration of the Clinical Chair of the Diseases of the Nervous System: nosology is that method "which argues from effect to cause, commencing with a study of disease at the bedside, as distinguished from the converse method of a prior reasoning, with the teachings of physiology for its base."[10] In other words, clinically observable facts are primary and theory is an additive, syntactic transcription of them. A good clinician is one who has a fineness of sensibility, which fineness shades over to an appreciation of art (Charcot's collaborative studies of art with Paul Richter,[11] as well as the classical look of beauty—defined by the carefulness of composition, from drapery to lighting—which distinguishes these photographs of the *Iconographie* from the other medical photographs of the period;[12] the final placing of the Rubens sketch in the first volume, the luminosity of its lighting an analogue to the aura of the previous photographs, all bear witness to this), and to the significance of the variations of forms rejected by the classificatory method. Variation, by this approach, could

8.   Quoted in Ernest Jones, *The Life and Work of Sigmund Freud*, New York, Basic Books, 1981, Vol. I, p. 208.
9.   A.R.G. Owen, *Hysteria, Hypnosis, and Healing: The Work of J.M. Charcot*, London, Dennis Dobson, 1971, p. 36.
10.   Charcot, *Lectures*, Vol. I, p. 9.
11.   *Les Démoniaques dans l'Art*, Amsterdam, Boekhandel and Antiquariaat. B.M. Israel, 1972 (Paris, 1887); and *Les Difformes et les Malades dans l'Art*, Amsterdam, Boekhandel and Antiquariaat. B.M. Israel, 1972 (Paris 1889).
12.   These are published in the multi-volumed *Revue Photographique des Hôpitaux de Paris*.

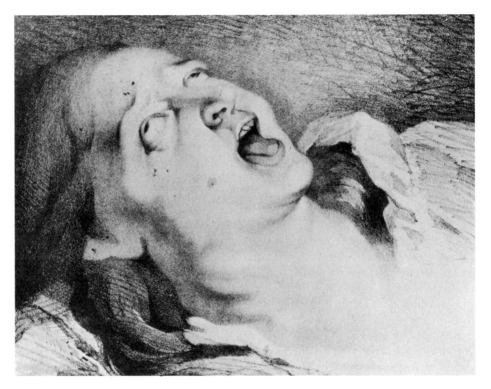

Iconographie, *Vol. II. Sketch by Rubens: Demoniaque.*

not be discarded in favor of the invariable as in the medicine of species. Instead the abnormal had to be accounted for and counted, added together with other abnormalities to form the normal. Foucault quotes this in evidence: "The study of monsters or monstrosities of the human species gives us an idea of nature's teeming resources and of the gap to which she can lend herself."[13] I quote Charcot's insistence on the importance to science of the work of artists who chose to copy, "not perfection, but deformities, infirmities, sickness, errors, deviations, aberrations of nature."[14]

Whereas Foucault analyzes this folding over of the one register onto the other, this adequation of seeing and knowing, in terms of the linguistic theories of the period, Sartre analyzes it in terms of the contemporaneous philosophical theories. His interest in the analytical method is, however, much more peripheral. His main concern in *Imagination: A Psychological Critique* is to examine the

13.   Michel Foucault, *The Birth of the Clinic*, New York, Vintage, 1975, p. 102.
14.   *Les Difformes et les Malades dans l'Art,* "Introduction," p. iii.

philosophical history of the concept of the image. He never mentions the anatomo-clinical method, but he does mention some of its practitioners, among them Charcot: "From 1869 to 1885, Bastian, Broca, Kussmaul, Exner, Wernicke, and Charcot laid down the classical theory of aphasia, which inclines to nothing short of differential centers of imagery."[15] The book is short because the history is (not short but) monotonous. Although Sartre differentiates three basic classical positions on the subject of images and their relation to thoughts, he finds that they are related in the way they treat images as things or, more accurately, inferior things immanent in the mind, copies of things outside. The classical positions are not controverted in the nineteenth century; instead this mistaken notion finds support from the method whose operation is dictated by the assumption of its validity. That is to say, associationism, the reigning psychological/philosophical discourse of the nineteenth century, which taught that concepts were formed from images which were repetitions of sensations, imprinted copies of things, found proof positive by the method of the clinicians, which was, though Foucault never names it, associationist. And where was this proof posited? In the brain, which during this period was discovered to be a differentiated and not a homogenous mass. Lesions and localization were thus the bedrock of the associationists. For, if areas in the brain could be located as original sites of images, then imagination and thought must be reducible to the elements found there and could not, *de facto*, be synthetic processes. Of course the argument was made more nuanced through particular debates like the one over hallucinations. The alienists still tried to maintain a radical separation between images produced by absent or nonexistent objects and sensations produced by real presences, but, for all intents and purposes, associationism held sway.

For the most part also we can agree with Sartre's placing of Charcot at the center and the avant-garde of this indexical neurology. Before electroencephalography, before electrocorticology, it was Charcot who, by direct linking of cortical lesions with motor dysfunctions, prepared the way for neurological surgery. The supplementary chain of illustrative images which accompanied his lectures might be said to have located their final point in the brain, just as in the 1875 version of the *Iconographie*, which is composed solely of images (the other three volumes contain a text which includes case histories and analyses of the hysterics), the series of photographs, primarily shots of heads of hysterical patients resting against pillows, is concluded with a photograph of a brain resting against a backdrop of drapery. Although Charcot never tried directly in his lectures to enter this debate over hallucinations, we see in the *Iconographie* that the four phases of the attack are not represented equally. There is instead a privileging of the third phase, the period of hallucinations. If there is a position taken, it is, of course, on the side of the body against the mind, on the side of this brain which

15. Jean-Paul Sartre, *Imagination*, trans. Forrest Williams, Ann Arbor, The University of Michigan Press, 1962, p. 24.

impresses itself on these faces to produce expressions of anguish, surprise, disdain, etc. It is on the side of the body of science which determines, as Charcot and Richter say in their introduction to *Les Difformes et les Malades dans l'Art,* the limits of the possible against the imaginative impossible. Included in this book of deformities are images only of natural deformities and not of invented forms like sphinxes or sirens which do not belong to nature but to, in their word, "scissors."

Hysteria, then, is a disease of the imagination, of the production of images cut off from the natural. The hysteric, receiver of impressions, inhabits a realm of imagination, of bodily passivity, anaesthesia, and paralysis. Charcot makes clear in Lecture XX that paralysis is thus necessarily, objectively real, a paralysis by the imagination and not an imaginary paralysis. The hysteric was lifted by the whole *weight,* as Freud said, of scientific authority from the scandal of malingering. For, as opposed to Janet, for example, who believed that paralysis was caused by a failure of imagination, a failure of the hysteric to form the image of his/her limb which was necessary to move it, Charcot believed that movement was inhibited by the action of a fixed idea, an image of paralysis or of the absence of movement which made the formation of an image of movement impossible. For both it was the production of an image which was necessary to execute a movement, but for Charcot it was the positivity of another, a counter-image, rather than the simple lack of an image, which was the condition of the disease. For Janet, lack of imagination meant also lack of intelligence; thus the hysteric was a "poor little thing." Charcot, who granted the hysteric more imagination also granted him/her more intelligence. Both, it is clear, linked imagination and intelligence, images and thoughts, through their common, that is, their sensory, origin. Thoughts which were always reducible to images, their elemental form, were at the same time superior to them, their coherent, discursive organization. When images got out of line, when they became unreliable echoes of the objects which had produced them, they could be brought back, made isomorphic with reality again by a force which was aimed precisely at the imagination. "Medicine for the imagination" is what Binet and Fere called the therapeutic method of the Sâlpetrière. "What has been done, can be undone," was Charcot's exact formulation of this undoing of the imagination through the imagination.[16] Hypnosis, suggestion, was meant to encourage the formation of fresh images in the patient which would counter the diseased ones. And because the formation of an image was conceived as a mechanical operation, the hypnosis was often mechanically induced by "concentrating the patient's attention on a fixed point . . . gentle pressure by the fingers on the eyeballs . . . noise, bright lights . . . the confusional technique."[17] The treatment, then, was the photographic image, the *"transfert"* of the disease. The third volume of the *Iconographie,* with its images of the phases of the hypnosis, is

16.   Charcot, *Lectures,* Vol. II, p. 258.
17.   Owen, p. 195.

presented almost as a reversal of the first, of the effects of the phases of the attack imaged in the first.

But not quite. That is to say, ideally, but not completely, not totally. It is this "not quite" which undermines the security of this reversal, this mensural principle of the analogical passion by which gradations of effect, perspectival figurations, trace and retrace the path between cause and effect, effect and cure. Where the ultimate photograph of Volume III—plate 40, "Lethargie. Contraction du Zygomatique," a photograph of a hysteric raising one side of her face toward an indicator which touches her cheek and is held by the in-frame hand of her hypnotist—may be viewed as an indexing of the index, lodging it as curator of these volumes of photographs, one must, nevertheless, abandon the "touching-touched" of this phenomenological reading if one considers these photographs as "participating in" the theory of hysteria.

For Charcot cannot quite, as Sartre has claimed, be credited with "laying down the classical theory of aphasia, which inclines to nothing short of differentiated centers of imagery."[18] Charcot "never developed any anatomical, pathologic documentation of his own for aphasia"[19] and remained until the end uncertain about Broca's theory of localization. Nor did Charcot employ theories of brain localization in his mapping of hysterical sites. Indeed, hysteria was seen as a disease which gave the lie to localization; it was a neuromimetic disease which could not be traced to any lesion of the brain. Instead Charcot defined a topography of the body, of hysterogenic zones located on the body, which when touched could produce or conclude a hysterical attack. This topography is analogous in impulse, of course, to the topography of the brain which neurophysiologists were trying to define at this time. But the dislodging of these zones from the brain and the shifting of them to the body began a displacement of the indexing of cause by the intermediary of the notion of the original site. This shifting, begun by Charcot, was to open a space for Freud and the jerrymandering which would result from the politics of his concept of the unconscious, the concept discovered as the resist which prevented the corrosive overlay of cause and cure.

As is clear from the photographs in Volume II, the three phases of hypnosis do not exactly reduplicate the four phases of the attack. It is important to remember that these four phases, discovered by Charcot at the Salpêtrière, were matter for considerable debate and were most consistently opposed by Bernheim of the Nancy School, who contested even the photographic "evidence" by proposing that hypnosis was all a matter of suggestion, that is, of external influence and thus not subject to the invariability of a regular sequence which physiological phenomena would produce. Freud, reporting the debate in "Hypnosis and Suggestion" (1888), sides with Charcot in the belief that hysterical symptoms are

---

18.   Sartre, p. 195.
19.   Georges Guillain, M.D. *J.M. Charcot 1825–93: His Life and Work,* trans. Pearce Bailey, New York, Paul B. Hoeber, 1959, p. 127.

governed by certain laws. But whereas for Charcot these were the laws of physiology, for Freud they were the laws of association. It is only later that Freud would understand them as the laws of the unconscious, but already he has defined a structure which resists pure suggestion, pure impressionability, a structure which resists finally, all appearances to the contrary, the pure associationism to which Sartre consigns him. It was in defining the mode of defense which hysterics exhibited towards association that Freud discovered an unconscious which was decidedly not the unconscious which Sartre attacked—not an inert repository of images, or the hypostatized *de jure* of thought which *must* exist to lend meaning to images, to supplement the essential poverty of images. Criticizing Freud as a naive realist, Sartre attempts to counter his supposed immanentism—by which images are seen as *things*, contents of consciousness—with his own immanentism—this time of meaning—by which consciousness is filled only with itself, is self-sufficient and thus independent of the existence of an unconscious, a latency.

It is clear that Sartre did not understand Freud, but he fought his battle with the unconscious on the proper ground—the imaginary. Sartre's work on the imaginary can be seen as part of the twentieth-century attack on the image, on associationism. The attack developed through the experiments of the Würzburg School, the philosophy of Bergson, and the intentional structure of consciousness introduced by Brentano. According to this structure, consciousness was directed at an object. No intermediary, no mental image separated the subject from the object of intention, for the ontological law which defined intention stated that there were only things in themselves and consciousness for itself. Images which were conceived as things in consciousness, that is, simultaneously in and for themselves, could not exist. It was on this ground that the unconscious was rejected as an impossibility. The imaginary replaced both images and the unconscious in the phenomenological system. The imaginary is a kind of consciousness, a way of apprehending, of presenting an object. The object and not the image is aimed at by consciousness and the image is nothing but the relationship of consciousness to the object. "Will and consciousness" were made the vortical reversal of the classical postulate which had described its subjects as receivers of impressions.

Freud's essay, "The Unconscious," was published in 1915, although the concept was outlined earlier in his other works. In 1928 Georges Politzer wrote his *Critique des fondements de la psychologie,* as a critique, basically, of this metapsychological concept. In 1936 Lacan's first essay on the mirror phase and Sartre's *Imagination* were both published. Four years later, Sartre extended his study in *The Psychology of the Imagination,* and five years after that, Lacan extended his in his second mirror phase essay. Politzer's critique, clearly a phenomenological one, is implicit (though never explicitly cited) in Sartre's, and Lacan's critque of the phenomenological critique, while implicit in his first essay, is in the second explicitly directed at Sartre, the philosopher of "being and nothingness." What this telescoped history marks is the imbrication of the concepts of images and the unconscious in French philosophical thought. The unconscious, a concept developed out of the work on the "imaginary" disease, hysteria, was displaced by the phenomenological concept of the imaginary. Lacan simply replaced back into the Freudian system this imaginary which it had attempted to reject. He demonstrated once again that the image, the Imaginary, is the precondition of the unconscious; that phenomenology, rather than being an adequate critique of the unconscious, was an orthopedic gesture, the prop of the possibility of the unconscious, which projected philosophy from the fantasies, produced by the associationists, of a fragmented body image to a form of the totality of a Being-in-the-world. Coming as they do before the birth of the concept of the unconscious, of psychoanalysis—wombed still in the study of neurology, medicine, the body—the images of the hysterics might be called the intra-organic mirror phase of psychoanalysis. That is, the specific premature birth of the subject of psychoanalysis was in these images of hysterics, these models of the corpus of medical knowledge. This first death of the body into an image was obscured for a time from its beholders by the dazzling beauty of the photographs, the aesthetic order of wholeness which it promised and which Sartre writes about in his conclusion to *The Psychology of the Imagination*. The second death comes from the theory of hysteria, from Lacan's reminder that this beauty, this wholeness is an imaginary synthesis which, despite Kant, Bergson, Sartre, and other manifold philosophers of the intensive intention, never, resisted as it is by the innervations from the unconscious, never *quite* takes place.

We must not forget that the theory of hysteria was from the beginning a theory of mimesis—of the hystrionics of the hysteric, their mimicry of physical diseases, and of the imitation produced by hypnosis. It is this fact which Lacan recalls in his elaboration of the mirror phase, which can only be seen as the grounding of the thetic, the positing and positioning of the ego and the object, in the theatrics of the Imaginary. There are, underlying the works of Sartre and Lacan, very different concepts of mimesis. Sartre's concept, defined by its antagonism to the associationists, can best be described by reference to their theory of mimesis:

(emotion in painter) (sensed) (work of art) (sensed) (emotion in viewer)
        1   2   3   4   5

What is important to recognize is that 1 and 3 are not equivalent. The immaterial emotion of 1 was embodied in 3, but between the two there is a radical separation. Sartre's "objective correlative" theory of mimesis looked much more like T.S. Eliot's:

            (object) (painter) (painting) (viewer) (object)
                1   2   3   4   5

Between 1 and 3 there is a relationship of equivalence; 3 is not the embodiment of

1, not the externalization of a mental state. As Sartre said in his earlier work, *Imagination*, psychologism, though it had made psychic images the copies in the subject of physical images outside, had in its aesthetic theories radically separated physical images such as paintings and photographs from psychic images on the basis of their material difference. Beginning with Husserl, who saw images as a way in which consciousness aimed at its objects, phenomenology, however, could view photographs as "hyletically ambiguous," that is, as either external objects or as imaginative consciousness. A photograph was equivalent to an imaginative consciousness when it de-realized itself, became disembodied:

> The painter does not realize his mental image on canvas at all; he has simply constructed a material analogue of such a kind that everyone can grasp the image provided he looks at the analogue. But the image thus provided with an external analogue remains an image. There's no realization of the imaginary, nor can we speak of its objectifica-tion. . . . The painting is an analogue, only what manifests itself through it is an unreal collection of new things . . . which do not exist in the painting nor anywhere in the world, but which manifest themselves by means of the canvas, and which have got hold of it by some sort of possession.[20]

We recognize in this notion of possession an earlier analysis which Sartre conducted of the impersonation of Maurice Chevalier by Franconay—an explicit critique of associationism and the illusion of immanence which it maintains. According to Sartre, there is no force of resemblance, no relation of metaphor and metonymy which bring Maurice Chevalier to consciousness when Franconay is perceived. Resemblance, that is, does not precede consciousness; rather conscious-ness apprehends all at once that Franconay is (that is, is possessed of) Maurice Chevalier. Resemblance is replaced by possession and the unconscious is banished as that shadowy area where resembling elements are stored, waiting to be discovered. We are not far, it seems, from that pre-Freudian analysis of hysteria by which possession, rather than the unconscious, was thought to underlie the spasmodic symptoms of the hysterics.

What is it, in Sartre's system, that is being possessed? Being. The imaginary is finally that form of consciousness which produces the object which it desires in a form that it can possess; the imaginary negates the object, dispossesses it of its reality in order to take possession of it(self). Thus, included in consciousness's Being-in-the-world is its freedom from it, its ability to negate it by bringing it in relation to itself. Consciousness is freed from the world because of this capacity for autoaffection: "It is not because the unreal object appears close to me that my eyes are going to converge, but it is the convergence of my eyes that mimics the

20.   Jean-Paul Sartre, *The Psychology of the Imagination*, London, Methuen and Co., 1972, pp. 220-222.

proximity of the object . . . My entire body participates in the make-up of the images."[21]

As opposed to this concept of mimesis as a matter of self-possession, Lacan describes it as a matter of self-dispossession. Instead of the world, it is the subject who experiences the "de-realizing effect" of mimicry. Where Sartre had made clear that it was "Being-in-the-world which is the necessary condition for the imagination," thus insuring the subject a place from which to act, Lacan describes the Imaginary as the necessary condition of Being-in-the-world, as the "dialectic which will henceforth link the *I* to socially elaborated situations." It is by becoming unreal, by being dispossessed of Being that the subject becomes inserted in the world (as meaning), that is, into a totality which exceeds it. Where for Sartre the subject's desire occasions the image, for Lacan the subject's assumption of an image occasions desire. The subject, that is, desires insofar as it is other, finds itself exteriorized in an image. Thus alienated from itself, the subject has, henceforth, a mediated relationship to itself and must seek validation by recognition from another. Mimesis, according to this theory, is no longer a matter of being impressed, or possessed of the positivity of another, but of covering up, camouflaging the gap which separates the other from itself.

The difference, to close this long parenthesis and to return to the photographs of the hysterics, is a matter of framing. According to the doctrine of phenomenology, consciousness has the ability to put the world in parenthesis; for Freudians it is consciousness itself which is put in parenthesis. Both Freud and Sartre inherited a critique of the copy theory of mimesis by way of Brentano's doctrine of "secondary consciousness." For Sartre this meant that consciousness was protected from being run through by the real by means of this secondary structure which was not a superadded power of consciousness but an essential part of its very realization. The world emerges out of the real, which is negated and presented to consciousness as imaginary. External perception results from this relationship of consciousness with itself and with its presentation of the implicit meaning of the real to itself. Freud, however, extended this doctrine of secondary consciousness into that of a second consciousness—the unconscious. His critique of the copy or inscription theory was thus carried out by doubling the inscription. Beginning with the "Project," we can see Freud's attempt to define the index or trace against the notion of analogical resemblance, and in the essay "The Unconscious," we see that analogy once again fails to grasp the structure of the unconscious, this second consciousness. The unconscious as an ungraspable structure is the condition of the impossibility of the subject to fulfill the two different functions of memory and consciousness. Between the two structures, consciousness and unconsciousness, there exists not a relationship of adequation—the unconscious as the meaning of the conscious manifestation, the

---

21.   *Ibid.*, p. 216.

superfluousness of consciousness's immanence—but of conflict. The subject, made up of separate mental agencies, is not the site of the inscription of psychic contents, but rather a conflictual structure of object relationships.

Consciousness's relationship with the world is not direct, but mediated through its relationship with the unconscious. Once again, it was Lacan who redefined the Imaginary in terms which made it not the replacement but the precondition of the unconscious. The subject, caught up in the lure of the Imaginary, projects itself out of itself. Thus the auto-perception which phenomenology describes must traverse this space, this internal foreign territory which separates the subject from itself. The world is returned not through consciousness, but through the unconscious.

Sartre's imaginary consciousness is turned towards the real in a defensive stance. The something which is negated, denied is the real which is surpassed, presented to consciousness as meaning. The image, according to Sartre (as well as Pound) is always the *adequate* symbol; the relationship of a dream, expression, symptom to its content is one of complete adequation, of simultaneous translation. Pleasure is manifest in a smile. Freud's consciousness defends itself from its unconscious, its introjected outside. Between these two forces there is a relationship of conflict and compromise; unconscious thoughts are displaced, condensed, converted by the conscious system. Dreams, symptoms are formations which result from a compromise between repressing and repressed ideas. There is no reading back from a dream or symptom to its simple presence, coextensive in the unconscious. For these formations are precisely displacements of lacunary eruptions of the unconscious which they expell. The Freudian concept of the unconscious eliminates the possibility of simple linear reversal as it institutes a structure of overdetermination into the process of the subject.

Hypnosis, once again, was related in its beginnings to the mechanical devices of *transfert*, of simple reversals of symptoms from one side of the body to the other. It was discovered one day at the Salpêtrière, while a patient was undergoing treatment with an "aesthesiogenism" (an agent which is employed for its action upon the patient's *sensations*), that while hearing was restored to the patient's hemianesthetic side, the loss was transferred to the other, the normal side. This phenomenon whereby paralyses, anesthesias, disorders of vision, hearing disappeared only to be replaced by their symmetrical other soon became identified as one of the salient characteristics of hysterical symptomology. At the same time as hypnosis was introduced as a method of investigation and treatment, metallotherapy, which drew symptoms, by means of large magnets, back and forth between the left and right sides of the body, was also being used to produce a primitive and mechanical, though "physiologically intelligible" (Freud refers to the phenomenon of *transfert*) form of abreaction. One of the most adamant champions of this method of treatment, this attention to mechanical reversal, was Paul Regnard, who, while an intern at the Salpêtrière, actually took the photographs for and, with Bourneville, coauthored the *Iconographie*, a kind of photographic staging of this very process of left-right reversal.

In as much as the *Iconographie* is imprinted by its own historical period, is grounded, in the first volume, in the associationists' debates over hallucinations, the differential diagnosis in the second, the mechanical aspects of hypnosis in the third; in as much as it is intent on registering the traces of this lubricious disease, hysteria; in as much, in short, as the *Iconographie* is an index of the *shift*ing symptoms of its hysterical subjects and an imprint of a counterbalancing therapeutic image, the photographic images are aligned, as they always have been by Western thought, on the side of presence. Images are deviated thoughts, a debased form of pure knowledge which thought secures. They are characterized by distortions, vagueness, and references to absent objects, and yet in spite of (or perhaps because of) their deviation (the "poverty of the image" giving the resource of thought that which it does not have—lack), they supplement thoughts by making present the distance they traverse, the distance which threatens presence with annihilation. For, by the commutative law of Western thought, the order of operations may be reversed, makes no difference. And in as much as Freud inherited this tradition, he had to abdicate his original title to the "Psychotherapy of Hysteria."

Yet the title does belong to Freud, nevertheless; it is his "original sin"—in the sense that Lacan uses this catholic term to describe the relationship of hysteria to psychoanalysis. The title, borrowed from the inscription of a medal, had its returns, its remuneration, in the theory of psychoanalysis, of the unconscious, Freud's unconscious, which is the other side on which this inscription is engraved. Freud's fascination with this inscription and his rejection of it reveals/disguises his unconscious desire for recognition, his desire that his work on hysteria be recognized as "germinal" and sustain him in his role as father of psychoanalysis. This original sin, related as it is to psychoanalysis, is problematically "original," problematically "sinful"—is, in fact, behovely, for it is the "stain" which allows the invisible unconscious to emerge in the conscious field. Freud wrote in *The Interpretation of Dreams*, "An unconscious idea is as such quite incapable of entering the preconscious . . . and it can only exercise any effect there by establishing a connection with an idea which already belongs to the preconscious, by transferring its intensity on to it and by getting itself 'covered' by it."[22] Psychoanalysis, it seems, was developed out of a deception perpetuated not only by the hysterical analysand, but also by the analyst. Mimicry, as it is elaborated by Lacan from the "Mirror Phase" to the seminars on transference, is just such a "cover up," a camouflaging which inserts the unconscious into a series of conscious thoughts by means of a *"méconnaissance"* (Lacan), or a *"mésalliance"* (Freud in *Studies on Hysteria*). Mimesis is related from its beginnings to the tragic flaw, the *hamarita*, that is, literally, the inevitable and productive "missing the mark." The drama of the subject is instituted by this Imaginary instance.

It is the transference which comes to replace in Freud's thought, in psycho-

22.   Freud, *The Interpretation of Dreams*, p. 377.

analytic technique, the notions of *transfert*, of hypnosis, of the techniques of photographic reversal. For the compromise between the forces pressing towards cure and those of the unconscious gathered to oppose it is another symptom of the resistance, another "artificial illness"—the transference. Hysteria's artificiality is thus raised (we see this clearly enough in the case of Dora) to another power, is projected out of itself and played out in another field—the field of the power of the other. "This," Freud says in "The Dynamics of the Transference," "is the ground on which the victory must be won," for "in the last resort no one can be slain *in absentia* or *in effigie.*" This Imaginary grounding of the subject, then, absents the subject from itself, makes of it an effigy of an effigy. This battleground, pictured as internecine, this new symptom, employs an image, a concept of the Imaginary which is alienated from any notion of presence or of a symptom as unambiguous, diagnostic indicator of an unconscious content with which it is copresent.

How, then, raised by these theoretical concerns out of the historical context in which the photographs were produced, are we to understand the relation of the *Iconographie* to the theory of hysteria? If not a pedagogic prop, then what? If we can not find there the tracings of the theory, what can we find? How can we say, as we have, that the theory of the unconscious is imprinted there? We would be hard pressed not to admit that the theory has found a support in these photographic images, that they have been a prop for this discussion as well as for Charcot and the theory of hysteria. But as a result of leaning on this function of the images, we have witnessed an important deviation of the theory of the image itself, a theory which founds the image in this deviation.

From the first viewing of the photographs of the *Iconographie*, what has seemed most striking is that it is the lack of parity between the first and the third volumes which makes the photographs parturient of psychoanalysis. This deviation can only be described as the effect of the gradual, metonymic intrusion of the analyst into the clinical picture—the tremendous deviation from the demands and practice of medical photographs taken in the Paris hospitals at the same time. The third volume depicts not only the hypnosis, the analyst's intervention in the disease, but the analyst himself; at first only metaphorically and metonymically by means of his hypnotic apparatus—*"bruit du diapson," "lumière vive," "brusque de la lumière"*—but finally in actuality, as his hand is revealed in the process. It is from the time that the analyst is caught up, mirrored in these images, that images enter the Imaginary. That is to say, what is important is no longer what is present in them so much as what is absent. The product of this Imaginary is, of course, the ego, that is, both a metaphor of the subject, a carrying over of the subject into the field of the Other, and a metonymy, a differentiated part, an agency of the subject. The product of the Imaginary, then, is a displacement, not a presence. It installs presence as an elsewhere, displaces it, as it displaces, is the displacement of associationism, which maintained that the subject sought and found objects by means of the laws of metaphor and metonymy, and the displacement of Sartre, who displaced the laws of metaphor and metonymy by the laws of intention.

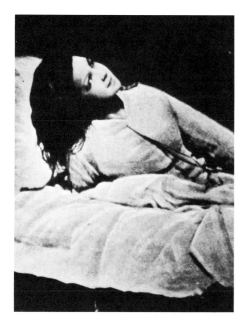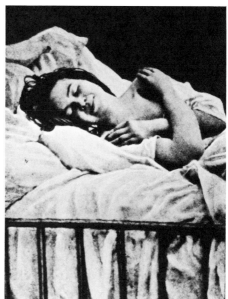

Iconographie, *Vol. I, Attitudes Passionnelles:*
Appel *(left),* Erotisme *(right). 1878.*

The object is no longer sought and found as a result of the concept of the Imaginary, but displaced, which is the precise meaning of the famous Freudian formulation, "The finding of an object is the refinding of it." The theory of hysteria uncovered the fact that the stigmatic loci of hysterics were not primary, but were conferred on any part of the body by sexual fantasies which displaced the object of the instinct by the representation of the drive. Hysteria names the recognition of this deviation of the object and "the hysteric," as Moustapha Safouan has said, "renounced being what men fight over,"[23] renounced, that is, being the object of their desire.

23.   Moustapha Safouan, "In Praise of Hysteria," in *Returning to Freud: Clinical Psychoanalysis in the School of Lacan,* ed. and trans. Stuart Schneiderman, New Haven and London, Yale University Press, 1980, p. 59.

Yet, something still remains in place, even in this final recognition in which it is implied, here as always, that the hysteric is a woman. This implication brings us to the final question about the relationship between the images and the theory: how, anyone who has seen the photographs may ask, how has she managed to discuss the *Iconographie* without mentioning that all the photographs are images of women? This is true. All the images are images of women, but I have avoided stating this obvious fact in this way. Which is not to say that it is neither here nor there. For it is—here and there, *fort* and *da*, man "thinking with his thing," attempting to master the gap opened up by the absence which sustains him. Although one of Charcot's main contributions to the study of hysteria was his demonstration that it is a disease found in men as well as women, although he exhibited hysterical men in his classroom and delivered long lectures on male hysteria, all the photographs in the *Iconographie* are images only of women.

My deliberate neglect of this fact as my starting point is to be taken as part of a strategy which refuses to sanction those discussions which continue to theorize hysteria as essentially a female disease, refuses to sanction a theoretical tradition which even Charcot, who, as we have said, initiated the break from it, continued in some ways to support. In the clinical lectures male hysteria is usually traced back to an accident, a physical trauma, while female hysteria is ascribed to a psychic trauma, the implication, even the explanation, being that the female is disposed constitutionally to the disease. Sometimes, more often in men Charcot is careful to say, hysteria is inherited, and in these cases the inheritance is through the mother, for it is her influence which is so "*delete*rious." Charcot often cites the caprices of hysterical patients, "even male ones," for hysteria is related to antic dispositions. The women patients, as the biographers have said, were often "excellent comedians." It is the same tradition which links women essentially to hysteria that also links women to humor, makes humor humoral, which this essay attempts to stem. Women must be theorized outside the "vapeurs" which, before Charcot's theory of hysteria, constituted her originally as sick. So too must she be thought outside the "poverty of the image" as the image is theorized in its relation to thought.

Nor can feminist theory continue to use the formulation "images of women" to name the site of its intervention without first examining the intentional structure of that formulation and the phenomenal illusion to which it binds the theory. This essay has been written in opposition to this structure, this placing of the subject on the one side and the object on the other. We must take care to examine how this structure, which is so seemingly natural, and so hale, makes itself vigorous through its exhalation of women, constituting them as the nonexistent objects of an imagining and purely subjective subject.

Of Mimicry and Man:
The Ambivalence of
Colonial Discourse*

HOMI BHABHA

Mimicry reveals something in so far as it is distinct from what might be called an itself that is behind. The effect of mimicry is camouflage. . . . It is not a question of harmonizing with the background, but against a mottled background, of becoming mottled — exactly like the technique of camouflage practised in human warfare.

—Jacques Lacan,
"The Line and Light," *Of the Gaze.*

It is out of season to question at this time of day, the original policy of conferring on every colony of the British Empire a mimic representation of the British Constitution. But if the creature so endowed has sometimes forgotten its real insignificance and under the fancied importance of speakers and maces, and all the paraphernalia and ceremonies of the imperial legislature, has dared to defy the mother country, she has to thank herself for the folly of conferring such privileges on a condition of society that has no earthly claim to so exalted a position. A fundamental principle appears to have been forgotten or overlooked in our system of colonial policy — that of colonial dependence. To give to a colony the forms of independence is a mockery; she would not be a colony for a single hour if she could maintain an independent station.

—Sir Edward Cust,
"Reflections on West African Affairs . . .
addressed to the Colonial Office,"
Hatchard, London 1839.

The discourse of post-Enlightenment English colonialism often speaks in a tongue that is forked, not false. If colonialism takes power in the name of history, it repeatedly exercises its authority through the figures of farce. For the epic intention of the civilizing mission, "human and not wholly human" in the famous words of Lord Rosebery, "writ by the finger of the Divine" [1] often produces a text rich in the traditions of *trompe l'oeil*, irony, mimicry, and repetition. In this comic turn from the high ideals of the colonial imagination to its low mimetic literary effects, mimicry emerges as one of the most elusive and effective strategies of colonial power and knowledge.

Within that conflictual economy of colonial discourse which Edward Said[2] describes as the tension between the synchronic panoptical vision of domination — the demand for identity, stasis — and the counter-pressure of the diachrony of history — change, difference — mimicry represents an *ironic* compromise. If I may adapt Samuel Weber's formulation of the marginalizing vision of castration,[3] then colonial mimicry is the desire for a reformed, recognizable Other, as *a subject of a difference that is almost the same, but not quite*. Which is to say, that the discourse of mimicry is constructed around an *ambivalence*; in order to be effective, mimicry must continually produce its slippage, its excess, its difference. The authority of that mode of colonial discourse that I have called mimicry is therefore stricken by an indeterminacy: mimicry emerges as the representation of a difference that is itself a process of disavowal. Mimicry is, thus, the sign of a double articulation; a complex strategy of reform, regulation, and discipline, which "appropriates" the Other as it visualizes power. Mimicry is also the sign of the inappropriate, however, a difference or recalcitrance which coheres the dominant strategic function of colonial power, intensifies surveillance, and poses an immanent threat to both "normalized" knowledges and disciplinary powers.

The effect of mimicry on the authority of colonial discourse is profound and disturbing. For in "normalizing" the colonial state or subject, the dream of post-Enlightenment civility alienates its own language of liberty and produces another knowledge of its norms. The ambivalence which thus informs this strategy is discernible, for example, in Locke's Second Treatise which *splits* to reveal the limitations of liberty in his double use of the word "slave": first simply, descriptively as the locus of a legitimate form of ownership, then as the

*   This paper was first presented as a contribution to a panel on "Colonialist and Post-Colonialist Discourse," organized by Gayatri Chakravorty Spivak for the Modern Language Association Convention in New York, December 1983. I would like to thank Professor Spivak for inviting me to participate on the panel and Dr. Stephan Feuchtwang for his advice in the preparation of the paper.
1.   Cited in Eric Stokes, *The Political Ideas of English Imperialism*, Oxford, Oxford University Press, 1960, pp. 17–18.
2.   Edward Said, *Orientalism*, New York, Pantheon Books, 1978, p. 240.
3.   Samuel Weber: "The Sideshow, Or: Remarks on a Canny Moment," *Modern Language Notes*, vol. 88, no. 6 (1973), p. 1112.

trope for an intolerable, illegitimate exercise of power. What is articulated in that distance between the two uses is the absolute, imagined difference between the "Colonial" State of Carolina and the Original State of Nature.

It is from this area between mimicry and mockery, where the reforming, civilizing mission is threatened by the displacing gaze of its disciplinary double, that my instances of colonial imitation come. What they all share is a discursive process by which the excess or slippage produced by the *ambivalence* of mimicry (almost the same, *but not quite*) does not merely "rupture" the discourse, but becomes transformed into an uncertainty which fixes the colonial subject as a "partial" presence. By "partial" I mean both "incomplete" and "virtual." It is as if the very emergence of the "colonial" is dependent for its representation upon some strategic limitation or prohibition *within* the authoritative discourse itself. The success of colonial appropriation depends on a proliferation of inappropriate objects that ensure its strategic failure, so that mimicry is at once resemblance and menace.

A classic text of such partiality is Charles Grant's "Observations on the State of Society among the Asiatic Subjects of Great Britain" (1792)[4] which was only superseded by James Mills's *History of India* as the most influential early nineteenth-century account of Indian manners and morals. Grant's dream of an evangelical system of mission education conducted uncompromisingly in English was partly a belief in political reform along Christian lines and partly an awareness that the expansion of company rule in India required a system of "interpellation" — a reform of manners, as Grant put it, that would provide the colonial with "a sense of personal identity as we know it." Caught between the desire for religious reform and the fear that the Indians might become turbulent for liberty, Grant implies that it is, in fact the "partial" diffusion of Christianity, and the "partial" influence of moral improvements which will construct a particularly appropriate form of colonial subjectivity. What is suggested is a process of reform through which Christian doctrines might collude with divisive caste practices to prevent dangerous political alliances. Inadvertently, Grant produces a knowledge of Christianity as a form of social control which conflicts with the enunciatory assumptions which authorize his discourse. In suggesting, finally, that "partial reform" will produce an empty form of "the *imitation* of English manners which will induce them [the colonial subjects] to remain under our protection,"[5] Grant mocks his moral project and violates the Evidences of Christianity — a central missionary tenet — which forbade any tolerance of heathen faiths.

The absurd extravagance of Macaulay's *Infamous Minute* (1835) — deeply influenced by Charles Grant's *Observations* — makes a mockery of Oriental learn-

---

4. Charles Grant, "Observations on the State of Society among the Asiatic Subjects of Great Britain," *Sessional Papers 1812–13*, X (282), East India Company.
5. *Ibid.*, chap. 4, p. 104.

ing until faced with the challenge of conceiving of a "reformed" colonial subject. Then the great tradition of European humanism seems capable only of ironizing itself. At the intersection of European learning and colonial power, Macaulay can conceive of nothing other than "a class of interpreters between us and the millions whom we govern — a class of persons Indian in blood and colour, but English in tastes, in opinions, in morals and in intellect"[6] — in other words a mimic man raised "through our English School," as a missionary educationist wrote in 1819, "to form a corps of translators and be employed in different departments of Labour."[7] The line of descent of the mimic man can be traced through the works of Kipling, Forester, Orwell, Naipaul, and to his emergence, most recently, in Benedict Anderson's excellent essay on nationalism, as the anomalous Bipin Chandra Pal.[8] He is the effect of a flawed colonial mimesis, in which to be Anglicized, is *emphatically* not to be English.

The figure of mimicry is locatable within what Anderson describes as "the inner incompatibility of empire and nation."[9] It problematizes the signs of racial and cultural priority, so that the "national" is no longer naturalizable. What emerges between mimesis and mimicry is a *writing*, a mode of representation, that marginalizes the monumentality of history, quite simply mocks its power to be a model, that power which supposedly makes it imitable. Mimicry *repeats* rather than *re-presents* and in that diminishing perspective emerges Decoud's displaced European vision of Sulaco as

> the endlessness of civil strife where folly seemed even harder to bear than its ignominy . . . the lawlessness of a populace of all colours and races, barbarism, irremediable tyranny. . . . America is ungovernable.[10]

Or Ralph Singh's apostasy in Naipaul's *The Mimic Men*:

> We pretended to be real, to be learning, to be preparing ourselves for life, we mimic men of the New World, one unknown corner of it, with all its reminders of the corruption that came so quickly to the new.[11]

Both Decoud and Singh, and in their different ways Grant and Macaulay, are the parodists of history. Despite their intentions and invocations they inscribe the colonial text erratically, eccentrically across a body politic that refuses to be

---

6.   T. B. Macaulay, "Minute on Education," in *Sources of Indian Tradition*, vol. II, ed. William Theodore de Bary, New York, Columbia University Press, 1958, p. 49.

7.   Mr. Thomason's communication to the Church Missionary Society, September 5, 1819, in *The Missionary Register*, 1821, pp. 54–55.

8.   Benedict Anderson, *Imagined Communities*, London, Verso, 1983, p. 88.

9.   *Ibid.*, pp. 88–89.

10.   Joseph Conrad, *Nostromo*, London, Penguin, 1979, p. 161.

11.   V. S. Naipaul, *The Mimic Men*, London, Penguin, 1967, p. 146.

representative, in a narrative that refuses to be representational. The desire to emerge as "authentic" through mimicry—through a process of writing and repetition—is the final irony of partial representation.

What I have called mimicry is not the familiar exercise of *dependent* colonial relations through narcissistic identification so that, as Fanon has observed,[12] the black man stops being an actional person for only the white man can represent his self-esteem. Mimicry conceals no presence or identity behind its mask: it is not what Césaire describes as "colonization-thingification"[13] behind which there stands the essence of the *présence Africaine*. The *menace* of mimicry is its *double* vision which in disclosing the ambivalence of colonial discourse also disrupts its authority. And it is a double-vision that is a result of what I've described as the partial representation/recognition of the colonial object. Grant's colonial as partial imitator, Macaulay's translator, Naipaul's colonial politician as play-actor, Decoud as the scene setter of the *opéra bouffe* of the New World, these are the appropriate objects of a colonialist chain of command, authorized versions of otherness. But they are also, as I have shown, the figures of a doubling, the part-objects of a metonymy of colonial desire which alienates the modality and normality of those dominant discourses in which they emerge as "inappropriate" colonial subjects. A desire that, through the repetition of *partial presence*, which is the basis of mimicry, articulates those disturbances of cultural, racial, and historical difference that menace the narcissistic demand of colonial authority. It is a desire that reverses "in part" the colonial appropriation by now producing a partial vision of the colonizer's presence. A gaze of otherness, that shares the acuity of the genealogical gaze which, as Foucault describes it, liberates marginal elements and shatters the unity of man's being through which he extends his sovereignty.[14]

I want to turn to this process by which the look of surveillance returns as the displacing gaze of the disciplined, where the observer becomes the observed and "partial" representation rearticulates the whole notion of *identity* and alienates it from essence. But not before observing that even an exemplary history like Eric Stokes's *The English Utilitarians in India* acknowledges the anomalous gaze of otherness but finally disavows it in a contradictory utterance:

> Certainly India played *no* central part in fashioning the distinctive qualities of English civilisation. In many ways it acted as a disturbing force, a magnetic power placed at the periphery tending to distort the natural development of Britain's character. . . .[15]

12. Frantz Fanon, *Black Skin, White Masks*, London, Paladin, 1970, p. 109.
13. Aimé Césaire, *Discourse on Colonialism*, New York, Monthly Review Press, 1972, p. 21.
14. Michel Foucault, "Nietzche, Genealogy, History," in *Language, Counter-Memory, Practice*, trans. Donald F. Bouchard and Sherry Simon, Ithaca, Cornell University Press, p. 153.
15. Eric Stokes, *The English Utilitarians and India*, Oxford, Oxford University Press, 1959, p. xi.

What is the nature of the hidden threat of the partial gaze? How does mimicry emerge as the subject of the scopic drive and the object of colonial surveillance? How is desire disciplined, authority displaced?

If we turn to a Freudian figure to address these issues of colonial textuality, that form of difference that is mimicry — *almost the same but not quite* — will become clear. Writing of the partial nature of fantasy, caught *inappropriately*, between the unconscious and the preconscious, making problematic, like mimicry, the very notion of "origins," Freud has this to say:

> Their mixed and split origin is what decides their fate. We may compare them with individuals of mixed race who taken all round resemble white men but who betray their coloured descent by some striking feature or other and on that account are excluded from society and enjoy none of the privileges.[16]

Almost the same but not white: the visibility of mimicry is always produced at the site of interdiction. It is a form of colonial discourse that is uttered *inter dicta*: a discourse at the crossroads of what is known and permissible and that which though known must be kept concealed; a discourse uttered between the lines and as such both against the rules and within them. The question of the representation of difference is therefore always also a problem of authority. The "desire" of mimicry, which is Freud's *striking feature* that reveals so little but makes such a big difference, is not merely that impossibility of the Other which repeatedly resists signification. The desire of colonial mimicry — an interdictory desire — may not have an object, but it has strategic objectives which I shall call the *metonymy of presence*.

Those inappropriate signifiers of colonial discourse — the difference between being English and being Anglicized; the identity between stereotypes which, through repetition, also become different; the discriminatory identities constructed across traditional cultural norms and classifications, the Simian Black, the Lying Asiatic — all these are metonymies of presence. They are strategies of desire in discourse that make the anomalous representation of the colonized something other than a process of "the return of the repressed," what Fanon unsatisfactorily characterized as collective catharsis.[17] These instances of metonymy are the nonrepressive productions of contradictory and multiple belief. They cross the boundaries of the culture of enunciation through a strategic confusion of the metaphoric and metonymic axes of the cultural production of meaning. For each of these instances of "a difference that is almost the same but not quite" inadvertently creates a crisis for the cultural priority given to the *metaphoric* as the process of repression and substitution which negotiates the difference between paradigmatic systems and classifications. In

16.   Sigmund Freud, "The Unconscious" (1915), *SE*, XIV, pp. 190–191.
17.   Fanon, p. 103.

mimicry, the representation of identity and meaning is rearticulated along the axis of metonymy. As Lacan reminds us, mimicry is like camouflage, not a harmonization or repression of difference, but a form of resemblance that differs/defends presence by displaying it in part, metonymically. Its threat, I would add, comes from the prodigious and strategic production of conflictual, fantastic, discriminatory "identity effects" in the play of a power that is elusive because it hides no essence, no "itself." And that form of *resemblance* is the most terrifying thing to behold, as Edward Long testifies in his *History of Jamaica* (1774). At the end of a tortured, negrophobic passage, that shifts anxiously between piety, prevarication, and perversion, the text finally confronts its fear; nothing other than the repetition of its resemblance "in part":

> (Negroes) are represented by all authors as the vilest of human kind, to which they have little more pretension of resemblance *than what arises from their exterior forms* (my italics).[18]

From such a colonial encounter between the white presence and its black semblance, there emerges the question of the ambivalence of mimicry as a problematic of colonial subjection. For if Sade's scandalous theatricalization of language repeatedly reminds us that discourse can claim "no priority," then the work of Edward Said will not let us forget that the "ethnocentric and erratic will to power from which texts can spring"[19] is itself a theater of war. Mimicry, as the metonymy of presence is, indeed, such an erratic, eccentric strategy of authority in colonial discourse. Mimicry does not merely destroy narcissistic authority through the repetitious slippage of difference and desire. It is the process of the *fixation* of the colonial as a form of cross-classificatory, discriminatory knowledge in the defiles of an interdictory discourse, and therefore necessarily raises the question of the *authorization* of colonial representations. A question of authority that goes beyond the subject's lack of priority (castration) to a historical crisis in the conceptuality of colonial man as an *object* of regulatory power, as the subject of racial, cultural, national representation.

"This culture . . . fixed in its colonial status," Fanon suggests, "(is) both present and mummified, it testified against its members. It defines them in fact without appeal."[20] The ambivalence of mimicry—almost but not quite—suggests that the fetishized colonial culture is potentially and strategically an insurgent counter-appeal. What I have called its "identity-effects," are always crucially *split*. Under cover of camouflage, mimicry, like the fetish, is a part-object that radically revalues the normative knowledges of the priority of race, writing, history. For the fetish mimes the forms of authority at the point at

18.   Edward Long, *A History of Jamaica*, 1774, vol. II, p. 353.
19.   Edward Said, "The Text, the World, the Critic," in *Textual Strategies*, ed. J. V. Harari, Ithaca, Cornell University Press, 1979, p. 184.
20.   Frantz Fanon, "Racism and Culture," in *Toward the African Revolution*, London, Pelican, 1967, p. 44.

OCTOBER: The First Decade

which it deauthorizes them. Similarly, mimicry rearticulates presence in terms of its "otherness," that which it disavows. There is a crucial difference between this *colonial* articulation of man and his doubles and that which Foucault describes as "thinking the unthought"[21] which, for nineteenth-century Europe, is the ending of man's alienation by reconciling him with his essence. The colonial discourse that articulates an *interdictory* "otherness" is precisely the "other scene" of this nineteenth-century European desire for an authentic historical consciousness.

The "unthought" across which colonial man is articulated is that process of classificatory confusion that I have described as the metonymy of the substitutive chain of ethical and cultural discourse. This results in the *splitting* of colonial discourse so that two attitudes towards external reality persist; one takes reality into consideration while the other disavows it and replaces it by a product of desire that repeats, rearticulates "reality" as mimicry.

So Edward Long can say with authority, quoting variously, Hume, Eastwick, and Bishop Warburton in his support, that:

> Ludicrous as the opinion may seem I do not think that an orangutang husband would be any dishonour to a Hottentot female.[22]

Such contradictory articulations of reality and desire—seen in racist stereotypes, statements, jokes, myths—are not caught in the doubtful circle of the return of the repressed. They are the effects of a disavowal that denies the differences of the other but produces in its stead forms of authority and multiple belief that alienate the assumptions of "civil" discourse. If, for a while, the ruse of desire is calculable for the uses of discipline soon the repetition of guilt, justification, pseudoscientific theories, superstition, spurious authorities, and classifications can be seen as the desperate effort to "normalize" *formally* the disturbance of a discourse of splitting that violates the rational, enlightened claims of its enunciatory modality. The ambivalence of colonial authority repeatedly turns from *mimicry*—a difference that is almost nothing but not quite—to *menace*—a difference that is almost total but not quite. And in that other scene of colonial power, where history turns to farce and presence to "a part," can be seen the twin figures of narcissism and paranoia that repeat furiously, uncontrollably.

In the ambivalent world of the "not quite/not white," on the margins of metropolitan desire, the *founding objects* of the Western world become the erratic, eccentric, accidental *objets trouvés* of the colonial discourse—the part-objects of presence. It is then that the body and the book loose their representational authority. Black skin splits under the racist gaze, displaced into signs of besti-

21. Michel Foucault, *The Order of Things*, New York, Pantheon, 1970, part II, chap. 9.
22. Long, p. 364.

ality, genitalia, grotesquerie, which reveal the phobic myth of the undifferentiated whole white body. And the holiest of books — the Bible — bearing both the
standard of the cross and the standard of empire finds itself strangely dismem-
bered. In May 1817 a missionary wrote from Bengal:

> Still everyone would gladly receive a Bible. And why? — that he may
> lay it up as a curiosity for a few pice; or use it for waste paper. Such
> it is well known has been the common fate of these copies of the
> Bible. . . . Some have been bartered in the markets, others have
> been thrown in snuff shops and used as wrapping paper.[23]

---

23. *The Missionary Register*, May 1817, p. 186.

Jean-Luc Godard. Two or Three Things I Know about
Her. *1966.*

Woman's Stake: Filming the
Female Body

MARY ANN DOANE

We know that, for want of a stake,
representation is not worth anything.
—Michèle Montrelay

To those who still ask, "What do women want?" the cinema seems to provide no answer. For the cinema, in its alignment with the fantasies of the voyeur, has historically articulated its stories through a conflation of its central axis of seeing/being seen with the opposition male/female. So much so that in a classical instance such as *Humoresque*, when Joan Crawford almost violently attempts to appropriate the gaze for herself, she must be represented as myopic (the moments of her transformation from spectacle to spectator thus captured and constrained through their visualization as the act of putting on glasses) and eventually eliminated from the text, her death equated with that of a point of view. Cinematic images of woman have been so consistently oppressive and repressive that the very idea of a feminist filmmaking practice seems an impossibility. The simple gesture of directing a camera toward a woman has become equivalent to a terrorist act.

This state of affairs—the result of a history which inscribes woman as subordinate—is not simply to be overturned by a contemporary practice that is more aware, more self-conscious. The impasse confronting feminist filmmakers today is linked to the force of a certain theoretical discourse which denies the neutrality of the cinematic apparatus itself. A machine for the production of images and sounds, the cinema generates and guarantees pleasure by a corroboration of the spectator's identity. Because that identity is bound up with that of the voyeur and the fetishist, because it requires for its support the attributes of the "noncastrated," the potential for illusory mastery of the signifier, it is not accessible to the female spectator, who, in buying her ticket, must deny her sex. There are no images either *for* her or *of* her. There is a sense in which Peter Gidal, in attempting to articulate the relationship between his own filmmaking practice and feminist concerns, draws the most logical conclusion from this tendency in theory:

> In terms of the feminist struggle specifically, I have had a vehement refusal over the last decade, with one or two minor aberrations, to allow images of women into my films at all, since I do not see how those images can be separated from the dominant meanings. The ultra-left aspect of this may be nihilistic as well, which may be a critique of my position because it does not see much hope for representations for women, but I do not see how, to take the main example I gave round about 1969 before any knowledge on my part of, say, semiotics, there is any possibility of using the image of a naked woman—at that time I did not have it clarified to the point of any image of a woman—other than in an absolutely sexist and politically repressive patriarchal way in this conjuncture.[1]

This is the extreme formulation of a project which can define itself only in terms of negativity. If the female body is not necessarily always excluded within this problematic, it must always be placed within quotation marks. For it is precisely the massive reading, writing, filming of the female body which constructs and maintains a hierarchy along the lines of a sexual difference assumed as natural. The ideological complicity of the concept of the natural dictates the impossibility of a nostalgic return to an unwritten body.

Thus, contemporary filmmaking addresses itself to the activity of uncoding, de-coding, deconstructing the given images. It is a project of de-familiarization whose aim is not necessarily that of seeing the female body differently, but of exposing the habitual meanings/values attached to femininity as cultural constructions. Sally Potter's *Thriller*, for instance, is a rereading of the woman's role in opera, specifically in Puccini's *La Bohème*, in terms of its ideological function. Mimi's death, depicted in the opera as tragedy, is rewritten as a murder, the film itself invoking the conventions of the suspense thriller. In Babette Mangolte's *The Camera: Je/La Caméra: Eye*, what is at stake are the relations of power sustained within the camera-subject nexus. The discomfort of the subjects posing for the camera, together with the authority of the off-screen voice giving instructions ("Smile," "Don't smile," "Look to the left," etc.), challenge the photographic image's claim to naturalism and spontaneity. And, most interestingly, the subjects, whether male or female, inevitably appear to assume a mask of "femininity" in order to become photographable (filmable)—as though femininity were synonymous with the *pose*.[2] This may explain the feminist film's frequent

1.   Peter Gidal, transcription of a discussion following "Technology and Ideology in/through/and Avant-Garde Film: An Instance," in *The Cinematic Apparatus*, eds. Teresa de Lauretis and Stephen Heath, New York, St. Martin's Press, 1980, p. 169.
2.   This calls for a more thorough dissection and analysis of the assumptions underlying the cliché that male models are "effeminate."

obsession with the pose as position—the importance accorded to dance positions in *Thriller*, or those assumed by the hysteric in Terrel Seltzer's *The Story of Anna O.*—which we may see as the arrangements of the body in the interests of aesthetics and science. In their rigidity (the recurrent use of the tableau in these films) or excessive repetition (the multiple, seemingly unending caresses of the woman's breasts in Mangolte's *What Maisie Knew*), positions and gestures are isolated, deprived of the syntagmatic rationalization which, in the more classical text, conduces to their naturalization. These strategies of demystification are attempts to strip the body of its readings. The inadequacy of this formulation of the problem is obvious, however, in that the gesture of stripping in relation to a female body is already the property of patriarchy. More importantly, perhaps, the question to be addressed is this: what is left after the stripping, the uncoding, the deconstruction? For an uncoded body is clearly an impossibility.

Attempts to answer this question by invoking the positivity or specificity of a definition have been severely criticized on the grounds that the particular definition claims a "nature" proper to the woman and is hence complicit with those discourses which set woman outside the social order. Since the patriarchy has always already said everything (everything and nothing) about woman, efforts to give those phrases a different intonation, to mumble, to stutter, to slur them, to articulate them differently, must be doomed to failure. Laura Mulvey and Peter Wollen's *Riddles of the Sphinx*, for instance, has been repeatedly criticized for its invocation of the sphinx as the figure of a femininity repressed by the Oedipal mythos. Femininity is something which has been forgotten or repressed, left outside the gates of the city; hence, what is called for is a radical act of remembering. The radicality of that act, however, has been subject to debate. As Stephen Heath points out,

> The line in the figure of the sphinx-woman between the posing of a question and the idea that women are the question is very thin; female sexuality is dark and unexplorable, women, as Freud put it, are that half of the audience which is the enigma, the great enigma. This is the problem and the difficulty—the area of debate and criticism—of Mulvey and Wollen's film *Riddles of the Sphinx* where the sphinx is produced as a point of resistance that seems nevertheless to repeat, in its very terms, the relations of women made within patriarchy, their representation in the conjunction of such elements as motherhood as mystery, the unconscious, a voice that speaks far off from the past through dream or forgotten language. The film is as though poised on the edge of a politics of the unconscious, of the imagination of a politics of the unconscious ('what would the politics of the unconscious be like?'), with a simultaneous falling short, that politics and imagination not yet there, coming back with old definitions, the given images.[3]

3.   Stephen Heath, "Difference," *Screen*, vol. 19, no. 3 (Autumn 1978), 73.

What is forgotten in the critical judgment, but retrieved in Heath's claim that "the force remains in the risk"—the risk, that is, of recapitulating the terms of patriarchy—is the fact that the sphinx is also, and crucially, subject to a kind of filmic disintegration. In the section entitled "Stones," the refilming of found footage of the Egyptian sphinx problematizes any notion of perceptual immediacy in refinding an "innocent" image of femininity. In fact, as the camera appears to get closer to its object, the graininess of the film is marked, thus indicating the limit of the material basis of its representation.

Most of this essay will be a lengthy digression, a prolegomenon to a much needed investigation of the material specificity of film in relation to the female body and its syntax. Given the power of a certain form of feminist theory which has successfully blocked attempts to provide a conceptualization of this body, the digression is, nevertheless, crucial.

The resistance to filmic and theoretical descriptions of femininity is linked to the strength of the feminist critique of essentialism—of ideas concerning an essential femininity, or of the "real" woman not yet disfigured by patriarchal social relations. The force of this critique lies in its exposure of the inevitable alliance between "feminine essence" and the natural, the given, or precisely what is outside the range of political action and thus not amenable to change. This unchangeable "order of things" in relation to sexual difference is an exact formulation of patriarchy's strongest rationalization of itself. And since the essence of femininity is most frequently attached to the natural body as an immediate indicator of sexual difference, it is this body which must be refused. The body is always a function of discourse.

Feminist theory which grounds itself in anti-essentialism frequently turns to psychoanalysis for its description of sexuality because psychoanalysis assumes a necessary gap between the body and the psyche, so that sexuality is not reducible to the physical. Sexuality is constructed within social and symbolic relations; it is most *un*natural and achieved only after an arduous struggle. One is not born with a sexual identity (hence the significance of the concept of bisexuality in psycho-analysis). The terms of this argument demand that charges of phallocentrism be met with statements that the phallus is not equal to the penis, castration is bloodless, and the father is, in any case, dead and only symbolic.

Nevertheless, the gap between body and psyche is not absolute; an image or symbolization of the body (which is not necessarily the body of biological science) is fundamental to the construction of the psychoanalytical discourse. Brief references to two different aspects of psychoanalytic theory will suffice to illustrate my point. Jean Laplanche explains the emergence of sexuality by means of the concept of propping or *anaclisis*. The drive, which is always sexual, leans or props itself upon the nonsexual or presexual instinct of self-preservation. His major example is the relation of the oral drive to the instinct of hunger whose object is the milk obtained from the mother's breast. The object of the oral drive (prompted by the sucking which activates the lips as an erotogenic zone) is necessarily displaced in relation to the first object of the instinct. The fantasmatic breast (henceforth the object of the oral drive) is a metonymic derivation, a symbol, of the milk: "The object to be rediscovered is not the lost object, but its substitute by displacement; the lost object is the object of self-preservation, of hunger, and the object one seeks to refind is an object displaced in relation to that first object."[4] Sexuality can only take form in a dissociation of subjectivity from the bodily function, but the concept of a bodily function is necessary in the explanation as, precisely, a support. We will see later how Laplanche de-naturalizes this body (which is simply a distribution of erotogenic zones) while retaining it as a cipher. Still, the body is there, as a prop.

The second aspect of psychoanalysis which suggests the necessity of a certain conceptualization of the body is perhaps more pertinent, and certainly more notorious, in relation to a discussion of feminism: the place of the phallus in Lacanian theory. Lacan and feminist theorists who subscribe to his formulations persistently claim that the phallus is not the penis; the phallus is a signifier (the signifier of lack). It does not *belong* to the male. The phallus is only important insofar as it can be put in circulation as a signifier. Both sexes define themselves in relation to this "third term." What is ultimately stressed here is the absolute necessity of positing only one libido (which Freud labels masculine) in relation to only one term, the phallus. Initially, both sexes, in desiring to conform to the desire of the other (the mother), define themselves in relation to the phallus in the mode of "being." Sexual difference, then, is inaugurated at the moment of the Oedipal complex when the girl continues to "be" the phallus while the boy situates himself in the mode of "having." Positing two terms, in relation to two fully defined sexualities, as Jones and Horney do, binds the concept of sexuality more immediately, more directly, to the body as it expresses itself at birth. For Jones and Horney, there is an essential femininity which is linked to an expression of the vagina. And for Horney at least, there is a sense in which the little girl experiences an empirical, not a psychic, inferiority.[5]

But does the phallus really have nothing to do with the penis, no commerce with it at all? The ease of the description by means of which the boy situates himself in the mode of "having" one would seem to indicate that this is not the case. And Lacan's justification for the privilege accorded to the phallus as signifier appears to guarantee its derivation from a certain representation of the bodily organ:

> The phallus is the privileged signifier of that mark in which the role of
> the logos is joined with the advent of desire. It can be said that this
> signifier is chosen because it is the most tangible element in the real of

---

4.   Jean Laplanche, *Life and Death in Psychoanalysis*, trans. Jeffrey Mehlman, Baltimore, Johns Hopkins, 1976, p. 20.
5.   See, for example, "The Denial of the Vagina," in *Psychoanalysis and Female Sexuality*, ed. Hendrick M. Ruitenbeek, New Haven, College and University Press, 1966, pp. 73–87; and *Feminine Psychology*, ed. Harold Kelman, New York, W. W. Norton, 1967.

sexual copulation, and also the most symbolic in the literal (typographical) sense of the term, since it is equivalent there to the (logical) copula. It might also be said that, by virtue of its turgidity, it is the image of the vital flow as it is transmitted in generation.[6]

There is a sense in which all attempts to deny the relation between the phallus and the penis are feints, veils, illusions. The phallus, as signifier, may no longer *be* the penis, but any effort to conceptualize its function is inseparable from an imaging of the body. The difficulty in conceptualizing the relation between the phallus and the penis is evident in Parveen Adams's explanation of the different psychic trajectories of the girl and the boy.

> Sexuality can only be considered at the level of the symbolic processes. This lack is undifferentiated for both sexes and has nothing to do with the absence of a penis, a physical lack.
>
> Nonetheless, the anatomical difference between the sexes does permit a differentiation within the symbolic process. . . . The phallus represents lack for both boys and girls. But the boy in having a penis has that which lends itself to the phallic symbol. The girl does not have a penis. What she lacks is not a penis as such, but the means to represent lack.[7]

The sexual differentiation is permitted but not demanded by the body and it is the exact force or import of this "permitting" which requires an explanation. For it is clear that what is being suggested is that the boy's body provides an access to the processes of representation while the girl's body does not. From this perspective, a certain slippage can then take place by means of which the female body becomes an absolute tabula rasa of sorts: anything and everything can be written on it. Or more accurately, perhaps, the male body comes fully equipped with a binary opposition—penis/no penis, presence/absence, phonemic opposition—while the female body is constituted as "noise,"[8] an undifferentiated presence which always threatens to disrupt representation.

This analysis of the bodily image in psychoanalysis becomes crucial for feminism with the recognition that sexuality is inextricable from discourse, from language. The conjunction of semiotics and psychoanalysis (as exemplified in the work of Lacan and others) has been successful in demonstrating the necessity of a break in an initial plenitude as a fundamental condition for signification. The concept of lack is not arbitrary. The fact that the little girl in the above description has no means to represent lack results in her different relation to language and

---

6. Jacques Lacan, *Écrits: A Selection*, trans. Alan Sheridan, New York, W. W. Norton, 1977, p. 287.
7. Parveen Adams, "Representation and Sexuality," *m/f*, no. 1 (1978), 66–67. Even if the phallus is defined as logically prior to the penis, in that it is the phallus which bestows significance on the penis, a *relation* between the two is nevertheless posited, and this is my point.
8. I am grateful to Philip Rosen for this "representation" of the problem.

representation. The work of Michèle Montrelay is most explicit on this issue: ". . . for want of a stake, representation is not worth anything."[9] The initial relation to the mother, the determinant of the desire of both sexes, is too full, too immediate, too present. This undifferentiated plenitude must be fissured through the introduction of lack before representation can be assured, since representation entails the absence of the desired object. "Hence the repression that ensures that one does not think, nor see, nor take the desired object, even and above all if it is within reach: this object must remain lost."[10] The tragedy of Oedipus lies in his refinding of the object. And as Montrelay points out, it is the sphinx as the figure of femininity which heralds this "ruin of representation."

In order for representation to be possible then, a stake is essential. Something must be threatened if the paternal prohibition against incest is to take effect, forcing the gap between desire and its object. This theory results in a rather surprising interpretation of the woman's psychic oppression: her different relation to language stems from the fact that she has nothing to lose, nothing at stake. Prohibition, the law of limitation, cannot touch the little girl. For the little boy, on the other hand, there is most definitely something to lose. "He experiments, not only with chance but also with the law and with his sexual organ: his body itself takes on the value of stake."[11]

Furthermore, in repeating, doubling the maternal body with her own, the woman recovers the first stake of representation and thus undermines the possibility of losing the object of desire since she has, instead become it.

> From now on, anxiety, tied to the presence of this body, can only be insistent, continuous. This body, so close, which she has to occupy, is an object in excess which must be 'lost,' that is to say, repressed, in order to be symbolised. Hence the symptoms which so often simulate this loss: 'there is no longer anything, only the hole, emptiness . . .' Such is the *leitmotif* of all feminine cure, which it would be a mistake to see as the expression of an alleged 'castration.' On the contrary, it is a defence produced in order to parry the avatars, the deficiencies, of symbolic castration.[12]

There are other types of defense as well, based on the woman's imaginary simulation of lack. Montrelay points to the anorexic, for instance, who diminishes her own body, dissolving the flesh and reducing the body to a cipher.[13] Or the woman can operate a performance of femininity, a masquerade, by means of an accumulation of accessories—jewelry, hats, feathers, etc.—all designed to mask the

9.   Michèle Montrelay, "Inquiry into Femininity," *m/f*, no. 1 (1978), 89.
10.   *Ibid.*
11.   *Ibid.*, p. 90.
12.   *Ibid.*, pp. 91–92.
13.   *Ibid.*, p. 92.

absence of a lack.[14] These defenses, however, are based on the woman's imaginary simulation of lack and exclude the possibility of an encounter with the symbolic. She can only mime representation.

Montrelay's work is problematic in several respects. In situating the woman's relation to her own body as narcissistic, erotic, and maternal, Montrelay insists that it is the "real of her own body" which "imposes itself," prior to any act of construction.[15] Furthermore, she does, eventually, outline a scenario within which the woman has access to symbolic lack, but it is defined in terms of a heterosexual act of intercourse in which the penis, even though it is described as "scarcely anything," produces the "purest and most elementary form of signifying articulation."[16] Nevertheless, Montrelay's work points to the crucial dilemma confronting an anti-essentialist feminist theory which utilizes psychoanalysis. That is, while psychoanalysis does theorize the relative autonomy of psychic processes, the gap between body and psyche, it also requires the body as a prop, a support for its description of sexuality as a discursive function. Too often anti-essentialism is characterized by a paranoia in relation to all discussions of the female body (since ideas about a "natural" female body or the female body and "nature" are the linchpins of patriarchal ideology). This results in a position which simply repeats that of classical Freudian psychoanalysis in its focus upon the little boy's psychic development at the expense of that of the little girl. What is repressed here is the fact that psychoanalysis can conceptualize the sexuality of both the boy and the girl *only* by positing gender-specific bodies.

Even more crucially, as Montrelay's work demonstrates, the use of the concepts of the phallus and castration within a semiotically oriented psychoanalysis logically implies that the woman must have a different relation to language from that of the man. And from a semiotic perspective, her relation to language must be deficient since her body does not "permit" access to what, for the semiotician, is the motor-force of language—the representation of lack. Hence, the greatest masquerade of all is that of the woman speaking (or writing, or filming), appropriating discourse. To take up a discourse for the woman (if not, indeed, by her), that is, the discourse of feminism itself, would thus seem to entail an absolute contradiction. How can she speak?

Yet, we know that women speak, even though it may not be clear exactly how this takes place. And unless we want to accept a formulation by means of which woman can only mimic man's relation to language, that is, assume a position defined by the penis-phallus as the supreme arbiter of lack, we must try to reconsider the relation between the female body and language, never forgetting

14.   This description is derived from Lacan's conceptualization of masquerade in relation to femininity. See *Écrits: A Selection*, pp. 289–290. Lacan, in turn, borrows the notion of masquerade from Joan Riviere; see "Womanliness as Masquerade," in *Psychoanalysis and Female Sexuality*, pp. 209–220.
15.   Montrelay, p. 91.
16.   *Ibid.*, p. 98.

that it is a relation between two terms and not two essences. Does woman have a stake in representation or, more appropriately, can we assign one to her? Anatomy is destiny only if the concept of destiny is recognized for what it really is: a concept proper to fiction.

The necessity of assigning to woman a specific stake informs the work of theorists such as Luce Irigaray and Julia Kristeva, and both have been criticized from an anti-essentialist perspective. Beverley Brown and Parveen Adams, for example, distinguish between two orders of argument about the female body which are attributed, respectively, to Irigaray and Kristeva:

> We can demand then: what is this place, this body, from which women speak so mutely?
>
> Two orders of reply to this question can be distinguished. In the first there is an attempt to find a real and natural body which is pre-social in a literal sense. The second, more sophisticated reply, says that the issue at stake is not the actual location of a real body, but that the positing of such a body seems to be a condition of the discursive in general.[17]

Although the second order of argument is described as "more sophisticated," Brown and Adams ultimately find that both are deficient. I want briefly to address this criticism although it really requires an extended discussion impossible within the limits of this essay. The criticisms of Irigaray are based primarily on her essay, "That Sex Which Is Not One,"[18] in which she attempts to conceptualize the female body in relation to language/discourse, but independently of the penis/ lack dichotomy. Irigaray valorizes certain features of the female body—the two lips (of the labia) which caress each other and define woman's auto-eroticism as a relation to duality, the multiplicity of sexualized zones spread across the body. Furthermore, Irigaray uses this representation of the body to specify a feminine language which is plural, polyvalent, and irreducible to a masculine language based on restrictive notions of unity and identity. Brown and Adams claim that "her argument turns upon the possibility of discovering that which is already there—it is a case of 'making visible' the previously 'invisible' of feminine sexuality."[19] While there are undoubtedly problems with the rather direct relation Irigaray often posits between the body and language, her attempt to provide the woman with an autonomous symbolic representation is not to be easily dismissed.

---

17. Beverley Brown and Parveen Adams, "The Feminine Body and Feminist Politics," *m/f*, no. 3 (1979), 37.

18. Luce Irigaray, "That Sex Which Is Not One," trans. R. Albury and P. Foss, in *Language, Sexuality, Subversion*, ed. Paul Foss and Meaghan Morris, Darlington, Feral Publications, 1978, pp. 161–172. This is a translation of the second essay in *Ce sexe qui n'en est pas un*, Paris, Minuit, 1977, pp. 23–32.

19. Brown and Adams, p. 38.

Irigaray herself criticizes the logic which gives privilege to the gaze, thereby questioning the gesture of "making visible" a previously hidden female sexuality. Her work is a radical rewriting of psychoanalysis which, while foregrounding the process of mimesis by which language represents the body, simultaneously constructs a distinction between a mimesis which is "productive" and one which is merely "reproductive" or "imitative"—a process of "adequation" and of "specularization."[20] An immediate dismissal of her work in the interests of an overwary anti-essentialism involves a premature rejection of "the force that remains in the risk."

The criticism addressed to Kristeva, on the other hand, is directed toward her stress on pre-Oedipal sexuality, allying it with a femininity whose repression is the very condition of Western discourse.[21] For Kristeva, the woman's negative relation to the symbolic determines her bond with a polymorphous, prelogical discourse which corresponds to the autonomous and polymorphous sexuality of the pre-Oedipal moment. Brown and Adams formulate their criticism in these terms: "Setting up this apolitical autonomy of polymorphous sexuality is, in effect, the positing of sexuality as an impossible origin, a state of nature, as simply the eternal presence of sexuality at all."[22] However, pre-Oedipal sexuality is not synonymous with "nature"; it already assumes an organized distribution of erotogenic zones over the body and forms of relations to objects which are variable (whether human or nonhuman). Both male and female pass through, live pre-Oedipality. Hence, pre-Oedipality can only be equated with femininity retrospectively, *après coup*, after the event of the Oedipal complex, of the threat of castration, and the subsequent negative entry into the symbolic attributed to the woman. Insofar as Kristeva's description of pre-Oedipality is dependent upon notions of the drive, it involves a displacement of sexuality in relation to the body. As Laplanche points out, the drive is a metonymic derivation from the instinct which is itself attached to an erotogenic zone, a zone of *exchange.*

> The drive properly speaking, in the only sense faithful to Freud's discovery, *is* sexuality. Now sexuality, in its entirety, in the human infant, lies in *a movement which deflects the instinct, metaphorizes its aim, displaces and internalizes its object, and concentrates its source on what is ultimately a minimal zone, the erotogenic zone.* . . . This zone of exchange is also a zone for care, namely the particular and attentive care provided by the mother. These zones, then, attract the first erotogenic maneuvers from the adult. An even more significant factor, if we introduce the subjectivity of the first "partner": these zones

20.   *Ce sexe qui n'en est pas un*, pp. 129–130.
21.   The critique of Kristeva is based on *About Chinese Women*, trans. Anita Barrows, New York, Urizen Books, 1977.
22.   Brown and Adams, p. 39.

> *focalize parental fantasies* and above all *maternal fantasies,* so that we
> may say, in what is barely a metaphor, that they are the points through
> which is *introduced into the child that alien internal entity* which is,
> properly speaking, the *sexual excitation.*[23]

The force of this scenario lies in its de-naturalization of the sexualized body. The conceptualization of the erotogenic zone as a zone of exchange demonstrates that the investment of the body with sexuality is always already social. Since it is ultimately *maternal* fantasies which are at issue here, it is apparent that, without an anchoring in the social, psychoanalysis can simply reiterate, reperform in its theorization, the vicious circle of patriarchy.

The rather long digression which structures this essay is motivated by the extreme difficulty of moving beyond the impasse generated by the opposition between essentialism and anti-essentialism. In the context of feminist film theory, both positions are formulated through a repression of the crucial and complex relation between the body and psychic processes, that is, processes of signification. From the point of view of essentialist theory, the goal of a feminist film practice must be the production of images which provide a pure reflection of the real woman, thus returning the real female body to the woman as her rightful property. And this body is accessible to a transparent cinematic discourse. The position is grounded in a mis-recognition of signification as outside of, uninformed by, the psychic. On the other hand, the logical extension of anti-essentialist theory, particularly as it is evidenced in Gidal's description of his filmmaking practice, results in the absolute exclusion of the female body, the refusal of any attempt to figure or represent that body. Both the proposal of a pure access to a natural female body and the rejection of attempts to conceptualize the female body based on their contamination by ideas of "nature" are inhibiting and misleading. Both positions deny the necessity of posing a complex relation between the body and psychic/signifying processes, of using the body, in effect, as a "prop." For Kristeva is right—the positing of a body *is* a condition of discursive practices. It is crucial that feminism move beyond the opposition between essentialism and anti-essentialism. This move will entail the necessary risk taken by theories which attempt to define or construct a feminine specificity (not essence), theories which work to provide the woman with an autonomous symbolic representation.

What this means in terms of the theorization of a feminist filmmaking practice can only be sketched here. But it is clear from the preceding exploration of the theoretical elaboration of the female body that the stake does not simply concern an isolated image of the body. The attempt to "lean" on the body in order to formulate the woman's different relation to speech, to language, clarifies the fact

23. Laplanche, pp. 23–24.

Laura Mulvey and Peter Wollen. Riddles of the
Sphinx. *1977.*

that what is at stake is, rather, the syntax which constitutes the female body as a term. The most interesting and productive recent films dealing with the feminist problematic are precisely those which elaborate a new syntax, thus "speaking" the female body differently, even haltingly or inarticulately from the perspective of a classical syntax. For instance, the circular camera movements which carve out the space of the mise-en-scène in *Riddles of the Sphinx* are in a sense more critical to a discussion of the film than the status of the figure of the sphinx as feminine. The film effects a continual displacement of the gaze which "catches" the woman's body only accidentally, momentarily, refusing to hold or fix her in the frame. The camera consistently transforms its own framing to elide the possibility of a fetishism of the female body. Chantal Akerman's *Jeanne Dielman, 23 Quai du Commerce—1080 Bruxelles* constructs its syntax by linking together scenes which, in the classical text, would be concealed, in effect negated, by temporal ellipses. The specificity of the film lies in the painful duration of that time "in-between" events, that time which is exactly proper to the woman (in particular, the housewife) within a patriarchal society. The obsessive routine of Jeanne Diel-

Sally Potter. Thriller. *1979.*

man's daily life, as both housewife and prostitute, is radically broken only by an instance of orgasm (corresponding quite literally to the "climax" of the narrative) which is immediately followed by her murder of the man. Hence, the narrative structure is a parodic "mime" that distorts, undoes the structure of the classical narrative through an insistence upon its repressions.

The analysis of the elaboration of a special syntax for a different articulation of the female body can also elucidate the significance of the recourse, in at least two of these films, to the classical codification of suspense. Both *Jeanne Dielman* and Sally Potter's *Thriller* construct a suspense without expectation. *Jeanne Dielman*, although it momentarily "cites" the mechanism of the narrative climax, articulates an absolute refusal of the phatic function of suspense, its engagement with and constraint of the spectator as consumer, devourer of discourse. *Thriller*, on the other hand, "quotes" the strategies of the suspense film (as well as individual films of this genre—for example, *Psycho*) in order to undermine radically the way in which the woman is "spoken" by another genre altogether, that of operatic tragedy. This engagement with the codification of suspense is an encounter with the genre which Roland Barthes defines as the most intense embodiment of the "generalized distortion" which "gives the language of narrative its special character":

> 'Suspense' is clearly only a privileged—or 'exacerbated'—form of distortion: on the one hand, by keeping a sequence open (through emphatic procedures of delay and renewal), it reinforces the contact with the reader (the listener), has a manifestly phatic function; while on the other, it offers the threat of an uncompleted sequence, of an open paradigm (if, as we believe, every sequence has two poles), that is to say, of a logical disturbance, it being this disturbance which is consumed with anxiety and pleasure (all the more so because it is always made right in the end). 'Suspense', therefore, is a game with structure, designed to endanger and glorify it, constituting a veritable 'thrilling' of intelligibility: by representing order (and no longer series) in its fragility, 'suspense' accomplishes the very idea of language. . . .[24]

It is precisely this "idea of language" which is threatened by both *Jeanne Dielman* and *Thriller* in their attempts to construct another syntax which would, perhaps, collapse the fragile order, revealing the ending too soon.

While I have barely approached the question of an exact formulation of the representation of the female body attached to the syntactical constructions of these films, it is apparent that this syntax is an area of intense concern, of reworking, rearticulating the specular imaging of woman, for whom, in the context of a current filmmaking, the formulation of a stake is already in process.

---

24.   Roland Barthes, "Introduction to the Structural Analysis of Narratives," in *Image-Music-Text*, trans. Stephen Heath, New York, Hill and Wang, 1977, p. 119.

Rhetoric

Richard Serra. Clara-Clara. *1983.*

A Picturesque Stroll
around *Clara-Clara**

YVE-ALAIN BOIS

translated by JOHN SHEPLEY

"When Smithson went to see *Shift*," Serra tells us, "he spoke of its picturesque quality, and I wasn't sure what he was talking about" (p. 181).[1] This incomprehension is quite comprehensible, at least if one sticks to early definitions
of the picturesque, all of which go back to the etymological origin of this word,
that is to say, the sphere of painting. For the pictorial is one of the qualities that
Serra would like to banish completely from his sculpture. In speaking of his
first *Prop Pieces*, he criticizes them for retaining pictorial concerns (the use of the
wall as background), since such a reminder detracts from their meaning (which
is prescribed by the way they are made) (p. 142). In speaking of the numerous
works created by laying out materials on the floor, works that appeared in the
late 1960s as a criticism of minimalism, in which he himself had participated,
Serra severely judges their debt to painting in this respect: "Lateral extension in
this case allows sculpture to be viewed pictorially — that is, as if the floor were
the canvas plane. It is no coincidence that most earth works are photographed
from the air" (p. 16). Which takes us back to Smithson: "What most people
know of Smithson's *Spiral Jetty*, for example, is an image shot from a helicopter.
When you actually see the work, it has none of that purely graphic character.
. . . But if you reduce sculpture to the flat plane of the photograph . . . [y]ou're
denying the temporal experience of the work. You're not only reducing the
sculpture to a different scale for the purposes of consumption, but you're denying the real content of the work" (p. 170). Far be it from Serra, of course, to
suggest that Smithson had approved such a reduction of his work to the plani-

*   This essay was first published as "*Promenade pittoresque autour de* Clara-Clara," in the *Richard
Serra* catalogue published by Centre Georges Pompidou, 1983. The author thanks Mirka Beneš,
Jacques Lucan, Monique Mosser, Baldine Saint-Girons, and Bruno Reichlin for the advice and
information that they so generously gave.
1.   Most of the quotations from Serra given here are taken from the collection of his texts
and interviews published in 1980 by the Hudson River Museum (*Richard Serra: Interviews, Etc.
1970–1980*). Reference will be made to it in the text by a simple page number; note numbers
will only appear for texts by Serra later than the publication of this collection, or for texts other
than his.

metric surface of a snapshot (we know that he found the movie camera, because it involves motion, to be a more suitable means for conveying the *Spiral Jetty*), but this animosity toward aerial photography plunges us into the very heart of the experience of the picturesque. Why this animosity? Because aerial photography produces a "Gestalt reading" of the operation, and reconstructs the work as the indifferent realization of a compositional *a priori* (Serra goes so far as to say that it is a kind of professional distortion peculiar to photography: "Most photographs take their cues from advertising, where the priority is high image content for an easy Gestalt reading" [p. 170]). Now all of Serra's oeuvre signals a desire to escape from the theory of "good form" (and from the opposition, on which it plays, between figure and background). Notice what he says about the *Rotary Arc*: no one who circumnavigates this sculpture, whether on foot or by car, "can ascribe the multiplicity of views to a Gestalt reading of the Arc. Its form remains ambiguous, indeterminable, unknowable as an entity" (p. 161). The multiplicity of views is what is destroyed by aerial photography (a theological point of view par excellence), and the multiplicity of views is the question opened by the picturesque, its knot of contradiction.

"I wasn't sure what he was talking about. He wasn't talking about the form of the work. But I guess he meant that one experienced the landscape as picturesque through the work" (p. 181). Serra's interpretation of Smithson's remarks is based on one of the commonplaces of the theory of the picturesque garden: not to force nature, but to reveal the "capacities" of the site, while magnifying their variety and singularity. This is exactly what Serra does: "The site is redefined not re-presented. . . . The placement of all structural elements in the open field draws the viewer's attention to the topography of the landscape as the landscape is walked."[2] As early as *Shift*, and then in connection with all his landscape sculptures, Serra has insisted on the discovery by the spectator, while walking within the sculpture, of the formless nature of the terrain: the sculptures "point to the indeterminacy of the landscape. The sculptural elements act as barometers for reading the landscape."[3] Or again: "The dialectic of walking and looking into the landscape establishes the sculptural experience" (p. 72).

I believe, however, that there is more than that in Smithson's remark, and that this remark clarifies all of Serra's work since 1970, that is, ever since he took an interest, starting with a trip to Japan where for six weeks he admired the Zen gardens of Myoshin-ji, in deambulatory space and peripatetic vision. *All* of Serra's sculpture, meaning not only his landscape sculptures, but also the sculptures erected in an urban setting and those he executes in an architectural interior. Indeed, although Serra himself makes a very clear distinction between these three types of sculpture — noting, for example, that while in his urban

2.   Richard Serra, "Notes from Sight Point Road," *Perspecta* No. 19, Cambridge, The M.I.T. Press, 1982, p. 180.
3.   Richard Serra and Peter Eisenman, "Interview," *Skyline*, April 1983, p. 16.

Richard Serra. Shift. *1970–72.*

works the internal structure responds to external conditions, as in his landscape works, "ultimately the attention is refocused on the sculpture itself" (p. 181) — all his work is based on the destruction of notions of identity and causality, and all of it can be read as an extension of what Smithson says about the picturesque: "The picturesque, far from being an inner movement of the mind, is based on real land; it precedes the mind in its material external existence. We cannot take a one-sided view of the landscape within this dialectic. A park can no longer be seen as 'a thing-in-itself,' but rather as a process of ongoing relationships existing in a physical region — the park becomes a 'thing-for-us.'"[4] Despite what he says about it, all of Serra's work is based on the deconstruction of such a notion as "sculpture itself." This is how Rosalind Krauss describes the relations between Serra's oeuvre and Merleau-Ponty's *Phenomenology of Perception*;[5] in order to describe in a different way the "identity crisis" operating in Serra's sculpture, I should like to stick to the notion of the picturesque, which, I might add, could only have been developed (in the eighteenth century, in England) after the critique of the relation of causality formulated by Hume, that forefather of modern phenomenology.

What does Smithson say? That the picturesque park is not the transcription on the land of a compositional pattern previously fixed in the mind, that its effects cannot be determined *a priori*, that it presupposes a stroller, someone who trusts more in the real movement of his legs than in the fictive movement of his gaze. This notion would seem to contradict the pictorial origin of the picturesque, as set forth by a large number of theoretical and practical treatises (the garden conceived as a picture *seen* from the house or as a sequence of small views — pauses — arranged along the path where one strolls). Even further, it implies that a fundamental break with pictorialism is put in place, most often unbeknown to its theoreticians, and in my opinion, Serra's art, more than two centuries later, furnishes the most striking manifestation of this break.

How does Serra work?

> The site determines how I think about what I am going to build, whether it be an urban or landscape site, a room or other architectural enclosure. Some works are realized from their inception to their completion totally at the site. Other pieces are worked out in the studio. Having a definite notion of the actual site, I experiment with steel models in a large sandbox. The sand, functioning as a ground plane or as a surrogate elevation, enables me to shift the building elements so as to understand their sculptural capacity. The

4.   Robert Smithson, "Frederick Law Olmsted and the Dialectical Landscape," in *The Writings of Robert Smithson*, ed. Nancy Holt, New York, New York University Press, 1979, p. 119.
5.   Rosalind Krauss, "Abaisser, étendre, contracter, comprimer, tourner: regarder l'oeuvre de Richard Serra," *Richard Serra*, Paris, Centre Georges Pompidou, 1983, pp. 29–35.

building method is based on hand manipulation. A continuous hands-on procedure both in the studio and at the site, using full-scale mock-ups, models, etc., allows me to perceive structures I could not imagine.[6]

Or again: "I never make sketches or drawings for sculptures. I don't work from an a priori concept or image" (p. 146).

In short, *Serra does not start with a plan*, he does not draw on a sheet of paper the geometric figure to be delineated by the aerial view of his sculpture. This does not mean that there are no drawings: they are done later (the Kröller-Müller museum owns a very "pictorial" drawing done by Serra *from Spin Out* and *after Spin Out* had been executed). It does not mean that there are no plans: these are the business of the engineers and of the firm that will carry out the material execution of the sculpture; they are the translation, *a posteriori* and into their own codes, of the elevation projected by Serra: "When you are building a 100-ton piece [the approximate weight of the piece commissioned by the Centre Georges Pompidou], you have to meet codes" (p. 121). Serra does not start from the plan, but rather from the elevation: "Even in pieces low to the ground, I am interested in the specificity of elevation" (p. 50). Now this is precisely where Serra comes together with the theory of the picturesque and where in a certain sense his work is closer to it than Smithson's (whose drawings are often ground plans of his sculptures). For the picturesque is above all a struggle against the reduction "of all terrains to the flatness of a sheet of paper."[7]

It may seem trite to say that a fundamental shift (from plan to elevation) should appear in an art of gardens based, at least in the beginning, on the imitation of the painting of Claude Lorrain or Salvatore Rosa. Indeed, painting, at least until recently, has never confronted the spectator as a horizontal plane[8] (one might suppose that an art wishing to imitate painting, the verticality of painting, would stress the elevation). It was not, however, something that happened by itself, and one only finds it expressed rather late in the theory of picturesque gardens. It was the Marquis de Girardin, patron of Jean-Jacques Rousseau, who first formulated it directly: "What has hitherto most retarded the progress of taste, in buildings as well as in gardens, is the bad practice of catching the effect of the picture in the ground plan instead of catching the ground plan in the effect of the picture."[9] The artificial arrangements of French

6. Serra, "Notes from Sight Point Road," p. 174.
7. René-Louis de Girardin, *De la composition des paysages* (1777), Editions du Champ urbain, 1979, p. 19.
8. The rupture performed, according to Leo Steinberg, by Rauschenberg (passage from the vertical plane of the painting to the horizontal plane of the "flatbed") precisely matches the one I analyze here, through the picturesque, as performed by Serra in the field of sculpture. As I will shortly do, Steinberg analyzes this pictorial turning point in Rauschenberg as a response to the modernist theories of Clement Greenberg. Cf. Leo Steinberg, *Other Criteria*, Oxford, Oxford University Press, 1972, pp. 82–91.
9. Girardin, p. 83.

gardens are condemned because they produce the effect "of a geometric plan, a dessert tray, or a sheet of cut-outs,"[10] as is symmetry because it "is probably born of laziness and vanity. Of vanity in that one has claimed to subject nature to one's house, instead of subjecting one's house to nature; and of laziness in that one has been satisfied to work only on paper, which tolerates everything, in order to spare oneself the trouble of seeing and carefully contriving on the terrain, which tolerates only what suits it."[11]

But the point is that Girardin is not content with these declarations of intention: he advises apprentice landscape gardeners to place on the site itself *full-sized* models of the various elements that they wish to include in it, "poles stretched with white cloth" for the masses of plants and facades of buildings, and white cloth spread on the ground to represent surfaces of water, "according to the outlines, extent, and position needed to produce the same effect in *nature* as in your picture."[12] In speaking of the architecture of constructions (but this also applies to the other elements), Girardin adds: "In this way, long before building, you will be able to contrive and guarantee the success of your constructions in relation to the various points where they ought to appear, and in relation to their form, their elevation. . . ; by this means you will be able to take into consideration all their relations and their harmony with the surrounding objects."[13]

Of course, there is no question here of reducing Serra's art to the contrivances of an eighteenth-century gentleman farmer, since Girardin's whole vocabulary shows that he clung to a scenographic view of the role of the landscape gardener (for him, groves of trees are stage flats, the surrounding countryside a backdrop). And, of course, no work by Serra seeks to create a picture (the idea of representation is foreign to him). But even though Girardin is content with a pictorial conception of the picturesque (his book is entitled *De la* composition *des paysages*), and even though the elevation of Girardin's constructions actually remains an illusion, his recommendation to use full-sized models testifies to a very early understanding of what distinguishes size from scale, and this distinction lies at the heart of Serra's interest in the "specificity of elevation."

We have long been aware of Serra's aversion for the monumental works of most contemporary sculptors, as well as his wish to make a sharp distinction between his own work and the production of monuments: "When we look at these pieces, are we asked to give any credence to the notion of a monument? They do not relate to the history of monuments. They do not memorialize anything" (p. 178); finally, we know he is irritated by architects who take only a utilitarian interest in sculpture (to adorn their buildings, to add something

10.   *Ibid.*, p. 17.
11.   *Ibid.*, p. 19.
12.   *Ibid.*, p. 31.
13.   *Ibid.*

soulful to their central banks and multinational headquarters). Serra calls this mediocre urban art, which has invaded our old as well as our modern cities, "piazza art." That he has no fondness for architects is certainly his right: he has often had a bone to pick with them, including one of the Beaubourg architects who suppressed his work.[14] But the chief reproach he directs at them deserves to be noted, for it is the same one that he directs at other creators of monuments, whether they be Moore, Calder, or Noguchi (their works do not have scale, since scale depends on context; only the size of these sculptures is imposing: they are small models enlarged). "Architects suffer from the same studio syndrome. They work out of their offices, terrace the landscape and place their building into the carved-out site. As a result the studio-designed then site-adjusted buildings look like blown-up cardboard models."[15] One can imagine the laughter and disdain of architects for a sculptor who presumes to tell them that they should make full-sized models of their buildings. There was a time when Mondrian, who cared much more for the process than for the plan, wondered how architects could avoid doing so ("how can they solve each new problem *a priori?*"[16]). One more difference between our period and Mondrian's lies in the fact that such a proposition would not then have seemed incongruous, and that it was even carried out directly by architects: in 1912, Mies van der Rohe, on the site chosen in The Hague, built a full-sized model (in wood and canvas) from his designs for a large villa for Mme Kröller-Müller; and in Paris in 1922, before Mondrian's very eyes a few months after he had written his text, Mallet-Stevens took the opportunity to erect at the Salon d'Automne at full scale a design for an "Aero-Club Pavilion." One can only say that Serra's sculpture, among other things, is a reminder to architects (a "*rappel à MM. les architectes,*" in Le Corbusier's words) of some forgotten truths. The relationship between architecture and Serra's sculpture is one of conflict: he says of his *Berlin Block for Charlie Chaplin,* placed in Mies van der Rohe's National Galerie in Berlin, that it was all done "so that it would contradict the architecture" (p. 127). Furthermore, ever since his first writings, he has insisted on the need to distinguish sculptural problems from architectural ones (pp. 16, 55, 128). And when, having enumerated different qualities of space operating in a number of his sculptures, he is asked where he has found "these concepts of space" (perceptive, behaviorist, psychological, cognitive, etc.), Serra replies: "They were the result of working through various sculptural problems. Some of my concerns may be related to architectonic principles — geometry, engineering, the use of light to define a volume — but the pieces themselves have no utilitar-

---

14.   On this point, see Serra's interview with Douglas Crimp, *Interviews, Etc.*, pp. 172–173.
15.   Serra and Eisenman, p. 15.
16.   Piet Mondrian, "De realiseering van het neo-plasticisme in verre toekomst en in de huidige architectuur," 2nd part, *De Stijl*, vol. V, no. 5 (May 1922), p. 67. On this point and what it implies in Mondrian's thought, see Yve-Alain Bois, "Du projet au procès," in *L'Atelier de Mondrian,* Paris, Editions Macula, 1982, pp. 34–35.

ian or pragmatic value" (p. 73). In this sentence I read a denial. Not only because architecture — fortunately — does not always limit itself to its "utilitarian or pragmatic value," but especially because the architectonic principles to which Serra refers have nothing, or very little, to do with his work (he even acknowledges his surprise, a few pages earlier in this same interview, at the role played by light inside *Sight Point* in Amsterdam [p. 66]). Serra, therefore, does not wish to be mistaken for an architect. Which does not keep his sculpture from being a lesson in architecture, or a criticism of architecture — something that he ended by admitting when an architect, to be exact, put him on the defensive:

> When sculpture . . . leaves the gallery or museum to occupy the same space and place as architecture, when it redefines the space and place in terms of sculptural necessities, architects become annoyed. Not only is their concept of space being changed, but for the most part it is being criticized. The criticism can come into effect only when architectural scale, methods, materials and procedures are being used. Comparisons are provoked. Every language has a structure about which nothing critical in that language can be said. To criticize a language, there must be a second language available dealing with the structure of the first but possessing a new structure.[17]

This is exactly the position in which Serra's sculpture finds itself in the presence of modern architecture: the former maintains a connection that allows it to criticize the latter. Both have a common denominator that allows them to communicate.

What is this common element? Serra doesn't say, although all his remarks about his work speak of it implicitly: this element is the play of parallax. "Parallax, from Greek *parallaxis*, 'change,' displacement of the apparent position of a body, due to a change of position of the observer" (Petit Robert dictionary). Serra uses the word only once (about *Spin Out, for Bob Smithson*) (p. 36), but all his descriptions take it into account. See, for example, how *Sight Point* seems at first "to fall right to left, make an X, and straighten itself out to a truncated pyramid. That would occur three times as you walked around" (p. 66). Or again, see how the upper edge of the *Rotary Arc* seems sometimes to curve toward the sky, sometimes toward the ground, how its concavity is curtailed before the moving spectator discovers a convexity whose end he cannot see, how this convexity is then flattened to the point of becoming a barely rounded wall, until this regularity is suddenly broken and in some way turned inside out like a glove when the spectator ascends a flight of steps (pp. 155–161). Other examples could be given; I prefer for the moment to go back to architecture.

In *Changing Ideals in Modern Architecture*, Peter Collins sees the new interest in parallax, in the middle of the eighteenth century, as one of the prime sources

17.   Serra and Eisenman, p. 15.

for the establishment of modern architectural space. People were interested at first in the illusionistic effects of parallax, hence the proliferation of large mirrors in Rococo salons, and later in architectural effects themselves: these effects did not occur frequently in existing architecture ("Before the mid-eighteenth century, the interior of a building was essentially a kind of box-like enclosure," Collins notes[18]), but

> they were invariably to be seen in ruins, and this may be one of the reasons why ruins became so popular in that period. Robert Wood, when visiting the ruins of Palmyra in 1751, was as much impressed by their aesthetic as by their archaeological qualities, and remarked that "so great a number of Corinthian columns, mixed with so little wall or solid building, afforded a most romantic variety of prospect." . . . The fondness at this time for multiplying free-standing Classical colonnades inside buildings, as well as outside buildings, may also be explained by the new delight in parallax. Boullée's most grandiose projects were to show many variations on this theme, but it had been exploited as early as 1757 by Soufflot in his great church of Ste. Geneviève. . . . Soufflot had noticed that in the cathedral of Notre-Dame, "the spectator, as he advances, and as he moves away, distinguishes in the distance a thousand objects, at one moment found, at another lost again, offering him delightful spectacles."[19] He therefore attempted to produce the same effect inside of Ste. Geneviève.[20]

And in a text that Collins mentions without quoting, Soufflot's successor as master builder at Sainte-Geneviève was to say that the chief object of that architect "in building his church, was to combine in one of the most beautiful forms the lightness of construction of Gothic buildings with the purity and magnificence of Greek architecture."[21]

At first sight the interest of a neoclassical architect in Gothic buildings would seem impossibly remote from our subject. The very strangeness of this interest, however, leads directly to it, since, as Collins notes, it is the result of this new taste for parallax that develops in this period. Collins's intuition is confirmed by a supplementary element: on September 6, 1764, on the occasion of the laying of the first stone for Sainte-Geneviève, Julien David Leroy, famous

18.   Peter Collins, *Changing Ideals in Modern Architecture*, Montreal, McGill-Queen's University Press, 1965, p. 26.
19.   Jacques-Germain Soufflot, "Mémoire sur l'architecture gothique" (1741), reprinted in Michael Petzet, *Soufflots Sainte-Geneviève und der französische Kirchenbau des 18. Jahrhunderts*, Berlin, 1961, p. 138.
20.   Peter Collins, pp. 27–28.
21.   Brebion, "Mémoire à M. le Comte de la Billarderie d'Angiviller" (1780), reprinted in Petzet, p. 147. This synthesis of Greek and Gothic was to be exactly the program expounded by Boullée in his famous *Essai sur l'art*.

for *Les ruines des plus beaux monuments de la Grèce,* a work he had published in 1758 and which marked the beginning of the Greek revival, presented a small pamphlet to the king. Now this little book, which ends with a panegyric on Soufflot's future church, is probably the first architectural treatise that "relies on an experimental knowledge of movement in space — *that metaphysical part of architecture,* as Leroy calls it in his letters."[22] The hymn to the varied effects produced by a peristyle is even more vibrant in this pamphlet than in his book on ruins, where Leroy had already addressed the question. But I would rather quote a less effusive passage in which Leroy, in order to explain his rejection of pilasters and engaged columns, then a great subject of debate among French architectural theoreticians, brings up the art of gardens. His demonstration is very simple:

> If you walk in a garden, at some distance from & along a row of regularly planted trees, all of whose trunks touch a wall pierced with arcades [as engaged columns do], the position of the trees with respect to these arcades will only seem to you to change very imperceptibly, & your soul will experience no new sensation. . . . But if this row of trees stands away from the wall [like a peristyle], while you walk in the same way as before, you will enjoy a new spectacle, because the different spaces in the wall will seem successively to be blocked up by the trees with every step you take.

And Leroy's description becomes surprisingly precise — as precise as the account given by Serra of one of the possible readings of the *Rotary Arc* — for one of the routes he suggests in his promenade: "You will soon see the trees divide the arcades into two equal parts, and a moment later cut them unequally, or leave them entirely exposed & conceal only their intervals; finally, if you approach or move away from these trees, the wall will seem to you to rise up to where their branches begin, or cut their trunks at very different heights." In short, despite the regular arrangement in both cases of tree and wall, "the first of the decorations will seem immobile, while the other, on the contrary, being in some way enlivened by the movement of the spectator, will show him a series of much varied views, which will result from the endless combination that he obtains of the simple objects that produce these views."[23]

Of course, the garden described by Leroy has nothing picturesque about it; what is picturesque is the importance accorded to the movement of the spectator, since it corresponds to that fundamental rule that Uvedale Price, one of the theoreticians cited by Smithson, called "intricacy." Indeed, for Price, the

---

22.   Richard Etlin, "Grandeur et décadence d'un modèle: l'église Sainte-Geneviève et les changements de valeur esthétique au XVIIIᵉ siècle," in *Soufflot et l'architecture des lumières,* proceedings of a conference held in Lyons in 1980, supplement to nos. 6–7 of *Cahiers de la Recherche Architecturale,* 1980, p. 30. I am wholly indebted to this text for having put me on Leroy's track.
23.   Julien David Leroy, *Histoire de la disposition et des formes différentes que les chrétiens ont données à leurs temples, depuis le règne de Constantin le Grand, jusqu'à nous,* Paris, 1764, pp. 56–57.

first so-called English gardens were not picturesque enough, for they neglected "two of the most fruitful sources of human pleasures: . . . *variety* . . . [and] *intricacy*, a quality which, though distinct from variety, is so connected and blended with it that one can hardly exist without the other. According to the idea I have formed of it," Price adds, "intricacy in landscape might be defined, that disposition of objects which, by a partial and uncertain concealment, excites and nourishes curiosity."[24]

To be sure, as Collins points out, theoreticians of the picturesque have never been able to extricate themselves from a veritable malaise engendered by a contradiction in their theory, by their stubborn determination to treat the scenic garden (promenade, temporal experience) and landscape painting as though they were one and the same thing.[25] Some, however, were aware of this contradiction, and it even became a stumbling block in their polemics. See Repton, responding to Price: "The spot from whence the view is taken is in a fixed state to the painter, but the gardener surveys his scenery while in motion."[26] Now it was the discovery of the play of parallax that made them specify the terms of the contradiction (static optical view/peripatetic view). Furthermore, it is in connection with architecture, the perception of architecture, that it appears most acutely in their texts:

> Avoid a straight avenue directed upon a dwelling-house; better for an oblique approach is a waving line. . . . In a direct approach, the first appearance is continued to the end. . . . In an oblique approach, the interposed objects put the house seemingly in motion: it moves with the passenger . . . seen successively in different directions, [it] assumes at each step a new figure.[27]

In short, despite the "pictorial" bias, it is necessary to break the assurance of the organ of vision, eliminate the presumption of "Gestalt," and recall to the spectator's body, its indolence and weight, its material existence: "The foot should never travel to [the object] by the same path which the eye has travelled over before. Lose the object, and draw nigh obliquely."[28] This is the great innovation contained in embryo in the picturesque garden:

> The Classical notion of design, whether in gardens or buildings, regarded the totality of such schemes as forming a single unified and immediately intelligible composition, of which the elements were

24. Uvedale Price, *Essays on the Picturesque, as compared with the sublime and the beautiful*, London, J. Mawman, 1810. Quoted and translated in the anthology entitled *Art et Nature en Grand-Bretagne au XVIIIᵉ siècle*, by Marie-Madeleine Martinet, Paris, Aubier, 1980, p. 249.
25. Peter Collins, p. 54.
26. Humphry Repton, *The Art of Landscape Gardening* (1794), Boston and New York, Houghton Mifflin, 1907. Quoted in Martinet, p. 243.
27. Henry Kames, *Elements of Criticism* (1762), quoted in Martinet, p. 171.
28. Shenstone, *Unconnected Thoughts on Gardening* (1764), quoted in Martinet, p. 12.

subdivisions constituting smaller but still harmoniously related parts,
[the picturesque garden was] on the contrary, designed in accordance with a diametrically opposite intention, for here the overall
concept was carefully hidden.[29]

Now if I said before that Serra's sculpture was a "reminder to architects,"
it is precisely because modern architecture was born of this rupture (analyzed
by Collins in connection with gardens)—a rupture that architects themselves,
perhaps under the influence of certain theoreticians, have almost completely
repressed. In his short book on modern architecture, Vincent Scully raises at
the outset (but one swallow doesn't make a summer) the question of the rupture: it is first of all necessary, he says, to "travel backward in time until we
reach a chronological point where we can no longer identify the architecture as
an image of the modern world."[30] And this point of rupture is situated in the
middle of the eighteenth century (it is surely not by chance that it exactly coin-
cides with the war conducted by the English garden against the symmetry of
the garden *à la française*): taking issue with Sigfried Giedion, Scully shows that
Baroque space (i.e., the architectural space that comes prior to this point of
rupture) is in no way the antecedent of modern space, and that modern space is
its negation. In the Baroque,

> order is absolutely firm, but against it an illusion of freedom is played.
> . . . It is therefore an architecture that is intended to enclose and
> shelter human beings in a psychic sense, to order them absolutely so
> that they can always find a known conclusion at the end of any jour-
> ney, but finally to let them play at freedom and action all the while.
> Everything works out; the play seems tumultuous but nobody gets
> hurt and everyone wins. It is . . . a maternal architecture, and cre-
> ates a world with which, today, only children, if they are lucky,
> could identify.[31]

Who brought about the rupture? asks Scully. It was Piranesi in his *Carceri*:
"In them, the symmetry, hierarchy, climax, and emotional release of Baroque
architectural space . . . were cast aside in favor of a complex spatial wandering,
in which the objectives of the journey were not revealed and therefore could not
be known."[32] Although one of the sources of the picturesque, Piranesi's art participates in the rupture that goes well beyond the picturesque that succeeds it.
And if Serra, because of the connotations of delicacy attached to this term *picturesque*, balked at its use to characterize his sculpture, I would say that in a certain sense he was right, for his art is the first response in sculptural space to the

29.   Peter Collins, p. 53.
30.   Vincent Scully Jr., *Modern Architecture*, New York, Braziller, 1965, p. 10.
31.   *Ibid.*, p. 11.
32.   *Ibid.*, p. 12.

questions raised about representational space more than two centuries ago by Piranesi.

The first point in common between the Venetian's engravings and Serra's work: space in them is not maternal, that is to say, it is not oriented, not centered.[33] There are indeed *some* axes in Piranesi's engravings, but as Ulya Vogt-Göknil has remarked, they are always multiple and either run parallel or mutually exclude each other.[34] Serra: "The work is not goal-oriented."[35] Or again, "the center, or the question of centering, is dislocated from the physical center of the work and found in a moving center" (p. 33). Or finally: "The expanse of the work allows one to perceive and locate a multiplicity of centers" (*ibid.*).

Another feature in common, which, as we have seen, was contained in embryo in the picturesque: both Piranesi's work and Serra's are based on the abolition of the prerogative of the plan. Let us dwell for a moment on the famous *Prima Parte di Architettura e Prospettive*, and look at plate 11 of that work, entitled "*Gruppo di Scale ornato di magnifica Architettura, le quali stanno disposte in modo che conducano a varii piani, e specialmente ad una Rotonda che serve per rappresentanze teatrali.*" Who of us, having been shown this image (elevation) and its title (isn't a rotunda circular, and doesn't it presuppose a completed geometrical space?), could have imagined that the floor plan, as patiently reconstituted by Ulya Vogt-Göknil, would turn out to be so architecturally formless, an apology for the fragment right there on the plan. It is as though Piranesi had not simply been content to break existing architectural rules (by the eccentric points of view adopted in his *vedute*), but had surreptitiously destroyed, *in the very elevations*, the identity of the plan. Now this is one of the essential strengths of Serra's sculpture. Clara Weyergraf has remarked about *Terminal*, a sculpture that stands today in Bochum and is related in principle to the one that Serra is in the process of constructing in La Défense, that "the information gathered from the construction drawings . . . cannot be verified in the experience of the sculpture."[36] And indeed the square opening of light that the spectator finds above him when he enters the sculpture cannot be inferred from his previous walk around the work (just as it is impossible for him to know, at any particular moment, that "*Terminal* is made of four trapezoidal slabs of steel of the same size" [*ibid.*], something specifically revealed by the construction drawings). The elevation cannot provide the plan, for as one walks around it, one finds no element that

---

33.   "The child's visual space is centered, inhabited by the body charged with libidinal interest from the mother. This space may be 'depopulated' and the boundaries where it loses itself become fascinating with their insecurity, their flow, their lack of guideposts, their boundless opening for the view, by a sort of extrusion of the gaze." Guy Rosolato, "Destinations du corps," *Nouvelle Revue de Psychanalyse*, Spring 1971, p. 12.
34.   Ulya Vogt-Göknil, *Giovanni Battista Piranesi: Carceri*, Zurich, Origo Verlag, p. 21.
35.   Serra, "Notes from Sight Point Road," p. 173.
36.   Clara Weyergraf, "From 'Trough Pieces' to 'Terminal,' Study of a Development," in *Richard Serra*, catalogue published by the museums of Tübingen and Baden-Baden, 1978, p. 214.

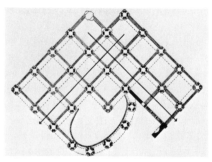

Piranesi. Prima Parte di Architettura e Prospettive, *plate 11.*

Reconstruction by Ulya Vogt-Göknil of plate 11.

has maintained a relation of identity with the others: "The decision to break with the expectations about the sequentialness of like elements make [*sic*] a dialectical relationship between inside and outside" (p. 86). *Terminal* is in some way a critique of the "narrative" space developed by *Sight Point* (three times three consecutive "views" when one walks around the sculpture), for the number of views of it cannot be counted. But Piranesi's principle of disjunction was already at work in *Sight Point*: even though this sculpture is constructed on a series of similar elements, nothing acts to forewarn the observer that it is, in Serra's words, a "truncated pyramid" delineating an equilateral triangle at its top. Or again, when Serra, with some reluctance, describes the placing of the three steel slabs of *Spin Out* in geometric terms, he says nothing about what the spectator's experience will be: he pretends to give a key to that experience, and this key is not the right one: "The plates were laid out at twelve, four and eight o'clock in an elliptical valley, and the space in between them forms an isosceles triangle" (p. 36). I have spent some time surveying *Spin Out*, trying in particular to determine whether some sort of geometry was at work there, and never was I able to come to that conclusion (on the contrary, it seemed to me that any *a priori* geometry was absent and that the work, like *Shift*, was a function of the topography). And Serra is right to express his reservations and prefer to speak of the work in terms of parallax and the progress of the spectator, since in no way does he work with a view to the recognition of a geometric form in his sculpture—he does not work, as he puts it, "for the sake of anything in that way" (p. 36).

The elevation does not provide the plan, and the plan cannot provide the elevation. Had it been erected in the place for which it was conceived, the piece commissioned by the Centre Georges Pompidou would have been the radical confirmation of this fundamental division. Because the work would have been placed in the pit of the Centre's entrance hall, the spectators would have had

Richard Serra. Spin Out (for Robert Smithson). *1973.*

from the outset an inkling of the plan in its symmetry (two equal arcs of a circle arranged as an X, one opposite the other): they would have first seen the work from above, and even if their view would not have been exactly aerial, let us say that their first apprehension of *Clara-Clara* would have been a "Gestalt" one. But this view would have been false. And it is fortunate that in the site actually occupied by the work at the time of its exhibition, between the Musée du Jeu de Paume and the Orangerie, something of this initial false impression can continue to exist, thanks to the sloping partitions that overhang the sculpture on each side. So at the Tuileries, as would have been the case at the Centre Georges Pompidou, the spectator of *Clara-Clara* had knowledge of the overall plan of the sculpture before going up to look at it more closely.

Geometrically, the two arcs of a circle are two identical segments of a section of a *cone* (and not of a cylinder), which means that the curved walls of these arcs are not vertical — the first fact that the plan doesn't tell us. Since the arcs

Richard Serra. Clara-Clara. *1983.*

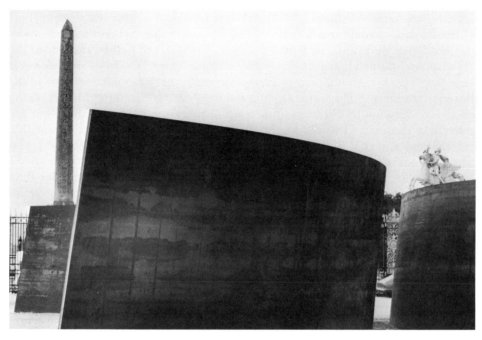

Richard Serra. Clara-Clara. *1983.*

are placed not parallel but opposite to each other (their convexity almost meeting in the middle), one logical conclusion would be to have the walls each lean in the opposite direction, each toward the inside of its own curve. But Serra's invention — the second element not apparent from the plan — lies in having broken this symmetry by using what forms the top of one of these arcs as the base for the other — in other words, in having put one of them upside down. Thanks to this reversal, the two walls lean in the same direction (one toward the inside of its curve, the other toward the outside), and this will increase, as one can imagine, the play of parallax. In walking inside *Clara-Clara*, going toward the bottleneck that these two arcs form at their middle, the spectator constantly has the strange impression that one wall goes "faster" than the other, that the right and left sides of his body are not synchronized. Having passed through the bottleneck, which reveals to him the reason for his strange feeling — although the slant of the walls is actually rather slight — he then sees the lateral differences reversed: the symmetry of this effect is foreseeable, but not the surprise that accompanies it.

To get back to Piranesi: William Chambers, one of the first theoreticians of the English garden and a critic of Price, reports that "when the students at the Académie de France in Rome accused [Piranesi] of being ignorant of the art of plans, he produced one of extreme complexity."[37] This *Pianta di ampio magnifico Collegio,* the only plan in Piranesi's oeuvre, is first of all a critique of the Baroque tradition. "The most singular feature," writes Monique Mosser, "may be the effort made by Piranesi to develop at the same time two ideas that are difficult to reconcile [I would say mutually exclusive]: that of a building with a central plan and that of the staircase as the dominant motif."[38] What Piranesi actually does in response to the students' accusation is to compose, to be sure, a centered plan, but this center, on the one hand, is considerably smaller than the rooms at the periphery (especially those at the four corners); on the other hand, *it is nothing but a thoroughfare*: its sole function is to provide access to eight staircases. From such a plan, swarming with useless and redundant stairways, which are conceived as elevation sections leading nowhere, from this falsely circular structure (going up/down/up), one can infer nothing but an endless rotary and vertical circulation. The center is a thoroughfare: as Ulya Vogt-Göknil had seen, this is the essential nature of Piranesi's architectural space—whether it be the space represented in the *Carceri,* of the *vedute* he provided of the Roman architecture he had before his eyes, or again of this school design.[39] The center is a thoroughfare, i.e., an indifferent place, with no other identity than the one conferred on it by the passersby, a nonplace that exists only by the experience of time and motion that the stroller may make of it. In a certain way, Piranesi can be understood to foreshadow not only the space of Serra's sculpture, but that of all modern sculpture as well. For, as Rosalind Krauss has shown, this space, from Rodin to Serra, is one of passage and displacement from the center, a space interrupted by the discontinuous time of involuntary memory, a slender space whose divergences it is up to the spectator to explore, while eventually connecting its threads for himself.[40]

In speaking of *Shift,* Krauss compares Serra's sculpture to Kuleshov's famous experiments in montage. In these experiments, the montage was revealed as an "index of difference or separateness within a prevailing matrix of sameness."[41] Kuleshov's montage demonstrated the perceptive primacy of spatial continuity, but at the same time expressed the fact that this continuity was *pro-*

37.   Quoted by Monique Mosser in the catalogue of the exhibition *Piranèse et les Français* (Villa Medicis, Rome, and Hôtel de Sully, Paris), 1976, p. 287.
38.   *Ibid.,* p. 288.
39.   Vogt-Göknil, pp. 22–23.
40.   Rosalind Krauss, *Passages in Modern Sculpture,* New York, Viking Press, 1977, passim. See especially pp. 280–287, where the question of the "passage" in Serra is directly examined. See also my review of this book, "Opacités de la sculpture," *Critique,* no. 381 (February 1979).
41.   Krauss, "Richard Serra: Sculpture Redrawn," *Artforum,* May 1972, p. 38.

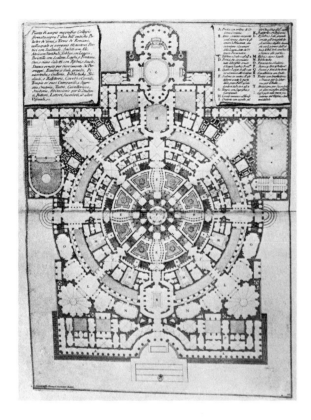

Piranesi. Opere Varie, plate 22: Pianta di ampio magnifico Collegio.

duced by means of discontinuity. This is exactly what Serra accomplishes in *Shift* and in many other sculptures as well.

One has only to reread the pages Serra has written on the *Rotary Arc* to be convinced that film fragmentation is an apt metaphor by which to describe his work: "Driving around the Rotary, both the Arc's convexity and concavity foreshorten, then compress, overlap, and elongate. The abrupt but continuous succession of views is highly transitive, akin to a cinematic experience" (pp. 155–156). The "transitivity" to which Serra here refers is the notion that he tried to work out his first films (an action perpetuated on an object, with no conclusion), in the sculptures in the *Skullcracker Series* (1969), and which he expressed in the simplest way of all by inscribing a list of verbs on the invitation announcement for one of his first exhibitions.[42] Now this very transitivity was discovered by Eisenstein in Piranesi when to the space in the *Carceri* he compared the sequence from *October* in which *"one and the same* piece showing the ascent of the head of state up the marble staircase of the Winter Palace has been cemented together in succession 'ad infinitum.' Of course, not really 'ad infinitum,' but in the course

42. On this subject, see Krauss, *Passages in Modern Sculpture*, pp. 272-276.

of the four or five variants in which this same scene was shot, which during the actual shooting was intended to be a very luxurious . . . episode."[43] Naturally the filmmaker's intention was ironical (to show that Kerensky's irresistible rise to power was built on sand), but that is not important here, since montage can express whatever it likes with "one and the same shot." What matters, on the one hand, is that this description of an almost endless repetition of the same gesture with no conclusion (climbing stairs for no other reason than to climb stairs) exactly matches the repetitive nonevent of Serra's first film, *Hand Catching Lead* (a hand tries to catch some falling pieces of lead, sometimes does catch one, and immediately lets it go: there is no "climax," no orgiastic release, as there is in the Baroque).[44] What matters, on the other hand, is that Eisenstein discovers this transitivity in Piranesi's work. Not only through the theme of an endless climbing of stairs (a romantic interpretation of the *Carceri*, and one that is a commonplace since the famous passage in De Quincey, quoted by the Soviet director[45]), but especially because in his opinion Piranesi works like a master of montage and bases his spatial continuities on discontinuity:

> Nowhere in the *Carceri* do we find a view in depth in continuous perspective. Everywhere the movement begun by a perspective in depth finds itself interrupted by a bridge, a pillar, an arch, a passageway. Each time, beyond the pillar or the semicircle of the arch, the movement of the perspective is once more resumed. . . . [But while] the eye expects to see behind the arch the continuation of the architectural theme preceding the arch normally reduced by perspective, [it is, in fact] another architectural motif that appears behind the arch, and moreover, in a reduction of perspective almost double what the eye had supposed. . . . Hence an unexpected qualitative leap from the space and the grand scale. And the series of planes in depth, cut off from each other by pillars and arches, is constructed in independent portions of autonomous spaces, being connected not by a single continuity of perspective, but as in the successive shocks of spaces of a qualitative intensity differing in depth.

This, says Eisenstein, is exactly the way montage operates in the cinema:

> This effect [in Piranesi] is constructed on the capacity of our eye to continue by inertia a movement once it has been given. *The collision of this "suggested" path of movement with another path substituted for it also*

43.   S. M. Eisenstein, "Piranesi, or the Fluidity of Forms," trans. Roberta Reeder, in *Oppositions* 11 (Winter 1977), p. 103.
44.   Cf. Krauss, *Passages in Modern Sculpture*, pp. 243–244. The analysis of *Hand Catching Lead* opens the chapter on the development of sculpture since the late 1960s.
45.   On the passage in the *Confessions of an English Opium-Eater* devoted to Piranesi and his influence on romanticism, cf. Luzius Keller, *Piranèse et les romantiques français: Le mythe des escaliers en spirale*, José Corti, 1966, passim.

produces the effect of a jolt. It is on the analogous ability of retaining imprints of a visual impression that the phenomenon of cinematic movement is built.[46]

Serra says somewhere (I have been unable to locate the exact wording) that he is interested in abrupt discontinuities: no doubt "the experience of shock," elsewhere described by Walter Benjamin as the experience par excellence of modernism, is what gives rise to his sculpture. As though echoing Eisenstein, he speaks of "memory and anticipation" as "vehicles of perception" for his sculptures,[47] both of them being dialectically opposed in order to prevent "good form," a "Gestalt" image, or a pattern of identity from taking over. One might say a good deal more about the relations between Eisenstein's montage and the art of Serra. We know that Eisenstein disagreed with Kuleshov (and others) on one fundamental point: he did not want montage, the experience of shock, to involve only "the element between shots," but wanted it to be "transferred to *inside* the fragment, into the elements included in the image itself"[48] — so that the dissociation between the shots would end by operating in the very interior of the shot, just as Piranesi's disjunction of plan and elevation surreptitiously destroyed the identity of the ground plan and its traditional domination over traditional space. Serra shares with Eisenstein this wish to introduce discontinuity into discontinuity itself, and this takes us back for one last time to the question of the picturesque. We have seen that *Terminal* constituted a sort of deconstruction of the narrative space created by *Sight Point.* Now the problem of narration unquestionably lies at the heart of Serra's enterprise: in his films as in his sculptures, he seeks to destroy that which has been the age-old foundation of narration, namely its conclusion. *Hand Catching Lead* is almost endless, "not actually endless, of course," as Eisenstein would say, but almost. And the descriptive account of his walk or drive around the *Rotary Arc* describes a complete circle: it begins and ends at an arbitrarily chosen — almost arbitrarily chosen — point, and could perpetuate itself indefinitely. When Peter Eisenman spoke of his sculptures as "framing the landscape," Serra bridled:

> If you use the word "frame" in referring to the landscape, you imply a notion of the picturesque. I have never really found the notion of framing parts of the landscape particularly interesting in terms of its potential for sculpture. Smithson was interested in the picturesque. . . . That's an interesting notion in terms of its relation to the narrative of seeing but it's not of particular concern to me.[49]

46.   Eisenstein, pp. 105–106.
47.   Serra, "Notes from Sight Point Road," p. 180.
48.   Quoted by Roland Barthes in "The Third Meaning," *Image–Music–Text*, trans. Stephen Heath, New York, Hill and Wang, 1977, p. 67.
49.   Serra and Eisenman, pp. 16–17.

I noted above this pictorial limitation of the theory of the picturesque, which made gardeners develop in their parks a series of small pictures to be discovered while walking. It is to this narrative conception of discontinuity that Serra is opposed, and it is this, more than anything else, that separates him from the picturesque. In December 1782, Hannah More reported to her sisters a conversation she had had with Capability Brown, the first great master of the English picturesque garden:

> He told me he compared his art to literary composition: "Now *there*," said he, pointing his finger, "I make a comma, and there," pointing to another spot, "where a more decided turn is needed, I make a colon; at another part, where an interruption is desirable to break the view, a parenthesis; now a full stop, and then I begin another subject."[50]

This, among other things, is what distinguishes Serra's art from that of landscape gardeners: he has no full stop. His art is not an art of punctuation (although often, while speaking of one of his sculptures, he draws on paper, at the rate of ten drawings a minute, a storyboard of its various aspects). It is an art of montage, an art that is not satisfied to interrupt continuity temporarily, but produces continuity by a double negation, by destroying the pictorial recovery of continuity through discontinuity, dissociation, and the loss of identity within the fragment.

Now what? This whole additional excursion into the eighteenth century just to be able to say that Serra and the picturesque are completely different? They're not completely different, although the use made by Serra of ideas developed two centuries ago could hardly be identical with what was done with them then, in that cult of rationality represented by the Enlightenment. One might therefore wonder why I have insisted on circumscribing my interpretation of his work in a vocabulary and a debate two centuries old. There are two fundamental reasons.

The first has to do with Serra's manifest hostility to architects. If this hostility is, in my opinion, wholly justified, if Serra can rightly say of *Terminal* that this sculpture reduces almost all the architecture surrounding it to the mediocrity of its "cardboard-model inventiveness" (p. 129), it is because he once again brings to bear on his work notions that appeared in the architectural debates of the eighteenth century, and which architects have since repressed. The history of this repression, which I have tried to trace here, has seemed to me indispensable if we are to understand the singular nature of Serra's work. It was never a question to my mind of unearthing sources for him, of seeking connections and

---

50.   Quoted by Dora Wiebenson, *The Picturesque Garden in France*, Princeton, Princeton University Press, 1978, note 86, p. 74.

Richard Serra. Terminal. *1977.*

influences. Quite the opposite, it was a matter of showing that the strength of his innovation was the raw one of the return of the repressed. Let us take another look at this aspect of architecture. After Leroy, the only theoretician who conceives architecture anew in terms of the effect it will produce on the moving spectator is Boullée. He does so in exactly the same way as Leroy, but he adds a word to his predecessor's vocabulary, a word to which I will come back: *sublime*. (I might add that a whole parallel could be traced between the idea formulated by Boullée of a *buried* architecture and Serra's sculptures that are sunk in the ground.) Following Boullée, but a century later, the historian Auguste Choisy was to be the first to reexamine this question of the peripatetic view. He did so in connection with a discovery very much his own (truly unheard-of and incomprehensible to architects trained at the Ecole des Beaux Arts, for it pointed directly at something they had obscured at the very heart of the example they wanted to imitate), that of "Greek picturesque" (namely, the asymmetrical arrangement of Greek temples, depending on the site).[51] Then came Le Corbusier, one of the few architects spared by Serra in his general anathema. Leaving aside the issue of whether the architectural concept of "promenade" invented by Le Corbusier is strongly influenced by Choisy's fantastic discovery—the important thing here is that, for the first time since Boullée, an architect speaks of the play of parallax for his architecture, if necessary borrowing from other cultures, as the cubists did from primitive art.

We know the text in Le Corbusier's *Oeuvres complètes* that accompanies his designs for the Villa Savoye:

> Arab architecture has much to teach us. It is appreciated *while on the move*, with one's feet; it is while walking, moving from one place to another, that one sees how the arrangements of the architecture develop. This is a principle contrary to Baroque architecture. . . . In this house [the Villa Savoye], we are dealing with a true architectural promenade, offering constantly varied, unexpected, sometimes astonishing aspects. It is interesting to obtain so much diversity when one has, for example, allowed from the standpoint of construction an absolutely rigorous pattern of posts and beams.[52]

Now here two things should be stressed. On the one hand, this "pattern of

---

51.   "The Greeks do not imagine a building independently of the site that frames it and the buildings that surround it. The idea of leveling the vicinity is absolutely foreign to them. They accept, while scarcely regularizing it, the location as nature has created it, and their only concern is to harmonize the architecture with the landscape; Greek temples are as worthy for the choice of their site as for the art with which they are built." There follows a description of the various groups of temples, especially the Acropolis in Athens, according to the effect produced on a moving spectator. "Le pittoresque dans l'art grec," *Histoire de l'Architecture*, vol. I (1899). My thanks to Jacques Lucan for having pointed out this text to me.
52.   Le Corbusier, *Oeuvres complètes*, vol. II, Zurich, Editions d'architecture, 1964 p. 24.

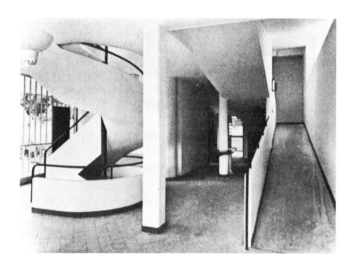

Le Corbusier. Villa Savoye. *1929-31.*

posts" is certainly not absolutely rigorous (contrary to what Le Corbusier says a little later, the posts are not "equidistant"). On the other hand, this disturbance of the plan has been made necessary by the first vertical breach constituted by the ramp, then further complicated by the displacement, in the planning stage, of the staircase (which became on this occasion a spiral one) — that is to say, in two different ways, by *thoroughfares.* It has sometimes been asked why Le Corbusier kept this troublesome ramp (he who claimed that the plan generated the architecture) when a simple staircase (especially a spiral one) would have posed fewer problems. Now the very *subject* of the Villa Savoye is the penetration of a vertical section into a horizontal grid (the "Do-mi-no" grid dating from 1914 and tried out in the designs for the Citrohan houses of 1920–22, in which the staircase was always conceived as exterior to the grid). It is this vertical penetration by the passageway into the arrangement of the plan, this disturbance of the plan by the elevation and by the movement of the stroller, that creates the richness and *intricacy* of the Villa Savoye (and in a certain way one could say that the aim of the free plan corresponds in Le Corbusier, despite what he says about it, to a wish to free his architecture from the generating tyranny of the plan). Le Corbusier, as his vocabulary shows, again takes up the idea of the picturesque, and tries to imagine what a picturesque architecture might be. But with him, as with Serra, it is a question of a modern picturesque, and not one of narrative and pictoriality. Hence the necessity, in the Villa Savoye, of a division of labor and a duplication ("one ascends imperceptibly by a ramp, which is a totally different feeling from the one provided by a staircase formed by steps. A staircase separates one floor from another, a ramp connects them"[53]). It is from this unequal duplication, this conflict between continuity

53. *Ibid.*, p. 25.

and discontinuity, that the experience of shock is born: quite late in the development of the project Le Corbusier pierced the stairwell, which had been
conceived at the beginning as a semi-cylindrical blind box, and bored openings
in it that are like the displaced projection onto the cylinder of the triangles delineated by the ramp. Why this give-and-take? Because the machine is not inhabited by a hermit: "It is most exhilarating when we can sense our movement
in relation to another person on another path, catching and losing sense of that
person, playing curve off straight and step off stride. Then we are acutely aware
of our own movement by its periodic relation to that of another participant."[54]
The fact that these remarks are by a present-day architect and critic in no way
detracts from my general thesis (that architects today have much to learn not
only from Le Corbusier but also from Serra), for just as Le Corbusier's kinetic
intelligence was something exceptional, so the understanding of that intelligence among architects today remains the thing least shared in the world. Now
it is just this, this attention to the effects of a dual movement, that makes Serra's
sculpture a lesson in architecture. At the time he was developing his ideas for
Shift, Serra spent five days walking about the site with Joan Jonas: the "boundaries" of the work were determined by the maximum distance that two people
could cover without losing sight of each other. "The horizon of the work," says
Serra, "was established by the possibilities of maintaining this mutual view-
point" (p. 25). Or again: "My open works [those that one can pass through] are
not concerned with internal relationships. They have to do with looking from
where they are into space, or from where they are to where the other one is
placed" (p. 51). Whether this "other one" is another element of the sculpture (as
in *Open Field Vertical/Horizontal Elevations*, ten steel cubes scattered in a seemingly huge park) or another spectator comes to the same thing, for here we are
dealing with an experience of reciprocity, of mutuality.

It is over this fracture of identity, this division of one into two, that the
history of parallax and of the picturesque promenade enters into Le Corbusier's
architecture and Serra's sculpture. Hence the necessity I feel to trace back the
discontinuous threads of this history, even though it might mean a temporary
retreat into the eighteenth century.

The second reason for this backward look in time is less direct but no less
essential.

Anyone concerned with the history of sculpture during these last twenty
years will recall the fundamental and vehement attack on minimalism published by Michael Fried at the end of the 1960s. In a certain way, all of Serra's
oeuvre is an implicit reply to Michael Fried's text. Here it is not a question of
going back over the terms of the discussion or even of summarizing "Art and

---

54.   Robert J. Yudell, "Body Movement," in Kent C. Bloomer and Charles W. Moore, *Body,
Memory, and Architecture*, New Haven, Yale University Press, 1977, p. 68.

Objecthood."[55] Let us merely say that, according to Fried, minimalist art sinks into "theater" (understood as the identification of the space of art with that of the spectator, daily life, and the world of objects), while for him the essential goal of modernist art, and of sculpture in particular, has been to affirm its autonomy in relation to this real space. More than just an attack on the confusion between two kinds of space—which would simply have repeated Adolf von Hildebrand's criticism of panoramas and Canova's tombs at the end of the last century[56]—Fried's text denounced in the minimalist work its implication of the *duration* of the spectator's experience. To Tony Smith's enthusiastic account of a drive on an unfinished turnpike (an account of a journey conceived as a model of the minimalist experience), Fried opposed the atemporality and instantly intelligible perception of the sculptors he was defending (*"at every moment the work itself is wholly manifest"*[57]). Fried opted for a *pictorial* conception of sculpture (following in this an idea of Greenberg's: sculpture is doomed to exist in the world of objects, and should therefore be as two-dimensional as possible in order to escape this condition of existence as much as it can[58]). "Pictoriality," on the contrary, seemed to Smith too narrow a framework to be able to produce experiences similar to the one he had had on the turnpike. The position termed modernist (both Greenberg's and Fried's, despite their differences) relies openly on Kant: an absolute distinction between the world of art and that of artifacts, immediacy of judgment about the beautiful, indifference to the object's *material* existence (Greenberg never speaks of texture, for example, or does so only in general terms). Furthermore, for Kant, the beautiful "is connected with the form of the object, which consists in having [definite] boundaries,"[59] and Fried tells us that it is the absence of *a priori* determination of their limits that radically distinguishes minimalist sculptures from modernist works of art. Indeed, in speaking of *Spin Out*, Serra states: "there isn't any definition of boundary" (p. 37). Finally, for Kant (as for Fried), "in the case of the beautiful taste presupposes and maintains the mind in *restful* contemplation."[60] Kant makes no reference, in his "Analytic of the Beautiful," to the duration of the spectator's experience (even when it is a question of music), nor to the movement of his body (especially when it is a question of architecture).

55.   Michael Fried, "Art and Objecthood" (1967), reprinted in *Minimal Art: A Critical Anthology*, ed. Gregory Battcock, New York, Dutton, 1968, pp. 116–147.
56.   Adolf von Hildebrand, *Das Problem der Form in der Bildenden Kunst*, 1903. For Hildebrand, Canova's funerary monuments, unlike those of Michelangelo, are to be condemned because in them there is no "boundary established between the monument and the public."
57.   Fried, p. 145.
58.   Cf. Clement Greenberg, "The New Sculpture," reprinted in *Art and Culture*, Boston, Beacon Press, 1965, pp. 143.
59.   Emmanuel Kant, *The Critique of Judgment*, trans. J. H. Bernard, New York, Hafner, 1951, § 23, p. 82.
60.   *Ibid.*, § 24, p. 85.

That the modernist aesthetic is Kantian through and through, no one will deny, nor that Fried's or Greenberg's interpretation of the first book of the first section of the first part of the *Critique of Judgment* is well founded. It is simply that this interpretation is singularly partial, in both senses of the word. It is as though modernism had obliterated that whole other side of the Kantian aesthetic, book II of the same portion of this work, entitled "Analytic of the Sublime." For although "the beautiful and the sublime agree in this that both please in themselves" (i.e., without conclusion), "there are also remarkable differences between the two."[61] While the beautiful, for example, concerns the form of the object, and thus its limitation, "the sublime, on the other hand, can be found in a formless object, so far as in it or by occasion of it *boundlessness* is represented in it, and yet its totality is also present to thought."[62] And while in the beautiful totality is immediately apprehended, the feeling of the sublime comes from the contradiction between apprehension (which "can go on *ad infinitum*") and comprehension (which quickly reaches a maximum, beyond which the imagination cannot go[63]). In other words, the feeling of the sublime lies in the separation between the *idea* of totality and the perceived impossibility of understanding that totality. The amazement of someone entering Saint Peter's in Rome for the first time is for Kant a sublime experience par excellence (it was *not sublime enough*, I might add, for a Leroy or a Boullée, for whom the church seemed much smaller than it actually was, due to the lack of attention paid to the play of parallax). Here is what Kant says about this virgin spectator penetrating to the heart of the papacy: "For there is here a feeling of the inadequacy of his imagination for presenting the idea of a whole, wherein the imagination reaches its maximum, and, in striving to surpass it, sinks into itself, by which, however, a kind of emotional satisfaction is produced."[64] (The pleasure I felt while walking in *Spin Out* did not occur in spite of my inability to grasp its geometric form, but because of that inability.) In a word, Kant, in his "Analytic of the Sublime," is forced to imagine a mechanism of perception quite different from the one he assumes in his theory of judgment about the beautiful. In particular, he is obliged to introduce the temporality of the aesthetic experience. Of course, for him, it is still a question, as Smithson remarks about all idealist theories of art, of a movement of the mind, but this movement is induced by the characteristics of the object ("the feeling of the sublime brings with it as its characteristic feature a *movement* of the mind bound up with the judging of the object"[65]). Why? Because the feeling of the sublime can only come from the grandeur of the object and the impossibility of controlling or understanding this grandeur by

61.   *Ibid.*, § 23, p. 82.
62.   *Ibid.*
63.   *Ibid.*, § 26, p. 90.
64.   *Ibid.*, § 26, p. 91.
65.   *Ibid.*, § 24, p. 85.

thought. From the impossibility, as Serra would say, of having a "Gestalt" view of it.

> For when apprehension has gone so far that the partial representations of sensuous intuition at first apprehended begin to vanish in the imagination, while this ever proceeds to the apprehension of others, then it loses as much on one side as it gains on the other; and in comprehension there is a maximum beyond which it cannot go.[66]

So far as I know, this is the only passage in the whole *Critique of Judgment* where Kant speaks in temporal terms ("begin," "goes forward," "next") of the mechanism of the aesthetic imagination, and one could call it a paraphrase of Serra's comments about his *Rotary Arc*. That it is a question of the "Analytic of the Sublime" and not that of the beautiful simply shows that the Kantian criteria applied by Greenberg and Fried in their condemnation of minimalism were inappropriate, since one cannot judge the sublime by the criteria of the beautiful.[67]

I can imagine Serra's negative reaction to Fried's indictment interspersed with Kant (since his work, even more than minimalism, falls under the hammer of this neo-Kantian diatribe). But it seemed to me that a brief return to Kant, by way of the sublime, was called for here. Not only because if the rupture of modernity actually took place in the eighteenth century, it is necessary for us today to go back over that past (that is, incidentally, what Michael Fried has done, endeavoring to describe, in order to shore up his position, what was produced at the time of this rupture, i.e., "in the age of Diderot"[68]). But also because the picturesque, as Smithson observed, flows from the sublime:

> Price extended Edmund Burke's *Inquiry into the Origin of our ideas of the Sublime and the Beautiful* (1757) to a point that tried to free landscaping from the "picture" gardens of Italy into a more physical sense of the temporal landscape. . . . Burke's notion of "beautiful" and "sublime" functions as a *thesis* of smoothness, gentle curves, and delicacy of nature, and as an antithesis of terror, solitude, and vastness of nature, both of which are rooted in the real world, rather than in a Hegelian

66. *Ibid.*, § 26, p. 90.
67. I find by chance an unexpected ally in the issue of *Perspecta* containing the article by Serra that I have quoted several times, in the person of Karsten Harries, who teaches philosophy at Yale University. In an article entitled "Building and the Terror of Time," Harries refers to Michael Fried's text and to an essay by the sculptor Robert Morris ("The Present Tense of Space," *Art in America*, January/February 1978). Although the differences between the art of the two sculptors are striking, I could have mentioned Morris's text often, for it brilliantly articulates certain ideas expressed aphoristically by Serra, and speaks in particular of Saint Peter's in Rome and of ruins. Harries concludes the passage in his text devoted to Morris with these words: "Just as Fried can refer to Kant to support his understanding of modernism, in the same way Morris can refer to the *Critique of Judgment*, but it is another section of the book that is appropriate, the 'Analytic of the Sublime'" (p. 68).
68. Michael Fried, *Absorption and Theatricality: Painting & Beholder in the Age of Diderot*, Berkeley, University of California Press, 1980.

ideal [it is this empirical basis of Burke's text that Kant criticized]. Price and Gilpin provide a *synthesis* with their formulation of the "picturesque," which is on close examination related to chance and change in the material order of nature.[69]

For Burke, the beautiful and the sublime were irreconcilable; they remained so for Price and Gilpin. But as Price wrote: "the picturesque appeared halfway between the beautiful and the sublime; and this may be why it allies itself more often and more happily with both than they do with each other."[70] There is thus a beautiful picturesque and a sublime picturesque: it is to this second category, if you like, that Serra's art belongs.

The word *picturesque*, says Smithson, is itself like a sublime tree struck by lightning in a picturesque English garden of the eighteenth century: "This word in its own way has been struck by lightning over the centuries. Words, like trees, can be suddenly deformed or wrecked, but such deformation or wreckage cannot be dismissed by timid academics."[71] It has taken all the support of Serra's work for a timid academic like myself to attempt to repair the damage.

69.   Smithson, pp. 118–119. On Gilpin, in quite another context, see also Krauss, "The Originality of the Avant-Garde: A Postmodernist Repetition," *October*, 18 (Autumn 1981), pp. 45–66.
70.   Quoted by Jean-Claude Lebensztejn, "En blanc et noir," *Macula*, 1 (1976), p. 13.
71.   Smithson, p. 118.

The Structure of Allegorical Desire

JOEL FINEMAN

Μῆνιν ἄειδε, Θεά, Πηληϊάδεω Ἀχιλῆος

My title should be read backwards and forwards, its *of* taken as objective and subjective genitive. On the one hand, I am concerned with the ways allegories begin and with the ends towards which they tend. In general, this is the problem of allegorical narrative, primarily a temporal issue regarding the way allegories linearly unfold, but also, as has often been pointed out, a symbolic progress that lends itself to spatial projection, as when the Temple translates the Labyrinth or the music of the spheres sounds the order of the stars. On the other hand, I am concerned with a specifically allegorical desire, a desire *for* allegory, that is implicit in the idea of structure itself, and explicit in criticism that directs itself towards the structurality of literature. This is not only to say that the notion of structure, especially of literary structure, presupposes the same system of multiply articulated levels as does that of allegory, but also that the possibility of such coherently polysemic significance originates out of the same intention, what I call desire, as does allegorical narrative.

I speak of desire in deference to the thematics of allegory and to describe the self-propelling, digressive impulse of allegorical movement, for example, the way the meandering *Canterbury Tales* begins by setting the scene and establishing the atmosphere in which folk properly "longen" to go on pilgrimages, that longing being motivation for each pilgrim's journey to Canterbury, but also the way the tales themselves set off towards the equally sacred center of their own allegorical space. I therefore psychoanalytically assume that the movement of allegory, like the dreamwork, enacts a wish that determines its progress—and the dream-vision is, of course, a characteristic framing and opening device of allegory, a way of situating allegory in the *mise en abyme* opened up by the variety of cognate accusatives that dream a dream, or see a sight, or tell a tale. On the other hand, with this reference to psychoanalysis I mean also to suggest that analysis itself, the critical response to allegory, rehearses the same wish and therefore embarks upon the same pilgrimage, so that psychoanalysis, especially structural psychoanalysis, by which today we are obliged to mean Lacan, is not simply the analysis, but the extension and conclusion of the classic allegorical tradition from which it derives—which is why psychoanalysis so readily assimilates the great archetypes of allegorical imagery into its discourse: the labyrinths, the depths, the navels, the psychomachian hydraulics.

I want to argue that there is for literary criticism a historical importance in the fact that psychoanalysis founds its scientificity on the hermeneutic circle traced by its own desire to know, as in the dream that begins psychoanalysis, Freud's dream of Irma's injection, whose wish is that its own interpretation be correct.[1] If psychoanalysis is the prevailing paradigm for critical inquiry today, it is precisely because *The Interpretation of Dreams* in this way develops itself as the dream, and therefore the desire, of interpretation itself. But in thus basing itself on its own critical reflection, desire becomes in psychoanalysis, as in allegory, both a theme and a structuring principle, and its psychology, its theory of the human, thus becomes, in the words of another and famously ambiguous genitive, the allegory of love, while its metapsychology, its theory of itself, becomes the allegory of allegory. I am concerned with the logic, presumably the psycho-logic—etymologically, the logos of the soul—that in our literary tradition links allegory, interpretation, and desire each to each, and with what happens to interpretation when its desire is no longer controllable by a figure.

That there should be formal reciprocity between allegory and its criticism is not surprising. Theoretical discussions of allegory regularly begin by lamenting the breadth of the term and relating its compass to the habit of mind that, as it is irritatedly put, sees allegory everywhere. Thus generalized, allegory rapidly acquires the status of trope of tropes, representative of the figurality of all language, the distance between signifier and signified, and, correlatively, the response to allegory becomes representative of critical activity per se. As Northrop Frye says, "It is not often realized that all commentary is allegorical interpretation, an attaching of ideas to the structure of poetic imagery,"[2] as indeed Frye's comment demonstrates, in its presumption of global, archetypal structure, which is already allegoricization whatever purely literary claims he may make for it. Often, allegory will internalize this critical mood that it evokes, and this is what gives it its characteristically didactic and sententious tone. This tendency on the part of allegory to read itself, for its theme to dominate its narrative, or, as Frye says, to prescribe the direction of its commentary, suggests the formal or phenomenological affinities of the genre with criticism.

More historically, we can note that allegory seems regularly to surface in critical or polemical atmospheres, when for political or metaphysical reasons there is something that cannot be said. Plutarch is generally instanced as the first to substitute ἀλληγορια for the more usual ὑπόνοια and he does so in the double context of defending poetry and demythologizing the gods.[3] In this he picks up the

---

1.   Sigmund Freud, *The Interpretation of Dreams, The Standard Edition of the Complete Psychological Works of Sigmund Freud* (hereafter cited as *S.E.*), ed. James Strachey, London, Hogarth Press, 1959, 4, pp. 105–121.

2.   Northrop Frye, *Anatomy of Criticism: Four Essays*, Princeton, Princeton University Press, 1971, p. 89.

3.   See Jean Pépin, *Mythe et Allégorie: Les origines Grecques et les contestations Judéo-Chrétiennes*, Paris, Aubier, 1958, pp. 87–88.

protoallegorical tradition of euhemerism that goes back to the third century B.C., or to Plato, or beyond that to the Pythagoreans, and whose importance for literary theory is not so much its dismantling of the pagan pantheon as, rather, the defensively recuperative intention it displays towards authoritative texts whose literalism has failed. The dignity of Apollo is deflated but the prestige of Homer preserved when the licentious intrigues of the gods are reinterpreted as philosophic, naturalistic, or scientific parables.

This deployment of allegory in the service of established literary tradition, a way of reviving prior literary authorities by making them new through critical revision—e.g., *Ovid moralisée*—forms the basis of Edwin Honig's theory of allegorical conception,[4] which has itself been forcefully revived and redeveloped in Harold Bloom's more psychoanalytical (allegorical?) *Anxiety of Influence*. It is as though allegory were precisely that mode which makes up for the distance, or heals the gap, between the present and a disappearing past which, without interpretation, would be otherwise irretrievable and foreclosed, as, for example, the pseudohieroglyphology of Horapollo, whose magic, hermetic graphesis was developed just at that moment when the legibility of hieroglyphs was lost.[5]

With the Patristics these allegoricizing perspectives and purposes turn into the dogma that lies at the base of all medieval and Renaissance critical theory. Again allegory is directed to critical and polemical ends, and again the motive for allegory emerges out of recuperative originology. The Old Testament is revived when interpreted as typologically predictive of the New, and the Gospels themselves receive the benefit of spiritualizing exegesis when the apocalypse they prophesy is indefinitely deferred. This is the major strain of allegoricizing sensibility in our tradition: the second- and third-century legacy on which the four- or three-fold medieval schemes will depend. Allegory becomes, for literature as for theology, a vivifying archaeology of occulted origins and a promissory eschatology of postponed ends—all this in the service of an essentially pietistic cosmology devoted to the corroboration of divinely ordered space and time, precisely the two matrices against which, as Erich Auerbach showed, the connotative nuances of figure, formal and chronic, develop.[6]

That allegory should organize itself with reference to these spatial and temporal axes, that, as it were, it should embody *figura*, follows directly from the linguistic structure attributed to the figure by classic rhetorical theory. The standard formulation, of course, is Quintilian's, which characterizes allegory as what happens when a single metaphor is introduced in continuous series. For grave Quintilian this is more often than not a defect, an excess of metaphor likely

4.   Edwin Honig, *Dark Conceit: The Making of Allegory*, Evanston, Northwestern University Press, 1959.
5.   Sir Alan Gardiner, *Egyptian Grammar; being an introduction to the study of hieroglyphs*, 3rd ed., London, Oxford University Press, 1957, pp. 10–11.
6.   Erich Auerbach, "Figura," *Scenes from the Drama of European Literature*, trans. Ralph Manheim, Meridian, 1959, pp. 11–76.

to lead to enigma. But whether avoided as a vice of style or assiduously "invented" for the sake of decorous amplification, allegory will be defined up through the Renaissance as the temporal extension of trope. As such, the procedure of allegory, and the relations that obtain between its spatial and temporal projections, are strictly circumscribed. Metaphor is the initial equivocating insight into the system of doubly articulated correspondences and proportions upon which depends the analogizing logic of any troping proposition. As the shepherd to his flock, so the pilot to his boat, the king to his realm, the priest to his congregation, the husband to his wife, the stomach to the body—metaphor will select from such a system of hierarchically arranged ratios (logoi) the particular similarity that, as Aristotle puts it, it chooses to see in differences. Developed at length, in narrative succession, the continued metaphor will maintain the rigor of the original conceit by appealing to the over-all structure that governs each term in the series, with the result that narrative logic directs itself towards introducing the fox, the tempest, the cuckold, or the canker as specifically structural predetermined consequences of the first metaphorization.

Thus there are allegories that are primarily perpendicular, concerned more with structure than with temporal extenson, as, say, illustrations of Fortune's wheel, or Fludd's famous diagram of the great chain of being. On the other hand, there is allegory that is primarily horizontal, such as picaresque or quest narrative where figurative structure is only casually and allusively appended to the circuit of adventures through time. Finally, of course, there are allegories that blend both axes together in relatively equal proportions, as in *The Canterbury Tales*, where each figurative tale advances the story of the pilgrimage as a whole. Whatever the prevailing orientation of any particular allegory, however—up and down through the declensions of structure, or laterally developed through narrative time—it will be successful as allegory only to the extent that it can suggest the authenticity with which the two coordinating poles bespeak each other, with structure plausibly unfolded in time, and narrative persuasively upholding the distinctions and equivalences described by structure. In Roman Jakobson's linguistic formula, which here simply picks up classic rhetorical theory (along with the awkward metaphoricity of the definition of metaphor itself), allegory would be the poetical projection of the metaphoric axis onto the metonymic, where metaphor is understood as the synchronic system of differences that constitutes the order of language (*langue*), and metonymy the diachronic principle of combination and connection by means of which structure is actualized in time in speech (*parole*).[7] (Taleus: "Continued *metonymia* is also allegory").[8] And while Jakobson goes on to associate metaphor with verse and romanticism, as opposed to metonymy,

7.   Roman Jakobson, "Linguistics and Poetics," *The Structuralists: From Marx to Lévi-Strauss*, eds. R. and F. DeGeorge, New York, Anchor, 1972, p. 95.

8.   Taleus, *Rhetorica* (1548), cited in Lee A. Sonnino, *A Handbook to Sixteenth Century Rhetoric*, New York, Barnes and Noble, 1968, p. 121.

which he identifies with realism and prose, allegory would cut across and subtend all such stylistic categorizations, being equally possible in either verse or prose, and quite capable of transforming the most objective naturalism into the most subjective expressionism, or the most determined realism into the most surrealistically ornamental baroque.

Thus defined, allegory fully deserves the generalization that renders it representative of language employed for literary ends, and at the same time we can see why for contemporary structuralism allegory would be the figure of speech par excellence. No other figure so readily lays itself out on the grid constructed out of the hypothesized intersection of paradigmatic synchrony and syntagmatic diachrony, which is to say that no other figure so immediately instances the definition of linguistic structure that was developed by Jakobson out of Saussure and the Russian formalists, and that has since been applied to all the so-called sciences of man, from anthropology (Lévi-Strauss) to semiotics (Barthes) to psychoanalysis (Lacan).

Several paradoxes, however, or apparent paradoxes, follow from this curiously pure structurality possessed by allegory, though taken singly none is at odds with our basic literary intuitions. On the one hand, as does structuralism itself, allegory begins with structure, thinks itself through it, regardless of whether its literary realizations orient themselves perpendicularly or horizontally, i.e., as primarily metaphoric or primarily metonymic. At each point of its progress, allegory will select its signifying elements from the system of binary oppositions that are provided by what Jakobson would call the metaphoric code, i.e., the structure, and as a result allegory will inevitably reenforce the structurality of that structure, regardless of how it manipulates the elements themselves. For Jakobson and for allegory, "The poetic function projects the principle of equivalence from the axis of selection into the axis of combination,"[9] and so it is always the structure of metaphor that is projected onto the sequence of metonymy, not the other way around, which is why allegory is always a hierarchicizing mode, indicative of timeless order, however subversively intended its contents might be. This is why allegory is "the courtly figure," as Puttenham called it,[10] an inherently political and therefore religious trope, not because it flatters tactfully, but because in deferring to structure it insinuates the power of structure, giving off what we can call the structural effect. So too, this is what leads a theoretician like Angus Fletcher to analogize the rhythm of allegory to that of obsessional neurosis: it is a formal rather than a thematic aspect of the figure, deriving directly from the structure that in-forms its movement.[11]

On the other hand, if allegorical themes are in a sense emptied of their

9.   Jakobson, p. 95.
10.   George Puttenham, *The Arte of English Poesie* (1589), facsimile edition, Kent, Kent State University Press, 1970, p. 196.
11.   Angus Fletcher, *Allegory: The Theory of a Symbolic Mode*, Ithaca, Cornell University Press, 1964, pp. 279–303.

content by the structure that governs them, if the particular signifiers of allegory become vehicles of a larger structural story which they carry but in which they play no part, they are at the same time ostentatiously foregrounded by the very structurality that becomes immanent in them. There is no clearer example of this than that of rhyme, which is precisely the poetic feature with which Jakobson illustrated his definition of the poetical as the superimposition of structural similarity on syntagmatic continuity. With rhyme we do indeed have "equivalence in sound, projected into the sequence,"[12] such that the principle of equivalent selection does indeed govern syntax; and the resulting literary effect is exactly that we hear the sound of the sound rather than the meaning of the meaning. The same holds for the other metrical and intonational means of marking poetic periods as isochronic, all of which render "the time of the speech flow experienced."[13] Thus, if before we saw signifiers lose their content when they were subsumed in a metaphoric structure to which they only obliquely referred, we here see them lose that content once again when they stagily embody that structure in sequential movement. We hear the sounds but not the sense when the signifiers, graded as similarity superinduced on continuity, point to themselves as signifers rather than to what they signify: poetic sense is exchanged for poetic sensuousness when the palpability and texture of the *signans* takes precedence over and even, as in doggerel, occludes the *signatum* altogether. Allegory would thus be exemplary of Jakobson's purely poetic function, namely, that message which, charged with reflexive poeticality, stresses itself as merely message. But this leaves us with the paradox that allegory, which we normally think of as the most didactic and abstractly moral-mongering of poetic figures, is at the same time the most empty and concrete: on the one hand, a structure of differential oppositions abstracted from its constituent units, on the other, a clamor of signifiers signifying nothing but themselves. Remembering the sententiousness of allegory, we are entitled to ask whether with such a structuralist description the thematic has not been "structured" out of court.

The paradox is, of course, only an apparent one, but I draw it out in this way so as to point to a real difficulty in structuralist poetics: namely, that in order to maintain any thematic meaning at all, structuralism, like allegory, must assume a meaningful connection between metaphoric and metonymic poles. That meaning is either what permits the two to join or the consequence of their juncture. What this means in practice is that Jakobson will pick up the tradition of Pope and Hopkins, or, for that matter, Wimsatt, and argue that sound is echo to sense. Jakobson does not, of course, intend the naive claim that there are different phonemes for different qualities—the notorious murmuring of innumerable bees—though he does accept studies which support Mallarmé's discriminations of

12.   Jakobson, p. 109.
13.   *Ibid.*, p. 95.

dark and light vowels. Rather, Jakobson wants to say that the structure of poetic sounds functions in relation to the structure of its poetic signifieds as a kind of Peircean index, a little like that to which it points, or, in negatively contrapuntal fashion, conspicuously, but equally indicatively, unlike. In pointing to themselves, therefore, as in rhyme, the sounds thus also point beyond themselves to the structure of their signifieds. The same goes for the signifieds themselves, which at a semantic and thematic level are again a structure of signifiers pointing both to themselves and to a structure of signifiers beyond themselves, all of them, alone or together, eventually pointing to the structure of language itself. This is the essentially Hegelian assumption that lies behind Jakobson's claim that "The history of a system is in turn also a system,"[14] i.e., that historical diachrony, the evolution of a language, reacts structurally upon the synchronic linguistic code. Once the signifier's relation to the signified, i.e., the sign as a whole, is in this way understood to be relatively motivated, rather than utterly arbitrary as in Saussure, it is possible to make the sign itself into an index pointing to the structure it embodies and supports. Thus all the levels of allegory, up through and including the thematic, will display themselves and each other with resoundingly poetic and emphatically structural effect.[15]

But this harmonious, now Leibnitzian structure, depending as it does on an utter idealization of the structure of the sign, occurs at a significant cost. "The supremacy of poetic function over referential function does not obliterate the reference but makes it ambiguous."[16] What this typically unbending aphorism means is that in a structuralist poem every signifier will be simultaneously metaphor and metonymy. Jakobson's example is the girl in the Russian folk tale who comes to be symbolized by the willow under which she walks. Ever after in the poem, girl and tree are metaphors each of the other by virtue of their metonymic intersection, just as the sequential movement of the poem is conditioned by their metaphoric equivalence. In classical rhetoric we would call this a synecdoche: the girl is represented by the tree or it by she in that one possesses the other. But in Jakobson's terms what we have is a metaphoric metonymy and a metonymic metaphor, and the result, not surprisingly, is allegory:

> Similarity superimposed on contiguity imparts to poetry its thoroughgoing symbolic, multiplex, polysemantic essence which is beau-

14. Jurii Tynianov and Roman Jakobson, "Problems in the Study of Language and Literature," *The Structuralists*, p. 82.
15. Similarly, because messages about the code are selected from the code, Lacan denies the possibility of a radical concept of metalanguage: "There is the relation here of the system to its own constitution as a signifier, which would seem to be relevant to the question of metalanguage and which, in my opinion, will demonstrate the impropriety of that notion if it is intended to define differentiated elements in language." (Jacques Lacan, "On a Question Preliminary to any Possible Treatment of Psychosis," *Ecrits*, trans. Alan Sheridan, New York, Norton, 1977, p. 185).
16. Jakobson, p. 112.

tifully suggested by Goethe's "Alles Vergängliche ist nur ein Gleichnis" (Anything transient is but a likeness). Said more technically, anything sequent is a simile. In poetry where similarity is superinduced upon contiguity, any metonymy is slightly metaphorical and any metaphor has a metonymic tint.[17]

Undoubtedly, poems, and allegories in particular, work this way; the question is, how can structuralism work this way? What does it mean for a metonymy to be slightly metaphorical, and what is this "tint" that makes a metaphor a little metonymic? If structuralism is the diacritical science because it begins with the difference around which binary oppositions assemble, what happens to its scientific status when its own most fundamental opposites, metaphor and metonymy, are from the very beginning already implicated one in the other, the difference between them collapsed for the sake of hierarchicized, structured, "symbolic, multiplex," allegorical meaning. If these seem merely abstract and theoretical issues, we can reformulate them again in terms of our original literary problem: how does time get into structure and structure into time; how does allegory begin, and why does it continue?

For reasons that will become clearer later, I want to illustrate the problem with the opening of *The Canterbury Tales*, which is an instance of the poetical whose structurality has never been questioned, and where the allegorical relationship of space and time is a straightforwardly thematic as well as a formal issue. This is the case in several ways, but for our purposes most importantly so with regard to the opening months and seasons description, which is the stylized convention by means of which the *Prologue* places itself squarely in a tradition of allegorical beginning. This months and seasons description is a long-established convention immediately evocative of and convenient to cosmological and metaphysical invention, a way of alluding through allegorical structure to the mysterious order of the cosmos and the position of God as unmoved mover within it. Here the *Prologue* can rely on a tradition that goes back to Lucretius and to Ovid and to Vergilian eclogue, and that is thoroughly alive and popular throughout the middle ages, whether in manuscript decoration, cathedral ornament, or various scientifically and philosophically inclined compendia. The details and history of this convention need not concern us now, save to the extent that they allow us to refer with some certainty to the explicitly allegorical intentions of *The Canterbury Tales* and to remark that here, as with any deployment of a convention within a literary tradition, we have precisely the joining of paradigm and syntagm by means of which a literary text will position itself within the structurality of literature as a whole (with the text presenting itself as either like or unlike others in the conventional paradigm—for Jakobson this would be the literary code, a structure of generic oppositions—at the same time as it actualizes the paradigm in

17.   *Ibid*, p. 111.

the temporality of literary history, though whether Chaucer's *parole* is here intended ironically remains an open question).

It is with reference to the complex tradition of allegorical literature and to the poem's burden of cosmological, theological, and scientific speculation, that we enter the work. And it is within this context that we discover in the *Prologue*'s first two lines, with the piercing of March by April, the metaphoric metonymy that for Jakobson constitutes the specifically poetic effect. That is, when April with its sweet showers pierces the drought of March, we have the code of the months, or more precisely the system of oppositions that makes up the code, translated directly into consecutive sequence, such that the binary oppositions between the months, rainy April versus dry March—but, of course, within the tradition there are other oppositions at stake besides the merely meteorological—are projected systematically onto the continuous progress of the months through the year: after March, then April, in a progression that completes and corroborates itself only when the entirety of the monthly paradigm unfolds itself through the temporal totality, or what we should here properly call the syntagm, of the year. Inevitably—and for the author of a treatise on the astrolabe, tautologically—this is picked up by the surrounding or encapsulating astrological references, which tell us again that we are in the first month, April, because the Ram has run through half his course and therefore, as with April and March, that the paradigmatic zodiacal opposition of Aries and Taurus is directly translatable onto, or as, the sequence of metonymy unrolled by celestial rotation.

All this is a rather complicated way of saying what for a competent reader should presumably go without saying; but for the sake of argument let us assume that the initial structural disposition of these first few images is then systematically repeated in the pattern of images that the poem develops throughout its opening few lines, so that the series of oppositions which we might summarize as wet and dry, up and down, sky and earth, male and female, fecundity and sterility, pagan and Christian, inside and outside, near and far, health and illness—all function structurally in relation to each other and to themselves as kinds of mirror images, indices, of the first metaphorico-metonymic structuring introduced by the intersection of March and April—each of them graded as structure superinduced on sequence. Let us even assume that the same thing happens metrically, so that the ictus on the unstressed position that we get in April is structurally related to the stress on the stressed position that we get with "March," and that this in turn sets up a stress structure of rhythmic and intonational patterning that the poem will reserve for specifically metaphorico-metonymic emphasis—e.g., "... with his shóurěs soote/ Thě dróughte...." Let us also assume—again only for the sake of argument and in pursuit of the ideal structural analysis—that the themes introduced by our now hypothetically structuralized *Prologue* imagery are in turn developed in the tales themselves, and that this enlargement proceeds with the same structural determinations as are sketched out in the first few lines, so that the implicit hierarchy presumed in the order of months is what finally lies behind the social hierarchy into which the pilgrims fit, from the Knight on down to the Miller (as well as the dictional hierarchy that governs the manner in which each tale is decorously related), and that the primacy of male April to female March is the structural source not only of the patriarchal orientation of the marriage tales, but also of presumptively analogous arrangements of cosmological and literary order that the tales regularly, allegorically ally with this—as, say, in The Wife of Bath's prologue and tale, where familial, sexual, theological, and literary "authorities" are all developed in terms of the hierarchicized sexuality already built into the piercing of March by the potent, engendering liquidity of April. Finally, so as to complete this imaginary, exhaustively structural analysis, let us assume that the relation of April to March, developed as structure superinduced on sequence, also describes the most general literary features of *The Canterbury Tales* as a whole, so that, in the same way that Jakobson's metaphorized metonymies point both to themselves as signifiers and to the structure of signifieds from which they derive, so too do we have in little with April-March a prototypical enactment of the procedure by means of which Chaucer characteristically manages to distance his text from its own textuality—whether in the way the tales comment upon each other by reference to their common frame, or the way they point to themselves by stepping out of themselves, as with the Pardoner's claims for his own rhetoric, or, in that culminating instance of self-reflection so dear to dialectical Chaucerians, the way the narrator's tale of Sir Thopas lapses into the allegorical prose of the *Tale of Melibee*, accomplishing thereby an instance of mirroring self-mockery surpassed only by the absolute duplicity of the *Retraction* itself, where Chaucer either turns Pardoner or steps out of literature altogether, but in either case piously and conventionally defers to the only moral imperatives that his allegorical system allows him in the first place.

Having now assumed so much—and I realize that to suggest the possibility or the shape of a completely successful, all-encompassing structural analysis of *The Canterbury Tales* is to assume a great deal—we are now entitled to ask in what way this structure accounts for the poeticality of the text. In what sense can our hypothesized structure explain either the pleasure or the meaning taken from, or generated by, a text organized by the projection of metaphoric equivalence onto metonymic succession? The poem tells us that when the sweet showers of April pierce the drought of March to the root, when Zephyrus inspires the crops in every woodland with his sweet breath, when small birds begin to make melody, "*thanne* longen folk to goon on pilgrimages." How does the structuring of the first few lines that we have now assumed manage to generate, or to justify, or to explain this longing? How does it entice a reader further into the poem, leading him on through and into its sequencing? How is structure extended, "longed," into time? In the terms of my title, how does the structure of the poem yield its allegorical desire?

For an answer, I turn to another famous essay by Jakobson in which he applies the procedures of structural analysis to phonemic patterning, and where he develops the theory of distinctive phonetic features, which remains the greatest achievement of structural linguistics, recognized as such even by linguists with entirely different theoretical perspectives.[18] We should say in advance that it is because of Jakobson's theoretical success with phonemes, a conceptualization that reduces the infinity of humanly producible sounds to a few significant phonological oppositions, that structural linguistics has become the prestigious model for disciplines whose fields are only marginally, or at least not obviously, related to language per se. All of them readily pay the price of analogizing their subject matter to language in exchange for the rigorous structurality that Jakobson's method provides.

In principle, then—and my account will be perfunctory paraphrase—Jakobson begins with Saussurean diacriticality, the thesis that we perceive positivities as systems of differences rather than as simple existents whose being immediately imposes itself upon our senses. We hear the structured differences between phonemes rather than the phonemes themselves, as we know from the fact that what is a significant sound to a speaker of one language may not even be heard by the speaker of another. For each language, then, Jakobson proposes that a system of binary phonological oppositions may be constructed whose systematicity can account for all the potentially significant sounds that can be produced within the language. This will be the phonological code of the *langue* that is actualized in metonymic *parole*. These systems naturally vary from language to language, depending on the phonological structure of each, but what concerns us now are features that, because of the structure of the human mouth, are universal phonological facts. Here, then, like a Ramist proposing his initial dichotomization, Jakobson applies structuralist methodology and searches out what would be the maximum binary opposition of which the mouth is capable, which he discovers in the first syllable, contrast of consonant and vowel, transcribed as /pa/. The constituents of this utterance, vocalic /a/ and the voiceless labial stop /p/, represent absolute phonological difference in the mouth: viz., with /p/ the buccal tract is closed at the front whereas in /a/ the tract is opened at the end as wide as possible. As a labial stop, /p/ exists for but a moment and requires a minimun of energy for its articulation; in contrast, /a/ is a continual voicing of sound and requires maximum energy. Where /p/ is the stopping of sound, /a/ is pure vocality. For all these diacritical reasons, /pa/ is plausibly identified as the largest binary opposition the mouth can articulate and as such, from a structuralist perspective, is conceptually the first syllable. This theoretical claim is in turn supported by studies in language acquisition and aphasia which report that /pa/ is both the first utterance children learn and the last that aphasics lose—striking empirical corroboration of Jakobson's structuralist claim that language begins

18.   Roman Jakobson and Morris Halle, "Phonemic Patterning," *Fundamentals of Language*, The Hague, Mouton, 1971, pp. 50-66.

and ends with the combination of vocalic /a/ with voiceless labial stop /p/ in the primal utterance /pa/.

The hypothesis is clearly ingenious, and if we assimilate voiceless /p/ to its twin labial stop, voiced /b/, sound and sense begin in Jakobson's sense to cohere structurally, as, for example, when we call the infant incapable of speech a *baby*, or when the Greeks call foreigners whose speech is strange *barbaroi* because they *babble*, as at the Tower of *Babel*, or when we begin our alpha-bets by joining *a* to *b*.[19] But /pa/ is only the beginning of a system. In order to build a structure at least two sets of oppositions are required so as to construct a series of proportions and logoi that can be actualized in speech. Thus Jakobson and the infant must identify a second binary opposition, structurally opposable to the first, so as to specify a paradigmatic code, and this they do by introducing the nasal consonant /m/. With the acquisition of /m/, the pure differentiality that was first presented by /pa/ is, as it were, plugged up, recuperated. As a nasal consonant, a continuant sound, /m/ combines the vocality of /a/ with the positionality of /p/ at the front of the mouth. As a little of one and a little of the other, /m/ is a kind of average or collapse or juncture of the original opposition, just as metaphor and metonymy seemed to collapse in Jakobson's theory. And once /m/ is articulated as a distinctive feature in its own right, we have the diacritical material with which to establish a structure of phonological sound: /p/ and /m/ being both opposed to /a/, while /p/ and /m/ are also opposed to each other. As Jakobson puts it: "Before there appeared the consonantal opposition nasal/oral, consonant was distinguished from vowel as closed tract from open tract. Once the nasal consonant has been opposed to the oral as presence to absence of the open tract, the contrast consonant/vowel is revalued as presence vs. absence of a closed tract."[20]

Again, there is striking cross-cultural empirical support for Jakobson's claim. In nearly every natural language that has been observed, some variation of *papa* and *mama* or their reversal, as in *abba* and *ema*, are the familiar terms for father and mother.[21] But what I am concerned with now, quite apart from whatever empirical power Jakobson's insight might possess, is how the first two terms of this series, /pa/ and /ma/, develop themselves as a structure. We remember that it is only with the introduction of the second opposition adduced by /ma/ that we can say we have a system. At that point, each term in the series can be seen as diacritically significant with respect to its opposition to another term in

---

19.   We are justified in thus assimilating /p/ with /b/ because at this stage the distinction between voiced and voiceless has not yet been made. "As the distinction voiced/voiceless has not yet been made, the first consonant may be shifting and sometimes indistinct, varying between types of /b/ and types of /p/, but still within a distinct 'family of sounds.'" (R.M. Jones, *System in Child Language*, Cardiff, University of Wales Press, 1970, II, p. 85). The collation shows itself in the orthography for the sounds.
20.   Jakobson and Halle, p. 51.
21.   Roman Jakobson, "Why 'Mama' and 'Papa'?" *Selected Writings*, The Hague, Mouton, 1962, I, pp. 538–45.

the structure. Until then, however, /pa/, insofar as it signifies anything, signifies only the sheer diacriticality through which the system as a whole is thought. But this original differential determination is thereupon lost, retroactively effaced, when the introduction of /ma/ "revalues" the first *valueless* contrast consonant/ vowel, or silence/sound, i.e., /pa/, as "presence vs. absence of a closed tract." In other words, /pa/ loses its original status as mark of pure diacriticality when it is promoted to the level of significant signifier within the system as a whole. This new significant /pa/ is utterly unrelated to the first simply diacritical /pa/ that it replaces, or, as Derrida would say, that it places under erasure. And it is precisely this occultation of the original /pa/, now structurally unspeakable because revalued as something else entirely, that allows the system to function as a structure in the first place. In short, the structure of significant sounds must erase the original marking of diacriticality upon which it depends and from which it emerges in order to signify anything at all. In a formulation whose resonance with contemporary literary criticism will be embarrassingly obvious, there is buried in the structurality of any structure the ghostly origin of that structure, because the origin will be structurally determined as a ghost, a palpably absent origin, by virtue of the very structurality it fathers. Every structure must begin with such an effacing, retroactive revaluation of its beginning, with such a murder of its diacritical source, just as Freud said when he identified the origin of human culture in the murder of the father, the primal /pa/, who lives on only in and as the guilty memory responsible for the structure of society.[22]

Turning back now to the opening of *The Canterbury Tales*—which it will now be clear I selected precisely because there in the intersection of *Ap*ril and *Mar*ch we have also the juncture of /pa/ and /ma/—we can answer the question of how an allegory begins and why it continues. What we can say is that with its poeticality defined as structure superinduced upon metonymy, allegory initiates and continually revivifies its own desire, a desire born of its own structuring. Every metaphor is always a little metonymic because in order to have a metaphor there must be a structure, and where there is a structure there is already piety and nostalgia for the lost origin through which the structure is thought. Every metaphor is a metonymy of its own origin, its structure thrust into time by its very structurality. With the piercing of March by April, then, the allegorical structure thus enunciated has already lost its center and thereby discovered a project: to re-cover the loss dis-covered by the structure of language and of literature. In thematic terms, this journey back to a foreclosed origin writes itself out as a pilgrimage to the sacred founding shrine, made such by murder, that is the motive of its movement. In terms of literary response, the structuring of the text holds out the promise of a meaning that it will also perpetually defer, an image of hermeneutic totality martyred and consecrated by and as the poetical. This is the

22. Sigmund Freud, *Totem and Taboo, S.E.,* 13, pp. 141-46.

formal destiny of every allegory insofar as allegory is definable as continued metaphor. Distanced at the beginning from its source, allegory will set out on an increasingly futile search for a signifier with which to recuperate the fracture of and at its source, and with each successive signifier the fracture and the search begin again: a structure of continual yearning, the insatiable desire of allegory.[23]

Perhaps this is one reason why, as Angus Fletcher has remarked, allegory seems by its nature to be incompletable, never quite fulfilling its grand design.[24] So too, this explains the formal affinity of allegory with obsessional neurosis, which, as Freud develops it in the case of the Wolf Man, derives precisely from such a search for lost origins, epitomized in the consequences of the primal scene, which answers the child's question of where he came from with a diacritical solution which he cannot accept, and which his neurosis thereupon represses and denies. But this would in turn suggest the affinity of psychoanalysis not only with obsessionality, but also with allegory.[25] For the theoretical concern of the Wolf Man case, argued out in the context of a polemic with Jung, is precisely to determine whether the scene of parental intercourse, the piercing of /ma/ by /pa/, observed by the Wolf Man was indeed a primal scene or instead a primal fantasy. And when Freud, relying on a hypothesis of universal, cross-cultural phylogenetic inheritance, tells us that it is a matter of indifference whether we choose to regard it as either, we may well wonder whether the theory of the primal scene, which is in some sense at the center of every psychoanalysis, is not itself the theoretical primal fantasy of psychoanalysis, a theoretical origin that the theoretical structure of Freud's thought obliges him to displace to the recesses of mythic history.[26]

23.   I am concerned here with the way literary structures are thought, and so feel no obligation to restrict my argument to cases which explicitly instance Jakobson's phonological thesis. Nevertheless, in the course of writing this essay I have enjoyed collecting concrete examples, as in the first line of the *Iliad*, from which I take my epigraph, where the wrathful Μη is joined to the stress on Πη in the first syllable of Lacan's and Achilles's Name of the Father. With regard to the pastoral tradition I focus on in the essay, from Chaucer's *Prologue* through Eliot, we should think of Marvell's *The Garden*, which opens with another Pa-Ma—"How vainly men themselves amaze/To win the palm, the oak, or bays"—and tells another nostalgic story of Eden lost through diacriticality: "Two paradises 'twere in one/To live in paradise alone." But there are also examples from the novel, e.g., *The Charterhouse of Parma (Parme)*, or *Mansfield Park*, or "Stately, plump, Buck Mulligan," or, my favorite, because its three syllables sum up Lacan's theory of the acquisition of language through the castration of the paternal metaphor: *Moby Dick*.
24.   Fletcher, pp. 174–80.
25.   The issue of Freud's and psychoanalytic obsessionality is a subject for another essay. It takes the hermeneutic form of attempting to plug up gaps. The culminating moment of Freud's analysis of the obsessional Rat Man comes when Freud's interpretation *participates* in the Rat Man's deepest homosexual fantasies: "Was he perhaps thinking of impalement? 'No, not that; . . . the criminal was tied up . . .'—he expressed himself so indistinctly that I could not immediately guess in what position—'. . . a pot was turned upside down on his buttocks . . . some *rats* were put into it . . . and they . . .'—he had again got up, and was showing every sign of horror and resistance—'bored their way in . . .'—Into his anus, I helped him out." ("Notes upon a Case of Obsessional Neurosis," *S.E.*, 10, p. 166). Professor Murray Schwartz suggested this reading of the Rat Man to me. I would say that we can follow out the same language and desire not only in Freud's biography, but in psychoanalytic theory and metatheory, a phenomenological sodomy.
26.   "From the History of an Infantile Neurosis," *S.E.*, 17, p. 97: "I should myself be glad to know

The question becomes perhaps more urgent when we recall the theoretical status of what for Freudian metapsychology is its own maximum binary opposition, namely, the instinct theory with its dualism of Eros and Death. For to the extent that these two instincts are different, it is only insofar as the recuperative, unifying impulses of Eros are provoked as response to the differentiating impulses of death, a /ma/ to the thanatotic /pa/. And even before this, death itself is already conceived by Freud as such a dualism, extended into time as the compulsive, obsessive repetition of its own diacriticality, i.e., the repetition compulsion, which is the vicious Freudian metonym of the metaphoricity of death. Is it any wonder, then, that for evidence of all of this Freud can in *Beyond the Pleasure Principle* but point to another piece of allegorical literature, to Plato's story of Aristophanes' story of divinely diacriticalized hermaphrodites, yet another case where desire originates in and as the loss of structure. And it is by no means accidental that Freud develops these same Aristophanic themes elsewhere, as in the allegory of his gender theory, with its unending quest by both hetero-sexes for the castrated phallus, powerful only in the division it teaches in its loss.[27] And so too with psychoanalytic interpretation, which completes itself only when it points mutely to that

> . . . passage in even the most thoroughly interpreted dream which has to be left obscure . . . a tangle of dream-thoughts which cannot be unravelled and which moreover adds nothing to our knowledge of the content of the dream. This is the dream's navel, the spot where it reaches down into the unknown. The dream-thoughts to which we are led by interpretation cannot from the nature of things, have any definite endings; they are bound to branch out in every direction into the intricate network of our world of thought. It is at some point where this meshwork is particularly close that the dream-wish grows up, like a mushroom out of its mycelium.[28]

Does this mean, then, that psychoanalysis as a science is "mere" allegory? Does the fact that the exposition of Freud's theory of the psyche acts out its own theorization mean that psychoanalysis is but a symptomatic instance of its own thwarted desire to know: a neurotic epistemophilia at the end of a bankrupt tradition of philosophy? It is thanks to Lacan that we can see in this theoretical self-reflection of psychoanalysis, mirror of Freud's original analysis of himself, both the historical necessity and the scientific validity of psychoanalytic allegoricization. For when Lacan makes the subject an effect of the signifier, when he defines

whether the primal scene in my patient's case was a phantasy or a real experience, but taking other similar cases into account, I must admit that the answer to this question is not in fact a matter of very great importance."

27.   In "The Dissolution of The Oedipus Complex," "The Infantile Genital Organization," and "Some Psychical Consequences of the Anatomical Distinction between the Sexes," *S.E.*, 19.

28.   *The Interpretation of Dreams*, *S.E.*, 5, p. 525. See also 4, p. 111n.

the unconscious as the "discourse of the Other" (let us note, a direct translation of the etymology of allegory: ἄλλος, other; ἀγορεύω, to speak), he establishes psychoanalysis as precisely that science whose concern is the split in the subject occasioned by the subject's accession to language. If psychoanalysis has discovered anything, it is precisely this loss of the self to the self that we vaguely refer to when we speak of the function of the unconscious. And what Lacan has taught us, in a series of blindingly lucid formulations still defensively resisted by the psychoanalytic establishment, is that in the same way that *The Canterbury Tales* is divided and directed when it enters language, so too is the psyche when it learns to speak.[29] This famous Lacanian barring of the subject—the loss of being that comes from re-presenting oneself in language as a meaning, correlative with the formation of the unconscious and the onset of desire, the construction of the Oedipal subject, and the acquisition of a place in the cultural order through the recognition of the Name of the Father—is what makes the psyche a critical allegory of itself, and what justifies psychoanalysis as the allegory of that allegory. It is in search of the meaning of this division of the subject through the dialectics of desire occasioned by the structurality of the logos that psychoanalysis finds its own epistemological project and its own initiatory desire.

If, then, the structure of Freud's thought, as it develops, becomes immanent as theme, if Freud's theory repeatedly valorizes those very images of loss which make his conceptual representations possible in the first place, this is to say no more than that Freud's hermeneutics are at one with the object of their inquiry. This is not the internalist fallacy: rather, it is the way psychoanalysis realizes itself as practice. For psychoanalysis is no empty theory; it is instead the operative science of the unconscious, and the unconscious is precisely that part of the self lost to the self by its articulation, just as Freud's theory embodies itself only through its endless, questing theoretical self-deconstruction. Or so the heroic, allegorical example of Freud and the rigorously figurative style of Lacan persuasively suggest.

This is to see in psychoanalytic structure and in psychoanalytic structuralism the conclusion of a search for wisdom that has motivated Western philosophy from its very beginning. In the declension of theoretical speculation about the order of order that begins as ontology, cosmology, theology, and that, starting with the Renaissance, is internalized in the sciences of man as anthropology, sociology, psychology, there occurs a completing or a breaking of the hermeneu-

29.   These themes run through all of Lacan's work. In *Ecrits*, see "The Mirror Stage as Formative of the Function of the I," "The Function and Field of Speech and Language in Psychoanalysis," "On a Question Preliminary to any Possible Treatment of Psychosis," "The Signification of the Phallus," and "The Subversion of the Subject and the Dialectic of Desire in the Freudian Unconscious." With regard to the occultation induced by metaphor, see especially Lacan's formulas for metaphor and metonymy in "The Agency of the Letter in the Unconscious, or Reason since Freud." See also my own "Gnosis and the Piety of Metaphor: The Gospel of Truth," forthcoming in *The Rediscovery of Gnosticism: Studies in the History of Religion*, ed. Bentley Layton, Leiden, Brill, 1980.

tic circle when psychology, defining the psyche as an effect of the logos, is itself transformed, in Kenneth Burke's phrase, into logology.[30] This is the Heideggerean theme straightforwardly developed in Lacan's thought. And, of course, it is precisely against this appeal to the order of order and the meaning of meaning that Derrida has directed his critique of Lacan, seeing in such a psychoanalysis nothing but the inherited aftereffects of Western logocentric metaphysics, where the phallus is the castrating, fascistic transcendental signified that condemns man's desire to a forever unsatisfying nostalgia for the lost origin of a chimerical golden age.[31] As an alternative, as we now all know, Derrida proposes instead a metaphysics and a psychoanalysis of difference itself, *la différance* of both structure and time, to be comprehended by a philosophy *avant la lettre*, before structure, before logos: in short, a philosophy of the effacing and trace of prelinguistic, diacritical /pa/.

But as Derrida is well aware, and as he repeatedly reminds the most enthusiastic Derrideans, this return to structuralist first principles can occur only *after* the structural fact, for it is only *in* structure that the origin and its loss emerges. The sign is always thought through difference, but it is always eventually thought out to the signifying conclusion that erases the difference upon which it depends, which is why "difference cannot be thought without the trace."[32] Thus, if Lacan is logocentric, it is because he characterizes the first logocentric lapse through which *différance* itself will be thematized and conceived, so that any criticism of Lacan will already have committed the Lacanian lapse. This accounts for the positivist illusion that there are things before differences, but it also explains the intrinsic belatedness of every deconstruction.[33]

This is also why any of the so-called post-structuralist critiques of structuralism, including Derrida's, must be seen as mere aftereffects of structuralism. They are already defined, by the criticism implicit in their *post* and in their hyphen, as the allegorical response to a metaphor of structure and a structure of metaphor in which they are already implicated and by which they are already implied. Whether the origin is perpetually displaced by Derridean *différance*, or whether it is

30.   Kenneth Burke, "Terministic Screens," *Language as Symbolic Action*, Berkeley, University of California Press, 1966, p. 47, and *The Rhetoric of Religion: Studies in Logology*, Berkeley, University of California Press, 1970.
31.   Jacques Derrida, "The Purveyor of Truth," *Yale French Studies*, 52 (1975), 31-113.
32.   Jacques Derrida, *Of Grammatology*, trans. G.C. Spivak, Baltimore, John Hopkins University Press, 1974, p. 57.
33.   For this reason, I think it is a mistake to assimilate Derrida and Lacan each to the other, and to see in the critical practice of both an equivalent response to textuality, e.g., Gayatri Spivak, "The Letter as Cutting Edge," *Yale French Studies*, 55/56, pp. 208-226; Barbara Johnson, "The Frame of Reference: Poe, Lacan, Derrida," *Yale French Studies*, 55/56, pp. 457-505. This is to reduce the historical importance that their confrontation represents both for psychoanalysis and for philosophy. Derrida is very much son to Lacan's father, which is why he attempts the critical parricide of "Purveyor of Truth" or *Positions*. In this sense, Derrida is quite right to characterize the Lacanian enterprise in terms of a dated and passé Hegelian project. On the other hand, in accord with the Freudian paradigm, Derrida's philosophical success only makes the mortified Lacan that much more authoritative.

historically located and crystallized by Girard's catastrophe of "no-difference" whatsoever, the thematic valorization of origin as loss survives.[34] And post-structuralism therefore gains its prestige only insofar as it thus pro-longs itself as the critical metonymy of the structuralist metaphor.

We must therefore stress again the sense in which the scientific thematization of structure that we find in psychoanalysis spells an end to the tradition of literary allegory as we have known it since first-century Alexandria. For when psychoanal-ysis itself turns into allegory, criticism for the first time in our tradition must admit to the irrecuperable distance between itself and its object. Having con-sciously formulated the allegory of its own desire, criticism must awaken from its dream of interpretation to a daylight where desire is but the memory of the night's desire. We have posited it as a law of literary form that the diacriticality effaced by literary structure emerges as theme in the register of loss. Our example has been the way pilgrimage is thematized in *The Canterbury Tales*, but we might have illustrated the point with any of a wide variety of texts. We may posit it as a second law that profoundly self-conscious texts eventually realize their responsibility for the loss upon which their literariness depends, and that when this happens this responsibility is itself thematized as sin. From silence to difference to loss to sin— and sometimes, in texts whose literary integrity is absolute, through sin back to silence once again, as in the *Retraction* with which *The Canterbury Tales* concludes. These laws of literary form also apply to the structure of literary history, whether we consider the development of an individual author or the evolution of a literary genre.

But this leaves open a way for poetry and for the history of poetry to remain literary even in their silence, whereas criticism ceases to be criticism when it turns mute. Because the things of poetry are words, poetry can, in a way that criticism cannot, conclude itself when it cannot continue. When poetry can find no new words with which to maintain the meaning of its longing, it can lapse into significant literary silence, thereby pro-longing its desire ad infinitum. But criticism, whose things are not words but the meanings of words, meanings forever foreclosed by words, will find in silence only the impetus for further speech and further longing, which it will thereupon thematize as its own responsibility for the loss of meaning. Where a poem can be closed poetically even by a gesture of self-abandon, criticism, dis-covering the futility of its pro-ject, can only go on and on, frustratingly repeating its own frustration, increasingly obsessed with its own sense of sin—unless, of course, in the psychoanalytic sense, it projects its own critical unhappiness onto literature, whose self-deconstruction would then be understood as criticism.[35]

34. René Girard, *Violence and the Sacred*, Baltimore, John Hopkins University Press, 1977.
35. See, for example, Gayatri Spivak: "I would like to suggest the possibility of conceiving poetry in

Thus it is that when the tradition of English pastoral that begins with Chaucer's *Prologue* finds its own conclusion, it remains literary even in its self-disgust. And Eliot, drawing the thematic structure of the genre to its absurdly melancholic, ultimate reduction, can still articulate a meaning pre-dicative of yet more poetic desire:

> April is the cruelest month, breeding
> Lilacs out of the dead land, mixing
> Memory and desire, stirring
> Dull roots with spring rain.

Eliot, with his habit of making a beginning out of ends, can imagine that the gap in landscape poetry that his poem proleptically prepares will become a significant silence in a perpetually meaningful literary tradition that will forever feed meaning back into his *Wasteland*. In contrast, Freud, whose Judaic thematizations of guilt and sin, as in *Civilization and Its Discontents*, are at least as forceful and serious as any of Eliot's Anglican regrets, can do no more than continue to repeat his themes with increasingly phlegmatic and precisely nuanced resignation, as in the fragment with which his corpus movingly concludes, prophetically and self-reflectively entitled "The Splitting of the Ego in the Process of Defence." [36] This is the insight into self-division and sin that psychoanalysis leaves as legacy to contemporary critical thought, which continues to repeat Freud's themes, though perhaps without the rigor of Freud's resignation. Here I refer to that note of eschatological salvation that sounds so strangely in current literary discourse, as when Girard looks forward to a revivification of difference through sacralizing violence, or when Derrida, telling us it is not a question of choosing, includes himself amongst those who "turn their eyes away in the face of

a totally opposite way to a common understanding that would see poetic language as that in which sign and sense are identical, as in music, as that which tends to maintain the distance between the sign and its semantic meaning. To support my argument, I will have recourse to the notion of allegory." (Gayatri Spivak, "Allégorie et historie de la poésie: Hypothèse de Travail," *Poétique*, 8 (1971), p. 427). In effect, I am suggesting that we are still entitled to retain the idea of the book, the poem, the artifact, as opposed to the infinite, indefinite, unbounded extension of what nowadays is called textuality. Thus I also maintain the validity of the distinction between literature and its criticism, though, in accord with my argument above, this distinction would only have become operative relatively recently with the conclusion of psychoanalytic hermeneutics. What distinguishes the literary from the critical is that the logocentric book or poem can effect the closure of representation precisely because it can structure silence into its discourse, just as language does with the combination of consonant and vowel. The result is a polysemic, structured literary universe. If contemporary criticism can do this, it chooses not to, and thus maintains itself only as the inconclusive textuality that it attributes to literature. I realize that Derrida would characterize the distinction between structure and time that structuralism proposes as dependent upon, in Heidegger's phrase, a "vulgar concept of time" (see *Grammatology*, p. 72). My concern, however, is with how these concepts have functioned and continue to function as decisively powerful metaphors in the Western literary critical tradition, regardless of how philosophically untenable they may have been for all these thousands of years.

36.   *S.E.*, 23, pp. 275-278. The essay takes up the "rift in the ego which never heals but which increases as time goes on" (p. 276). Freud's illustrative example is castration disavowal.

the as yet unnameable which is proclaiming itself and which can do so, as is necessary whenever a birth is in the offing, only under the species of the non-species, in the formless, mute, infant, and terrifying form of monstrosity."[37]

It would seem by the rules of the endgame Beckett wrote in *Waiting for Godot* that contemporary thought here turns pastoral nostalgia for a golden age into the brute expectations of a sentimental apocalypticism. But we will wait forever for the rough beast to slouch its way to Bethlehem; so too, for a philosophy or a literary criticism of what the thunder said: DA.[38]

37.   Jacques Derrida, "Structure, Sign, and Play in the Discourse of the Human Sciences," *The Languages of Criticism and the Sciences of Man,* eds. Richard Macksey and Eugenio Donato, Baltimore, John Hopkins University Press, 1970, p. 265. If Girard is the theoretician of an unthinkable sacred Origin, and Derrida the philosopher of an indefinitely deferred Origin, then Foucault, with his inexplicable transitions between *epistemic* frames, is, despite his disclaimers, the post-structuralist of missing middles. And Foucault shares post-structuralist millenarianism: "In attempting to uncover the deepest strata of Western culture, I am restoring to our silent and apparently immobile soil its rifts, its instability, its flaws; and it is the same ground that is once more stirring under our feet." (Michel Foucault, *The Order of Things*, New York, Vintage, 1970, p. xxiv.)
38.   See Lacan, "Function and Field of Speech and Language," *Ecrits*, esp. pp. 106-107.

The Body

A Portfolio of Photographs
of Trisha Brown's Work

BABETTE MANGOLTE

Accumulation, 1971

Locus, 1975
Dancers: Trisha Brown, Elizabeth Garren, Judith Ragir, Mona Sulzman.

Line-Up, 1977

Dancers: Trisha Brown, Elizabeth Garren, Lisa Kraus, Wendy Perron, Judith Ragir, Mona Sulzman

Water Motor, 1978

Glacial Decoy, 1979
Dancers: Trisha Brown, Elizabeth Garren, Lisa Kraus, Nina Lundborg.

Blue Poem
for B.

PETER HANDKE

TRANSLATED BY MICHAEL ROLOFF

Deep at night
it became bright again
Crushed from the outside
I began to curdle
in full consciousness
Unfeeling my cock twitched
larger
from breath to breath
"Don't wake up now!" I thought
and held my breath
But it was too late
Nonsense had struck again

Never before had I felt so
in the minority
Outside the window
nothing but omnipotence
At first a few birds sang
then so many
the singing
became a racket
the air an echo chamber
without pause or end
Such a down
suddenly no memory
no thought of the future.
I lay stretched out long in my fear
did not dare

open my eyes
relived the winter night
when I did not turn once
from one side
to the other
gnarled by the cold then
now stretched out
illiterate from the horror outside me—
The air
how high it shrilled!
And then
all at once
quite near the window
a low whistling in the bird racket
a juke box tune
"A human being!" I thought
spelling out each letter from deathly fear
and withered
without moving
"The one who has been murdered
   by the disembodied monster
in the unpeopled predawn light
Fear billowed up from the cellar stairs
and the COMMON-SENSE PERSON inside me
listened:
the tune was repeated
was repeated—
"No bird whistles that monotonously
the phantom wants to ridicule me
its grinning
with pitchblack lips

"I" thought
The light
when I squinted
had the color from the time
when I still believed in hell
and the whistling monster by the window
soundlessly rattled its wrists
as if it now meant business

"Didn't Freddy Quinn sing that back then?"
I thought
"But which bird?" the common-sense person
Then child woke up in the next room
and shouted
that she couldn't sleep
"Finally," I said
went to her
and calmed her down
full of egotism
A garage door slammed
the first early riser had to go to work
The evening of the next day I left

The unleveled rolling plazas
in the large graceful city
this repetition of the open country
with its horizons of hills
amid the houses
the land
prolonged into the city
onto these plazas
where you were overwhelmed as nowhere else
by horizon-longing
When I climbed out of the subway
even the dog shitting on the sidewalk
struck me as magicked
I shuddered with disbelief
suddenly I was THE OBJECTIVELY LIVING THING
My cock lay strangely forgotten
between my legs
Joy rose
from the deepest depth
and replaced me
"I can be happy!" I thought
"Why don't you envy me!"

For days I was beside myself
and yet as
I wanted to be.

I ate little
talked just to myself—
needless so happy
unapproachable so full of curiosity
selfless
and self-confident
in one
the self-confidence
as the INMOST
of the self-lessness
I as inspired machine
Everything happened by chance.
that a bus stopped
and that I got on
that I rode my ticket's worth
that I walked through streets
until the neighborhood changed
that I walked on in the new neighborhood.
I lived
as it came
no longer HESITATED
reacted IMMEDIATELY
experienced nothing SPECIAL
—no "Once I saw"—
merely experienced
The cats sniffed around in the mausoleums
of the large cemeteries
Very small couples sat in the cafes
and ate Salade Niçoise together . . .
I was in my element
clucking

But in my dreams
I hadn't yet lost all interest
Straggling slime track
of the snail person.
I was not ashamed
was only angry.
I made myself wishless
by drinking too much

The twitching eyelids became irksome
The passersby were walk-ons
who behaved like stars
"Levi's-Jeans-people!" I thought
"Ad-space bodies!"
—"Which says everything about you"
I thought
without the earlier sympathy.
I became superficial with crossness
Whatever I saw
I also felt I touched
it seemed
so bristly
and perverse
Once when I was paying
the bill crinkled
at the salesman's breath
like a caterpillar
on a hotplate.
I did not feel well
in my skin
everything itched.
I no longer sweated as nonchalantly
The features
in the wrong places . . .
And the boulevards
doodled with dogshit . . .
"What impudence
of you fellows imported from Africa
to sweep the gutter before me
with such animally absent eyes!"
I gave up
and left for another city
where I had friends

Unfeeling transport object
within means of transportation
Self-forgotten
but for my hand's susceptibility to smell
of the butter

and of the coldcuts
lying there like that forever
under the plastic cover
and of the towellettes!
Cared for
yes
as someone who pays
Lodged
yes a part of a unit
In any case:
a DIFFERENT nonsense
without deathly fear
My heart throbbed for no one
and the city was foreign to me again
from all its familiar landmarks
The housedoors were locked as of eight PM
and I telephoned
to get in
in a friend's dark apartment
I sat absentmindedly
my ears buzzing
and heard my soulless own voice
Being happy all I could remember
was happiness
being unhappy merely unhappiness
Indifferently I recounted
how okay everything had been with me

Then we talked about fucking
The sexual expressions
provided us with the unabashedness
for everything else
Anyone joining us we greeted
with obscenities
and let loose
they lost their strangeness
Even while entering
the suburban wine cellars
we prolonged our fantasies there
where we had dropped them

looking for a parking place
Everything without horniness
In the upper deck of the bus
the total strangers grinned
when they listened to us
and felt at home with us

What exhibitionism
as soon as one of us
suddenly mentioned something!
But there was always someone
who found the hint of sex
in the allegedly other . . .
Yet no one talked about himself
we only fantasized
never the embarrassment of true stories
How the surrounding flourished then
and the pleasure in nothing but the present:
the heartiness of the sour wine in the
cylindrical glasses
Don't stop
please don't stop!
The indescribable particulars
of the grim new age
found the order of their lost connection
in the dirty stories
Hello
meaning is back!
Not to have to see my worried face
at midnight any more
Even left alone
I sat well guarded
in my afterthoughts
Calmly I watched the outstretched heel
twitching from my heart beat.
I felt well
by feeling nothing of myself
"My prick" I said
impersonally

Then it got serious
and the seriousness hit so quickly
that it didn't want to be me
who was meant
Then I became curious
then ruthless
I would take a woman to the next best toilet
No more flirting
no more obscenities
no more touches
instead of "fucking" I now said
"sleep with you"
—if I said anything at all.
I pared my fingernails
so as not to hurt you too much
In my horniness
I could suddenly call nothing
by its name
Before I had found a metaphor for sex
in the most unsuspecting things
now
during the experience
we experienced the sexual acts
as metaphors for something else
The movements reminded me
of what?
The noises were the noises from the world of things
it smelled of . . .
I didn't even have to close my eyes
to experience completely different events
than those before me
and to describe the "real" pictures
the "facts"
was optional
for
only the "other" pictures
into which the "real" ones
rocked me more and more
were for real

and the "other" pictures
were not allegories
but moments
from the past
set free by the good feeling
—as I remember just now
a hedgehog in the grass
with an apple
impaled on its quills
Dragging signs
with your breath
out of the depth of your consciousness
Thus I could be tender
without loving
and the skin at the heels
the pale navel
and the blissful smile
were no contradiction
and each thing by itself
intertwined with the other:
the leaves by the window
the child singing himself awake
a framework house at dawn
the light blue on the wayside shrine
from the time when you still believed in eternity
"Yes, swallow that!"
"Beauty is a kind of information" I thought
warm from you
and from the recollection
"You force me
to be
as I want to be" I thought
To exist
began
to mean something to me—
Don't stop!
I faltered just now
when I noticed
how suddenly the poem ended

Georges Méliès. L'éclipse de soleil en pleine lune. *1907.*

On the Eve of the Future:
The Reasonable Facsimile and
the Philosophical Toy

ANNETTE MICHELSON

In preparing these first, tentatively framed reflections on that intersection marked by the invention of the toy termed philosophical, I have had quite constantly in mind my friend, the late Hollis Frampton. To him the larger project, of which this forms a beginning stage, is dedicated.

It is, of course, the cinema, and particularly its prototypes — the phenakistoscope, most notably — which were referred to as toys both philosophical and scientific. These terms, their conjunction, are the product of an era in which science and its technological applications could still be identified with philosophy, and the scientist held to be the natural philosopher. For an early and significant text, for the *locus classicus* on the scientific toy, I turn, therefore, to Baudelaire's *La morale du joujoux* (*The Ethic of the Toy*), written in 1859:

> I think that children generally do exert influence on their toys, that their choice is directed by inclinations and desires, which, however vague and unformulated, are nevertheless, very real. Still, I would not deny the contrary, that is to say, that toys act upon the child, particularly upon one with literary or artistic inclinations. One would hardly be surprised to see a child of that sort, whose parents take him to the theater, already coming to consider the theater as beauty in its most entrancing form.
>
> There is a kind of toy recently on the increase, and upon which I shall pronounce no judgment of value. I mean the scientific toy. Its principal defect is its high cost. But it can provide extended amusement and develop within the child the taste for surprising and wonderful effects. The stereoscope, which renders a flat image in depth, is of this sort. It has been around a few years now. The phenakistoscope, which is older, is less well known. Let us suppose that a movement of some sort — that of a dancer or tumbler, for example — is divided and decomposed into a certain number of motions. Suppose that each of these motions — twenty in number, if you like — be rep-

resented by a single figure of juggler or of dancer, and that they are all drawn around a circle of cardboard. Adjust this circle, and that of another, pierced with twenty small windows, equidistant from each other, to a pivot at the end of a handle, which you hold as you might a screen before a fire. The twenty little figures, representing the decomposed movement of a single figure, are reflected in a mirror placed opposite you. Set your eye at the level of the little openings, and turn the circles rapidly. The rapidity of the rotation transforms the twenty openings into a single circular one, through which you see reflected in the mirror twenty dancing figures, all exactly alike and executing, with fantastic precision, the same movements. Each small figure has benefited from the nineteen others. On this circle it turns, and its rapidity renders it invisible. In the mirror, seen through the turning window, it stays in one place, executing all the movements distributed amongst the twenty figures. The number of pictures that can be thus created is infinite.

Such was the prototype of the cinema, that toy Baudelaire termed scientific, and others, philosophical, in an era prodigal of natural philosophers, among them the magi of electricity: Ampère, Faraday, Coulomb, Clerk-Maxwell, Edison.

Science, then, as natural philosophy and the inventions of technology as philosophically inspired are the ground of our concern. And our protagonist is Edison, the central figure of a fable composed a century ago, by Villiers de l'Isle-Adam, the student of Baudelaire and the master of Mallarmé. *L'eve future* is a late work, written between 1880 and 1886, published three years before Villiers's death in 1889, the year of Edison's visit to the great Exposition Universelle, organized in celebration of the centenary of the French Revolution.

I will propose a reading of this text, in the knowledge that it has not gone wholly without mention within the cinematic context. Its place, however, and its force as epitomization of the dynamics of representation issuing in the invention of the cinema have been utterly neglected. For Bazin, whose single allusion to it in *The Myth of Total Cinema* is laconic, it is a merely peripheral and curious episode in the evolution of realism. My project is genealogical, and I will claim for the text the status of a greatly privileged instance in the formation of our arsenal of mechanical reproduction, initiated, as it were, by photography, extended by telegraphy, phonography, cinematography, holography, television, and the computer. Its fuller understanding will demand, however, that we locate its anticipatory instances, embedded and dispersed within the epistemophilic discourse which traverses the art of the Renaissance and of the Enlightenment until the crisis of modernity. The poetics and metaphysics of symbolism which articulate that crisis mark, as well, the point of cinema's invention, and of the inscription, within its invention, of desire. To speak of that inscription is, of course, to speak of the perversion at its source. But it is this perversion — characterized as fetishistic — which informs symbolism in its highest and most seminal instances, that of Mallarmé, as that of Villiers, guardians of the Orphic in the era of industrial capitalism, Hegelian idealists in the parish of Auguste Comte.

Our protagonist is Edison, the Faust of industrial capitalism, the wizard of Menlo Park. He is already, when the tale begins, *"le Papa du phonographe."* But let Villiers set the scene:

Twenty-five miles from New York, surrounded by a web of electric wires, enclosed within broad and lonely gardens, there stands a dwelling. Its façade looks out upon a luxuriant lawn crossed by sanded walks, leading to a large and isolated cottage. To the south and to the west, two long avenues of ancient trees cast their shade upon this cottage. It is numbered "one" in the village of Menlo Park. Here dwells Thomas Alva Edison, the man who has taken Echo captive.

Edison is a man of forty-two. His physiognomy, some years back, strikingly recalled that of a celebrated Frenchman, Gustave Doré. He had almost the artist's visage translated into that of a scientist. Kindred aptitudes, of different application. Mysterious twins, these two; at what age might the resemblance have been complete? Perhaps it never was. Their two photographs fused, at that time, in stereoscopy, produced the impression that certain effigies of a higher species are realized only through the coinage of faces, scattered far apart amidst the human race.

As to Edison's face, it is, when studied in relation to old prints, the spitting image of Archimedes, of the Syracusan medallion.

Now, towards five o'clock of a recent autumn evening, the wonderful inventor of so many wonders, the Magician of the Ear (who, nearly deaf himself, like a Beethoven of Science, had created that imperceptible instrument which, adjusted to the ear drum's orifice, not only causes deafness to disappear, but further refines the sense of hearing), Edison, I say, retired into the depths of his private laboratory, within the cottage set in seclusion from his castle.

The engineer had, that evening, dismissed his five acolytes, his foremen — devoted, learned, and skilled workers whose rewards were princely and whose silence he commanded. Alone, seated in his American armchair, leaning on his elbows, a Havana cigar between his lips — the tobacco transforming his virile projects into reveries — staring distractedly ahead, his legs crossed, wrapped in his already legendary garment of purple-tasseled black silk, he appeared lost in the depths of meditation.

To his right, a tall window, wide open to the West, aired the vast den, casting a glow of reddening gold upon all its contents.

Here and there, piled upon the tables, were the outlines of precision instruments, the works of unknown mechanisms, of electrical equipment, telescopes, reflectors, of huge magnets, of piped receivers, of vials filled with mysterious substances, and of slates covered with equations.

Outside, over the horizon, the sunset, piercing the distant curtains of foliage on the maple and pine-wooded New Jersey hills, brightened the room for an instant, with a patch of purple or a flash of light. At those instants there streamed, from every side, metallic angles, crystal facets, the curves of batteries.

The wind was cooling. The day's storm had drenched the garden grass — and bathed, as well, the heavy, heady Asian blossoms in their green sheathes, beneath the window. Dried plants hanging between pulleys depending from the ceiling's rafters, released, as it were, reminders of their former perfumed forest life. Under the subtle action of this atmosphere, the dreamer's thought, usually vigorous and lively, relaxed and gave itself up to the seduction, to the pull, of reverie and of dusk.

Into this Faustian sanctum steps Lord Celian Ewald, an old friend of Edison's. He is in love with Miss Alicia Clary. Although a mere "virtuoso" (or, as we would say, performer), she is of the most unique and exquisite beauty. Let us attend to the particulars of her description:

> Miss Alicia is barely twenty. She is svelte as the silvery aspen. Her movements are slow, and delicious in their harmony. The lines of her body form an ensemble such as one finds in the greatest sculpture. Their fullness is sheathed in the warm pallor of the tuberose. Here is truly the splendor of a humanized Venus Victrix. Her thick dark hair has the sheen of the southern night. Often, when emerging from her bath, she will tread upon these shining tresses which even water cannot straighten and, tossing them from one shoulder to the other, will cast luxuriant shadows before her, as if from the folds of a mantle. Her face is the most seductive of ovals. Her cruel mouth blooms like a bleeding carnation drunk with dew. Moist lights linger playfully upon those lips, which reveal in dimpled laughter the brilliance of her strong young animal teeth. And her eyebrows quiver at a shadow. The lobes of her delightful ears are cool as April roses. Her nose, exquisite, straight, with lucent nostrils, extends the forehead's plane. . . . Her hands are pagan rather than aristocratic; her feet as elegant as those of Grecian statues. This body is lighted by two fine, dark eyes which glimmer through their lashes. A warm fra-

grance issues from the breast of this human flower, its perfume that of a meadow; its scent is burning, intoxicating, ravishing. The timbre of Miss Alicia's speaking voice is so penetrating, the inflections of her singing voice are so vibrant, so deep, that whether in tragic or noble recitation, or in superb song, she never fails to set me shuddering with a wonder which is, as you shall see, strange indeed.

Such is the catalogue or inventory of Miss Alicia's beauties. And yet, and yet. . . . Lord Ewald cannot rid himself of the awareness of that indelible, essential inner life which confers upon every creature its character, which governs its details, impressions, whether sharp or vague, which shapes experience and reflection. To this substratum of sentience he gives the name of "Soul."

Now, between Miss Alicia's body and soul, he perceives no mere disproportion, but an overwhelming, a total disparity—as if her beauty, which he terms "divine," were alien to her self. Her inner being proclaims a contradiction with her form, so that he finds himself inclined to wonder if, in that which he calls "the Limbo of Becoming" (Yes, Villiers has a Hegelian past, but that is still another story), if then, in the Limbo of Becoming, this woman had somehow strayed into a body which did not belong to her.

Lord Ewald goes on to speak of his sense of that body as a temple (it is Greek, no doubt) profaned by the spirit that now dwells within it. And that spirit, how is it to be described? Its description answers exactly to that of the Absolute Bourgeois, detailed in other of Villiers's polemical tracts, most particularly the portrait of Tribulat Bonhommet, Villiers's own compiler of a Dictionary of Received Ideas, first cousin to Monsieur Homais, to Bouvard and Pécuchet.

Looking and listening to Miss Alicia, Lord Ewald has the impression of a temple profaned, neither by rebellion nor the bloody torches of the barbarian invader, but rather by calculating ostentation, a hard insensitivity, an incredulous superstitiousness. She is, as it were, the priestess of bourgeois positivism, of that belief in progress founded in the materialism of a rising middle class, with its eye to advantage, its meanness and intolerance of excess, its philistinism: the ideology, in short, of commodity fetishism against which Villiers shored up defense together with Baudelaire, his master, and those to whom he was master, Mallarmé and the symbolists.

For Miss Alicia is afflicted with reason. Were she unreasoning Lord Ewald could understand and accept. The marble Venus, after all, has made no compact with reason. The goddess is veiled in mineral and in silence, and her aspect seems to proclaim her beauty incarnate, to declare, "I think only with the mind of the beholder. In my absolute state, all concepts are self-cancelling, limits are dissolved; they collapse, intermingled, indistinct, identical, like waves of a river entering the sea. For the man who reflects me, I am of such depth as he can bestow upon me."

It is Lord Ewald's lament which impels Edison to hasten to completion the great work upon which he has been engaged lo! these many years. And Villiers's tale becomes the narration of the creation—the fabrication—of a simulacrum, an android in which Miss Alicia's beauty, reproduced in accurate and complete detail, is informed with mind, with spirit. The simulacrum's name will be Hadaly—Arabic, we are told, for Ideal. Lord Ewald, in the climactic passage of the tale, will come to mistake her for Miss Alicia, and his rapture at this fusion of body with spirit is ended only by the destruction of Hadaly in a storm at sea, as they journey to a life of secluded bliss on his ancestral estate in England.

The text is organized on two parameters: the narrative of Lord Ewald's plight and of its resolution, and that of Edison's discourse on method. And this discourse serves persuasion, elaborated in the register of casuistry, all enveloped in a paean to electricity as the Promethean fluid of vivification, pitched to an extremity of lyricism that borders on the pastiche. Tale and discourse converge in the climactic moment of induction of misprision, followed by Lord Ewald's acceptance of the simulacrum for the model.

To pursue our reading, we return to the manner of Villiers's rendering of the female body in its glory of perfection, to its particulars of description. Composed, as one notes, of details, it proceeds, one also notes, downwards, from shining tresses to elegant feet, rather like the male glance of inspection which, as in French, *toise d'un regard*, takes the measure or stock of its object. Detailing, inventorying, cataloguing the body with, of course, the lingering, descending glance at not only the Venus Victrix (as the Venus of Milo, then thought to be a figure of Victory, was then known), but also, by inference, at the Venus of Botticelli, her hair swirling about her shoulders as she rises from the sea. The sculptural ideal of Greece and the pictorial paradigm of the Italian Renaissance are fused in the canonical stereoscopy of this living Venus.

For the rhetorical model of this litany (and it is one of many which punctuate the tale at regular intervals), for the sources of its syntax, we do well to press somewhat further on toward the anticipatory instance generated by the sixteenth century, in that moment marked by erotic art of the high Renaissance in France, in both its poetic and pictorial instances: that of the School of Fontainebleau under François I. For it is here that the notion of the erotic assumes, with a paradigmatic power, a distinctly fetishistic aspect, in its analytic view of the female body. One sees this in the celebrated double portrait of Gabrielle d'Estrées and the Duchess of Villars in their bath (c. 1594)—itself a reference to those of Venus and of Diana—in which the Duchess, naked, like her sister, points to and encircles the nipple of her sister's breast. "What," an old friend asked many years ago as we strolled through the Grande Galerie of the Louvre, "is the Duchess doing to her sister?" She announces, the iconographer tells us, Gabrielle's coming maternity, confirmed by the allusion to the coming birth of the Duc de Vendôme, for whom, in the painting's furthest plane, a nurse prepares a layette. But that ostensive gesture, indicating, pointing, and marking off, is, in its ambiguity, deeply consonant with Fontainebleau's eroti-

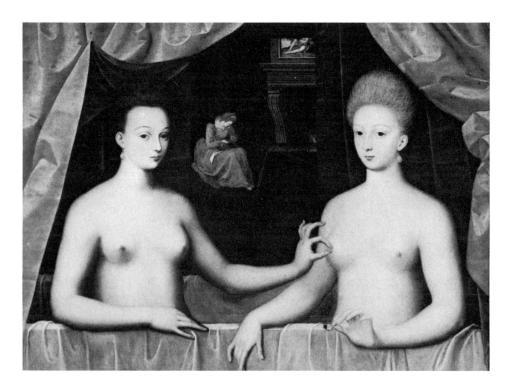

School of Fontainebleau. Gabrielle d'Estrées and the
Duchess of Villars in Their Bath. *c. 1594.*

cism: one which marks, dissects, delimits the body, charting, mapping the zones of pleasure. It is thus that the cultural order is inscribed on the body, through clothing, jewels, cosmetics, and, in other civilizations, through scarring, tattooing, extension or binding of the body and its members. This is the work of fetishization, of the mapping of the body in parts, of *la carte du tendre*. Its expression in the sixteenth century of the high Renaissance in France will find poetic instantiation in the invention of a new and highly developed, scandalous, controversial genre: the *blason du corps*, the blazon — or escutcheon — of the female body, in which the poets — among them Clément Marot, its inventor, Michel d'Amboise, Gilles d'Aurigny, Estorg de Beaulieu, Antoine Heroet, François Sagon, Lancelot de Carle, and the foremost of them, Maurice Scève — will fragment and glorify the body of woman. *Blason des cheveux, du front, blason du sourcil, blason de l'oeil, blason de l'oreille, blason du nez*, and, in Clément Marot's celebrated founding work, *Le blason du beau tétin* or *Blazon of the Comely Tit*.

A glance at that founding instance will well repay our attention. The blazon as a form originates during Clément Marot's exile from Fontainebleau. Finding refuge at the court of the Duchesse Renée in Ferrara, he devoted himself, far from the court of François I, to the composition of apologetics and the translation of the Psalms.

The Psalms, lyrics of perpetual praise, articulate, in their enumerative structure and cumulative metaphors, the rhetoric of the Old Testament. Marot, then, impelled by his study of the Psalms, composes his own, but they are secular, to say the least. They are, as we should say, profane. Such was the *Blazon of the Comely Tit*, and the success of this form at the court of François I was such, it is recounted, that not only poets such as Scève, but also the lettered members of the court, the magistrates, the booksellers — and many of the clergy — produced blazons. And their subject was single, central; it was woman, her body already denuded by the artists of Fontainebleau, her seduction evident, her charms half-hidden, her force secret. The tradition of sacred poetry was, then, redirected in the service of the most profane of subjects, for *la femme blasonnée* was not spiritual, but carnal, and each member, every part of her body was precious, venerable. For the fetishistic veneration of the holy relic, the *blasonneurs*, as they were known, substituted the cult of the living detail. Or, one might say, for *le corps glorieux*, the glorified Body of Christ, they substituted the female body. An eroticism in the mode of castration and veneration, fragmenting and glorifying. Woman, subjected to the analytic of dissection is then reconstituted, glorified in entirety and submission: as Marot says in his *Blason du beau tétin*, "He who shall with milk make you swell, makes of a virgin's tit that of a woman, whole and fine."

We have seen that body, a stereoscopy of Greek sculpture and Renaissance painting, generated in conformity with the aesthetic canons of the nineteenth century, submitted to inventory by the lover's eye. Let us now consider how it is constituted, simulated by Edison in the fabrication of Hadaly, the android.

We are told in Chapter One of Book V, entitled "The First Appearance of the Machine in Human Form." Edison speaks:

The Android is subdivided into four parts:
1. The live, internal System, which includes Balance, Locomotion, Voice, Gesture, the Senses, possible facial Expressions, the inner action regulator, or if you prefer, "the Soul";
2. The plastic Mediator, which includes the metallic envelope insulated from the epidermis and the flesh tint, a sort of armor with flexible articulations to which the internal System is firmly attached;
3. The Carnation (or properly speaking, imitation flesh), superimposed upon and adhering to, the Mediator, which (penetrating and penetrated by the animating fluid) includes the traits and lines of the imitated body, with that body's particular personal emanation reproduced, the responses of the skeleton, the modelling of veins, musculature, the model's Sexuality, all bodily proportions, etc.;
4. The Epidermis or human skin, which includes and controls the Complexion, Porosity, Features, the sparkle of the smile, the imperceptible creases of Expression, the precise labial movements of speech, the hair and the entire pilose system, the ocular set, together with the individuality of the Glance, the Dental and Ungular systems.

We are reminded of those medical drawings and anatomical models with layered articulations of nervous, digestive, and circulatory systems, among which those commissioned by the naturalist Felice Fontana in the eighteenth century for the Royal Cabinet of Physics and Natural History in Florence are preeminent. It was the close collaboration of Fontana with designers and modellers, the mobilization of the extraordinary technical prowess of Clemente Susini, which produced, in an era increasingly bent on the scrutiny of the female body, the Waxen Venus. Here is the fastidiously and voluptuously modeled woman in the flush of youth, nude, recumbent, suave and tender of aspect, her digestive, pulmonary, circulatory, and genital systems revealed and resolved into detachable elements. Her balance, her posture, her ever-so-slightly parted lips, her long, gleaming tresses, her pearl necklace, the tassled silken coverlet upon which she lies — these and the presence of pubic hair (none of these indispensable for the purpose of anatomical demonstration) — fashion an object of fascinated desire in which the anatomist's analytic is modulated by the lambent sensuality of Bernini. This Venus yields, responds, one feels, to the anatomist's ruthless penetration with the ecstatic passivity of Saint Theresa or the Blessed Ludovica Albertoni to the ministrations of the Holy Spirit.

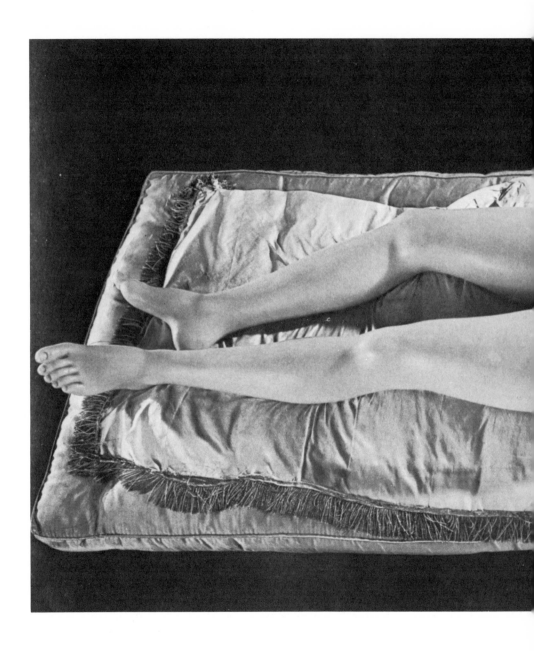

Clemete Susini and Giuseppe Ferroni.
La Donna della Specola di Firenze. *1782.*

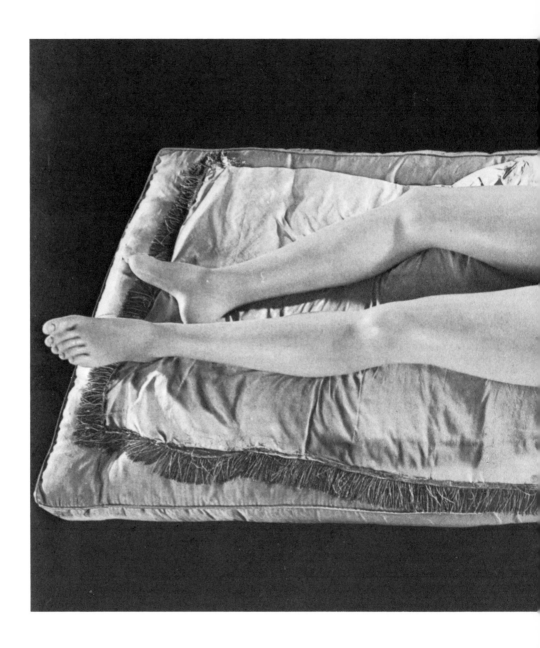

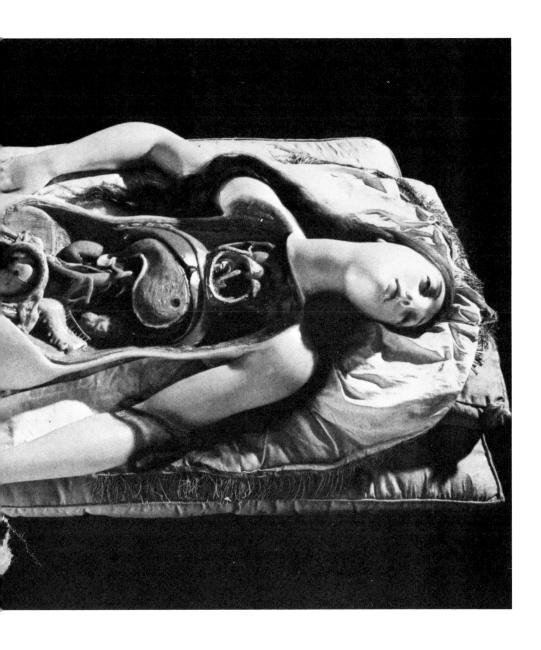

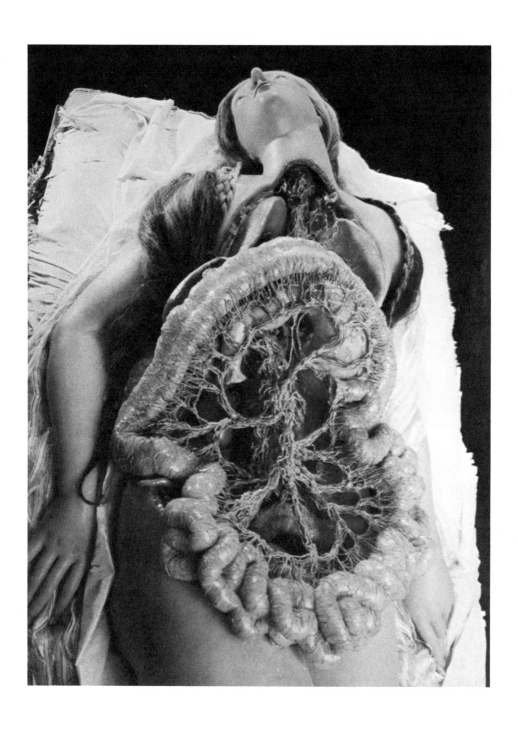

"But," says Edison, "the Android presents nothing like the frightful spectacle of our own vital processes. In her everything is rich, ingenious, and somber. Look!" And he presses his scalpel on the central apparatus riveted to the level of the android's cervical vertebrae.

> "Here," [he continues] "is the locus of Man's vital center. One prick here and we die instantly. . . . You see that I've respected nature's example here. These two inductors, insulated at this point, match the play of the Android's golden lungs. . . . It is due to the mystery generated in these metal disks and emitted by them that warmth, movement, and strength are distributed through Hadaly's body via this intricate mesh of shining wires, exact replica of our nerves, arteries, and veins. . . . This extremely powerful electro-magnetic motor which I have reduced in size and weight controls all the adjustments of the inductors.
>
> "This spark, bequeathed by Prometheus, harnessed to flow around this truly magic wand, produces respiration. . . . I have even thought of the deep sighs which sorrow elicits from the heart. Hadaly, being of a gentle and silent nature, is aware of them and is no stranger to their appeal. Any woman will acknowledge that these melancholy signs are easily counterfeited. . . .
>
> "These two gold phonographs on an angle inclined towards the center of the chest are Hadaly's two lungs. Between them pass the metallic leaves of her harmonious, I might say, celestial chatter. They operate like sheets of paper run through printing presses. A single ribbon of tinfoil will hold seven hours of speech. These have been composed by our greatest poets, our subtlest metaphysicians, the deepest novelists of our century—geniuses—upon my commission. These never-to-be-published marvels are worth their weight in diamonds. I therefore claim that in Hadaly Intellect is replaced by Intelligence."

We might say, then, that Hadaly has intelligence of the corpus of occidental culture. She is a palimpsest constituted in a synthetic text of Edison's inscription.

> "And" [continues Edison], "See, here they are, two imperceptible styluses of pure steel trembling on grooves which rotate due to the unceasing motion of the mysterious spark. They await only Miss Alicia's voice, I assure you. They will capture at a distance, while she, unaware of their action, as an ordinary actress recites scenes incomprehensible to her, the marvelous unknown roles wherein Hadaly will be forever incarnated."

After Villiers's description of other recording devices for gesture, speech, labial movements, balance — and for all the modulated depths of subtle expression, regulated with perfect precision — Hadaly's scenes, so to speak, are set in place. Hadaly becomes that palimpsest of inscription, that unreasoning and reasonable facsimile, generated by reason, whose interlocutor, Lord Ewald, has only to submit to the range and nuance of mise-en-scène possible in what Edison calls the "great kaleidoscope" of human speech and gesture in which signifiers will infinitely float. "And never will her speech deceive your expectations. It will be even as sublime as your inspiration to elicit it. With her you need never, as with the live model, fear misunderstanding. You will have only to remember the rests engraved between the words. Nor need you even articulate the words yourself. Hers will reply to your thoughts and to your silence."

It is a comedy for all time that Ewald is asked to rehearse, and it will take the shock of direct and inadvertent encounter with the completed and perfected android to change his horrified refusal into eager, ardent acceptance, to transform his rejection of mimesis into assenting seduction by the simulacrum.

If, then, Miss Clary is but an empty vessel, Edison's text, whose complex articulations, fine tolerances, and inscriptions will fill that vessel, vivifies the statue's body, fragmenting, analyzing, then restoring, through inscription, this body. We have seen that impulse animating the *blasons d'amour*, the erotic poetry of the high Renaissance, denuding, fragmenting, restoring the painted body of Venus. Where, however, shall we find the model of its inspiriting? Where but in the celebrated image of that statue which founds the epistemology of the ideologues of the Enlightenment, in that statue which Condillac proposes as the sentient, knowing subject in *The Treatise of Sensations* (1754)?

Let us recall something of Condillac's project. It is generated by his need to trace knowledge back to its first elements, employing not direct observation, but a hypothetical and analytic construction. Condillac had, prior to its publication, worked to systematize and popularize Locke's theory, holding that nothing inheres in the intellect which is not given in and by the senses. The source of knowledge was twofold: sensation and reflexion. It was by sensation that we apprehend external phenomena, and by reflexion, internal phenomena. In *The Treatise of Sensations* we have the completed and definitive exposition of Condillac's epistemology. Departing from Locke, he maintains that there exist not two sources of ideas, sensation and reflexion, but one only, sensation. From this he derives the activity of mind. His critique of Locke centers on what he considers to be an insufficiently radical deployment of the natural methods of analysis. If knowledge is sentience, we must trace the process of its generation to its source. We must first resolve it into its elements. Next we must show how these elements will account for the activity of the human soul in all and every form. The faculties of the soul are not innate; they have their origin in sensation itself.

For his analysis of the genesis of our faculties, Condillac, as is quite generally known, made use of a fiction, a fantasy wholly in keeping with the sensibility of the time. He imagined a marble statue (it was Greek, no doubt) with the complete organic structure of the human body, but insentient. He then proceeded to analyze the knowledge such an imaginary being would develop were its senses to be awakened one at a time. He began by allowing it smell. Here is the initial stage of this awakening:

> Our Statue being limited to the sense of smell, its cognitions cannot extend beyond smells. It can no more have ideas of extension, shape, or of anything outside itself, or outside its sensations, than it can have ideas of color, sound, or taste.
>
> If we give the statue a rose to smell, to us it is a statue smelling a rose, to itself it is smell of rose. The statue therefore will be rose smell, pink smell, jasmine smell, violet smell, according to the flower which stimulates its sense organ. In a word, in regard to itself, smells are its modifications or modes. It cannot suppose itself to be anything else, since it is only susceptible to sensations.
>
> Let the philosophers, to whom it appears so evident that all is material, put themselves for a moment in its place, and then imagine how they could suspect the existence of anything which resembles what we call matter.

Condillac, in a systematic strategy of *ascription*, then successively endows his statue with taste, hearing, then sight, and so on, with touch the last of the senses. Sensations themselves are referred to that which is external to ourselves. It is something like a theory, say, of intentionality, and our sensations become our ideas of things. Attention, memory, judgment are produced by these sensations, in their interrelations; the emotions and passions—hope, fear, love, hatred, volition—are sensations transformed. For Condillac the nature of thought was wholly unproblematic; it followed from sensibility. Sense is sensibility. *To feel is to think.*

We had recognized in Alicia Clary the lineaments of Venus Anadyomene. Do we, as well, discern in Hadaly, the subject formed by Edison's textual inscription, that marble statue endowed by Condillac's systematic ascription with the parameters of sentience?

We will want once more to note that assiduous, relentless impulse which claims the female body as the site of an analytic, mapping upon its landscape a poetics and an epistemology with all the perverse detail and somber ceremony of fetishism. And may we not then begin to think that body in its cinematic relations somewhat differently? Not as the mere object of a cinematic *iconography* of repression and desire—as catalogued by now in the extensive literature on dominant narrative in its major genres of melodrama, *film noir*, and so on—but rather as the fantasmatic ground of cinema itself.

We will then wish to consider once again, and somewhat differently, those acts of magic perpetrated upon the female subject, as by Edison and Méliès in the films of the primitive period (1900–1906), for the mutilations, reconstitutions, levitations, and transformations performed upon her body are to be read not, as has been suggested, as instances of male envy of the female procreative function. We may rather understand them as the obsessive reenactment of that proleptic movement between analysis and synthesis which will accelerate and crystallize around the female body in an ultimate, fantasmatic mode of representation *as* cinema.

The female body then comes into focus as the very site of cinema's invention, and we may, in an effect of stereoscopic fusion (like that of the two Venuses, like that of Edison and Doré, artist and natural philosopher) see the philosophical toy we know as the cinema as marked in the very moment of its invention by the inscription of desire.

For the moment of Lord Ewald's surrender to his Eve-to-be is that of a world, assenting, on the eve of its future, to that synthesis of the parameters of mechanical reproduction figured as simulacrum of the female body, for whose interlocutor (or spectator) the scene is already set. And this world, assenting, murmurs, "I know, but. . . ."*

---

* Among the sources consulted in the preparation of this text are: Villiers de l'Isle-Adam, *L'eve future*, Éditions Jean-Jacques Pauvert, Paris, 1960; Etienne Bonnot de Condillac, *Traité des sensations*, Paris, 1754; Maria Luisa Azzaroli Puccetti, Benedetto Lanza, and Ludmilla Bontempelli, "La Venere Scomponibile," *Kos*, No. 4 (May 1984), 65–94; Lucy Fisher, "The Lady Vanishes: Woman, Magic, and the Movies," *Film Quarterly*, Fall 1979, 29–40.

*Jehanne d'Alcy, actress and later wife of Georges Méliès, in
1897.*

GEORGES BATAILLE

translated by ANNETTE MICHELSON

The life of civilized peoples in pre-Columbian America is a source of wonder to us, not only in its discovery and instantaneous disappearance, but also because of its bloody eccentricity, surely the most extreme ever conceived by an aberrant mind. Continuous crime committed in broad daylight for the mere satisfaction of deified nightmares, terrifying phantasms, priests' cannibalistic meals, ceremonial corpses, and streams of blood evoke not so much the historical adventure, but rather the blinding debauches described by the illustrious Marquis de Sade.

This observation applies, it is true, mostly to Mexico. It may be that Peru represents a singular mirage, an incandescence of solar gold, a gleam, a troubling burst of wealth, but this does not correspond to reality. Cuzco, the capital of the Inca empire, lay on a plateau, at the foot of a sort of fortified acropolis. This city was massive, of a heavy grandeur. Tall, thatched houses, built in squares, of enormous rocks with no exterior windows, no ornamentation, gave to the streets a somewhat dreary, sordid look. The architecture of the temples which looked down upon the roofs was equally bare; only the pediment was wholly covered with a plaque of beaten gold. To this gold we must add the brilliantly colored fabrics which clothed the rich and elegant, but nothing could quite dispel the impression of wild seediness and, above all, of deadly uniformity.

Cuzco was actually the seat of one of man's most rule-ridden, thoroughly administered states. After important military conquests made possible by the meticulous organization of an immense army, the Incas' power spread over a considerable part of South America: Ecuador, Peru, northern Argentina, and Chile. Within this area opened up by roads, an entire people obeyed official orders as if soldiers to officers in a barracks. Work was distributed and marriages made by officials, the land and harvests belonged to the state. Celebrations were those of the state's religious festivals. Everything was planned ahead in an airless existence. This organization is not to be confused with that of present-day communism; it was essentially different, since it was based on heredity and on class hierarchy.

Given these conditions, it is not surprising that the Inca civilization is relatively dull. Cuzco is not even particularly striking in its horror. Infrequently, victims were strangled with cord in the temples, in that of the Sun, for instance, whose solid gold statue, melted down after the conquest, retains, in spite of all, a magical charm. The arts, although quite brilliantly developed, are nevertheless of secondary interest: fabrics, vases in the shape of human or animal heads are remarkable. It is not, however, among the Incas in this territory that we must seek a production really worthy of interest. The celebrated Gate of the Sun at Tihuanaco in northern Bolivia already points to an art and architecture attributable to a far distant era; pots and shards are stylistically linked to this thousand-year-old gate. It was, even in the Incas' own time, the coast-dwellers of a far more ancient civilization who produced the most curious objects.

In the era of conquest, Columbia, Ecuador, Panama, and the West Indies were also civilizations whose art today astonishes us. Moreover, many of the fantastic statuettes, the dream faces which are responsible for our present pre-occupation with pre-Columbian art, must be attributed to the people of these regions. Nevertheless, we must immediately make clear that, in our view, nothing in bygone America can equal Mexico, a region in which, moreover, we must discern two very different civilizations, that of the Maya-Qui'tche and that of the Mexicans, properly called.

The civilization of the Maya-Qui'tche is generally held to have been the most brilliant and interesting of all in extinct America. It is probably her production which does indeed most nearly approach that which the archaeologists have come to consider remarkable.

It developed several centuries before the Spanish conquest, in eastern Central America, in the south of present-day Mexico, more precisely in the Yucatan peninsula. By the time of the Spaniards' arrival, it was in full decline.

Mayan art is certainly the most human in America. Despite its lack of influence, it impels comparison with Far Eastern art of that same time, that of Khmer, for example, with its luxuriant and heavily vegetative look. Both, in any case, developed under leaden skies in overheated and unhealthy climates. The gods of Mayan bas-reliefs, although human in form, are heavy, monstrous, highly stylized, and, above all, very uniform. One can see them as extremely decorative. They actually formed part of quite marvelous architectural wholes, enabling the American civilizations to be placed beside the great classical civilizations. In Chichen-Itza, Uxmal, and Palenque, one still finds the ruins of temples and palaces, both impressive and richly wrought. We know the religious myths and social organization of these peoples. Their development was certainly a strong and largely determining influence upon later civilization in the high plains, and yet their art seems somewhat stillborn, plainly ugly, despite the perfection and richness of the work.

For air and violence, for poetry and humor, we must look to the peoples of central Mexico, who attained a high degree of civilization shortly before the conquest, that is to say during the fifteenth century.

The Mexicans that Cortez found were doubtless only recently civilized barbarians. Coming from the north, where they wandered like Indians, they had barely and not very brilliantly assimilated borrowings from their predecessors. Their system of writing was inferior to that of the Mayan, which it resembled. No matter; of the various American Indians, the Aztec people, whose extremely powerful confederation had seized almost all of present-day Mexico during the fifteenth century, was nonetheless the liveliest, the most seductive, even in its mad violence, its trancelike development.

Stockade of skulls. Codex Vaticanus 3738.

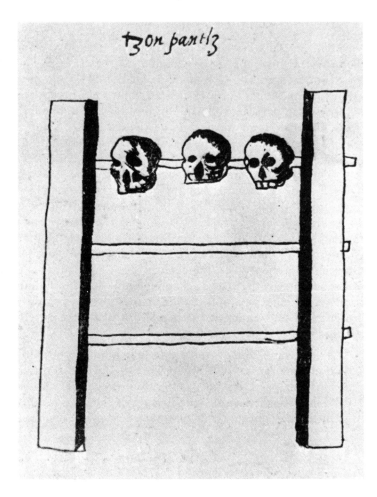

The historians who have dealt with Mexico have remained, for the most part, utterly uncomprehending. If, for example, we consider the literally extravagant manner of representing the gods, we find their explanations disconcertingly weak.

> In casting an eye [says Prescott] over a Mexican manuscript, or map, as it is called, one is struck with the grotesque caricatures it exhibits of the human figure; monstrous, overgrown heads on puny, misshapen bodies which are themselves hard and angular in their outlines, and without the least skill in composition. On closer inspection, however, it is obvious that it is not so much a rude attempt to delineate nature as a conventional symbol, to express the idea in the most clear and forcible manner; in the same way as the pieces of similar value on a chessboard, while they correspond with one another in form, bear little resemblance, usually to the object they represent.*

This interpretation of the gruesome or grotesque deformations which troubled Prescott now appears inadequate. If, however, we go back to the time of the Spanish conquest, we find an explication of this point that is truly worthy of interest. The monk Torquemada attributes the horrors of Mexican art to the demon which possessed the Indian mind. "The figures of their gods," he says, "were like their souls in their endlessly sinful existence."

A comparison between the Christian representation of the devil and the Mexican representation of the gods is obviously in order.

The Mexicans were probably as religious as the Spaniards, but their religion included a sentiment of horror, or terror, joined to a sort of black humor more frightful still. Most of their gods were savage or weirdly mischievous. Texcatlipoca seems to take an inexplicable pleasure in a certain sort of hoax. His exploits, as related by the Spanish chronicler Sahagun, form a curious counterpart to the Golden Legend. The honey of Christians contrasts with the bitter aloes of the Aztecs, the healing of the sick with evil pranks. Texcatlipoca walks out amidst the crowd, cavorting and dancing to a drum. The crowd becomes a dancing mob and rushes madly toward chasms in which their bodies are crushed and changed to rock. Another of the Necromancer god's nasty tricks is reported by Sahagun:

> There was a rain of stones and then a huge rock called *techcalt*. From that time on, an old Indian woman traveled through a place called Chapultepec Cuitlapico, offering little banners for sale and calling, "Little flags!" Anyone who had resolved to die would say, "Buy me a little flag," and once it had been bought he would go to the place

---

*   William H. Prescott, *History of the Conquest of Mexico*, New York, Modern Library, p. 56.

of *techcalt* and would be killed, and no one would think of asking, "What's happening to us?" And they were all as if gone mad.

Clearly the Mexicans seem to have taken some disturbing pleasure in this sort of practical joke. Probably these nightmares and catastrophes in some way even made them laugh. One then begins to have some direct understanding of hallucinations as delirious as those of the gods in the manuscripts. *Bogeyman* or *mute* are the words associated with these violent characters, evil pranksters, brimming with wicked humor, like the god Quetzalcoatl sliding down slopes of the high mountains on a little board. . . .

The sculptured demons of European churches are to some degree comparable (surely they are involved in the same basic obsession), but they lack the power, the grandeur, of the Aztec ghosts, the bloodiest ever to people the clouds of our earth. And they were, as we know, literally bloody. Not a single one among them but was not periodically spattered with blood for his own festival. The figures cited vary, but it is agreed that the number of victims annually numbered several thousands at the very least in Mexico City alone. The priest had a man held belly up, his back arched over a sort of large boundary marker, and with one fell blow of his knife of shining stone, cut open the trunk. The skeleton thus severed, both hands reached into the blood-filled cavity to grasp the heart, wrenching it out with a skill and dispatch such that the bleeding man continued for a few seconds to quiver with life over the red coals before the corpse, flung away, tumbled heavily down to the bottom of a staircase. Finally, at night, when the corpses had been flayed, carved, and cooked, the priests came and ate them.

And they were not always content with a blood bath for themselves, the temple walls, the idols, and the bright flowers piled upon the altars. For certain sacrificial rites involving the immediate flaying of the man chosen, the priest, transported, would cover his face and body with the bloody skin and body. Arrayed in this incredible garment, he prayed ecstatically to his god.

And it is here that the amazingly joyous character of these horrors must be clearly stressed. Mexico City was not only the streaming, human slaughterhouse; it was also a city of wealth, a veritable Venice, with canals, footbridges, ornamented temples, and, above all, flower gardens of extreme beauty. Flowers were grown even in the water, and they decorated the altars. Prior to the sacrificial rite, the victims danced, "decked out in necklaces and garlands of flowers." And they carried flowering and scented reeds which they alternately smoked and inhaled.

One easily imagines the swarms of flies which must have swirled around the streaming blood of the sacrificial chamber. Mirbeau, who had already dreamed of them for his *Torture Garden*, wrote, "Here amongst flowers and scents, this was neither repugnant nor terrible."

Death, for the Aztecs, was nothing. They asked of their gods to let them

Aztec sacrifice. Codex Vaticanus 3738.

receive death in joy, and to help them to see its sweetness, its charm. They chose to see swords and arrows as sweetmeats. And yet these savage warriors were simply pleasant and sociable, like any others, fond of gathering to drink and to talk. There, at the Aztec banquets, one frequently got drunk on one of a variety of drugs in common use.

It would seem that this people of extraordinary courage had an excessive taste for death. They surrendered to the Spaniards in a sort of mad hypnotic state. Cortez's victory was won not by strength, but rather by the casting of a true spell. As if this people had vaguely understood that once they had reached this degree of joyous violence, the only way out, both for them and for the victims with which they appeased their giddy gods, was a sudden and terrifying death.

They wished until the end to serve as "spectacle" and "theater" to these capricious characters, to "serve for amusement," for their "distraction." Such was their conception of their strange excitement. Strange and delicate, since they died suddenly, like crushed insects.

1928

Erotic Predicaments for Camera

HOLLIS FRAMPTON

It has been widely alleged that a picture is worth some reasonably large but finite number of words. It has been widely believed that a photograph is as plausible as — or approximates to the plausibility of — that swarm of events that we are accustomed to call the real world. And indeed the entire photographic literature of eroticism depends very heavily on exactly that supposed plausibility. I have chosen, therefore, to attempt to believe what is believed, to attempt to generate those words that the photograph is supposed to be worth, in four instances of erotic predicaments for camera, using my possibly defective understanding of the method of Robert Browning.*

*

The year is, or is about to be, or has recently been, 1855. I am in France. This part of France is delicately colorless, and faintly metallic in texture; if I adjust my position slightly, I may find my own fragmentary image reflected in the darker parts of the scene before me. Light here is diffuse, shadows transparent. Either the time is approximately local apparent noon, or I am indoors: the locale is indeterminate. In what may be the distance, I find only a vague, uniform mist — but that distance may amount to no more than a blank wall whose junction with the floor is elided. Nearer, and to my right, I find a semi-solid entity the size of a large boulder, but a little more complex in shape.

About half the space before me is occupied by two anonymous strangers. They are quite clearly a woman, who faces me, and a man, who presents to me his left profile. Both are mesomorphs, both sustain their weight on the left foot, both are quite naked. The man's right leg is extended behind the woman's left leg, as if encountering her in mid-stride. They embrace. The woman's left arm

*   These prefatory remarks are not contained in the typescript of Frampton's text. They were added when Frampton presented the text at a symposium entitled "The Pornographic and Erotic Image — Toward Definition and Implication," at the International Center of Photography, New York, April 17–18, 1982.

encircles the man's upper torso: the fingertips are visible below his left shoulder blade. Her right arm crosses her body horizontally; the extended fingers nearly touch, or touch lightly, near the lower insertion of the left pectoralis major muscle. The man's right arm encircles her and emerges below her right arm; the splayed fingers partially enclose her right breast. His left hand is pressed against her abdomen, the thumb fourteen centimeters below her navel, the palm guarding the vulnerable passage of the femoral artery into the thigh, the fingers reaching the pubic symphysis. The woman flexes her right knee, resting her foot on a barely visible thing as thick as a plump pillow; her left hip inclines toward the man, her head away. He closes his eyes and kisses her cheek. She lowers her eyelids, and averts her gaze from me, looking above me and to my left. I make a quarter plate daguerreotype of this scene, trusting that neither person will move during the long interval required by the exposure, and that the man will sustain, unwavering, his very enthusiastic erection. The couple vanishes, or I vanish. Was their encounter arranged for my benefit, their postures rehearsed, the space evacuated to enhance their visibility? Or did I merely chance to witness an occasion that would have transpired in any case? Did my intervention inject uncertainties into the event? Would they have behaved differently had I not been present, or if I had brought no camera? Did I leave too soon, or arrive too late? Am I entitled to suspect that I failed to record something of interest? To suspend and memorialize all these irresolutions, I shall mount the little picture in an elegant frame of tortoise shell, lined with gold, and leave it, for more than a century, in a bureau drawer. About myself, I know only that I am a mature adult, whose name is F. J. Moulin.

*

The year is 1878, and it is high summer. I am in England, probably in Oxford, where the University has not closed its doors since the time of Dante Alighieri; the light here is typical of our fine English days. Hazy, but permeant, it illuminates a hand-painted tropic world nearing twilight. In a distant seascape, the black skeleton of a derelict ship is half-submerged. A slight foamy chop in the water suggests a breeze I cannot feel. Nearby, to my right, the tip of a rocky promontory slopes into the water, lightly overgrown with a sketchy greenery that looks like mimosa. Two perfectly real children, nicely tinted, are entwined within the brushwork, which mainly surrounds their outlines, appearing behind them in atmospheric perspective, but somehow encroaches before them, as well, to conceal their respective loins with a ragged cloth and a bit of foliage. Nearer still, painted wavelets splash without wetting the children's feet.

It is as though this fragment of the universe had been created using two different methods, or sets of rules, each foreign to the other but mutually inextricable, like that landscape, at once nonsensical and plausible, through which

I have walked, in dreams recorded with a special instrument of my own invention.

That the children are girls I infer from their fine features, long tresses, pensive demeanor. One, on the left, sits on the rock and rests her right hand on it. Her right leg is drawn up and crossed so that the ankle rests on her left knee; her left hand, then, rests on the ankle. The other stands, the width of a body apart from her, leaning against the same rock, hands on hips.

Both girls look to the left, at right angles to my own sightline, but they direct their attention to two different things, neither of which is known to me. The seated child seems melancholy, the standing, expectant. Neither appears to notice the wreck behind them, or to require from it any of those comforts that Defoe's Crusoe salvaged and patched together into a threadbare cartoon of civilization. Indeed, they seem unaware that they are castaways in a menacing island of artifice; one might more easily suppose them at rest after hours of playing naked in the sunshine among our lawns and hedgerows.

To record my own puzzlement at finding them in such contradictory surroundings, I photograph the scene before me with a collodion wet plate I have freshly prepared, whereupon the environs disappear, but the children remain. And now I recall the circumstances that brought me this fanciful vision. My colleague, Patrick Henderson, a Fellow of Wadham College, had left with me his daughters Annie, aged eight, and Frances, younger by a year, for an afternoon chat and tea. To my delight, these innocent little creatures thought nothing of showing themselves to me, and to my camera, in their natural state. I delight especially in the company of little girls, to satisfy whose boundless, prankish curiosity I am always ready to invent a new puzzle, rebus, word game, or nonsense story. Indeed two stories, which I made up to amuse Alice Liddell, the daughter of the Greek lexicographer in Christ's Church, have been published here and abroad. What momentary aberration, then, could have caused me to imagine, so vividly, Annie and Frances in such wild surroundings? I must make an albumen print of this picture, and give it to Mrs. Hatch to paint over in oils according to that fancy, so that I may contemplate it at length. Convinced of my artistry, she might then allow me to photograph her daughter Evelyn Maud, of whom I would like to do an infantile version of Goya's *Maja Desnuda*.

In fact I am, by profession, neither storyteller nor photographer, but a logician. Personally, I so much hate the idea of strangers being able to know me by sight that I refuse to give my photograph, even for the albums of relations and friends, who know that my name is Rev. Charles Lutwidge Dodgson, and that I am called Lewis Carroll.

*

The year is 1885, on an afternoon in early November. I am in London, in Whitechapel, a teeming slum just north of the city, where the circumstances of life are so vile that even the fearless Jack London, come to study, left, sickened, after a few months. I am in room 13, off a foul alleyway in Miller's Court. I am told that the whole space is no more than twelve feet square, and contains only two chairs, a table, and a bed, but I can see only the last named item, and a corner of the table beside it, and behind it, very near, the lower part of a closed door. The rent, which is four shillings a week, is three months in arrears.

The light is dim, and will need to be augmented with magnesium. Today, mercifully, the world is colorless, odorless, tasteless as distilled water. On the bed, still wearing portions of a linen undergarment, lies what remains of a woman. The throat has been cut straight across with a knife, nearly severing the head from the body. The left arm, like the head, is attached to the body by skin only. The nose has been cut off, the forehead flayed, and the thighs stripped of flesh. The abdomen has been slashed with a knife both across and downward, and the viscera wrenched away. Both of the breasts have been cut from the body. The flesh from the thighs, together with the kidneys, nose, and breasts, have been placed on the table, and the liver placed between the feet. An amputated hand has been pushed into the stomach. The eyes are intact. Blood, from the severing of the carotid artery, is everywhere, but the bedclothes, which have been rolled aside, are surprisingly unstained.

Because it is my duty to do so, as it is my duty to be here in this place at all, I make a single photograph of this shambles. The scene vanishes.

This is my fifth such encounter in recent months, and it is destined to be my last. After the first, it was given out to the papers that, through the photograph's power of minutely detailed observation, Scotland Yard expected to determine the murderer's identity with all speed. Formerly, known miscreants were routinely photographed as part of an immense project that was to delimit the criminal type of physiognomy for good and all. Here and in France, vast libraries of these photographs have accumulated, but not one man has been remanded to Dr. Bentham's famous Panopticon in Newgate Prison on the strength of their information. It would seem that what such photographs will teach us, if, in time, they teach us anything, is the precise location of the boundary between knowledge and understanding—assuming that those two principalities of the mind border on one another.

Thus my work has not, in fact, illuminated our pursuit of the murderer, of whom it is known only that he is right handed . . . and that from medical evidence alone. But it has not been, I fear, without its miserable effect, because, knowing that the result of his own work is to be photographed, he has come to perform for my camera. In each successive instance, he has become more thorough, painstaking, ingenious in his ghastly craft. In the first case, he probably accomplished his business in a minute or two, but the coroner has estimated that he spent three hours arranging this final and most spectacular masterpiece, like an artist who would rearrange anatomy to his whim, in whom all affection for that grand edifice, the human body, has soured and rotted. But may there still be hope that the camera will come to our aid? It is rumored that a new technique has been invented, in Germany, to develop the retina of the eye, like a photographic negative, and retrieve the ultimate image perceived by the dying. To that end, the body of this piteous victim will be desecrated yet once more, and this time in the name of science. Will we understand that photograph any better than we have any of the others we have made, of everything under the sun? Not long ago, the man we seek sent a letter to the Chief Inspector, dated, with perfect correctness, "from Hell." Our incomprehension of these pictures, which we so desperately need to comprehend, has made for us a Hell of our own. At least, out of our need to know the murderer's name, we have conferred one upon him: he is called Jack the Ripper. My own name is unknown, even to myself; my photographs will be hidden away for three generations, and when they come to light again the meaning that we seek in them will be no plainer than it is at this moment. Perhaps they mean something else entirely.

*

The year is 1980, and the season indeterminate except that an abbreviated patch of sky, visible through a far window, seems bleakly overcast. I am in something like Boston, where there are still turn-of-the-century houses of a spacious cut, in a white room in such a house. The floor is of polished hardwood; there is a handsome fireplace, and a rug before it that looks like fur; brass electric sconces and chandelier are extinguished. The space is otherwise as replete as a Victorian parlor. On the left, an open grand piano displays albums of Chopin and Mozart. Its bench is ornate. On the right, a magnificent big cabinet of Far Eastern design supports a much smaller one, from beneath which dangles a silk stocking. Three modern chrome and leather chairs are disposed as if for conversation, with a matching chrome and glass coffee table. Two large embroidered cushions, numerous exotic plants, African and Asiatic objets d'art, and a few things that I cannot identify, fill the scene, throughout which, arrayed on floor, walls, and furniture, with rectilinear, geometric precision, I see scores of minor oral mollifiers in the shape of bars of Hershey's Milk Chocolate (with Almonds) and sticks of Juicy Fruit chewing gum, and twice I distinguish, on small plastic signs a trifle larger than the gum, and of the sort posted on office doors, the name G. I. FREUD.

In the middle of this plethora, a young oriental woman kneels, naked, on one of the cushions. Her left hand rests on her left thigh, and her right hand encircles, just above the knee, the left leg of a standing naked man in his midthirties. The man's left arm is behind his back, his right foot advanced, his right arm raised so that the forearm is level at the latitude of his navel. He is clean shaven, and holds an open straight razor in his right hand. Both of these personages face me in aggressively direct eye contact. I choose to regard the woman's expression as mildly surprised, and the man's as mildly annoyed. Although their postures occasion a minor difficulty for such an act, the woman is fellating the man.

There is an instantaneous, blinding burst of light, as if from an electronic flash, and I realize that a photograph has been made. Now I find myself elsewhere, at my worktable, examining a print of this photograph, and trying to decide who made it. There are two possibilities. I may be a genial professor of art in an upstate New York university, the photographer Leslie Krims; but if, as I suspect, the man who has just been photographed is himself Leslie Krims, then my pretense that I have been other than a nameless spectator is invalidated, and the maker of the piece, synonymous with its prime watcher, is watching himself and his friend performing the act of making the photograph. But if that is true, what rationale can obtain for annoyance or surprise on the part of the performers? On the other hand, if I am the photographer, then my intrusion at this private amorous moment justifies both those emotions, but I cannot fail to question their stances, which suit the necessities of the camera far better than the convenience of erotic enjoyment.

Therefore, I will keep this photograph, taking pleasure in the ways it criticizes my every attempt to include my own contemplation in a system of which it is, itself, both center and limit, knowing that its intellectual economy partakes of a class of problems that may never be resolved, because it is congruent with an instance in which we touch the limit of our reasoning powers. That limit may be best generalized in a letter of 1885, written by Lewis Carroll to a mathematician:

> Let a geometrical point move from A to B. In so doing, it passes through intermediate positions. Now, of these positions, either (1) there is a position through which it passes first after leaving A, or (2) there is not such a position. These propositions are contradictories, so one of them must be true. But neither is conceivable.

Buffalo, New York
April 1982

Fragment from the Rodin Museum

ROBERT MORRIS

Gravel formal rectangles pathways yellowish brown like along Champs Elysées asked them to bring it over dead shrubs cut square around pool seventy-five feet long twenty-five feet wide water dead unfrozen winter water motionless concrete wall just above ground level foot wide pathway surrounding pool then dead hedge two feet high then expanse of yellowish brown pea gravel under feet air a whir a whirring sound from traffic one hundred yards away along parkway moving consistent 5pm blurs traversing distance beside pool sound of gravel below away sound of whir steady unchanging back of pool ground damp off gravel ground black dead unfrozen wet winter ground cold 5pm light fading back of pool first step sound of gravel stopped two sounds foot on granite block below drifting whir traffic parkway sitting above granite stairs (her) legs slightly apart eyes half closed legs and eyes slightly apart immobile watching pool below hearing foot immobile passing her above her top stair twelfth her thighs press seventh down seven yellowish gravel pool somewhere a word inscribed gravel word unreadable at distance whir and 5pm light directly in front green vertical expanse bronze in and out focus representations pushing falling stretched strained naked metal stops space stepped along gravel sound thighs against granite stops against second gated world of congealment.

(Cue: Oompah band keeps heavy time with each word)—Spirits, genii, angels, nymphs, satyrs, bacchantes, sirens, centaurs, dancers, bathers, Satan, Adam, Eve (before and after the Fall), Christ, St. John, Mary Magdelen, Bacchus, Psyche, Orpheus, Ariadne, Ugolino, Aphrodite, Apollo, Mercury, Perseus and Medusa, Pygmalion and Galatea, Paolo and Francesca, Romeo and Juliet, Ovid and Dante, sin, melancholy, sorrow, despair, desire, embraces, abductions, rapes, sleeps, fatigues, awakenings, reveries, meditations, self-sacrifices, muses, maternities, incests, perils, slitherings, pulsing, throbbing, sagging, tumescent, bulging, hacked, slicked, gouged, polished, ripped, probed, kneeded, torn (Cue: cut Oompah band) are not the first stirrings of an animated clay so much as a population melting down into . . .[1]

1.   Dog shit was my first response and the whole thing went like this: ". . . not the first stirrings of an animated clay so much as a population melting down into dog shit. Maybe. Green dog shit. The impression given is of a state of affairs existing in the first moments after some basic molecular process

Within the triangular enclosure. Cold granite below. Taut line of insulating wool skirt above. Two curves (bulges) of flesh either side. A chamber in which temperature was equalizing itself. I entered the door on the left into a cramped vestibule. Opened the heavy bronze door and entered the dark hallway. Turned to the left, away from the green bronze meringue. Wanting to descend five stairs and place my hand on the cold granite. Shifted my weight to the left, walked the three steps to the bronze door which was deep brown. It was heavy but swung smoothly on its hinges. A step. A step up and I was before a small, high counter or desk where a crudely pencilled notation read, "Adults: $1.00." The door swung further open than I had expected. From the inertia of its weight. I had trouble keeping it from swinging into the wall. My torso twisted to the left, carried by the inertia of the door. It was a moment of struggle in which I turned to the left away from a brown counter to my right. Having decided to bother no further with the green upright bronze plaque, I turned sharply to the left and glanced over my shoulder at the leg projecting out over the seventh step as my right hand went out against the mullion of the heavy bronze door. My left hand pressed down with too much force on the handle whose brown patina had been worn to a brassy shine. The door began to swing inward and I began to pull back slightly, anticipating that its inertia would carry it into the wall with a force I had not at first suspected. The admission sign was taped with scotch tape to the brown wood. Rather it had been taped several times. Possibly whoever taped it had suspected the tape of poor adhesion and had taped and taped again. An aging female, slightly gray. Slightly transparent. Veiled with a patina of nothingness in my mind's recollection, stood behind the tongue and groove, brown painted kiosk. I suspected her as the taper. She and the tape, transparent but yellowish in my recollection. I turned on my right heel and entered the great hall. From below the sound of the foot against the terrazzo. Even with the eyes closed one would have sensed . . . what? Something about the change of pressure. More as though the air were old and heavy. Companion to the water outside. Heavy, unchanged, inside winter air. A sudden weariness behind the eyes. Want to roll up into head. Knees beginning to buckle as (Cue: low angle slow motion shot of moment of impact of large heavy object hitting highly polished stone floor) weight of fatigue pulls heavy slow. I waded into the great hall. That and the light. The light of skylights at 5pm winter. The light of a translucent skylight at that hour. Fatiguing as the air. Not bothering with the catalogue at the end of a gray transparent arm, I leaned my weight to the right. Three steps and I was into the thickening light of a great arched hall full of

has gone awry. An instant. Before we are all melted back into the earth as piles of green dog shit. No pain. Just a faint kind of buzzing sensation. And a powerful, confused sense of difference. "This my hand? What? Slightly green and . . . it smells. Good God, I'm turning into dog shit." Yet the tone of that was not right. Something scatological was wanted. But what? The sad truth is that the mind is faced with a poverty of terms when it turns to consider what might follow the phrase, "a population melting down into . . ." Cup grease? Karo syrup? The real problem is to be found in the preceding sentence. Specifically, the very phrase, "population melting down into" is the clinker. Why wouldn't "frozen into" do? Or even the clumsier, far weaker, "distorted into" is wide open for followers.

broad, plain mouldings and dados the color of dark bronze. The walls were white. A resistance to the eye. Something in my body turning slightly. Perhaps preparing for one of its seven year renewals. From below the sound of the foot on the stone. And at a distance. In the mind. It seemed high up. The sound of mumbled conversation. Or the muffled sound of pigeons under an eve. The triceps muscles of the right arm were contracted, thrusting the arm straight downward and slightly away from the body. The forearm was bulging with ligaments forcing the hand into a fist with the index finger pointing at the ground. Five steps and my eyes were at the level of his sex. The only relaxed muscle in his body. I imagined it otherwise. His right hand gripped (her) left calf at the point where the stocking ended. I moved toward the figure and the sound of steps on the flagstones from below. The neck was forced down and forward against the left shoulder. The torso pivoted slightly to the right so that the chest and arms were in one plane. The hips and legs in another. The body was tense and motionless. Stood rooted there. Allowing her to heave against. Skirt around waist. I waded through the heavy dense air not hearing the sound of the foot against the rough stone. Vision moving down its own tunnel. Fixed ahead on the bunched muscles of the bronze belly. Brown and polished like the water outside. Like the winter pool outside which had brown leaves at the bottom. But if drawn to it, also drawn past it. To the window beyond. Small paned and with bronze mullions running up and down. Past the bronze mid-section to the metal rectangle. Through its squareness the corrugation of granite stairs fanning out below. And there. At the seventh. The wool stocking caught on the polished rigid index finger. Behind me the great hall. Its stale air. Its broad and plain brown moldings following the curves of its white arched ceiling. I stood for some seconds before the window. Dead center. Five thin bronze mullions to the right, five to the left. From the corner of my right eye I sensed rather than saw a room. Or a hallway. Or an alcove. Or a darker space. I stretched my right arm down stiff. Against my body. I felt the triceps muscle at the back of the arm contract and press against the shirt. I twisted from the waist. The shoulders and the chest faced toward the room, the hips and legs addressed the glass for a moment before turning. The head dropped against the left shoulder resisting the turn momentarily as the vision caught on the leg projecting from the seventh step below. It was a hallway. Or an alcove. And a darker space. And a room. Beyond it, or through it, on the right stood a glass case edged in bronze. Unlit. Against the wall of the alcove stood a second massive case. The lower third was of bronze. The upper section was formed by four large panes of glass. Within was a model of the green bronze Gate which stood outside. A passageway connected the great hall, its light now like smoke, to the smaller room. A wall of granite. On the one side the green bronze Gate. The outside. On the other side a miniature of the same in red clay. The inside. The same fistless three atop the red. Even tinier figures writhing in the throws of death, orgasm, or ray-gun transformation into . . .

"And the light?" he inquired after so long a pause. "Dark," I said. Suddenly he looked weary, almost as though he withheld the expression of a secret pain gnawing at some part of his body. He held himself stiffly. Pivoted his upper body around to face me while his lower legs remained facing a different way. "The fists?" We both knew. "Fistless," I replied, feeling infected with his weariness. "Fistless, I could see that much even in the light,"[2] I continued. Somehow I wanted to convince him. I recall that he had no eyes. Only hollows of deep shadow. And projecting brows. The weight was thrown back. The belly vast and slung forward. A heavy robe covered the massive torso. The hands were beneath the robe. The left gripped the right wrist. The right fist appeared to hold the sex. The hands were not visible. The figure was raised up on a high pedestal. I waited for him to speak of another unseen fist. But he turned, sunk back into himself. Or leaned his weight back and merely peered down at me. Squat and massive. Thick with flesh. Heavy with muscle in the process of losing its tone. An abandoned body. Gross and full. The bulk was leaning back. The weight was back on the heels. The right fist pulled the flesh forward against the lean. Away. Somewhere. The aforementioned sound. Pigeons. And below. As I circled the bulk. The sound of one foot sliding across the stone. Then the other coming to rest beside it. Sideways locomotion. The robe thick as felt. The robe draped over squat flesh. The robe bulging over the right fist. The heavy plaster robe was covered with a fine patina of dust and, in places, dirt. The plaster figure covered with dust. The light suited it. It suited the light. The dust. Where the air had sagged and died. The plaster was hard and angular. Nearly planar in places. To the left a small, narrow, single paned window framed in bronze, gave out onto the wet earth and a corner of the stair. The way the flesh of fat people can look. The way the expanse of flesh and

2.   Had the fist been nearby it would have had the status of a 'fragment'. Had the body been armless and had the arms been nearby, they too would have been addressed as fragments of the body. Or, had the body not been nearby, we would simply have 'arm fragments'. Does a once-whole figure when equally divided, as though by sword from crown to crotch, yield two fragments? More than likely two halves have been produced. At what point in a progressive removal of parts do we encounter the threshold, the dividing line, beyond which we no longer have a figure and its fragment(s)? Somewhere less than half, no doubt. Yet a bust is not a fragment so much as a part. Fragment, of course, is a kind of part. But a bust is not that kind of part. The fragment kind. A nose, an ear, a finger, a cock, a foot, a slice of back (how fitting 'slice' is to fragment; they were made for each other) are fragment type parts. But assume the fist had been nearby, having fallen from the figure. Assume further that in striking the ground (nothing to do with anger, but pulled down by the heavy hand of gravity, so to speak) the knuckle of the second finger had broken off. Do we now posses a 'part' of a fragment? Had the fist broken neatly into two parts weighing equal amounts, in spite of a certain asymmetry, would we then have two halves of a fragment? Or do we begin over? Taking one half of the fist at a time, we are back to dealing with 'fragments' of the figure pure and simple. But here Rilke chides that "the feeling of incompleteness does not rise from the aspect of a thing, but from the assumption of a narrow-minded pedantry, which says that arms are a necessary part of the body . . ." Nothing here of fists falling off like roof tiles. On the contrary, Rilke saw in the drawers at Meudon: "Hands that rise, irritated and in wrath; hands whose five bristling fingers seem to bark like the five jaws of a dog of Hell. Hands that walk, sleeping hands, and hands that are awakening; criminal hands, tainted with some hereditary disease; and hands that are tired and will do no more, and have lain down in some corner like sick animals that know no one can help them . . ." Perhaps what that missing fist was hiding in its clutch was reason enough for its removal.

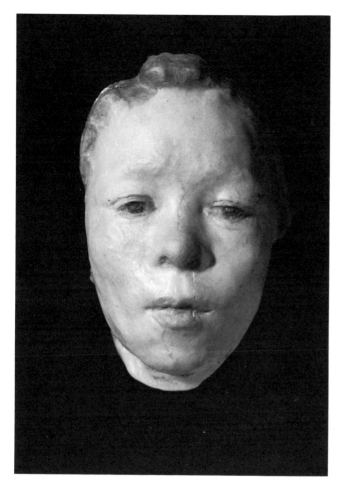

Auguste Rodin. Mask of Hanako, The Japanese
Actress. *1911. Pâte de verre. (The Rodin Museum,
Philadelphia.)*

hair of fat men can take on the appearance of powerful animals. Elephants and
rhinoceros or hippos. Beneath the expanse of encasing hide and hair and fat one
senses the powerful muscles. Without his robe he had that look. Legs spread.
Rather legs astride. Astride of what I could not say. But his heavy thighs were
astride a shape. A shape started beside his ankles and thrust upward in a tapering,
pyramidal form coming to rest between his legs. Spearing his groin. A large prop.
An aid which both held him up and . . . I had again felt the fatigue. As though I
had been knocked down from above. The feeling behind the knees. The eyes
wanting to roll back. The desire to give in (Cue: color shot, medium closeup, 23
frames only, of the heavy sword beheading in one stroke a black bull in the
Malaysian New Year festival) and sink down onto the granite in a deep sleep.
Well, I was not blessed with a prop like his. Blessed? Perhaps it was not a prop but

rather a sort of geometric hernia which sagged out of him. To the very earth. And which his long robe sometimes covered. Perhaps. I had lost all interest in him. I shifted my weight, the left foot coming to rest beside the right. Nothing between the legs. Nothing but dead air. It hung there. In the space. Palpable. A slightly dirty light filtering down from the arches of the great hall. It deposited, particle by particle, a patina of fine dust and, in places, built up to a layer of dirt over the bronze flesh. Figures. Lurching. Leaning. Straining. Rotating. Six. Seven. More? Pressing. Milling. Confined. Space too small. Pressing. Six. Seven. More. Twelve legs. Fourteen? More? Confined. Circling. Circling her? Milling. Pressing. Wool. Thighs. Enclosing. Pushing. Damp. Bronze. Mumbling. Wet. Pressed. Pressed in. Pushed and flattened. The face was grotesque. Not a full face. More like a mask. Several. Several of the same face. Three of the same face. There behind the high glass of the case. Sitting well back in the bronze case, overly large for what it displayed, were three rough masks or modeled faces in pinkish terra cotta. These were placed on a rumpled, pinkish, faded velvet whose wrinkles led one to suspect an attempt by a curator long since gone to give a careless but suave style to the swirl and folds of the cloth. Perhaps further handiwork of the transparent taper . . . Dead cloth. As dead appearing as the objects within, the air without, and, one could not help but assume, the air within. The edges of the glass plates met in bronze corner mullions. Undoubtedly it was airtight. One suspected that the entire contents would collapse into dust particles should the case be opened. The faces. Both hacked and modeled. Smoothed in places, gouged in others. As though made in the spirit of a sketch. Or a study. Or a studied sketch. As though trying for those contours, those planes, those eccentricities of shape and line, which in themselves tread dangerously near the lump, but taken all together (and how else can a face be taken?) catch the look of the subject. Oriental. The eyes without the upper folds. And flattened out. The whole of the thing more in one plane than most faces. The bridge of the nose quite low. The mouth slightly parted. Those touches of roughness, those small gouges, pits, scratches, hacks and lumps gave to the face not only its verisimilitude but its expression of terror. It had witnessed the flesh melting, the skin peeling, the fire spreading, the bodies bloating, the blood clotting. My face was pressed against the glass. I felt the bridge of my nose flatten as I stared into the other faces. At my left, around the bronze corner and pressing against the glass perpendicular to my glass, a flattened face was reflected, the bridge of her nose nearly in a plane with the cheek bones. Lips parted and wet against the glass. The dark, like dust, settling on her back. Hands against the pilaster. Skirt pulled up. The curve of her hip visibly pressing against the dark bronze. Hands forcing the arch in her back. Still as statues. Partly hidden by the darkness settling in the niche. High up. In the recesses. Where the 5pm winter light died in the motionless air. Where the dead air hung. Where the sound of a foot on stone drifted upward to be met by the sound of mumbled conversations. Or pigeons. Drifting down. Where midway in the numbed space the sounds met. Interpenetrated. Blended into an irregular sighing sound . . .